THE
WILKOMIRSKI
AFFAIR

THE
WILKOMIRSKI
AFFAIR

A STUDY IN BIOGRAPHICAL TRUTH

STEFAN MAECHLER

TRANSLATED FROM THE GERMAN
BY JOHN E. WOODS

PICADOR

First published 2001 by Schocken Books, a division of Random House, Inc., New York
and simultaneously by Random House of Canada Ltd., Toronto

First published in Great Britain 2001 by Picador
an imprint of Macmillan Publishers Ltd
25 Eccleston Place, London sw1w 9nf
Basingstoke and Oxford
Associated companies throughout the world
www.macmillan.com

isbn 0 330 48726 4

A CIP catalogue record for this book is available from
the British Library.

Typeset by North Market Street Graphics, Lancaster, Pennsylvania
Printed and bound by R. R. Donnelley & Sons, Co., Harrisonburg, Virginia

CONTENTS

Foreword   vii

The Story of Bruno Grosjean   3

Wilkomirski Tells His Story   22

The Origins of *Fragments*   84

A Global Literary Event   111

The Plunge into the Abyss—Autobiography or Fake?   129

Tracking Down the Truth—The Historical Research   165

The Truth of the Biography   263

The Truth of the Fiction   274

Afterword   309

Epilogue   310

Notes   319

Select Bibliography   368

Permissions Acknowledgments   373

Fragments   375

PUBLISHER'S NOTE

The first text in this book consists of the report by the Swiss historian Dr. Stefan Maechler, who was commissioned by the Liepman Literary Agency in Zurich to research the authenticity of Binjamin Wilkomirski's memoir *Fragments*. In order to allow the reader to weigh Dr. Maechler's exploration of all the elements that make up Mr. Wilkomirski's book against the memoir itself, the complete text of *Fragments* is also included.

FOREWORD

Binjamin Wilkomirski's *Fragments* (*Bruchstücke*) was published by the Jüdischer Verlag, a division of Suhrkamp, in 1995. In it the author describes how as a young child in Riga he fled from the Nazis, survived two concentration camps, and after first spending a period in orphanages in Kraków, came to Switzerland. The book received wide attention and was translated into nine languages. On 27 August 1998, Daniel Ganzfried, a Swiss writer, wrote an article for the weekly *Die Weltwoche* in which he accused Wilkomirski of having invented his autobiography. He was, Ganzfried wrote, "never confined to a concentration camp," but rather is the same person as one Bruno Grosjean, born in the Swiss town of Biel in 1941. The charges were picked up by the media worldwide.

In early April 1999, I was engaged by the literary agency of Liepman AG in Zurich, which had assigned the rights to *Fragments* to publishers around the world, and asked to investigate, as a historian, the book's claims of authenticity. In my contract with the agency I was assured complete independence as regards both content and methodology.[1] The present book is the result of that research.

In the opening chapter of his book, Wilkomirski wrote: "My early childhood memories are planted, first and foremost, in exact snapshots of my photographic memory and in the feelings imprinted in them, and the physical sensations." He is not a poet or a writer. "I can only try to use words to draw as exactly as possible what happened, what I saw; exactly the way my child's memory has held on to it."[2] The reader is to proceed under two assumptions. (1) The first-person narrator has personally experienced everything he describes. This assertion is the chief object of my investigation. (2) The author presents his "shards of memory," while giving up on "the ordering logic of grown-ups," since "it would only distort what had happened." Wilkomirski proceeds from the idea that memories are stored in our brains as objects that can be brought unchanged into the light of the present. This assumption stands in opposition to the view that memory is subject to influences and changes because it is always constructed or reconstructed within the context of the present.

Within the historical sciences there is a comparable debate as old as the discipline of history itself. In brief, it revolves around the question of whether a historian registers past events in simple passivity, without reflecting his or her own agency, or adds something new to the presentation whenever she or he constructs a true story out of evidence left by the past. Ultimately it is a question of the relationship between the form of a given history and historical realities. Which facts does the historian choose to tell a given history? Which are omitted? Is the history written on the basis of these facts something the historian finds at hand, or does he or she invent it? Does the form in which it is told create a meaning commensurate with historical reality?

Such questions are of the greatest importance for the present case. After all, Binjamin Wilkomirski has been accused of mixing fact with fiction in his story and, what's more, of turning the Shoah itself into fiction. This study in particular, then, will not allow me as a historian to dodge these complex problems. I have therefore made every effort to investigate all relevant evidence without bias and with the greatest care. All my descriptions and conclusions—whether relating to specific events, statements of individuals, or a weather report—are based on documents, audiovisual materials, and conversations in which I took part. Every detail included here has its connection to historical reality. To be sure, by its very nature oral history deals not just with evidence already at hand but also with evidence created by the interview process itself, for it is only by posing certain questions to selected witnesses that the historian generates such material at all. Primarily for that reason, I have chosen to give this account the form of a journalist's report and have attempted to achieve a transparency that will allow readers to examine my procedures, constructions, and results and to keep in mind my position as a researcher and writer when forming their own opinion.

The genesis of *Fragments,* its success and the regard paid to its author, the public controversy following Ganzfried's article, and the sudden transformation of respect into disdain are all phenomena of analytical interest far transcending the person of Wilkomirski. Questions arise about the history of child survivors and foster children, about the therapeutic production of memory, about the function of a literature of contemporary witnesses, about the treatment of the Shoah and all the perils of its being instrumentalized, about the aesthetics of a literary work's reception, and last but not least, about the actions of the media. All of that, however, was not part of my commission, nor would it have been possible to pursue such issues within the framework of a few months' work. But in order at least to provide a basis for such analyses, I have attached great importance to providing as solid a description of these events as possible.

My report would not have been possible without the help of countless eyewitnesses and informants. Offering many working hours to assist in the project, Eva Koralnik of the Liepman Agency was indispensable, as was Claudia Sandkühler, who edited my text with impressive dedication and a meticulousness matched only by her great talent. To all of them, my deepest thanks.

March 2000   Stefan Maechler

THE
WILKOMIRSKI
AFFAIR

THE STORY OF BRUNO GROSJEAN

In the State Archives in Bern can be found transcripts of interviews, investigation reports, and court records that have remained unnoticed since they were first put to paper.[1] My reading of these documents shows that they reveal in rich, atmospheric detail the circumstances that shaped the life of a central figure in my investigation.

A FATEFUL EXCURSION

A gentle breeze passed over the lake that extended along the forested lower slopes of the Jura. In the distance the snow-capped peaks of the Alps were visible, and vineyards grew along the opposite shore. The stillness was broken now and again by the sounds and voices of countless bicyclists following the lakeside road, and more rarely by the noise of a car. It was early August 1940, with no reminders here of the war and terror raging in the countries all around and leaving only little Switzerland untouched.

Three women had better than half of their trip behind them. They had set out from their home in Biel on their bike excursion early that morning. All three friends were on vacation—the first worked as a housemaid, the second as a waitress, the third in a watch factory—and they were taking a ride around the entire lake. Yvonne, the one who worked in the factory, had borrowed a bike from her boyfriend's mother for the trip.

The women had just passed through Neuenstadt, a town marked by its medieval origins, and were proceeding at a leisurely pace toward the next small village of winegrowers, on the border between the French- and German-speaking regions of Switzerland. As they headed back now toward Biel, their own shadows cast by the evening sun seemed to point the way home. On the right, between the road and the shoreline, were railroad tracks; on the left, the road narrowed because of mounds of dirt where sewers were being laid.

Two young men on a tandem bicycle approached the trio from behind and began to pass them. A train was thundering toward them, and to avoid the noise the women moved near the middle of the road but not far enough to obstruct a swiftly approaching car they had noticed sometime before. They were still waving handkerchiefs at the passengers on the train when the fellows on the tandem shot past in such a hurry that they saw the oncoming car too late, and as they maneuvered quickly back in front of Yvonne, their tandem grazed her front wheel. She lost control, and as she tottered she was struck by the car's front fender and pulled off the bicycle, which went hurling through the air. She was left lying in the middle of the road, bleeding and unconscious, her face battered.

The police and the physician on call were notified, but they took their time getting there. One of Yvonne's friends decided she couldn't be left out on the road any longer, and with the help of a farmer who was passing by, she carried her to the nearest house. The harried doctor who had finally arrived from Neuenstadt declared her skull fractured and ordered that the seriously injured woman be taken to the hospital by ambulance. The car involved in the accident, a 1939 Ford five-seater, had come to a stop a dozen yards beyond but was undamaged. The driver, an elderly factory owner who had been on the road all day, was perhaps overly tired or had simply been blinded by the sun, for he had not even noticed the accident until he heard people shouting behind him.

The accident report—printed between a notice about an unruly cow that had pushed a soldier off his bike and a retirement announcement—appeared in two terse sentences in the *Bieler Tagblatt* of 3 August: "A young woman from Biel was struck by a car in Schafis yesterday. Suffering severe injuries, she had to be taken to the district hospital."

The accident victim remained unconscious for several days and only gradually, over the next four weeks, emerged from the deep coma that followed. The doctors found a double fracture of her skull, paralysis of the left side of her face, and a loss of her sense of smell. Once the patient was fully conscious, she learned from the doctors that she was a couple of months pregnant.

The documents I found in Bern and in Biel[2] indicate that the unfortunate woman was a twenty-six-year-old named Yvonne Grosjean who had been employed for three years at the Omega watch factory in Biel. She told the doctors that she had lost her parents early on, had grown up with foster parents who were now deceased, knew of no living relatives, and was quite alone in the world.

During a visit with Max Grosjean, Yvonne's brother, at his home near Zurich in the spring of 1999, I learned that after the death of their mother (allegedly of grief over their father's drinking), the family was broken up by the civil authorities, who did not wish to leave the children with their alcoholic father.[3] The children were hired out to strangers. At age four Max was sent to a farm in the Emmen Valley, while his six-year-old sister, Yvonne, was shipped to the canton of Solothurn, though he did not know to whom or what her life had been like there—just as he knew almost nothing else about her. He had only recently learned from the newspapers that she had died years before. But he certainly remembered a great many very sad things about his own childhood, about beatings, forced hard labor, and terrible loneliness. The best time of his life had been at age seven, when a woman visiting his master happened to discover that Max was suffering from life-threatening pleurisy, and he was sent to a hospital, where for the first time in his life he had toys to play with.

I could not help thinking of works like *Mirror of the Peasants* and *Needs of the Poor* by Jeremias Gotthelf, a nineteenth-century writer from the Bern region who castigated abuses in the child-labor system: how orphaned children were offered for sale like cattle and auctioned off to farmers; how local authorities awarded contracts to those farmers who demanded the least for boarding children; how farmers haggled over these children because they wanted cheap labor, certainly not because they wished to raise them and make their lives better.[4] The same sort of thing had gone on in his own foster home, Max explained—the less money his foster father received to board him, the harder he worked him.

Many years later, as a young adult, Max had gone in search of Yvonne, whom he had not seen since he was four. Following a tip from the police, he finally found his sister in the district hospital at Biel, but upon entering her ward he did not recognize her among the other women and had to ask a nurse which one she was. This reunion must have taken place in 1941, when Yvonne was once again in the same hospital where she had been brought the summer before—though this time she was there to give birth. The previous October she had been released to the home of the parents of the young man who had gotten her pregnant—too soon, as it turned out, for after barely two weeks she was forced to return to the hospital for care, and she had remained there a few more months after the birth.

To avoid the physical dangers of childbirth, the doctors had opted for a cesarean section and, to their own astonishment, delivered a healthy child. This occurred at 3:30 on the morning of 12 February 1941, as attested by the standard birth certificate issued by the registry office.[5] The child's name was entered as Bruno Grosjean, with only the name of the mother listed under the rubric for parents; the space for the father's name was left empty.

Since my knowledge of Bruno's birth and his first years comes only from documents and the scant information gleaned from his uncle Max, I hope to find further elucidation from his father, Rudolf Z. I meet him in the summer of 1999 at a restaurant in a city in central Switzerland.[6] He is willing to help shed light on the Grosjean matter, but prefers anonymity. He has never seen his son, for he broke off contact with Yvonne well before the birth. I ask him if he knew of the accident at the time.

"She was already in the hospital when I learned of it. It was in the paper."

When had he last seen Yvonne? I inquire.

"I can't really say, but before the accident, in any case. As it was, there was nothing after that."

During Yvonne's brief stay with his parents, he had been in the military. Max Grosjean, however, had told me that the expectant father had visited her in the hospital and then, horrified by her disfigured face, had made himself scarce. Whom should I believe? It seems pointless and presumptuous of me to confront this elderly man—who has himself undergone several operations and is rather upset at having this old business turn up again—with the conflicting claim.

At the time of their affair, Rudolf Z. had been in training as a fine mechanic at the Omega watch factory, prior to continuing studies as an engineering student at the Advanced Technical Academy of Biel. He became acquainted with Yvonne during this apprenticeship; she worked at the same factory and was always passing his window. But he was first introduced to her by his own mother, who likewise worked at Omega and who invited Yvonne to visit them at their home.

Yvonne was amusing, happy, and very devoted, "a pretty girl, always dressed very elegantly"; a man could be seen with her anywhere. She was his first love, and he was proud of the fact that she was older than he. Their relationship was anything but a "one-night stand"; it lasted at least two years. They had had a lovely time together, and he had always regretted their breakup.

There were two problems: the damned war, because his military service demanded he be gone all the time; and his parents, who sternly objected to his relationship with Yvonne. "Why was that?" I ask. Well, because of the child—they wouldn't have objected otherwise. They were afraid of the disgrace, afraid of what people would say. It was different back then; an illegitimate child was a scandal. And his father was unfair besides, and let pride get in the way. He would have done better to explain the facts of life to his son, because he had been a "real greenhorn." But when the child welfare office notified his father about the child, he came out to the recruit barracks in Payerne to haul Rudolf over the coals. There was a horrible argument; they didn't speak to each other for a good year. His father threatened not to pay for his studies if he didn't break it off with Yvonne. One day Rudolf went into the kitchen and turned on the gas to take his own life, but his father barged in just in time.

I read to him from the paternity records of 1941, which describe how Yvonne, seven years his senior, seduced Rudolf, then still a minor, behind his parents' backs and despite great resistance on his part, even secretly slipping him pills to induce him to have sex with her. I read aloud the passage that raises doubts as to whether Rudolf was her exclusive sexual partner and thus, in fact, Bruno's father.[7] Rudolf Z. is amazed at this representation of the matter—which he himself had signed. His memories of Yvonne were very different. The story about pills and Yvonne's ostensible promiscuity had definitely been the work of his father, who wanted to discredit the woman and palm the child off on someone else.

In an out-of-court settlement, Rudolf Z. was obliged to pay monthly support, but only a small sum, in consideration of his future status as a student. He never saw Yvonne again.

In cases of illegitimacy the law at the time demanded that parental power be taken from the mother and transferred to a guardian. The guardian selected for Bruno Grosjean was Walter Stauffer, head of the Biel Child Welfare Office.[8] According to the records cosigned by Stauffer—and therefore presumably representing his point of view as well—the mother of his new ward was a woman who had seduced a minor by every indecent means possible. One can imagine with what skepticism he must have viewed her.

From then on Yvonne had to deal not only with her child's guardian but with the courts as well, since the accident in which she had innocently been involved had left irreparable damage, and those responsible needed to be found. Her facial paralysis had improved thanks to electrotherapy, but some disfigurement remained. She had lost her sense of smell, and the damage to her brain made her easily fatigued and slowed down her reaction time. All this was detrimental not only to her health and social life, but also to her employability. Because of her limited judgment in the wake of the accident, she was granted a legal adviser to represent her interests, who now sued the driver of the car, accusing him of gross negligence resulting in grievous bodily injury. But the driver was a reputable manufacturer from Neuenburg, and in reading the court records, it is hard to avoid the impression that this was a case where social class came before justice. That had already been ensured by the statement of the police, whose investigation was curiously superficial, consisting of a telephone call to the driver of the car four days after the accident, in which only a minimum of information was requested. The interests of a working girl, who had been raised as an indentured orphan besides, were obviously outweighed by those of a manufacturer. It should come as no surprise that the driver was declared innocent all the way up the chain of appeal.[9]

Following the difficult birth, Yvonne had to remain under hospital care for another three months, and for now it was pointless for her to think of returning to her old job. In an evaluation addressed to Yvonne's insurance company, which surely had a material interest in her being able to work, the doctor wrote: "The child, a boy, is developing well. During her long hospital stay, Fräulein Grosjean has also been presented with opportunities for planning for her future; she and the child can move in with a married couple who will supervise and care for the child while she resumes her work, as soon as she is able to do so." But for now he would recommend a stay at a convalescent home, to be paid for by the insurance company. She should also be able to take the child with her, "something we must regard as of therapeutic and psychohygienic importance; caring for the child is the best and most natural means of keeping her busy and diverted, and it trains her better for resuming work than if she were to be consumed with longing for her child during her convalescence. On the other hand, it must not be forgotten that the patient is still nursing the child and a separation would be detrimental to the child as well."

The doctor also had good things to say about Yvonne and her relationship with little Bruno. Her initial depression had been "replaced by the joy of motherhood"; she now had a "thoroughly positive, even cheerful affect; she is proud to be a mother and happy to have found a real meaning for her life in raising the child."[10]

Stauffer, the child's guardian, was more skeptical. He wrote the Langnau Convalescent Home in the Emmen Valley, where Yvonne and Bruno had since taken up residence, asking for information: "As you are aware, the young woman suffered a serious automobile accident and has since been handicapped. Nevertheless she wishes to care for the child herself. It is my impression, however, that she does not possess qualities necessary for this, and/or that it would be irresponsible to act in accordance with her wishes. I beg to ask you in confidence to observe Fräulein Grosjean's behavior toward the child and her ability to care for it during her stay at your institution and to inform us once she has departed whether it is your opinion that the boy may be left with her." The home's administrator wrote back that mother and child had been with them for twenty-eight days now: "During that entire time we have found nothing to criticize about her, and she is very good at looking after the boy. She is evidently very fond of him, and it would be more correct to say that she spoils him a little by constantly carrying him around and the like. But of course we do not know what the circumstances are, whether she can devote herself entirely to the child or will have to earn her own living."[11]

As a single mother entirely on her own, it is out of the question for Yvonne to look after the infant exclusively and not to have to earn a living for them both. Soon after her return from the convalescent home, her legal adviser presses her to return to work. In September 1941, more than a year after the accident, she is given part-time employment by the Omega Watch Company in Biel. This is piecework to be done at home, since, as her insurance company's doctor writes, she ostensibly cannot be employed at the same factory as the mother of the man who got her pregnant.[12] Since pay for such part-time work is poor and quite inadequate for her needs, Yvonne appeals to the child's guardian: "Try as I may, it is impossible for me to support my child and myself all on my own. I am currently earning circa 100 Swiss francs a month doing piecework at home for Omega, while room and board for the two of us costs 135 francs a month. There is no possibility of my wages being increased in the foreseeable future. In addition, my compensation suit for damages is not yet settled, so that I find myself in a serious predicament and must ask for assistance."[13] Yvonne receives 30 francs a month from the Child Welfare Office. That is what the child's father was supposed to provide in child support, but he was a student with no income and his father refused to pay in his stead.

The Guardianship Authorities keep an eye on the situation. A coworker of the child's guardian visits Yvonne in the spring of 1942 and reports: "Bruno is a sweet little boy. His mother appears to devote the necessary attention to his care." That autumn the same woman voices the opinion that the boy is developing normally and that his mother is "trying to raise Bruno correctly." That is the full extent, and brevity, of her visitation reports. But one can imagine the plight of this single mother: Yvonne has long since lost every foothold in life, and symptomatic of her difficulties is her inability to keep a room anywhere for long. Her legal adviser complains that she pleads each time with him and Stauffer for permission "to board with a family with whom she is allegedly good friends, and each time, within a few days and at most within two weeks, has moved out just as suddenly, after allegedly not being able to get along with the previously so highly touted family."[14] And in fact there is a period when the mother and her baby change addresses every few weeks: the registry office entries read like the records of a homeless person.

Bruno is almost two years old. Until now his mother has cared for him by herself, but she now finds herself with no choice but to hand his care over to strangers. On 1 February 1943, he is taken in by a childless couple named Schluep in the neighboring village of Port. Ten months later he returns to Biel and a family named Rossel. And now the problems grow worse. In the spring of 1944, Stauffer's coworker determines that the foster mother is having trouble with Bruno—he is very lively, somewhat stubborn, and a tight rein must be kept on him. But he seems to be well cared for, and the woman appears to be a good housekeeper. While the authorities can find no fault with his external circumstances, Bruno (and with him, his mother) has become a problem. Stauffer's early doubts appear to have been justified. After a conversation with the foster mother, he notes that Fräulein Grosjean is "not very" concerned about the child. "If on a given Sunday she is supposed to care for him, she always has an excuse. The boy is a bad bed-wetter," and "the foster mother consulted with Dr. Tanner about it today. The cause: neglect." A dangerous word has now been spoken. The mother, whose "quite abnormal inconsistency of character" was censured early on by her legal adviser, dare not give cause for any further complaints.

DOUBLY UNLUCKY

On 11 June 1944, Yvonne places her three-year-old son with a family named Aeberhard in Nidau, a village in the vicinity of Biel. Bruno will live here for nine months.[15] Also living with his new foster parents at the time is their eighteen-year-old son, René. He emigrated after the war and now lives in the United States. He remembers Bruno very well, he says in our telephone conversation. He had a mischievous face and curly hair; there must still be photographs of him. There had been major problems with his—René's—mother, which was why later on they had had to give Bruno up to a doctor in Zurich.[16]

I schedule a meeting with René Aeberhard in early June 1999, at his daughter's home in Nidau, not far from the house where his family had lived. Speaking in the broad dialect of a Bern native, but lacing his speech with Americanisms, he tells about the first time he saw Bruno. He had been tending cows for several months on the slopes of the nearby Tessenberg, working for a farmer whose hands had all been drafted to guard the border, and one Sunday his parents came to visit. "They had a little boy with them, he was three maybe. They said that this was Bruno."[17] He was a little surprised that they had taken on a foster child so soon, and assumed that they did it to help them get over his own absence from home.

Aeberhard says he remembers how his family gave Bruno their own children's toys to play with and went sledding with him in winter. They borrowed a Davos sled from father Aeberhard's boss, and went up on the Hueb, a hill behind their house.

"We watched to see who could go the farthest, all the way down to the canal." (He laughs.) "Considering there was a war on, it was a wonderful time."

Bruno's mother was a beautiful woman, Aeberhard recalls; she was slender and carried herself well, though her mouth was a little skewed—from a car accident, he believes—and could walk only slowly. He saw her several times because she visited Bruno regularly, every other Sunday at least. No, she never picked Bruno up to take him anywhere, just always came out for afternoon coffee. She was nice to him and interested in how he was doing. And Bruno was glad to see her, too. It was a normal relationship. It must have been sad for her not to be able to see him later on, Aeberhard says, looking back. And he felt sorry for Bruno, too, who got bounced around a lot during his childhood.

When asked for the precise reasons Bruno was sent away, Aeberhard replies, "My mother had moments when she almost wasn't in her right mind." He doesn't evade my questions, but I can tell that I have touched on some painful experiences whose effects still linger. He is cautious in his responses, as if trying to avoid sharp-edged memories that might wound him or his long-dead mother. There were times when she was crazy, he says. Later, after Bruno had left, she underwent psychiatric treatment; she finally was put in a clinic, where she took her own life in the early 1970s. Her condition was totally unpredictable. Sometimes she would fly into a rage and demolish everything, and other times she would sit in a corner, sobbing. But if someone knocked on the door she would be normal, just like that. And even when she flew into a rage, it was suddenly all over. She had never hit anyone; there was no threat to life. His brother and he had both grown up under the same conditions.

I read to him from a report written by Bruno's guardian, dated 17 February 1945: "Herr René Aeberhard shows up at the Child Welfare Office in Nidau and declares: 'We have been caring for Bruno Grosjean for several months. Unfortunately, it is no longer possible for us to keep the boy. First, because my mother is not well, and second, because the boy is hard to raise. He is not easy to handle in a lot of ways, which doesn't do my mother's health any good. I am therefore asking that the child be placed somewhere else.' "[18] Aeberhard says today that "hard to raise" was not the right way to put it. Frau Aeberhard's seizures had intimidated Bruno and in his fright the boy had crept into a corner. That sort of thing was hard for a little boy to deal with: "You don't need to hit him, that's not necessary. He just shies away. That's what happened to Bruno, too. He was simply afraid, and then afterwards, when they would try to dress him or say something to him, he would get almost hysterical. He had some sort of anxiety complex." "This was fear of everyone, of you, or your father?" I ask. "He was never afraid of me, or of my father, either. It was my mother, when she was in a rage— all hell would break loose then."

The only person who might have shielded the little boy from his foster mother was his natural mother. But she was having to fight for her own life. Yvonne's brother Max says that he was given military leave after being called to Biel because his sister was seriously ill in the hospital. They feared the worst for her. She had punctured her uterus in an abortion attempt and almost hemorrhaged to death. On one of his hospital visits she told him that her son was being sent to Adelboden.

I read for Aeberhard the crucial letter that the Child Welfare Office sent the boy's mother as she lay in the hospital: "As you are aware, for reasons of health Frau Aeberhard could no longer keep Bruno. It appeared to us that the best thing was to place the boy temporarily at the Sonnhalde Children's Home in Adelboden. A change of air will certainly do the boy good. In the meantime you will have regained your health and then together we can discuss the child's future. Wishing you a speedy recovery, we send you our best wishes and regards."[19]

Aeberhard cannot remember either Yvonne's severe illness or Bruno's being sent off to Adelboden. He knew only that Bruno was being well cared for by a doctor's family in Zurich. His parents had no doubt learned this from Yvonne. I ask whether Bruno had visited her while she was in the hospital. Aeberhard doesn't know, but says it surely would have been possible—it was only a forty-five minute walk from their home to the district hospital.

We look at some photographs that are in his daughter Marijke's possession. There are no shots of Bruno among them. Aeberhard is disappointed, but says he has a lot of photos at home in California and will go through them all as soon as he returns.

After our conversation, I take a look around the area. In Bruno's day, the Aeberhards lived in what was once a farmhouse, on a street that bears the fitting name of Grasgarten (grass garden). The house itself has changed little since then, but what were once broad fields and meadows have now all been built up. Directly before the front door flows the Nidau-Büren Canal, which redirects the Aare's water out of Lake Biel and on toward the Rhine. Farther downstream is a dam, and from a distance one can hear shots from a rifle range. I walk downstream, past single-family homes built after the war. This is where Bruno would have walked and played with his mother. I can't help asking myself whether before his final departure for Adelboden he might have visited his mother one last time as she laying fighting for her life in the hospital. But who would have taken him to see her? The guardian, who had hundreds of wards to look after? His foster mother, who from one moment to the next could make his life hell?

FROM A CHILDREN'S HOME TO NEW PARENTS

On 8 March 1945, Bruno was taken by train to Adelboden, a village in the Bernese Oberland.[20] Sonnhalde Children's Home was, like most all child-care facilities at the time, a private institution. The surrounding area is known for its many religious sects, and the home was administered by two deeply devout women, one born into a local dynasty of hoteliers, the other a registered nurse. It was not an orphanage, but a home where children from families in crisis could be sent for rest and recreation. An advertising brochure praises it as a "small, excellently managed home—a modern, solid structure in the local chalet style built in a wonderful, quiet, dust-free setting near a forest, with panoramic views. Especially suited for children needing rest and recuperation, from infancy on, and for girls up to age seventeen. Recognized for its fine food (only butter is used in cooking). Medical instructions and regimens conscientiously followed. Tubercular patients not admitted."[21] Photographs show a large sun terrace with a view of the mountains, a well-lighted room full of deck chairs, as well as game rooms, bedrooms, and baths, whose sterility is reminiscent of a sanatorium.

One reads, of course, in the guardian's files that due to ill health Frau Aeberhard was no longer able to keep the little boy. It is doubtful, however, that the authorities were aware of just how catastrophic the situation was at his last foster home. Stauffer, Bruno's guardian, evidently saw the boy's problem as lying with his mother, Yvonne; it was because of her, he wrote, that the child twice had to change foster homes. After all, he had always had his reservations about her ability to raise the child. By mid-May 1945, he could no longer simply stand idly by, so he presented a prepared text for her signature: "The undersigned Yvonne Grosjean, of Saules, in Biel, authorizes the Biel Child Welfare Office to offer her child, Grosjean, Bruno, born on 12 February 1941, to a childless married couple so that they may care for and raise him, at no further charge, and later adopt him. I hereby waive my personal rights to him and to any knowledge of his whereabouts. I grant permission as of this date for an adoption." Because Stauffer wanted the mother to renounce any future personal contact as well, he went further than current law provided for in such cases. Yvonne, however, refused to sign, saying that it was impossible for her to give up her child.[22]

Three weeks later a Kurt Dössekker, M.D., of Zurich applied to the Biel Guardianship Authorities: "As a childless married couple (born in 1893 & 1901) we would very much like to raise & adopt a nice, healthy child between 2 and 10 years of age; preferably a girl & an older child.—A specialist in practice for 22 years, well-situated, single family home on the Zürichberg."

Biel's routine inquiry to local authorities concerning the Dössekkers raised no red flags: the man in question—his wife was mentioned only in passing—was a well-known specialist in dermatology and urology, with his own prosperous practice, residing with his wife and a housemaid in a large villa and living in ordered, affluent circumstances. People spoke well of him; he was an active officer in the Swiss army. Both husband and wife possessed "the requisite kindheartedness and the capability of providing an adopted child with an upbringing and education as desirable as can be imagined."[23]

Stauffer informs Kurt Dössekker that he will be sure to let him know as soon as he has a suitable child to release to them, which, however, is not the case at the moment. Two days later he has another conversation with Yvonne; this time he persuades her to sign the statement waiving her rights to the child. One can guess at both the tone and the substance of their discussion from a promise Stauffer requires of the woman only five days later, when she pledges in writing that she will "strive to maintain proper conduct in the future" and says she is aware that if she "should not keep her word," she "will be assigned a court-ordered guardian as previously threatened." Stauffer obviously believes that the thirty-year-old woman should be disciplined after all. All the more so, since in the same document Yvonne announces that she will be moving to Bern because she has several acquaintances there—"none of them men"—and admits that it would "definitely be advantageous" for her "to leave Biel."[24]

On 2 July 1945, Dössekker is informed by Stauffer that he

has a boy named Bruno Grosjean, age four and a half, to give away: "He is a pleasant, intelligent child, with whom I am sure you will be happy. The boy is illegitimate. His mother sees no possible way that she can ever care for and educate him herself and has therefore decided, though with a heavy heart, to give him to a childless couple for the purpose of later adoption."[25] Stauffer then informs the Sonnhalde Children's Home that Fräulein Grosjean, "given her state of ill health, has decided to put Bruno, now living with you, up for adoption. A childless physician and his wife have already expressed interest in the boy and will be calling on you later in the month in order to see the boy and to be informed by you as to his qualities."[26]

Within three weeks, the Dössekkers have made their decision. "We sincerely hope that in Bruno we have found the child we seek," the husband writes to Stauffer, who in turn says he is delighted that his ward "has pleased you and you have decided to take him into your home for now on probation. You may now take your time making preparations and determine for yourselves the date on which you want to take him in. A few weeks either way will make no difference."[27]

Max Grosjean and his fiancée (and later wife), Trauti, had also thought about adopting Bruno.[28] When Max learned from his sister that the boy was in Adelboden, his fiancée decided to ride her bike out to visit him. When she got there, she learned to her surprise that it was too late for them to adopt the boy: there was already an agreement with another couple, who had visited Bruno several times and taken him out for the day. He would be picked up for good within about two weeks. At that point, Max says, he tried to intervene with Stauffer. The man was "blown away" by this brother suddenly showing up: Fräulein Grosjean had lied to him when she said she had no one left. The guardian told Max that Bruno's adoption had already taken place and could not be reversed. A doctor and his wife had visited the child frequently and taken every opportunity to observe him and test his intelligence; presumably they were looking for a successor for the doctor's practice. And then, Max says, he had an angry argument with his sister because she had not told him about the adoption. He later lost track of her entirely.

By this time Bruno was so confused by the many changes in his life that he introduced a visitor whom he had never seen before to the other children as his mother. His real mother had moved to Bern by then, where she took a factory job. A few years later a snapshot of Bruno would be passed on to her by way of his guardian.[29]

On October 13, Bruno joined his foster parents in Zurich. The child of a young working woman who herself had grown up without parents, he was now living in a grand villa with a highly respected family rich in tradition: he had indeed been thrust into another world. Stauffer was convinced that his ward had been "well placed." But after his first official visit at the end of the same month, he had to record that there were problems. He noted in his report that Dössekker had confronted him about "misbehavior" that indicated the boy had been "poorly raised." "It had certainly been high time, I was told, that this intelligent child found a solid home, where he could be raised with the necessary understanding and with goals in mind. [Dössekker] said Bruno had his good qualities, too, and was very attached to them. There could be no question of returning him at the present, nor was such a thing likely in the future, either."[30]

When the boy arrived at the Dössekkers' he was leaving behind a terrible past: conceived in ignorance, born with death hovering nearby, he had been bounced around from place to place from the start, ultimately landing in a children's home. While still unable to speak, he had known a loving mother, someone who had herself been abandoned and bruised and who slowly but surely drew away from him. Then for a time he had been put in the care of another woman, who erupted erratically into his world. Finally, amid the constant chaos of ever-changing places and faces, his mother had been lost to him entirely before he ever really knew her. Had he at last found a secure home with this physician's family in Zurich?

Stauffer, his guardian, visited him in his new home a second time before the year was out, but either he wrote no report or the report he did write has since vanished from the files. The next visitation report dates from February 1947,[31] more than a year later.

WILKOMIRSKI TELLS HIS STORY

It was during those years that Bruno Grosjean vanished from the Dössekker household, and, as Binjamin Wilkomirski tells it, he himself became Bruno's successor. He tells me this when I first visit him in his present home in a rural village fifty miles northeast of Zurich.

Wilkomirski resides there with his life partner, Verena Piller, in a very old farmhouse they have renovated. It is a half-timbered building, common in the area; there are, however, a few small, unusual tokens—such as a Star of David—to indicate that the residents are Jewish. The current owners have turned the adjoining hay barn into a concert hall and work studio—he is a clarinetist, music teacher, and builder of musical instruments, and she is a classically trained vocalist and also a music teacher. As we sit conversing in the enchanting interior courtyard, buzzards circle soundlessly above our heads at times, along with gliders towed into the air from a nearby small airfield. Wilkomirski's gentle facial features are framed by prominent, long, light-brown sideburns and an unruly head of finely curled hair that is starting to thin along the brow and at the crown. I spend several days with Wilkomirski so that he can tell me his story. The following is based on these conversations, on interviews he has given other people, and on texts he has written himself.[1]

This is the story as Wilkomirski himself tells it.

THE EXCHANGE

He can still clearly recall his arrival at the Dössekkers', Wilkomirski says. He came from a children's home, presumably somewhere in French-speaking Switzerland, since most of the kids there spoke French. The home overlooked a large lake—it may have been Neuenburger Lake or Biel Lake, because the sun rose from across it, and the direction from which light falls has always helped get his bearings.

A strange woman who had previously visited him in the home took him with her on the train. In his little parcel he had two items that he always kept with him, remnants of a story that was branded in the marrow of his bones. One was a spoon on a long chain, stamped "KL Lublin" on the back, where someone else had also scratched "Blockov 5," although he does not know what those marks mean. He still has the spoon "from there." The other item was a costume for the festival of Purim, an open jacket and black puffy breeches. He can vaguely recall having taken part in the observance of Purim in Kraków. He does not know who it was that sewed the costume and gave it to him.[2]

Carrying his bundle and accompanied by the strange lady, Wilkomirski says, he entered the Dössekker home, a villa on the slopes of the Zürichberg. "It was a big house, in a big garden, and there weren't any other children. But the husband of the strange lady was there. He greeted me with a rather awkward smile. Apart from him, there didn't seem to be anybody in the house."[3]

It was evening by then, and he was given something to eat; the food was unfamiliar, served in a lot of bowls—it was all very odd. Then it was time for sleep, and the strange lady wanted to teach him how to say good night properly. He didn't know what that was. The woman explained that he had to say, "Good night, Mother." "No, I won't!" he cried, upset. She wasn't his mother, he knew where his mother had gotten left, and he wanted to go home. But she kept saying that he had to forget that—"Forget it, like a bad dream." She was his mother now.

After joining his new family, he had to forget not only his mother but also his own name, because the Dössekkers gave him the name of his predecessor, Bruno. In order to avoid confusion in the present context, however, we shall continue to call him Binjamin.

Presumably it was soon after his arrival that the box with the objects from Lublin and Kraków disappeared. He was always told that it belonged to him, but that he couldn't have it just yet. He had found the items again when clearing out his foster parents' residence after their death, and he still has them today. His life partner told me this, because Wilkomirski does not want to talk about these relics anymore, though he did show them during a videotaped interview in 1997, asking if any viewer might be able to explain their origin.[4]

Wilkomirski explains how the woman who wanted to be called Mother led him through the house the next day and told him all the things he wasn't allowed to do: tread in the flower beds, sit on the grass, pull fruit from the trees, climb the fence, and so on. The same day, his foster father called him into the library and explained that he and his wife had taken him in because they could not have children of their own. He said he came from a family of doctors and was himself a doctor, and that they expected Binjamin to be bright enough to study medicine one day and continue the dynasty. That was what interested him, he said; he didn't really like children, they made him nervous. Binjamin should keep his distance and not disturb him.

It must have been in these early days that Binjamin noticed a room in which baby food and a lot of used toys were stored. Who had been there before him? he asked his foster parents. Dismayed by his question, they turned pale, and instead of giving him an answer, made the topic itself taboo.[5] Only many years later would he understand the meaning of his remarkable discovery. Several experiences would prove decisive for his realization.

There was a boy in the Swiss children's home, Wilkomirski says, who looked a lot like him but had a totally different personality. "He never stopped talking and was constantly up to something; as we would say today, he was the alpha animal." The other kids called him and this other boy brothers. The other boy thought that was funny, but it irritated Binjamin immensely.

He was about seventeen, Wilkomirski says, when by chance he happened to run into this boy again in Zurich. On two occasions they just greeted each other from a distance. The third time they ended up on the same trolley-stop island and could not avoid speaking. Just as he had done long ago, the boy "started in with a long song and dance" about how fabulous it was at his foster parents'. He wasn't in school anymore, because he was about to emigrate with his foster father to America, and he couldn't wait. "At the end he said something very curious— at the time it annoyed me no end, but I didn't think anything of it until later when I remembered it, and then it seemed even more curious to me. He said to me, 'I'm really glad I didn't stay on with your foster parents.' And I thought, Damn it all, you don't even *know* my foster parents, what's all this stupid stuff! It was some time later that it all strangely came back to me."

Wilkomirski is now convinced that he was exchanged with the other boy. It was only after a second experience years later, he says, that he understood more of what lay behind it all. He had begun to study medicine in Geneva, and his foster father requested that he call on a friend, Dr. Jadassohn, who lived there. This Polish Jewish doctor had occasionally visited the Dössekkers, although Binjamin had never seen him because he would always be sent to his room then. It was said that Jadassohn had often acted as an adviser during adoptions. His foster father always praised him as having done him a great favor, but never explained what that favor was.

Binjamin was invited to lunch with the doctor in Geneva.

Dr. J. sat across from me, scrutinizing me. Suddenly he asked what it had been like having his friend as a father. I was surprised and stammered that it hadn't been exactly a wonderful time and that I could never accept him as my father—he had tried to no avail to erase my memories from before. But I didn't say a word about their being Jewish memories. And then Dr. J., who was a very old man, flew into a rage. I had been anxious to avoid the word *Jewish*. And it was Dr. J. who started in about it, without my ever mentioning it. He shouted that anti-Semitism hadn't died with the war, it would happen all over again, there was nowhere in the world where Jews had a chance to survive, and would I please take note that he was telling me this as a scientist. Our only chance to survive was by going geneti- cally underground, by total social assimilation. It was a hor- rible thing to keep the awareness of being Jewish alive; there ought to be a law forbidding Jewish parents to tell their children they were Jews—that was the only way. One had to use every means possible to keep Jewish children from ever knowing they were Jews. He looked at me as if I had turned out to be a huge disappointment. All that bit- terness just made me freeze. I couldn't reply and escaped to my next lecture. I wasn't invited ever again, either. My only thought was, So that's what you did, you two doctors! The longer and more often I recalled that old face, the stronger my suspicion became that Dr. J. had been one of the visitors in the children's home.[6]

Wilkomirski remembers how, along with the other boys, he was examined at the home by a doctor—presumably by this same man, Jadassohn. Dr. Jadassohn had then provided the papers of the Swiss Christian boy Bruno Grosjean for the foreign Jewish boy Binjamin, so that he could lead a secure life in Switzerland under a false identity.

I ask Wilkomirski why it was that his non-Jewish foster

father had taken part in this. He says that presumably things had just not worked out with the other boy. He was "an out-and-out rascal and scalawag," constantly up to something, and could never have possibly fit in with his conservative and frightfully old-fashioned foster parents, who were determined to have a successor for the medical practice. I recall Stauffer's report of his first visit, in October 1945, when Bruno's foster father complained about his misbehavior and evidently also discussed the possibility of giving him back.

Wilkomirski points out to me that there are no other reports after that until February 1947. During that whole period, Wilkomirski says, his guardian makes no reports at all, whereas previously two per year had been the rule. In 1947, moreover, he describes a totally different child. In fact Stauffer's brief judgment is one of complete satisfaction, without a word of any problems. "The boy is healthy and cheerful and is developing nicely. He is a joy to his foster parents. His care and education are impeccable in every regard."[7] It is also revealing, Wilkomirski says, that each time his guardian visited, he would be sent out of the house with orders not to return before six o'clock, or put to bed with the excuse that he had something catching. He had never seen his guardian face-to-face. His foster parents had even arranged for Stauffer not to be present at the official act of adoption.

Wilkomirski is as certain of this exchange of children as he is of the rest of his story. Why else would he have the panic attacks that suddenly overwhelm him? Or the misshapen bump at the back of his head and the scar on his forehead? Or the nightmares that constantly plague him?

THE FLIGHT FROM RIGA — THE EARLIEST MEMORIES

On his very first night at the Swiss children's home his sleep was interrupted by a nightmare, Wilkomirski says. "I was in half darkness, and I was the only child on earth. No other human being, no tree, no grass, no water—nothing. Just a great desert of stone and sand. In the middle of the world, a cone-shaped mountain loomed up against the dark sky. The peak of the mountain was capped with a black, metallic, glinting, ominous helmet." Coal cars were moving up to the peak on a narrow rail track. In the cars were dead people, who were dumped into a gaping jawbone. Bugs were crawling all over the dreaming child. "I awoke with a sense of despair, and the absolute certainty that there was no way out. Any relief is not real, it's the last false hope before the inevitable arrival of death."

He lay there awake for a while; everything was quiet in the home, and he had to think about his experiences in the concentration camp. "The nightmare would repeat itself mercilessly in the years that followed, image by image, detail by detail, night by night, like an unstoppable copying machine."[8] These were images of another world that could not be reconciled with the here and now—experiences that he could not understand or give any sense of order to, pain for which he had no words. Only much later would he understand it better, discover that names like Riga and Lublin were not just imagined but designated real places, and gradually be able to put the various fragments of memory into a context—some of them, at least. But at the time he was trapped by a child's limited perspective and could not have told his story the way he can today.

He has neither a mother nor a father tongue, Wilkomirski says, so the origins of his language must lie in the Yiddish of his brother Mordechai. He can only guess at his place of birth, presumably somewhere in the region of Riga, or it might be southern Estonia. He knows his year of birth only from doctors: probably 1938 or 1939. He cannot even be certain of his name; he recalls only that he was once called Binjamin Wilkomirski; in the orphanage in Kraków they called him Bronek, short for Bronislav.

Wilkomirski tells of his first clear memories. "It must have been Riga, in winter. The city moat was frozen over. I'm sitting all bundled up with someone on a sled, and we're running smoothly over the ice as if we're on a street. Other sleds overtake us, and people on skates. Everyone's laughing, looking happy. On both sides tree branches are bright and heavy with snow. They bend over the ice; we travel through and under them like through a silver tunnel."

But these happy memories are soon banished by agonizing images. Uniformed men are screaming at a man who has just smiled sweetly at him, and then they lead the man out the door. A cry of terror in the staircase: "Watch it! Latvian militia!" Binjamin watches as the uniformed men in their transport crush the man against the wall of a house. Maybe it was his father.[9] As he tries to go on, he falters, tries again, sobs.

> We were able to flee somehow at night; it was simply a chaotic situation. I remember also that I'm sure I was being carried—because I remember a street sign suddenly at eye level, and that isn't normal, so evidently I was carried partway through the city—and that I must have been horribly cold and wet through and that somehow we got to the harbor. And we waited there all night, and then when it was almost morning and there was a bit of light, we could board a little boat. I was picked up and set down among the ropes, and the ship pulled out. And then by the light of the oncoming dawn I saw the silhouette of the town, and then I may have fallen asleep, I don't know anymore. But that silhouette has remained in my memory as a very, very strong image, and so I made a drawing of that silhouette. It can only have been Riga, because no other city on the Baltic or North Sea has that typical silhouette with those typical, special spires and in that arrangement, and I recognized it at once when I went to Riga a few years ago.[10]

Wilkomirski sometimes speaks broken German—with unusual syntax, missing articles, an increasing number of grammatical mistakes, and an occasional Yiddish word (e.g., *dorten*)—

drawing out his vowels and talking in a rhythm that gives it all an Eastern sound. Are these remnants of Yiddish, breaking through in the height of emotion? I ask him later whether he can explain these variations to me, since he speaks and writes perfect High German, and I can't hear the least accent in his Swiss German, either. He suggests that it may have something to do with his inability to distance himself from our topic, but he has no more precise explanation.

Later he found himself on an endless journey in an over-crowded train. Maybe to Lemberg; at least, he has a vague recollection of that name. In a little town a woman took him by the hand and dragged him from door to door, talking to people. "Finally we were at the end of this little town somehow and then she said to me, we visited now nine places or nine families or nine people to look where we can get you, but nobody wants you, so we have to go on. I was very astonished—why does nobody want me? I didn't understand that."[11]

HIDDEN ON A FARM NEAR ZAMOŚĆ

Then comes a gap in his memories, Wilkomirski says. Next come images of a farmstead where he was in hiding with his brothers.[12] The barn and stable were empty, there was a horsecart minus its horse, and the farm was no longer functioning. A canal ran past nearby; a narrow footbridge across a weir led to the other side and a meadow where they were sometimes allowed to play. Crossing it, he was afraid of the deep, whirling water.

The only person on the farm besides the boys was the farmer's wife. She supervised the children and fed them; he can recall porridge in a big pot. The woman was strong and rough, with an angry look in her eyes and a loud, frightening voice—they all feared her punishments.

Binjamin's older brother Mordechai, or Motti, was his protector, comforting him, providing him with warmth and safety. Motti had put together a glider out of paper and sticks. On rare evenings they were allowed to climb a nearby hill and let the glider float down to a meadow bordered by woods. Much later Binjamin would fight off his nightmares by imagining he was in that meadow beside the woods again, where Motti had thrown the glider into the air. He tried to reestablish the connection as a way of protecting himself somehow.[13]

It was during this period that he learned from Motti that there was a war on, Wilkomirski says. "One day we heard a man's voice, loud and deep, half-singing, half-roaring in front of the house. In spite of it being forbidden, we peered furtively out of the window. Motti said it was a soldier and explained to me what a soldier was." The man began yelling, put his fist through the windowpane, and climbed into the kitchen. "Out, get out!" the farmer's wife screamed at the children. "We ran into the living room and listened. We heard terrible noises, crashing and blows, the woman screaming, the man cursing in his deep voice. Then it was silent." Finally the children returned to the kitchen. The room had been demolished—the dishes broken, the cupboard tipped over, the table's legs ripped off. The farmer's wife was sitting on the floor, "her clothes all torn and her hair in a mess, and she was crying. The farmer's wife could cry! The farmer's wife, this strong woman who could be so bad-tempered and frightening. The stern judge who ruled us children and thought up such painful punishments—she could cry?" This was how war began for the children.[14]

They could leave the house only rarely. One exception was a visit by a lady. This was a great event; Binjamin was beside himself with joy. They walked over the footbridge to the meadow on the other side of the river, where there was a hill with tall grass. "It was incredible, it was beautiful," and he ran around and shouted until the others had to tell him not to make so much noise. "The big thing was that that lady was there and I only remember that I was rolling through the grass and shouting for joy and then running to the farm woman and this lady and holding on to both by their skirts." Wilkomirski recalls only that the visitor was a very important person; he does not know who she was.[15]

"Then one day it happened," Wilkomirski writes. "The war reached us." They heard sounds of gunfire, the rumble of approaching engines, then a dull explosion. The whole house shook. "The racket died down, there were one or two more scattered shots—then silence." Binjamin went to the adjoining outhouse and out of curiosity looked out the window, although that was forbidden. A gray-black vehicle had crashed into the wall of the house; he saw the bodies of three dead soldiers. The furious farmer's wife ran in and pulled him away from the window, slapping him in a way she had never done before. "I'm going to lock you up alone in the cellar for this."[16]

The next day Binjamin managed to free himself from the cellar, but there was nobody to be seen. "None of my brothers, and not the woman either. I went through the empty house, all the doors were open and the pot still had some of yesterday's porridge in it." After two or three days, he heard a roaring sound and a truck with men in green uniforms pulled into the courtyard, followed by a group of strange men on foot. A woman dressed in a gray uniform, with a skirt and boots, came over to him and pushed him toward the others waiting there. He asked her where they were going. "Majdan Lublin—Majdanek!" she replied. He would be able to play there and see his brothers again. She smiled, then grinned; he wasn't sure what to make of it. " 'Majdanek, Majdan Lublin, Majdanek,' I said, over and over again. The name was pretty." In Polish the word means "camp," and he thought of a beautiful place where he could be with his brothers, where he could play with them in a big sunny field. "Motti must certainly have taken his handmade glider with him, I thought, and maybe the ball, too. I couldn't wait."[17]

"MAJDANEK IS NO PLAYGROUND"

After one or two days' traveling, they came to a valley with a lot of long houses built of wood, Wilkomirski says. Wooden towers and a gate came into view. For the first time in his life he saw barbed wire, which surrounded everything. There—in his German speech Wilkomirski uses the Yiddish word *dorten*—they waited. Then they went in small groups. He tugged at a soldier standing beside him; quick as a flash the soldier turned around and gave him a lash of his whip across the face. He understood then: "The gray lady was lying: Majdanek is no playground." No one knew anything about his brothers. The block wardens just ran around shouting, and so he stopped asking.

He was led into a cubicle, heard the German word *schliesst* (close) for the first time, and could not get out again, he says. After that he lived in a barracks, in the so-called children's quarantine, where the inmates were all children, some younger, some older.[18] They were always locked in, even during the day.

The worst thing for Wilkomirski was that there was no toilet. There was a washroom at the end of the barrack but the stone basins had no running water so the older ones encouraged the children to relieve themselves in the middle aisle. You could hardly breathe because of the stench. That's how he got to know Jankl. He had jumped down from his bunk to the floor and practically sank up to his knees in excrement. He got a terrible shock and began crying. "Stop moaning," someone reprimanded him in a strict, forceful voice. "Be glad that you can stand in the warm excrement at night so your feet don't freeze so quickly. It's the best protection." (Wilkomirski stammers and sighs.) His name was Jankl, he said. He was a very tall, strong boy. Wilkomirski was impressed by how much he knew. He spoke a different language so they usually communicated using gestures. From that moment on they were constantly in each other's company and Jankl remained his friend for a long time.[19] Wilkomirski falters, then begins to cry.

Jankl, who had been there a long time already, became his counselor and protector. The older boy knew how and where you could steal food, and sometimes used a low wall buttress adjoining a yard with two little trees to sneak away. When he came back he would untie the strings he had tied around the bottom of his trouser legs, and what food he had found would fall out. And Jankl would share it with him, Wilkomirski says.[20]

When asked what else there was to eat, Wilkomirski sighs. Usually, but not always, there was soup. It wasn't brought by the block wardens but by gray figures. They were the women from the neighboring barrack who put the pot outside the door. The children had to stand in line, and then a block warden came and dished it out somehow, he can't really remember exactly how it worked. Wilkomirski had a small mug which he held out. He also had a spoon which he always carried with him on a chain around his waist. It was huge for a child because one spoonful was enough for two swallows, but that was an advantage. You could only stand in line once, but it didn't mean you would always get something. It all depended on the block warden. Wilkomirski sighs. Perhaps she liked you, perhaps she didn't, or perhaps she was in a bad mood. He carried the spoon, his single most precious possession, under his shirt, along with the mug.[21]

One day, Wilkomirski writes, he was locked up inside a dog kennel. "If only they don't bring the dogs back, I thought, frightened, if only rats don't come once it gets dark. Rats were what I was most afraid of, because they came when you were asleep. To drive them away, I began to stamp my feet in a steady rhythm, the way Jankl had showed me." The rats were the children's deadly enemies, attacking at night, leaving painful wounds that never healed and made their very flesh rot away. But the worst thing that night wasn't rats; it was bugs. The kennel was full of them. Lice crawled over Binjamin's face. Triangular beetles buzzed at his head, crept into his clothes, and gave off a horrible smell.[22] Even today, Wilkomirski says, those beetles from the kennel pursue him, and he always moves his feet when he sleeps for fear of rats. And the large bump on the back of his head—he touches the spot—that comes from Majdanek. One winter day they were driven out of their barracks. He stumbled, rolled down an embankment, and sank into the snow. "I raised my head to find myself looking straight at the tip of a black boot that was aimed at my face. I was quick enough to turn away, so it only hit the back of my head. The blow lifted me and threw me clean back onto the path."[23]

One day, Wilkomirski reports, he watched in horror as a bull-necked man in uniform cracked open a little boy's skull with a ball-shaped object, killing him. He knew the little boy was dead.

Rage and despair explode in me, I can't think anymore.

Kill him, kill him, I'm screaming inside me, and I can see bull-neck's slack arm right above me and his self-satisfied, grinning face.

Do it like a dog—a dog! Kill him—the voice inside me screams again.

Yes—I'm a dog now, I'm a wolf.

Hands out, I take a flying leap. I grab the bare forearm, open my jaws as wide as I can, and bite with all my strength.

Harder! Deeper! You've got to kill him, I think, my jaws grinding as best they can.

Then I want to let go and run away. I loosen my hands, want to let myself drop, but my jaws won't open, they feel locked shut. They're still grinding, independent of my control. So I'm hanging from this arm by my teeth and it's pulling me upward by brute force, then coming down again, then it's carrying me away and the roaring and screaming is deafening.

He feels his back being slammed hard against something. Here the memory fades out. He does not know how he got away.[24]

At night no one was allowed to go to the latrines, and so each evening a bucket was put out in the passageway. One day a new boy arrived, pale, small, and very shy. That night he began to moan and hold his stomach in pain, but the bucket was already gone. The new boy started screaming, and his screaming could mean they would all be done for. In a panic Binjamin told him, "Just go in the straw, right where you are." The next day a uniformed Ukrainian discovered the filthy straw and killed the new boy. Binjamin realized that he himself was responsible: "I crawled into the darkness of my bunk. I felt the finality of what I'd done and the irredeemability of my guilt."[25]

One bright afternoon, Wilkomirski writes, the barracks door was opened. "Binjamin! Is there a Binjamin here? Come out! Quick!" The rough woman's voice belonged to a block warden, who wore the same gray uniform as the woman who had brought him to Majdanek from the farm. "Today you can see your mother, but—only dahle." He didn't understand what she had said. What did "mother" mean? He couldn't remember. The block warden forbade him to talk: "Not now, not when you see your mother, not afterward either." She made a terrible gesture over his head, and he knew that if he disobeyed, she would kill him.[26]

She led him along the road around the edge of the camp, down to two large barracks. Today he knows that these were the gas chambers.

> She opened the gate and pushed me inside and told me to go down along the wall on this side, and then closed the door behind me, and I was inside. At first the room seemed empty. And then I saw that there were no bunks, or anything, but that people were lying on the floor on both sides. And they were all women, moving very slowly, like in slow motion, like people who haven't had anything to eat.

And I walked to the end, to the far wall, and turned around, and then I saw: someone was lying there, and the someone, a woman's head—[he swallows hard and sighs] and a lot of curly dark hair, and shiny in the dark. And I just stood there, because I wasn't allowed to speak, and I just looked. I didn't know what it all meant, and—[he sighs very deeply] and she didn't speak either, just sat up a little, looked a little. And then I heard something at the door, and light was coming from the door. And I knew that it—that the time was up, and I'd have to leave soon. And at that moment the woman made a motion on one side, the side to the wall, sort of like this [Wilkomirski makes a beckoning motion], and then held something out to me, motioning for me to come. I was terribly afraid to get any closer, but I finally did move closer. And she put something into my hand. And I could see that her face was all wet, as if she'd been crying. But she didn't say a word. And then I went outside and was clutching the object tight. I didn't know what it was, but it was very hard and very rough and jagged.

And the block warden grabbed hold of me, to drag me back. And then I asked, "What do I have, what is this?" And she explained that it was bread and that I should dunk it in a mug of water and it would get soft and then I could eat it.[27]

Afterward he was not taken back to Field 5 but smuggled into Field 3, among the Polish and Christian peasant children. This change, as he would come to understand only years later, saved his life, for in November 1943 every single child in Field 5 was killed.[28]

Wilkomirski repeats the story of meeting his mother several times. This is what haunts him most, at every hour of the day— "because the memory is incomplete. Because even today I'm not able to recall her face exactly. No matter how hard I concentrate."

"Is the memory more a feeling or an image?" I ask.

"I no longer have any clear notion of a face in my visual memory, just an outline. My wish is to be able to remember that face someday, so that in looking at a photograph I could say, *That* is the face. But I can't. The visual memory is missing. It's simply missing. An outline is all that's left in my memory."

"So it's primarily a feeling?" I say.

"No," Wilkomirski replies. "There's a very clear visual memory. Bound up, of course, with feelings, some that arose later, too. Still do, even now. Sometimes when I hear about something a mother has done for her child, or see how a mother relates to her child, it amazes me: Ah, so that's it. Then I think what memories I have of that, and maybe understand a little bit more about what was taken away from me. It's hard to put into words."

"But," I probe further, "don't you first have to have some experience of it, in order later to understand it?"

"I don't really know what I understand, whether it's right. . . . Sometimes I have the feeling that I understand things emotionally as well, and I believe, at least, that during my infancy I sensed something of it, and maybe something is left of that."

"A mother who loved you?"

"Yes. Yes. Otherwise she would never have given me the bread. I didn't understand any of it at the time, I was merely afraid. I regret to this day that I didn't go beyond that fear, didn't look more closely."

Wilkomirski says he was forever asking people about the meaning of the word *dahle*. Only recently someone explained to him that it's Latvian or Ukrainian and means "not from up close" or "only from a distance." He presumes this was the reason for his terrible fear of getting too close to his mother, which is so painful for him to remember.

I remark that for a small child, closeness comes not just from physical contact but also from a dependable and steady relationship—day in, day out, month in, month out.

"But that didn't exist for me. There were always different people."

"Right," I go on, "if a little child sees a person only one time, he doesn't retain the image of the face, no matter how close that person is to him."

"Yes, otherwise I might not have been so afraid. I can only remember my terrible fear."

THE VICTIM'S SHAME—
BIRKENAU CONCENTRATION CAMP

He spent one more winter with the Polish children in Field 3, Wilkomirski says, and it was dreadfully cold. The next spring he got away from Majdanek; he doesn't know how exactly. His memory is confused here, with a great many gaps, and only picks up again with wintry images of another place, no longer hilly, but very flat. Beyond a big fence he saw a birch forest that was usually lost in the fog. Only the barracks were the same; they seemed to follow him everywhere. He had lost all orientation, he says: "There were always new children around me. I could almost never understand what they were saying, and even less from the grown-ups. Everything seemed to be dissolving, murky, a blur."[29] It was only a few years ago, he says, that an expert explained that without doubt he had been in the concentration camp at Birkenau. He reacted to this statement with shock and fury, hadn't wanted to accept it at first.

"Why were you so furious, why did you reject his explanation?"

Wilkomirski hesitates. "It's a difficult question, but maybe because I felt that from there I have some memories I [he pauses] I really absolutely didn't want to have." He confronted these memories only recently. They have to do with people in clean white smocks and with the disappearance of almost all the other children. All that were left were a dozen very blond and blue-eyed youngsters, of whom he was one and whom the men used for medical experiments. "I was so ashamed of what they did that I couldn't speak about it. I couldn't even . . . didn't dare to think about that."[30] Of all the ordeals the children suffered, the thing with the eye drops was the most harmless. Wilkomirski stammers as he describes how the children had to line up and have caustic drops put in their eyes.

I ask whether Dr. Mengele participated. He says no, and instead gives the names Fischer and König. He identified Dr. Fischer from a book with pictures of concentration camp doctors, which he looked through with Miriam, a survivor his own age. Miriam had been at the same place and also recognized Fischer's face. He associates the name König with a later childhood experience in Switzerland. He had to see a doctor, a Dr. König, about an eye problem, and was told to pass along his parents' best wishes. He panicked and made a terrible scene—it had to be a confusion with someone from before.

A few years ago he also met Laura, another fellow victim, Wilkomirski says. He can still remember how in the old days her hair had been almost snow-white blond. She is doing very badly now, he adds; she doesn't want to speak to anyone. It's remarkable, he says, that almost all of these particular survivors have a similar unspecified blood problem and a fractured coccyx bone. I ask what the doctors did to him. "I can only recall a bent needle that gave me the idea that they wanted to get in behind the eyeball. But that is something I don't talk about." He still dreams of it even now, Wilkomirski says with a long sigh.[31]

Wilkomirski says he endured these tortures shortly before the end of his imprisonment in the concentration camp. Then some men hid him somewhere in a hole or a box, and after that he was taken to a room full of huge piles of rags and clothes where women were working. They made a hollow within one of these piles and pushed Wilkomirski inside. Sometimes he would watch them through the legs of a long, large table that stood in the middle of the room. He could see only calves moving back and forth. The nest under the clothes was his new home. There was a strong chemical odor—certain soaps remind him of it even today.[32]

Then came a chaotic period, Wilkomirski says. There was no sense of order, no more commands and roll calls; the block wardens, camp workers, and soldiers vanished; a soothing quiet lay over everything. Groups of prisoners moved toward the fence, where it was forbidden to go. Suddenly a woman he didn't know detached herself from the others and ran toward him, calling, "Binjamin!" Suddenly it hit him; he finally understood that this was his name. The woman, whom he must have known from before, led him out of the camp, right past uniformed guards who paid no attention. They walked for a very long time, but sometimes they rode in a horse-drawn cart, and at last they came to Sandomierz, a small town set on a promontory east of Kraków. "It was spring already, the snow had melted, and I watched all the birds flying over the valley and the river below me. I daydreamed about flying with them, soundless and free."[33]

One day the strange woman set out with him for Kraków, Wilkomirski says. They waited there for several days outside the Miodowa synagogue. Finally the huge doors opened. "An impressive-looking man in a long black coat and a big black hat looked down at me and smiled. The woman spoke to him vehemently. I only understood the first words she said. 'I'm bringing you the little Wilkomirski boy, Binjamin Wilkomirski.' She took me by the shoulders and pushed me forward, so that he could see me better. He nodded."[34] That was how Binjamin heard his last name for the first time.

The man brought him to two other men in black. They were sitting at a table with papers in front of them, and they began to ask him questions. Then something extraordinary occurred: he began to talk, although he had lost his voice back in Majdanek. "I talked like a waterfall, but I have no idea anymore what I said. But at some point it was enough, there was only a sick feeling in my throat, I stopped talking and everything inside me was quiet

again, the way it was before."[35] He was led to the entrance and
told to wait. The woman who had known his name was gone. "I
was very deeply disappointed. So it was again an adult that first
was nice and then dropped me."[36]

RELEASED AGAIN AND PURSUED — IN KRAKÓW

Wilkomirski cannot remember where they took him then or
who took him; it's all a blur in his fragmented memory. He
remembers being in different places which he shared with different groups of other children but that he always felt out of
place and kept trying to find his way back to a camp again,
because that was the world he knew. Running away only
brought punishment from the adults. He retreated into a silent
fantasy world in which he made up his own language and lost all
sense of communication with people around him. This confusion probably accounts for the different versions of the story that
Wilkomirski tells about his stay in Kraków, with various homes
getting confused. I shall follow the version that seems most
plausible to me.

They placed him in a home on Długa Street, Wilkomirski
says. However, he found it unbearable. All these people were so
fat and strong that he was afraid of them. These people, who
had warm food and lived in beautiful houses, were on the
wrong side; he didn't belong with them, but with the barracks
people. The grown-ups had lied to him; the best thing was not
even to listen anymore. He ran away; he lived out on the street
and begged. His biggest handicap was that he was mute: Language was merely a fantasy for him. He imagined how he
would speak, and how he would imitate the people he heard.
But in Kraków he only managed to get one or two words out on
very few occasions. Was it really him who had spoken though,
or was it simply someone else saying aloud what he was thinking?[37] Not even Karola[38] could give him an answer as to why

he felt he'd been lied to, Wilkomirski says.[39] Karola was older than he.

> We knew each other from somewhere, from one of the many barracks probably, we weren't sure anymore, and we never talked about it.
>
> We just looked at each other, and that was enough.
>
> Just once, I asked her what had happened when she was taken away with her mother, and this, more or less, is what she told me:
>
> They were already moving in the column of people who were being led from the barracks through the camp, Karola and her mother, with uniforms in attendance, all selected to die.
>
> It was a long way, the column kept stopping and starting, past unfamiliar barracks, and mounds of bodies, then more barracks and more mounds of bodies.
>
> Then the column had to halt again. Karola and her mother stood still and waited.
>
> They were standing next to a stacked pile of corpses. The SS men were patrolling impatiently up and down.
>
> Then something completely extraordinary happened. A uniform, a young one, came slowly up beside Karola's mother, looked her up and down for a moment, then grabbed hold of her and with a single heave threw her on top of the corpses that were next to them. Karola was being held tight by her mother's hand, so she was carried along with her.
>
> They lay there, frozen with terror, on the cold bodies. They didn't understand what had happened, or why; it had all happened so fast. But they did understand that now there was a way out.
>
> They lay there, playing dead, absolutely still so as not to be discovered, all day until night came. Once it was dark, they slid down and mixed themselves back in among the

living, but as fake living people, struck off all the lists, because they were supposed to be dead.

It was hard, because they didn't dare to be recognized either dead or alive.

Later Karola and her mother got separated after all, and neither got further news of the other.

Now, in Kraków, Karola searched everywhere, inquiring about her mother, Wilkomirski says.

At least part of the time the two of them were together in the same orphanage, Wilkomirski says. He no longer knows whether he lived there full-time or just came for the day to eat and play. "I was afraid of the other children, they were older than I, and their games were often cruel and dangerous. They imitated the uniforms, and were obviously practicing to be grownups. If that's how it is, I don't ever want to grow up, I thought, and being with Karola gave me some sense of safety and peace. I don't know why, but nobody ever dared come near her to do anything bad, she never got trapped into quarrels, she was untouchable."[40]

In one orphanage—maybe on Augustiańska Boczna, Wilkomirski says—he took part in a Purim festival in 1946 or 1947. "Lots of children were sitting squashed around a long table by candlelight. I beat with my stick as hard as I could, and didn't want to stop, until two soft hands took hold of my arms from behind, and a voice spoke to me soothingly." This was where he was given the costume he would take to Switzerland.[41] Many years later, in Kraków, Wilkomirski would find some of these streets he had lived in again. He also remembered a Misia and an Olga, who took the children for walks.[42]

The general mood in Kraków at the time was anti-Semitic. A cart that was supposed to bring food to the orphanage was stoned. People often spat at the children. Once they went on an excursion to Rabka or Zakopane. The orphanage or vacation camp there was guarded by young men with machine guns under orders to protect the children against anti-Semitic attacks.[43] The memory of these hostilities enabled Wilkomirski to recognize the orphanage on Długa Street when he visited Kraków several years ago. "It's today something else in this building, but people said that in those days it was an orphanage for small Jewish children. And it was—I remember because it was the street when I was looking down into the street which makes a slight curve around this house. I saw masses, black masses of excited people running through this street shouting something I didn't understand and having wooden and so sticks and make like this into the air and then I heard in the house one of the nurses screaming, 'Oh, they are killing the Jews again.' " That happened during a cool autumn, Wilkomirski says.[44]

A short time after that, Frau Grosz appeared. She was a nurse at the orphanage, or maybe just someone who frequently helped out there. She asked if Binjamin wanted to come with her; she was going back home to Switzerland and would pass him off as her son. Switzerland was a beautiful country, she said.[45]

THE INTRUDER—
THE FOSTER CHILD IN SWITZERLAND

During this period, Wilkomirski says, a great many Jewish children were smuggled into the West so they could be sent on to Palestine. They were gathered in the French cities of Lyon and Besançon, near the Swiss border. It was there that Jewish doctors decided which children could undertake the rigorous journey and which were too weak; the latter would preferably be smuggled into Switzerland. Wilkomirski later learned from someone who had taken part in just such an illegal action exactly how it was done: they watched as the Swiss Red Cross took children from France or Alsace for vacations in Switzerland, and they simply slipped Jewish children in with these groups, knowing that they would not be expelled again.

And so he arrived with a group at the dark train station in
Basel. They were all led into a waiting room. A woman with a
list called each child one by one. He was terribly afraid remembering the gray uniforms who had also shouted names from a
list. The children were taken out of the room but he did not
know where to. In the end he was the only one left behind. His
name wasn't on any list, the label with the red border hanging
around his neck had nothing written on it, and Frau Grosz had
vanished. Finally a woman came, tried to question him, to no
avail, and left again, taking his label. After a long time, another
woman appeared and declared that they had found a place for
him at an orphanage.[46]

Wilkomirski says they put him on a train that took him to a
Swiss orphanage. He stayed there two or three weeks. He was
confused; he thought of all the places that now lay behind him,
of Frau Grosz, who had abandoned him, and compared that
world with his new one. "No matter how hard I tried, I couldn't
pull these two worlds together. I hunted in vain for some thread
I could hold on to." Mostly he just sat off by himself, not want-
ing to join in games with the others. Happily, Swiss German
was closely related to Yiddish, and very soon the mute boy
began to speak again. One day a doctor came and examined him;
he would discover many years later that it was Jadassohn, the
friend of his future foster parents. Shortly thereafter he was
taken away by a woman from Zurich. Later he would ask himself why he had not at least ended up in a Jewish family, and
would reproach his Jewish friend who had taken part in these
illegal rescue operations for what had happened. What could he
be thinking? the fellow would respond; in those days they had
had to put all their efforts into making sure the children survived somehow.[47]

His foster parents were quite old, already of the generation of
grandparents, Wilkomirski says. "They were childless and were
very much embarrassed to admit to others that I was adopted. If
a visitor said, 'What, you have a son this big; did you take him

in, then?' my foster father would often say, 'No, no, he's always been here.' And if the visitor said, 'But I've never seen him before,' he would say, 'He's often sick, that's all.' Which was true. If I objected to remarks of that sort or replied before they could, there'd be a slap on the mouth and hell to pay. 'You don't say things like that!' But usually I would get locked in my room if a visitor came. 'Children disturb grown-ups,' they would say."

Once he was taken along to a family celebration for his foster father's parents, then in their nineties. It was held in a hotel dining room. "A long table was already set and people took their seats. My foster mother made a timid remark about how my setting and chair had been forgotten. My foster father's mother banged her fist on the table and shouted in a very loud and angry voice, 'I don't allow unbaptized savages at my table—there's the place for him!' and pointed to a corner of the room, where there was a little table far away from everyone else. That was where they put me, leaving me to curious looks from the other hotel guests, who had heard the whole uproar."[48] What do you do as a child, Wilkomirski asks, when you're the disgrace of the family?[49]

He lived in a state of chronic anxiety for decades, Wilkomirski says. He feared that his illegal status in Switzerland would be discovered and he would be deported as a Jew and an undesirable.[50]

Wilkomirski shows me some of his foster parents' correspondence, including two letters from the summer of 1946. The sender was Kurt Dössekker's father, who was very upset, "because you *never said one word* about your *intention* of taking in a child, let alone about the *adoption* you are evidently planning in the near future." Angered by their secrecy, he asked, "Why is it that you have been so incomprehensibly tight-lipped with us, with those closest to you, your parents, who have always been lovingly ready to support you in everything? You will *never* be able to free yourselves of the reproach of having to lie in the bed you have made for yourselves. Don't be too angry with me &

please send me an answer that will settle my nerves."[51] The conflict would remain unresolved five years later. "We *urgently* beg you," both fathers of Wilkomirski's foster parents would write, "to decide *for once and for all* against adopting Bruno. If you provide Bruno with a good education, a lovely home, and the skills to enter a profession of his choice, you will surely have done a fine work of Christian charity—and you may choose to do other things as well. But the thought that as a result of an adoption Bruno will be your *sole, legal heir* after your passing, that he will come into possession not only of *all your* property but also of *half of both our inheritances,* becoming a millionaire while still a young man without having lifted a finger, is *intolerable to both of us.*"[52]

His foster parents were not Jewish, Wilkomirski says, and though they knew of his origins, they made them taboo. They constantly hammered into him that he had to forget the past, that he had only dreamed it. "If I said that wasn't so, they would shout me down: 'Children have no memory, children quickly forget.' That was one of their standard maxims. And these scenes always ended in angry shouting and weeping. I would give up, resign myself, and babble their maxims after them in the hope that they wouldn't send me back—I still had a roof over my head and a certain measure of security. Things would go on like that for a while, until at some point I would lose control again and accuse them of lying."[53]

There were two Jewish girls at his school. His foster parents strictly forbade him to walk with them, although they all went home the same way. If he disobeyed, they punished him severely. Why did they forbid him to do all these things? he asked them. It was only for his protection, they said. Once his father shouted at him that people in Switzerland didn't like Jews either, and he shouldn't have any contact with them.[54]

"Once," Wilkomirski says, "I discovered a magazine with pictures of war ruins and lots of barbed-wire barricades. I ran screaming to my foster mother. 'You see, that's where I come from! From there!' and pointed to the pictures. 'I don't come from where you always tell me I do. Look here! Please tell me where that was, please!' She strictly forbade me to look at any more picture magazines. Then she said the usual thing: 'You just dreamed it.' But I wouldn't let it go, and I begged her to tell me whether she knew anything, if she knew where I came from. And in the end she grew weary and suddenly said, 'That was so awful, such a horrible place, that no one should even speak about it.' "[55]

The rule of silence made every sort of security seem illusory. "Nobody ever said right out to me, 'Yes, the camp was real, but now it's over. There *is* another world now, and you're allowed to live in it.' So I said to myself, All right, you're still stronger than I am. I'll pay constant attention, I'll learn the rules of your games, I'll play your games, but that's all I'll do—play them— I'll never become like you. You people, you profess to take these rules seriously. You preach honesty, and you're liars. You preach openness, and you won't tell me the truth. . . . The good life is nothing but a trap. The camp's still there![56]

Wilkomirski would often carry on such conversations with himself as he sat in a tall old fir tree in his foster parents' garden. He had built himself a perch there with a view out over the city. He was safe there, he wouldn't be disturbed, no one would follow him, no one would hear him. For hours on end he would repeat all the details of his past that he could remember, because he lived with the idea of escaping and returning to where he came from. And for that he needed to keep all the details in his head—what a road looked like or a certain corner of a house— otherwise he would be lost. When he started school and learned to write, he put down everything he knew. He filled a little book bound in brown linen with his texts and drawings. His foster parents appeared in it, too, but not in a flattering light. For a long time it was his best-guarded treasure, but at some point his foster mother found it, and it disappeared into his foster father's desk.[57]

THE BEGGAR BOY AND WILLIAM TELL—
TWO SCHOOL EXPERIENCES

He entered Switzerland in early 1947 or 1948 and was sent to school that same spring, Wilkomirski says. He presumes he was nine years old at the time. But he had hardly grown at all over the last few years; he still looked like a five-year-old and was the smallest boy in his class. They called him "dwarf" and treated him accordingly, which was hard for him to bear, given his earlier experiences.[58] They talked an awful lot in school, Wilkomirski says, but no one had the faintest idea about life. And now came a bad time for him: "Mostly, I couldn't understand a thing. I could understand most of the words quite quickly, but when I put them together, they made no sense, no shape that I could project. So I dozed along in class, mostly baffled by what was going on around me."[59] It was a wonder that they even let him remain in school. He will always remember the time before his exams when all the other children's notebooks were full, but his were all empty.[60]

A few weeks after he entered school, Wilkomirski says, his teacher took the class to a Folk Fair. He was excited, but also afraid that he might betray his past, that someone might become suspicious that he was one of those who had no right to share in all these comforts. Unsure of himself, he walked through the fairground with its unfamiliar booths and amusements. A chestnut vendor gave him a "round hot brown thing," and Wilkomirski tried to eat it shell and all; the man roared with laughter when he spat out the shell. Then he was terrified by children aiming guns and shooting at a painted lady.

There were stalls with marvelous sweets. Wilkomirski started to feel hungry, but he had no money to buy things with. He remembered how he had sat on a street corner in Kraków and stretched out a hand, his cap at his feet. Since he had no cap, he used a handkerchief instead. "What sort of disgusting behavior is this?" a man roared, and pulled him to his feet. "People don't beg! It's forbidden!" News of Wilkomirski's outrageous behavior spread throughout the whole school; his foster parents also learned of it and were scandalized because he had disgraced them. Months later the children were still taunting him as a "beggar kid."[61]

One day, Wilkomirski says, the teacher unrolled a large colored poster and asked the class what they saw. "William Tell!" they all called from their benches. The teacher ordered Wilkomirski to describe what was in the picture. He looked in horror at the poster, which showed a man who was evidently named Tell—a hero—and who was aiming a strange weapon at an unsuspecting child. " 'I see—I see an SS man,' I say hesitantly, 'and he's shooting at children,' I add quickly." The children burst into laughter, the teacher's face turns red with rage. Wilkomirski is totally confused, cannot interpret what is going on. "I look straight at her face. I see the glittering eyes, the angry, twisted mouth—it's the block warden. There she stands, legs apart, sturdy, hands on her hips. The teacher's a warden— our block warden. She's just in disguise, she's taken off her uniform." She has been trying to trick him, Wilkomirski thinks, and will now hand him over to Tell, who will lead him away and take aim at him. Where the blackboard had been, he sees the big smoking chimney, the teacher's red sweater has become a huge fire. "The class has gone wild, they're all yelling. The girls are laughing right out loud now, high mocking laughter, and tapping their foreheads, while the boys point at me and make fists and yell: 'He's raving, there's no such thing. Liar! He's crazy, mad, he's an idiot.' " After school the students fall on him like a swarm and beat him up. Wilkomirski cannot understand why they are fighting with him, and no one helps him. "Then, to save myself, I fly away in my head, and soar through the air, over the houses and roofs, over the evil city and away, following the

birds, far away over endless birch forests, lakes, and rivers, I circle pure white clouds and fly on over hills and valleys, I wave at
Motti, my eldest brother, who's in a sunny field throwing his
handmade airplane—and it's all beautiful. Motti waves back."
At some point he realizes that the blows have stopped, and he
goes home.[62]

"THE CAMP'S STILL HERE"—
GROWING UP IN SWITZERLAND

He found no help at home, Wilkomirski says. His foster parents'
strict ban on speaking of his past reinforced not only his certainty that he had come from a very bad place, but also his conviction that he was to blame. This confusion had begun with his
arrival at the Dössekkers' home, when his foster mother showed
him the fruit racks in the cellar and he was immediately afraid
because they reminded of the bunks in the concentration camp.
What was going on, what were they hiding from him? When
she led him to the coal furnace, his thoughts began to tumble:
"The camp's still here."[63] Later—he was perhaps ten years old—
he panicked during a winter vacation when he heard the menac-
ing roar of an engine. Children were hanging from wooden
double hooks that were being pulled up the mountain by a thick
steel cable. "The death machine," he heard himself saying, and
instinctively threw himself into the snow. "In those days ski
lifts in Switzerland were driven by Saurer engines. A survivor
from Majdanek has told me that at the entrance to the gas
chambers were two trucks for producing the gas and that they
were driven by rebuilt Saurer engines. And just as a child nowadays can distinguish the engines from among different kinds of
cars, that sound had been so deeply imprinted in my mind that
it was able to frighten me to death later in Switzerland." And
just as such recollections could overtake him during the day, his

nights were constantly tormented by nightmares. Primarily these were of lice and insects that attacked him and could not be shaken off.[64]

He could not keep the two worlds apart and assumed that all children had grown up in barracks. A schoolmate once said something about kindergarten, and Wilkomirski took that to be another term for "child quarantine," the children's barracks in the camp. He began to ask the schoolmate whether he had ever been beaten, how he had survived, how many had died. The boy ran off in a panic. There was a big scandal; parents forbade their children to play with him anymore. Each time he timidly attempted to share his memories with someone, the person would tap his forehead—Binjamin was crazy. He began to doubt his own memories, to believe he wasn't normal, was perhaps a bad person. It was too dangerous for him to confide in anyone, since he had been brought into Switzerland illegally. In his despair he attempted suicide several times—the first at age ten by eating mushrooms he thought were poisonous.[65] His sole source of support was the Dössekkers' housekeeper, Hermine Egloff. She had taken the position with the family only because she saw it as her religious duty to save the child. She had immediately realized that the family was dysfunctional and that there was something wrong with the boy.

His foster parents, on the other hand, were "terribly old-fashioned," Wilkomirski says. His foster father "was a quick-tempered, authoritarian person who thought that money and his doctor's degree allowed him to do whatever he wanted." He was a proponent of Prussian precepts when it came to child-rearing; the boy was often spanked and had to change his clothes three times a day. Wilkomirski considered his foster parents hypocrites. They always had smiles for the outside world; the most important thing was what other people thought. When he wanted to learn to play the violin—his greatest wish since arriving in Switzerland—they would not permit it. "Fiddling" was not appropriate in their social circle. They had a grand piano, which they considered a more suitable instrument for people like themselves. When Wilkomirski was thirteen, he borrowed a clarinet from a schoolmate; unlike a violin, it could be hidden under his mattress. He secretly taught himself to play it and did not start regular lessons on the instrument until about four years later. When his foster parents learned that his classmates were organizing parties and were allowed to go on vacations without chaperons, they permitted him to do the same, for the sake of appearances.[66]

In high school Wilkomirski began to understand his story better: "Not until I was thirteen, fourteen, fifteen did I slowly find the words for things, but not for all of them. I realized for the first time what the images meant." He read in newspapers about the trials of old Nazis in Germany and Austria. He could not bear the ridiculously light sentences and scandalous not-guilty verdicts they received. "During this period I began to have horrible revenge fantasies. I swore that someday I would take revenge on the whole world for what had been done to me." He hung out in dubious pubs and made contacts with the underworld to find out how to get hold of explosives and weapons. He had already made a few friends who might possibly form a group with him to carry out his plans for revenge, Wilkomirski says.

During this period, however, there was an incident that pulled him up short. Because of unsatisfactory grades, he was transferred from the academic *gymnasium* to a standard high school. A classmate—a large, fat boy with a cold smirk—was always making fun of him because of his poor grades in math. The thought crossed his mind: Damn it, I know that grin, it's the grin that kills people. He exploded, pummeled him down a whole flight of stairs, and left him lying at the bottom. The boy was so badly beaten that he ended up staying in the hospital for three weeks—Wilkomirski hadn't known that he had asthma. He had come close to killing him and was almost expelled from school because of it.[67] Reality, the fact that he himself could hurt or even kill another person, had caught up with his fantasies. It terrified him—if he kept this up, he would become like his block warden.

He saw only one countermeasure—to learn more. His foster parents allowed him to attend a private *gymnasium* so that he could pass the national final exams. They proposed a deal: they would pay for his future education, but he must accept their last name for once and for all and later study medicine. Although he had been living with the Dössekkers for a long time, he still had the legally less binding status of foster child. In the spring of 1957, they went to the municipal authorities to finalize the adoption. Now he finally belonged to the couple with whom he had thus far spent only unhappy days and whose name he hated. "It was really terrible, I felt in a way blackmailed, but it was the only thing to save me."[68]

At the private *gymnasium* he met two teachers who became important to him, Wilkomirski says. They helped him understand his nightmares a little better and to put his memories in a historical context for the first time. One of them was Werner Keller, his history and German teacher, whom he revered. The old, white-haired gentleman had himself been driven out of Germany by the Nazis, and so he had his own reasons for teaching students about the Nazi system and World War II. "I soaked up every word he said, asked endless questions, followed up every suggestion to get hold of additional books, which I then secretly read. My foster parents must not find out."[69]

But the more he concerned himself with his own memories, it seemed, the more elusive became the sense of what had happened. "It made me despair. Why had I, in particular, survived? I hadn't earned that right. I had brought too much guilt on myself for that." He thought of the new boy in the camp, who had been killed for acting on his advice that night; of friends at the orphanage in Kraków whom he'd left to their fate; of his mother, whom he'd betrayed by calling a stranger Mother. His class was shown a documentary film about the Allied liberation of the concentration camp at Mauthausen. He was horrified—that wasn't how he remembered it, those happy faces, that wasn't true. It was a trick. Then he became uncertain: "Perhaps it's true—somehow I missed my own liberation."[70] Wilkomirski never told his history teacher the reason for his interest. The only person he could confide in was Salvo Berkovici, his physics teacher.

"Why did you feel you could open up to him?"

"Just how he looked. He looked very Jewish, and I thought, Oh, that's one of us."

"He looked Jewish?"

"Yes, yes, he came out of a very, very old Romanian family of rabbis and was the first who didn't become a rabbi, but he had about five or six doctorates."[71]

The wise old man understood him and made him feel safe. He was his guide and mentor, the kind of father he would have wished for himself.[72] When he visited him for the last time before his death, Wilkomirski was feeling completely exhausted, had lost all lust for life, felt like cold ashes. He told Berkovici that after passing his exams he would study chemistry so he could use his knowledge to burn the whole world down. The old man's reaction made him aware that he would only be destroying himself that way, and somehow that restored his hope: "He just said under these ashes there's still a little fire—that he can feel it and see it. Such little remarks became very important, because I knew he's telling the truth. He doesn't tell it just to comfort me."[73]

Thanks to these two teachers, Wilkomirski realized that he was not crazy. That was what was most important for him at the time. The candid way in which they dealt with the past provided an acknowledgment of his memories for the first time, and that saved him. Until then he had had only one means of assuring himself that he wasn't imagining things: he could touch the scar on his forehead and the bump on the back of his head and tell himself, "Nothing comes from nothing."[74]

MUSIC AND HISTORY

Wilkomirski says that his foster parents (despite his adoption, he almost always refers to them by that term) sent him upon his graduation to Geneva to study medicine. But he didn't last long at that, and soon informed them that instead he was attending physics lectures and had registered for clarinet lessons at the Geneva Conservatory. His decision caused a rift between himself and his foster parents. He sought no contact with them for a long time. He chose music because it was the only way he could express himself and find the hearing systematically denied him elsewhere. No one wanted to hear the language that he had spent so much time learning, he thought. But they had to listen to his music. After graduating from the conservatory and making his first recording, he received a scholarship from the canton of Zurich for two years of study at the Vienna Academy of Music. And so he became a musician and music teacher.[75]

He married early, but the marriage was not without its complications, Wilkomirski says. "When I visited my foster father at his medical office to tell him I wanted to get married—my girlfriend was from a 'prominent' Protestant home and was expecting a child—he completely lost control, slapped me, and shouted what an idiot I was not to have found myself a Jewish girl, that I would come to regret that. I was speechless and thought, Now you've given yourself away!" This slip confirmed for Wilkomirski that despite the family taboo, his foster father had always been well aware of his past. A second difficulty came from the civil authorities. For reasons unknown, the official papers did not arrive in time for the wedding—to the bridegroom it seemed a "debacle." A bad beginning for any marriage, and this one would fall apart two decades later.[76]

When he returned to Zurich after his stay in Geneva, Wilkomirski decided to do graduate study in history. His aim was not to follow the career of a historian but to put his story into context and to understand it. He knew that as a student he would have greater access to many archives than he would have otherwise. "So, finally I've also chosen the subject of my thesis so that I could with some detours combine that with my personal researches." The subject of his research, begun in the mid-1960s, was Jewish migration in central and eastern Europe between World War I and the Refugee Conference at Évian in 1938.[77]

Wilkomirski traveled to Poland several times, but in the 1960s and 1970s it was very difficult to gain access to archives there because the Polish minister of the interior was a fanatical anti-Semite. When he went to Warsaw and Kraków in 1968, he met a Pole named Sylwester Marx on the train. As they passed through Czechoslovakia, which had recently been occupied by Soviet troops, the Polish man noticed Wilkomirski's anxiety and surmised that he had no idea what lay ahead. He invited Wilkomirski to visit him and his wife at their home in Katowice. Wilkomirski stopped in Warsaw for a few days to find out what archives were available to him, and then traveled south. On the way back he visited Marx and his wife, Christine. A friendship developed, and Sylwester became his interpreter, accompanying him everywhere and showing him how to get around in a country under a totalitarian regime. In 1973, Wilkomirski went to Kraków and Warsaw a second time. Because he failed to report to the authorities every day, he was stopped, deported, and punished by being forbidden to reenter the country. It was not until 1993 that he made his next trip to Poland, when he no longer needed a visa, Wilkomirski says.

Although he found abundant materials, he had to give up on his doctorate shortly before completing it. The research weighed too heavily on him; besides, he had a family to feed, which is not an easy task for a musician. When at age forty he was diagnosed with a spleen tumor and a blood disease with symptoms similar to those of leukemia, it seemed more doubtful than ever that he would finish his doctorate. And so in the mid-1980s, he donated the more than one thousand documents he had collected to Yad Vashem, the Institute for Remembrance and Research, in Jerusalem.[78]

Even as he was engaged in his research, he was still trying to come to grips with his own personal past. While studying at the Vienna Academy of Music, he had frequented used-book stores that were run by Russian émigrés who also dealt in objects from Eastern Europe. He gave particular instructions to one of the dealers, with whom he had struck up a friendship, to let him know if he ever ran across anything with a connection to the name Wilkomirski or to the city of Wilkomir (or Ukmerge, in Lithuanian), from which all the Wilkomirskis originally came. One day while Wilkomirski was still in Vienna, the dealer phoned to tell him he had something interesting for him. It was a portrait of a rabbi from the city of Wilkomir, painted in the year 1848. Wilkomirski bought it and took it with him back to Zurich.

IMPOSED IDENTITY — A LIFE IN TWO WORLDS

In the 1960s, Wilkomirski says, he read Jerzy Kosinski's *The Painted Bird*.[79] The author had arrived in Switzerland after the war and begun to write his book there. Wilkomirski was given a few episodes to read by one of his fellow students even before the book was published. "[Kosinski] was the first person ever to write about children and their experiences when they were little in Poland. Very matter-of-fact, just as he saw it, whether he understood it or not. It was the most touching and most shocking thing I had ever read," he recalls. Kosinski had been twelve years old at the time he experienced these things.

"In a camp?" I ask.

"He wasn't in a camp. He was shuttled around underground."

"Is he Jewish, too?"

"He doesn't know for sure whether his origins are Jewish or Gypsy. A lot of people take him for a Jew."

Wilkomirski explains the book's title. Rural Poland was rife with superstition and brutality. The last time he had been in Rytro with Sylwester, who had a vacation home there, he had experienced it himself: the stupid cruelty, as if the average Pole still lived in the Middle Ages. Kosinski describes huge flocks of birds that move across the countryside. Village boys think it's fun to catch a bird and paint it, then let it go and watch as it is no longer recognized by its own flock. "It looks different, it smells different because of the paint. It's rejected as a foreign body and pecked to death. That was the village sport. And it's from that episode, included in the book, that the title comes."

"Does this metaphor apply to you as well?" I want to know.

"What do you mean, to me? It happens to so many; child survivors feel that way, too."

"What affected you so much about the book?" I ask.

"I didn't recognize the events, but the truth of the atmosphere that was rampant in those days. He experienced it somewhere entirely different in Poland, but still within the framework of the Shoah."

Wilkomirski says that decades later he again met his childhood comrade Karola. It was a chance meeting on a train in France. She was working as a translator. Together they went to the hospital to visit her mother, whom she had lost track of during the war, but later found again. After that he and Karola met regularly and became friends. They never spoke about the past they shared—the children's home in Kraków, or other things— for fear of touching the real bond between them. "She doesn't talk about it even today, at most just hints at it," he says. I ask him whether he could put me in contact with this woman. He refuses. I don't quite understand his arguments; perhaps he wants to protect her from any unpleasantness.[80]

In the autumn of 1979, Wilkomirski met a man who from

then on was to be his closest friend and his companion on his journeys into the past. This was Elitsur Bernstein ("Eli" to German speakers), an Israeli psychologist who had been living in Zurich for almost two decades. One day Eli telephoned Wilkomirski and said he wanted to learn to play the clarinet. During his first free trial lesson, Wilkomirski's new student turned toward the wall and asked, "Who's looking down at me so sternly there?" He had noticed the portrait Wilkomirski had bought in Vienna. That was the rabbi of Wilkomir, he was told. Bernstein became very excited and asked if he could call his father in Israel. "Do you know who I'm taking clarinet lessons from?" he asked on the telephone. "From someone who owns a portrait of the rabbi of Wilkomir." It turned out that Bernstein's father had attended a yeshiva in Wilkomir, Wilkomirski says.

In the 1980s he began to search for possible relatives. One day he discovered that there were at least thirty-six families named Wilkomirski in Israel. He learned this from Bernstein, who in the meantime had returned to Israel. Among his Israeli namesakes there had been a Mordechai, who had died in about 1978, or so Wilkomirski was told. He had come from the Baltic, had slipped away from one of the transports, and had, incredibly, managed to escape. That was the only time Wilkomirski ever heard of anyone who had the same name as his older brother.

He was disappointed that news of this Mordechai reached him after his death, Wilkomirski says. He did not dare follow the trail any further. It takes courage to brave the past, and Wilkomirski could not simply cast aside a burden forced upon him since early childhood. He had long since learned to fit in with people's expectations of him and "tried to be a good actor" so that no one would ever suspect his true identity. "I did not really live the part. I always knew that I was someone else, but I was playing a good Swiss boy, the good Swiss citizen," he has said. Or again, "That I was only playing a role wasn't as clear to me at the time as it is today. But it explains for me why that sort of life can't be kept up for decades. At some point one's real self breaks through, as does the need to finally stand up for oneself and stop playing hide-and-seek."[81] It was no longer possible for him to research the Shoah without tying his work to his own individual experience.

"The repression of this traumatic experience suddenly no longer worked?"

"This repression can be halfway successful between twenty and fifty, but then it simply didn't work anymore, keeping the lid on my childhood." He "cautiously kept lifting it more and more," since those around him "allowed and wanted" him to, and he found the strength to do it.[82]

He has Verena Piller to thank for his finally pursuing his memories, Wilkomirski says. When he first became acquainted with her in 1982, he was still feeling the effects of surgery and had only recently separated from his wife. They met at the school where they both gave music lessons. "I felt the first moment, she was able to create a sort of atmosphere of security and that I from the beginning could tell her first a little bit and then more and more . . . about all my nightmares and where they come from and what I remember. And she had incredible patience and loved to listen, listen again and again, and that was during the time I was ill and it was due to her that I survived that, because I already [had given] up. I saw no chance anymore to survive this illness." Verena Piller told him that his physical problems were related to his memories and that he had to do something about them.[83]

His foster parents, with whom he had never been able to talk, both died in 1985. On paying his annual courtesy call some years before that, he had seen that they were totally alone and had subsequently taken care of them for two and a half years, cooking for them once a day. When they began to require more intensive care, he had had to find a place for them in a nursing home. At this point, there were problems with Rosie Berti, who had been his father's longtime assistant in his practice and who now insisted on the "most luxurious nursing home" possible for the two old people, Wilkomirski says.

He made several discoveries in the papers they left. He found letters revealing that his foster father had been disinherited: Kurt Dössekker's father had refused to allow "one single hard-earned Swiss franc to end up in the hands of such a good-for-nothing, half-naked scoundrel as Binjamin Wilkomirski."[84] Wilkomirski also found the parcel of objects he had brought with him from Kraków, though his hope of finding the little book in which he had written down his story the first time at age ten was met with disappointment. But he did make another discovery.

> In their papers I found a book belonging to my foster father about the psychological and psychiatric treatment of children and young people from concentration camps, by one of the first psychiatrists who concerned themselves with this problem after the war. I was more than amazed, because my foster father had had no use whatever for psychology or psychiatry—it was a red flag for him, and he had never allowed books of that sort in his house. It was totally amazing to me that I found this book, the only one on the topic. And he had evidently studied very thoroughly various cases discussed there, and had underlined certain things, certain place names and certain details, again and again, and then at the end of the book had jotted down symptoms and underlined them.[85]

Wilkomirski shows me what he is talking about. It is a well-known text by William G. Niederland, *Folgen der Verfolgung: Das Überlebendensyndrom Seelenmord* (The consequences of persecution: the survivor syndrome—murder of the soul), a milestone in psychoanalytic literature about the Holocaust, containing documentation of his examinations of Shoah victims who had filed compensation suits.[86] I page through and read the passages highlighted by italics or marginal marks.[87]

Something *new* had evidenced itself here: *chronic*, extremely *stubborn* complaints that therapy had little effect on, *underachievement* . . . psychologically deeply rooted *personality change* [p. 9] . . . *frequent and acute fear of death* and dying [p. 10]. . . . *He was unable to work at all for many years*, because he could not stay calm or even sit still. *He felt he was being followed.* [p. 13] . . . *Persistent depression from being uprooted* was common; *not a few committed suicide as a consequence.* [p. 16] . . . He recalled . . . having been taken "from place to place," including an orphanage, and having been a "difficult child," who was frightened, disoriented, and *restless*, who never spoke to anyone, *did not respond to questions.* [P. 29] . . . *He complained of general nervousness, insomnia, stomach pains*, anxiousness, of being *very easily frightened.* [p. 31] . . . The feeling of being uprooted, the loneliness and difficulty in adapting to a new country, can be seen in the fact that despite satisfactory intelligence, he had considerable difficulties at school and *remained "a poor student."* . . . that he retains only a shadowy but nonetheless fear-filled recollection of many of these places ("shoved from place to place"). [p. 41] . . . *Consequences of disturbed, hostile identity relationships* [p. 43] . . . On the basis of my own observations I *consider the impact on a child to be pathological* if, along with a familial atmosphere filled with fear and anxiety, there is the sudden and repeated removal of the child from one milieu only to be thrust into another unfamiliar milieu, frequent change "from place to place," and the shock of being separated from the mother, even if for only a limited time. [p. 44] . . . kept hidden . . . by a Polish farmer [p. 66] . . . a small but unattractive *scar at the hairline on the right* [p. 71] . . . *Riga* [p. 96] . . . *Out of a fear of nightmares, which recurred every night or every other night, she was afraid to go to bed.* [p. 102] . . . transported to *Auschwitz concentration camp* [p. 169] . . . He says: *"I try to be alone . . . I bear the memory of what I experienced with me and in me . . . I cannot talk about it."* [p. 170] . . . so-called *hypermnesia*, i.e., the extremely sharply focused *capacity for remembering*, under strong emotional affect, a traumatic persecution experience and the psychological shock associated with it. Hypermnetically retained events of terror tend—whether they occurred inside or outside the concentration camp—to return *especially just before sleep or during medical questioning, with an agonizingly sharp focus of both memory and image*, and present a new shock to the person formerly persecuted. [p. 230f.]

"He wrote a description of me and the way I had reacted as a child at home. Very curious," Wilkomirski says. He asks me, rhetorically, why his foster father would have underlined things of no medical importance: Riga, Kraków, geographical terms in general. He shows me a map on which he has drawn the routes indicated by the underlining, leading from Riga to Majdanek and Birkenau.[88]

The map hangs in his renovated farmhouse, where a large archive has been set up on the second floor, containing countless books and files on the Shoah, including notebooks filled with drawings and lists of children. It is as if these extensive historical materials were slowly crowding out living space; even a bedroom is now crammed with bookcases, desks, a copy machine. Wilkomirski is well equipped for his work, with computer, printer, scanner, satellite dish, video equipment, and fax, for he has become a hot line for survivors from around the globe who are researching their own history. On occasion he has even given courses and seminars on the Shoah.[89]

Wilkomirski leads me to the adjoining renovated barn, where he has his workshop for making clarinets. He shows me a few pieces currently under construction and explains how it's done. He learned the craft on his own. From his remarks one can sense the satisfaction he takes in this work.

His instrument-making was the main theme of a film project put together by the Colla brothers, Wilkomirski says. In the early 1980s, Fernando and Rolando Colla, students at the time, saw his workshop and had the idea of making a kind of music film that would show the process of turning a piece of raw wood into an instrument out of which melodies are coaxed for a concert. Although the filmmakers took some shots of Wilkomirski playing with a philharmonic orchestra, they were never able to complete their project. In response to my request to see the script, he shows me a copy of its cover—*Binjamin* is the title, and beneath it is a picture of a clarinet. He also gives me a letter written by Fernando Colla requesting grant money from the government for the project. Colla writes that Wilkomirski's workshop is unique, since all the other clarinets in the world are produced in factories. Along with the instruments and the music, Colla also proposes to document "Binjamin's childhood in Poland." He is "not interested in depicting the horrors of the concentration camp where Binjamin spent a part of his childhood, but rather in finding images that show Binjamin as a victim of this terrible period: images of his search for an identity, his attempt to work through his own repressed childhood experiences. Images, too, for his speechlessness, for the somatic illness that has threatened his life for two years now and that he interprets as resulting from chronic repression." It seems to me that Wilkomirski's past played a larger role in the project than he now claims. Moreover, I'm intrigued that Colla mentions only one concentration camp. I ask Wilkomirski to give me the entire script. But he fails to see the point of my request.[90]

Wilkomirski says that the film project with the Colla brothers had not been so important to him, and that it had been initiated solely by the filmmakers themselves. Rather, for him the decisive experience was the 1984 television film *Der Prozess* (The

trial) by Eberhard Fechner, documenting the trial of SS executioners from Majdanek concentration camp.[91] It showed interviews with witnesses, defendants, defense lawyers, and judges,
as well as historical material. "It was the first time I had ever
seen pictures of Majdanek. There was not even any literature
about it; it was a forgotten camp. During the trial at Düsseldorf
they showed historical photographs for the first time." These
confirmed the images in Wilkomirski's memory; he recognized
things, some of which he had already told Verena Piller about.

"Were there surviving children in the film as well?" I ask.

"No, there were only reports about children. There was a segment—but a very large one at that—about the so-called children's actions that took place there."

JOURNEYS INTO THE PAST

Wilkomirski says that in the meantime he had pursued his historical researches like a long-term hobby. In the early 1990s,
however, the real reason for his studying history in the first place
asserted itself stronger than ever. He decided to try to analyze
his memories by using historical methods and scientific ratio-
nality. He was so sober, in fact, that he approached his analysis
as if it were someone else's story. In addition to his own extensive reading—over the course of thirty years he has plowed his
way through roughly two thousand books, plus twice as many
files—he now went back to visit the localities in his own story.[92]

In the summer of 1993, he returned to Poland for the first
time since 1973. Joining him this time were his girlfriend, Verena Piller, and the entire Bernstein family, as well as Remigius
Marx, the son of his Polish friends Sylwester and Christine Marx.
They had a video camera with them, operated by Avi, one of the
Bernstein sons.[93] In Kraków, Wilkomirski visited with the former rector of the university, a biologist named Janowski, who
was considered an expert in the history of the concentration

camps and was now working with former prisoners. Wilkomirski wanted to show him some drawings and plans he had created on the computer as part of the therapy he had started by then. Although still skeptical of Janowski, he let him see several sketches he had made from memory, indicating where the barracks stood, what they looked like, from which side the sun came, and so on. Wilkomirski himself was fairly certain that these memories were associated with Majdanek. "[Janowski] very quickly laid several of the drawings on their side, gave them back, and said, 'Go to Majdanek. You will find it there.' Then I knew I was right. It was the confirmation that I wanted to have from an independent person."[94]

The next day Wilkomirski visited Janowski once more, and this time he was introduced to a very old man who had been interned in many camps and knew them in every detail. When Wilkomirski presented some drawings dealing with his memories from the period when he had become fully disoriented, the old man said, "That's Birkenau!" Wilkomirski fiercely denied it, but the man persisted, saying that the hydrant included as a detail in the sketch was something he could have seen only at Birkenau. "That was simply very difficult to accept, that idea, because I had always disputed it. I didn't want to have anything to do with it."[95]

The group traveled to the two neighboring camps at Auschwitz and Birkenau (or Auschwitz II). Wilkomirski says he had never been back to Birkenau since the war because the Communist regime had made it taboo to discuss the persecution of Jews. When Wilkomirski asked his friend Bernstein why his recollection of his experiences in this camp was less clear than earlier memories, Bernstein explained that it was due to his increasing exhaustion as a child after years of duress. The videotape made of this visit shows Wilkomirski searching for site after site in the camp. In one hand he holds a map. His face looks strained. The group arrives at a spot where everything fits: the corner, the outline—but the light is coming from the wrong side. Finally Bernstein's sons discover that Wilkomirski's drawing should be read as if in a mirror. Wilkomirski says that Bernstein attributes this to the fact that until age seven or so children's brains do not definitively differentiate between left and right, so that optical memories are often stored in their memory as mirror images.[96]

Various barracks are shown on the tape, and Wilkomirski explains to me how he hid under the laundry in one of them. Three years earlier, he met a survivor from Lodz who had once worked in this barracks and who confirmed his description of what had happened there. Wilkomirski told him how a few days before the Russians liberated the camp, he left with a woman and walked to Sandomierz. "He became very excited: What, what! Yes, that was well known, so I'd been the one!" I ask for the name and address of this witness from Lodz, but Wilkomirski never wrote it down and doesn't think the man is still alive.[97] In answer to my question as to exactly when he left Birkenau, he says it was 22 or 23 January, and refers me to the *Auschwitz Chronicle*. During a later visit I ask Wilkomirski for the book, since I know he has it in his archives. The entry in question is marked and matches his description: around noon a group of women and children left without being molested and were able to walk to the train station at Auschwitz.[98]

On the way to Majdanek, the group stopped in Sandomierz, where Wilkomirski wanted to film the house in which he had lived with the woman after their flight from Birkenau. He found what he was looking for. A large blanket was hung out to air from the dormer window. "Just like back then. The room is just big enough for a bed," Wilkomirski says. From up there he used to look down into the valley and see birds below him. "That sticks with you," he says with a grin.[99]

This first return to Majdanek was the most decisive experience of the trip, Wilkomirski says. The film shows him during his tour of the grounds, a yarmulke on his head. In one hand he has a handkerchief, which he holds to his nose, as if the smoky stench of burning corpses were still in the air; in the other hand he holds his drawn plans. His eyes wander; he tries to remember, seeking some detail or other; he hurries in various directions. His face looks somehow harried, distant, as if he were moving about in a nightmare.

"Although most of the buildings were no longer standing, I immediately got my bearings again," Wilkomirski says. "And then I ran right up the hill to where my barracks had stood and where the foundations were still visible. My companions, who had all conducted themselves with reverence, were horrified by my running, and even more so when I said, 'This was my home.' "—in Field 5, the second barracks to the right of the west entrance. "Every person feels at home where his memories have taken root. And as dreadful as it may sound to others, home for me was simply a barracks."[100]

The film shows Wilkomirski searching in the overgrown field for the washbasin that almost never had any water in it, and finally finding a damaged stone trough. Later the group goes to the huge memorial monument, in the middle of which is a basin with a mound of human ashes, a low flame flickering around its edge. Wilkomirski weeps in Bernstein's arms for a long time.

The group then proceeded to the camp archives to ask for more information about the "children's quarantine." But the historians there laughed at Wilkomirski. There had never been anything like that here, they told him—him of all people, when he had found the location of his barracks on just that spot. "They made me look really stupid. It was a very rotten thing to do." In the museum bookstore he bought a book in Polish, in which he discovered a photograph of his barracks. Visible in the same picture, directly across from the "children's quarantine," were two newly planted trees and a low wall surrounding an open square. Wilkomirski could remember both features: sometimes the children would play there, and that was where Jankl used to slip away to look for food. A guard had banged Wilkomirski's head against that little wall once; that was how he'd gotten the scar on his forehead. The picture was his confirmation. He knew now for sure that he had been there, and his memory took on a chronology.[101]

About a year after this trip, Wilkomirski chanced upon a musician whose grandmother had survived Majdanek and made exact sketches of the camp. The grandson handed the files over to Wilkomirski; the complete edition of them is to be found only in his archive. He shows them to me. These are the papers of Eugenia Deskur, frequently quoted in the research literature. On a plan drawn on square-ruled paper and with hand-printed labels, the children's barracks is placed just as Wilkomirski described it. "From that moment on," he says, "I knew that I could depend more on my memory than on what is said by the so-called historians, who never gave a thought to children in their research."[102]

He and his companions then traveled east from Majdanek to the area of Zamość. He is fairly certain that it was somewhere near there that he was hidden away on a farm. "I know that I went south in the direction of Lublin, with the sun at my back. And my sense of distance is not so bad. I now know the various regions and only in this region did I find farms with the typical style elements, the canals running through rolling countryside, the appropriate vegetation, and the typical smell of the area." On the videotape, the group is shown standing on a dam as the water plunges into the depths below. Wilkomirski tells his companions about his memories of just such a small footbridge over deep water.

He explains how events that occurred there during the time in question also correspond to his recollections. The Nazis did in fact carry out their program of Germanization in the area. They "cleansed" Zamość of every Jew and Pole; according to Polish sources, some 30,000 children were taken to Majdanek. (On another occasion Wilkomirski shows me a book from his archive, in which the "cleansing" of the region and the deportations to Majdanek, including those of peasant children, are described in detail.)[103]

In the autumn of the same year he returned to Majdanek, this time with Sylwester Marx. First they went to Lublin, which is not far from the concentration camps, and visited with Ewa Kurek-Lesik, a historian who had written her dissertation on the children in Majdanek and its environs and who they hoped could solve one of the riddles in Wilkomirski's recollections. His barracks at Majdanek was not far from the crematorium—the children suffered from the smoke and the stench, their eyes burning and their skin turning oily—but after he was taken to see his dying mother, the crematorium had suddenly seemed farther in the distance. Kurek could explain this remarkable change. All the children in the quarantine in Field 5 had been murdered in a massacre in November 1943. The camp had been corrupt, however, and thanks to bribery a few children had been moved from Field 5 to Field 3, where they were smuggled in with the Christian peasant children and thus survived. During their visit to the camp afterward, Wilkomirski and Marx established that this shift in perspective of the crematorium did in fact match the change of location.[104]

Wilkomirski says that he flew to Riga in August 1994, accompanied by Eli Bernstein and Verena Piller. They took the video camera along this time, too. Even from the plane, he recognized the city—which he had not seen since fleeing it by night more than fifty years before—by its unmistakable silhouette. First they went to the harbor, where Wilkomirski had long ago left the city by boat. He found the little bollard where he had had to stand waiting in the freezing cold until their departure. Then he tried "to go back in his mind, in the direction from which we had come to the harbor that night. Eli and Verena had to walk behind me so that I wouldn't be distracted." The three of them walked for four hours, until suddenly on the Iela Katolu (Catholic Street) they were standing in front of a house that Wilkomirski remembered.[105] He immediately stormed up the steps to the second story. On the videotape is the sound of Wilkomirski saying in Swiss German that it was this "jumble" of doors that he recalled, he was certain of that. "We found it all just as I had described it beforehand. The front gate, the house entrance on the right, the stairway on the left leading up into the house, the door off the first landing, where the shout 'Watch it: Latvian militia!' had come from, the second floor with its two apartment doors, so close together that only one door could be opened at a time . . . the view from the house to the street, where you could see a church steeple and the towers of an orthodox church." It was by these towers that Bernstein knew at once that this was the right place, because Wilkomirski had told him, before their trip, about a library with a clock and the view of church towers. At the time Bernstein had thought these towers out of place in a ghetto, so the image had stuck with him, Wilkomirski says.[106]

The next day they spoke with a local historian named Marģers Vestermanis, who had survived the Riga Ghetto as a young man and now in large measure confirmed Wilkomirski's recollections. He explained that the house on Iela Katolu had been included within the Ghetto for a single month. For ages it had been home to a Jewish charitable organization, a kind of first stop for Jews new to the city and trying to get their bearings. When Wilkomirski described the murder of the man who might have been his father, the historian interrupted and said, "I know what you're talking about. I was there." The Latvian militia had liquidated the Large Ghetto, he said, on the night between 29 and 30 November 1941.[107]

GENES AND FILES—
BINJAMIN'S FATHER, BRUNO'S MOTHER

In the months immediately following his trip to Riga in the summer of 1994, Wilkomirski participated in the making of an

Israeli documentary film. Entitled *Wanda's List,* it was produced for the Israeli television network Kol Israel by its director, Vered Berman, and was broadcast on 22 November 1994.[108] The film documents how Jewish child survivors with no sure idea of their origins have searched in archives and among eyewitnesses for traces of their own past. The historical research was done by an Israeli named Lea Balint, originally from Poland, for whom children without identities have been a major concern. She knows the problems of such survivors from personal experience: she herself survived the war, after fleeing the Warsaw Ghetto, by hiding in a cloister under an assumed identity. Balint asked Wilkomirski if he wanted to be involved in the film.

Irena Dombrowska, one of the main figures in the film, was tossed out of the train to Auschwitz as a baby, and so survived, Wilkomirski says. She and he were later in the same orphanage in Kraków, but he does not remember her. The video shows her original name being recovered from her falsified passport: it reads Erela Goldschmidt.

Wilkomirski, wearing a yarmulke, is seen in the film visiting the research center Yad Vashem with his friend Eli Bernstein. He says that he first heard his name in Kraków, but he tells a member of the archive staff that he cannot be absolutely certain it is his true name.

Following an inserted sequence showing Wilkomirski locating his barracks in Majdanek, the film records a meeting with Julius Löwinger, who lived as a child after the war in the home on Augustiańska Street and who now lives in Israel. Löwinger shows several photographs, one of a group of children and others of various buildings. His questions are translated by Bernstein. Wilkomirski says in Swiss German, "I remember a kind of carpet-beating pole, a high bar." He motions with his arms as if trying to pull himself up on a high bar. "Right, there was one," Löwinger says in Hebrew, nodding vigorously. (Wilkomirski has a copy of the group shot from Löwinger's album dating from 1946 or 1947; he shows it to me and points to a boy in the middle of the second row: "That's me." Unfortunately, no one could tell him anything about this particular boy—he means about himself—which is not surprising, since he was never in one spot for long.)[109]

In another scene, Wilkomirski and Erela Goldschmidt sit across from an old, white-haired lady, with photographs spread out on the table in front of them. Wilkomirski has evidently mentioned the name Bruno, for the old woman asks about a Bruno Jas—"That wasn't you, was it?" He shakes his head. The woman is named Misia Leibel, and she worked as a children's attendant at the Augustiańska orphanage. Wilkomirski explains to me that he recognized her from a photo. He has negative memories of the meeting. "She was very grumpy, very cranky. She had her problems, was constantly arguing with her daughter, who accused her of having taken care of everyone except her. She didn't want to hear about any of it anymore." She couldn't remember Wilkomirski then, though four weeks later he heard in a roundabout way that she did remember him after all.[110]

The camera follows Wilkomirski during a strenuous search for his orphanage in the streets of Kraków. At last he finds a building he thinks he knows and points to where the playground was. (It later turned out, Wilkomirski explains to me, that he wasn't correct; this building was only similar to the right one.)

In one moving scene, Frau Goldschmidt finds the Christian couple who had hidden her in Poland. The film is both fascinating and touching in that it portrays eyewitnesses from those days discovering their own lost origins bit by bit. Wilkomirski, however, is unsuccessful in his search. A final summary sequence includes video shots of the house that Wilkomirski found on Iela Katolu in Riga; the commentator repeats that even Wilkomirski's name cannot be determined with certainty. He asks viewers to forward to the station any pertinent information concerning those portrayed in the film.

The first program elicited such a strong response, Wilko-

mirski says, that a sequel to *Wanda's List* was broadcast in July
1995. A woman named Sarah Genislav had called him from
New York, saying that she had likewise been in the orphanage
on Augustiańska Street. Her mother was the Frau Grosz he had
mentioned in his story. Frau Grosz had been a frequent visitor to
the orphanage and was always brought in when a child needed
to be told something difficult. She had been a patient woman,
with more time to give than the attendants. She might well
have brought him to the train station in Kraków, but it was
not possible that she had accompanied him to Switzerland. Presumably, Wilkomirski tells me, his memory has merged two
different women into one.[111] In the film we see Frau Genislav
greeting former residents of the orphanage at her apartment in
Israel. Those who have gathered there share reminiscences and
look at photographs. Wilkomirski is also present, but he looks
lost somehow. When I ask him if Frau Genislav had recognized
him, he reacts testily. That same old question, asked again and
again, only reveals total ignorance of the situation, he says; one
surely should not expect so much from young children—she had
been just nine years old at the time.

One older woman speaks directly into the camera, her words
animated and yet almost solemn. This is Sarah Lerner, Wilkomirski says; she had also responded after the first broadcast, and
now there was no getting rid of her. She claims to recognize
Wilkomirski as her sister's son, who was named Benjamin (but
not Binjamin) and who disappeared into the concentration
camp at Majdanek. His mother had died, but his father, Yakov
Maroko, survived in Field 4.

The film shows a taxi, its passengers a woman and three men,
all in black clothes and hats, two younger men with *payess* at
their temples and an old man with a snow-white beard. Wilkomirski says this is Yakov Maroko, with his second wife and
sons. Maybe heaven has sent a miracle, Maroko says from the
backseat, quoting Wilkomirski. "How can a child still live after
fifty, fifty-two years?" They enter a hospital, the father in the

lead, closely followed by his two scowling sons. A very short man, he is there to have blood drawn. Wilkomirski says he did the same in Switzerland. In the wake of Sarah Lerner's conjecture that he was Maroko's lost son, the two men had established contact. They wrote and telephoned each other often. Then someone suggested that the surmised relationship could be determined by a DNA test.

In another scene, Maroko sits in his living room and reads aloud a letter to Wilkomirski. His excited face disappears at times behind the sheet of paper. "After so many years I hear the voice of my little child," he says. Sarah Lerner holds up a photograph; a young woman with braids stares into the camera. This is, we learn from what is being read, Maroko's first wife. "I have to end my first writing to you, my so dear baby. For me you are my baby. Your father, Yakov Maroko." His voice breaks, his hand drops heavily to the table, his eyes are moist.

Maroko and his family return to the hospital; he makes a joke to hide his nervousness. Without further ado, the doctor reveals the finding: Bruno cannot be Maroko's son; it is biologically impossible.

"Who first came up with the idea of a blood test?" I ask Wilkomirski.

"There was just a feeling that a test would make sense, because a lot of things in our two stories matched, but other things didn't." It is not a clear answer to my question.

"The DNA test was conclusive for you?" I ask.

"Pretty conclusive."

"And for Maroko as well?"

"It was an ethical and religious question as to how one should react."

In the film, Maroko's family, along with some journalists and other people, are shown waiting in the arrival hall at Ben Gurion airport. A voice off-camera quotes Maroko as saying Bruno is his son—he has spoken with several rabbis, and all of them have confirmed this for him. A few people discuss the similarity between photographs of Wilkomirski and Maroko's first wife. A doctor sees no resemblance whatever to the putative mother but some similarity to Maroko's sister-in-law. He is asked, "You're a doctor. Medical science says no, what do you think?" "I say yes!" he responds. Wilkomirski appears, wearing his yarmulke, with a printed shawl around his neck. Maroko falls into his arms, sobbing for joy. Wilkomirski embraces the younger men. "My brother, my brother," says one of Maroko's sons.

Wilkomirski walks among huge stone slabs at Yad Vashem, the Institute for Remembrance, each inscribed with names of vanished Jewish committees. He stops at the one for Ukmerge, the city from which the Wilkomirskis come. The negative results of the blood test are not so important, he says into the camera. "The most important thing, I think, is that we met, we were in the same situation, at the same places. We found out now that we have so many memories, the same memories of the time from these places; it's a very strong feeling not only of solidarity but really the feeling to belong together, that we belong together, and the biological thing is in the background. The important thing is the human feeling you have. He was looking for his son, I was looking for my father, and he was ready to accept me, and these are circumstances in a beautiful, beautiful way."[112]

In a later film, Wilkomirski says that Maroko remains "totally convinced" that he is his child. For the first time he has felt from Maroko a father's love that is deep and genuine. In decades past he was always trying to reconstruct a picture of his mother from his memory; he never even thought of having a father as well. It was simply incredible to experience something like this at his age: "It really was like a miracle."[113]

I ask Wilkomirski if he has researched events in Switzerland as systematically as he traced things back to Riga, Kraków, or the concentration camps.

"That was less important to me. Why should I have done that?"

"So that you could reconstruct your history," I explain.

"We tried that with no success after the wedding debacle."

The registry office in Biel, he says, was mysteriously evasive and refused to give him his birth certificate. "But that's not normal. I'm a Swiss citizen," he protested. "Yes, but you see, in your case—" the official explained. Wilkomirski insisted: "But I would like to see any documents on file about me." The official remained implacable. That was impossible; he was not allowed to look at them, and as far as the official could tell, that prohibition would not be lifted. He also refused, Wilkomirski says, to put the substance of their conversation in writing or to provide an alternative document. An inquiry directed to the Zurich city hall likewise yielded nothing. It was beginning to seem quite eerie, and Wilkomirski spoke about it with a Jewish acquaintance. "He said that Switzerland was just as corrupt as other countries; it was simply more expensive here. I should be careful and diplomatic about it, otherwise I'd undermine my own legal status in Switzerland. And I decided to let things be."

He did not, however, give up completely, Wilkomirski says. "I tried several times in the late seventies to find Yvonne Grosjean, the woman listed as my 'mother' in my documents. At the time I suspected she was the woman who had 'left' me at the Basel train station. I went to Biel and Tavannes more than once. But I could get no information from the civil authorities, only 'hearsay': that was the woman who had ended up in a mental clinic, and there was no talking with her. And so I came back home empty-handed each time. I was never able to establish contact with the woman, and never saw her." He also went to Adelboden, since his foster father had "served up" a story about his having been in a children's home there. He first heard of this at age twenty-two, but didn't believe it since his foster father always changed the story each time he told it. "I have examined pictures of the place and the general area—and I can't recall ever having seen such a place, or an area even vaguely like it!"[114] The exchange with Bruno Grosjean took place in a children's home located somewhere else, Wilkomirski says.

THERAPY AND WRITING— PATHS TO PERSONAL HISTORY

No sooner had he completed filming *Wanda's List* in Poland, Wilkomirski says, than he took off for another visit to the east in October 1994, to take part in a conference on the Shoah held in Ostrava, in the Czech Republic. He had been invited by a member of the board of the Association for the Advancement of the Chair for German Studies at the university there. "As the result of a forty-year ban by the Communists on research into the history of Judaism in Galicia—Ostrava lies just to the south—students there have a great need to make up for lost time and are especially interested in studying the multicultural roots of their own history," he has noted. These new contacts resulted in Wilkomirski's deciding to return to Ostrava the following year to give "seminars on the cultural and historical aspects of the mutual relationships between Christians and Jews and questions of Shoah research."[115]

In April 1995, he gave a "guest lecture series on the topic 'Problems of the Shoah (Holocaust)' " at the University of Ostrava. In it he called attention to the "most neglected" segment of contemporary historical research: the "study of that part of history that has left no written traces, so-called 'oral history,' which demands a special technique for questioning contemporary witnesses." In October 1995 he elaborated from the same lectern on the nature of this technique. "The Child's Memory as a Historical Source in Contemporary History, as Exemplified by Surviving Children of the Shoah" was the title of his talk, aimed at "both historians and psychologists."

In his lecture he first turned to the "preconditions necessary for successful questioning of an adult about his or her childhood memories. For this, I urgently advised interdisciplinary co-operation between a trained historian and a psychologist. Since in our case we are dealing with witnesses to the Shoah, memories connected with it are usually accompanied by very serious trauma often extremely agonizing to talk about. To prevent the historian from causing further trauma with his questions, he himself, along with the witness, requires the support of a psychologist versed in the field."

Using practical examples, Wilkomirski then spoke of "several fundamental types of childhood memory, based on diverse examples, ranging from the physical, 'preverbal' memory of very young children to the purely visual and those first intellectually verbalized memories that are to be 'reverbalized.'" Finally he "discussed the most common forms in which a child's memory of traumatic experiences are stored, . . . in order to call the historian's attention to possible difficulties and the dangers of misinterpretation."[116]

His talk became the "basis for a lecture" that he would deliver several times along with Eli Bernstein, first in June 1996, at the World Congress of Psychotherapy in Vienna.[117] Wilkomirski says he developed the concept of interdisciplinary therapy they presented there "both as a survivor and as a historian," more or less as "experiment on himself," and came to realize that it might help others to regain their lost identities. In Israel this approach has been employed in therapy with fifty people to date.[118]

In fact, all the examples given in the talk relate to his own story, for example, his flight from Riga: "After more than a year of being therapeutically assisted in concentration exercises, a client who had very vague recollections initially recalls a scene that takes place outside a building in a city he associates with the name Riga and in which a man, possibly his father, is murdered—." The client also recalls a nighttime flight to the harbor and sailing off in a boat. When visiting the place, he is able to identify individual elements from his memory and to have them confirmed by a local historian, who finally declares:

> "It snowed that night; that was why you were wet and half frozen. We also know of a boatman in Riga harbor who, as best we can tell today, smuggled more than sixty people to the other side of the Daugava that night." The client mentions his family name, which he can remember. In a "house book" from 1927, the historian finds that the only family of that same name listed lived in close proximity to the house identified by the client. The client, who has suffered from regular and severe migraines for many years, is instantly relieved of them from that day forward.[119]

Wilkomirski says that at the start of their friendship, Piller suggested that he write down his memories. She saw a connection between his illness and the repressed fears and aggressive thoughts that were turning destructively on his own body. Because of the nightmares he was having, she urged him to go into therapy. Not until the early 1990s, however, did he finally realize that he needed help. He went to a therapist on an irregular basis, sometimes several times a week and sometimes not at all. His therapist taught him to remain calm and to concentrate on his memories and not get them jumbled up. He now began to write them down and show the texts to his therapist. "Look, I have found a language, now I can translate it," he told her. The process allowed him to bring order to his memories.[120] They are not the product of therapy, Wilkomirski emphasizes; he had written them down the first time as a child. "I simply wanted to get a precise fix on it all and concentrate on what was still in my memory, be it important or unimportant." He also wrote them for those closest to him. He had three children from his marriage; they should know more about their father than just that he was born on the far side of Poland. He wanted more understanding from those who often reproached him for his strange reactions to things, his hypersensitivity, his fearfulness, and panic attacks. He had had enough of "strict self-control" and "playing hide-and-seek."

He wrote chapter after chapter and gave them to those closest to him to read. Sometimes they would talk about them, sometimes not. Despite his writing, he did not think of himself as a writer: "I never polished my text. I just wrote a chapter in half an hour, in one hour, and that was it."[121]

Wilkomirski says that it was his younger son's encouragement that made him decide to write a book that might reach an audience of people with similar experiences, and that the book has now appeared in sixteen languages.[122]

This, then, is Wilkomirski's version of his story.

THE ORIGINS OF *FRAGMENTS*

FINDING A HEARING — WILKOMIRSKI'S GIRLFRIEND,
VERENA PILLER

Verena Piller-Altherr is a slender, dark-haired woman of about fifty who has her own grown children from her first relationship. She says she first knew Wilkomirski as Bruno. She was aware of the name Binjamin, but he did not make an issue of being called that. Even for her, the name Binjamin tends "to make him smaller." She doesn't want to see herself "constantly confronted by this little boy"—his life, too, has moved on. "For me he is Bruno and Binjamin, but I actually live with Bruno."[1] In my presence she watches over him solicitously, as if to guard him from undue stress.

Although during my visits she usually stays in the background, I have the impression that the preoccupation with his story and her concern for him have become the center of her life. I feel the omnipresence of the past in both their lives as somehow frightening, and I speak to her about it the first time I sit down with her alone.[2] It was like that from the start, she responds. She talks about all the symptoms that are part of his story: the insect phobia, the way his feet move when he sleeps, the way his body constantly remembers things, the images in his mind of medical instruments. She remembers their watching the film about the Majdanek trial in Düsseldorf: "For the first time ever I saw how he retreated into this childlike posture, absolutely turning to stone. You could touch him, but you had the feeling he didn't notice, because he was staring at the dog kennels on the screen."

Of all the trips she has taken with her partner, for Verena Piller the one to Majdanek was the most terrible experience. "He ran up the hill to where the barracks had stood. . . . I thought it would be a horrible shock for him. But he said, 'It's like going back to someplace where you lived as a child.' And yet he was in a state of near-collapse. I saw him weep for the first time at such a place. And I was glad that Eli [Bernstein] was there, he was his mainstay. I felt very lost. I realized that I didn't really belong to this story; that was quite clear. It's such a vile place, I don't ever want to go back there."

Piller stresses how important it was for her to take Wilkomirski seriously: "I don't think he's experienced that in his life very often." She didn't block what he was saying, as people had done with him before. And in that way his past, she concedes, may have gained a greater priority. But his being preoccupied with his past was nothing new; he had searched for it before. "He says he has always had these images. They didn't first appear when I got to know him and he could talk about them." Not until ten years after their relationship began did he write them down: "That took a lot of courage."

"Did you have to encourage him?" I ask.

"I told him it was important. I didn't want to push him." She doesn't think that his writing them down was "the only reason the images were released. It was simply time for it to happen." Otherwise he might simply have perished from "his ghastly images." She describes how Wilkomirski was totally changed whenever he wrote, as if he were in the grip of something he had to get rid of. "Then he'd usually read it aloud to me. I knew that I didn't dare cry, because then he would stop." She had learned from him that his ex-wife had always cried, and then he would take back what he had told her and say that it wasn't all that bad, just so she would stop crying.[3]

In 1984, Piller and Wilkomirski visited their friend Bern-

stein in Israel. On their arrival, Bernstein says, Piller took him
to one side. "Do you think Bruno is a Jew?" she asked. "Why do
you ask?" Bernstein replied. She explained that she had been
warned by Bruno's former friends and his ex-wife that he was
lying, that he was a pathological liar and not the person he pre-
tended to be. It was worrying her and she wanted Bernstein's
opinion. This was at a time when Wilkomirski was also com-
plaining to his friend about the horrible nightmares he was having, which were all about being followed. Bernstein's response
to her was, "I've never approached the matter in any legal sense,
and I don't have the knowledge of historical details, but I
believe him intuitively." And, Piller says, her own inner voice
tells her, too, that "it might very well be possible."[4]

THE JEWISH FRIEND —
THE PSYCHOLOGIST ELITSUR BERNSTEIN

Just from the way he looks, Bernstein seems predestined to be a
staunch friend to the obviously fragile Wilkomirski. He has a
broad build, his massive head is framed by a reddish gray beard,
and his gray hair is combed back, making his brow look even
higher and more angular. We meet in a restaurant at the Zurich
main station, where he has only just arrived from Israel. His
handshake is strong, and he greets me in almost perfect Swiss
German.

Born in Israel, Bernstein came to Zurich in 1961 to study
medicine at the university, but after a few years he switched to
psychology. Even before he was awarded his Ph.D. in 1980, he
had worked in the field, first as a school psychologist, then at
Schlössli, the renowned psychiatric clinic near Zurich. When
asked, he says that he does not belong to any particular school of
psychology. He works on a psychoanalytical and psychodynamic
basis, but has also been trained in behavioral methods and group
therapy. He returned to Israel in 1982 and nowadays practices in

a Tel Aviv suburb. He flies back to Zurich regularly to teach at the IAP, the Institute for Applied Psychology. When he is in Zurich, he stays in Wilkomirski's town apartment, the same one where he had his first clarinet lessons twenty years ago.

Bernstein emphasizes that he still calls Wilkomirski Bruno, as he has always done. He prefers to refer to him that way with me, too: "If I don't to have to talk about Binjamin here, it will make it more authentic." His friend once asked him to call him Binjamin, but Bernstein replied, "Listen, I met you as Bruno, there are plenty of Jews named Bruno, for me you're Bruno, just as you've always been."

The issue of whether Wilkomirski was or was not a Jew played no role in their friendship, Bernstein says. After discovering the portrait of the rabbi from Wilkomir in his clarinet teacher's apartment, he made a decision never to press him with questions: "Everything I know about him came spontaneously from him. I never asked." In September 1980, Bernstein visited him in the hospital. Wilkomirski had undergone surgery that morning and was still delirious. He was muttering incoherent things about Leibniz's mathematical worldview and phrases in Yiddish. Bernstein was taken aback. "Yiddish is my second mother tongue. There was crazy stuff, too, but there were fragments that made perfect sense, like '*Ich will nish*' [I don't want to] or '*Losst mich ob*' [Let me go]." He left the room without disturbing the patient. When Bernstein got home and told his wife what had happened, she said, "Don't you want to ask him if he's Jewish?" "Don't touch it," he responded. Today he's very glad he didn't do it, Bernstein says. It had been more the psychologist within him speaking. And he thought, "If there's something to it and he wants to talk about it, it will come on its own. I don't want to initiate it and certainly not to influence it by suggestion." He was intuitively afraid he might set off something in Wilkomirski that "could suck him into the vortex, which happened later in any case."

In December 1981, Wilkomirski had to be hospitalized

again. When Bernstein visited him that time, he saw two Yiddish books on the nightstand. In response to his surprised question, Wilkomirski said that he spoke Yiddish but wanted to
increase his knowledge. From then on, Bernstein's conviction
grew that his friend needed therapy. "Above all, it was obvious
that he was recovering very slowly. I saw a subdepressive, for-
getful, somewhat volatile man. So I asked if he'd ever thought
of trying psychotherapy. He turned me down flat. He wanted
nothing whatever to do with a psychotherapist. That wouldn't
help him at all; his problems were of a much larger nature."

The following spring, Bernstein and his wife invited Wilkomirski to join them on a Friday evening for Sabbath dinner.
"We had a very lovely evening together. I had the impression he
was clinging to the atmosphere of our home. It was almost a revelation to him." Bernstein thought he could sense an affinity in
Wilkomirski, something strange and amorphous that was lying
fallow. "We sang a lot together. If you hear a piece of music
whose style is strange to you, you usually feel some annoyance or
are put off. I had the impression, He's familiar with this style
but has no real knowledge of it. He knows that there are prayers
before, during, and after the meal, but none of the particulars."

Bernstein's return to Israel put an end to the clarinet lessons,
but not to his friendship with Wilkomirski, with whom he was
now on a first-name basis. Wilkomirski told him about his
nightmares, which were getting worse by that time. In the
early 1990s, he had an especially bad night. He dreamed that
he was sleeping, heard a horrible racket, ran to the window, and
saw a lot of people being burned alive. It was at this point that
Wilkomirski agreed to start therapy.[5] He went to see the psychologist Monika Matta, with whom an acquaintance of Verena
Piller had put him in contact. Bernstein knows Matta from his
student days and recalls her as being a very sensible and obser-
vant woman. He says that while her orientation is psychoanalytic, she does not practice classic psychoanalysis. Wilkomirski

has told him that she also works with nonverbal techniques, in which drawings and the awareness of the body's emotions play a large role. For nearly ten years now, there has been a heated argument in the United States about therapies that claim to bring patients to a conscious awareness of repressed traumatic memories (the so-called recovered-memory debate). When I question him about this, Bernstein explains that Wilkomirski's therapy did not include hypnosis, hallucinogenic drugs, or any other such methods. Like Wilkomirski (and Piller as well), he emphasizes that this therapy did not belong in that controversial category and was in no way the soil from which the book had grown.[6]

During a visit to Switzerland in July 1991, Bernstein heard that Wilkomirski was writing down his memories.[7] "He asked me what I thought about it, as a friend and as a psychologist. I said, 'As a friend, I say do it. As a psychologist, I say do it. It will be very helpful when you're talking with Frau Matta about your memories.' One night in September, around two in the morning, the fax rings. . . . I jump up out of bed to see what it is. And there are the first pages he's written." It was the story about meeting his mother in the concentration camp. The next morning he telephoned Wilkomirski, who asked, " 'So what do you think? Should I go on writing? Can it have been like that?' I told him I didn't know if it could have been like that, but if he was writing on the basis of his memories, it probably had been that way, and he should go on writing."

That same night Bernstein read the text to his wife. They were both horrified to learn that Wilkomirski had lived through an experience like that. Over time they received more of the stories; one or two of them they had heard before, "but their being written down in this way was new to us."

"Do you think all the stories were already there before?" I ask.

"I don't know. I read a lot of new things in the pages that were faxed to me, but for me they fit into the whole picture."

He was most deeply moved by the accounts of Wilkomirski's meeting with his mother, the rats, and his life in hiding on the farm, where the child is suddenly left absolutely alone. "In the story of his being with his brothers on the farm there's a vacation mood, there's kindly Motti, who comes back again and again as a key figure in his life. And suddenly everything comes to a stop." Bernstein found these descriptions so agonizing because they told of life circumstances that bordered on a kind of normality and then suddenly turned into the horror of naked force. The final story he received was the one about the new boy in the camp whom Wilkomirski told to relieve himself in his bunk, as there was nowhere else. Wilkomirski is still haunted by guilt over the incident, because the guards killed the boy as a punishment. That time, Bernstein says, Wilkomirski did not ask what he thought, but whether he could be held accountable as a murderer. According to Bernstein, it was this concern that caused Wilkomirski to have reservations about the book's being published in a Hebrew translation.

By that time, Wilkomirski's texts had already been published in several languages. Wilkomirski, seconded by Bernstein and Piller, insists even now that there was originally no thought of publication. Piller says, "I didn't urge him to write a book, but to get his memories out and put them down where they could be viewed from the outside." Bernstein says that both his and Verena's reaction to the notion of publication had been "one of great reserve," and that even Wilkomirski had "in fact resisted the idea at the start." Wilkomirski reiterates that he originally wrote the texts just for his children and those closest to him. So why were they published? I ask him. "Because people persuaded me and said to me, look, under certain circumstances this will help other survivors who are totally isolated and living without any contact with other survivors."[8]

In January 1994, Wilkomirski gave his texts to Eva Koralnik, an agent who helps to find the right publishers for manuscripts. They were entitled "Embers Under the Ashes: Days of Childhood 1939–1947: Fragments of Memory."

A SINGULAR SUCCESS — A PUBLISHER IS IMMEDIATELY FOUND FOR THE MANUSCRIPT

Eva Koralnik is one of the owners of the Liepman Literary Agency, with offices in an old Zurich villa only a few minutes' walk from the street where Wilkomirski grew up. I have come there to meet with Koralnik and have her explain to me how Wilkomirski's manuscript came to be published. Hers is a very prestigious agency, handling manuscripts and books translated from many languages, primarily English, French, Dutch, and Hebrew. It represents the interests of authors from all over the world[9] and oversees a number of important literary estates, including those of Erich Fromm, Anne Frank, and Norbert Elias. It is not just by chance that the Liepman Agency represents many Jewish authors and books dealing with World War II. Ruth Liepman, who founded the agency in Hamburg in 1949, was forced to leave Germany in 1934 because she was Jewish and there was a warrant out against her for her political activities. After moving to Zurich in 1961, she found in Eva Koralnik a partner whose life likewise bears the stamp of the Nazi era. Koralnik's mother was a Swiss Jew who in marrying a Hungarian had lost her Swiss citizenship. When Hungary was occupied by the Germans in 1944, the family was threatened with deportation from Budapest, but was saved thanks to the personal intervention of a courageous Swiss diplomat, who helped both the mother and her two little daughters flee at the last minute.[10]

Such a background more or less predestined Liepman AG to be the agency of choice for manuscripts about the Shoah, and Eva Koralnik tells me she receives memoirs from a great many

survivors. "Most of them are not publishable. I've just come
back from a book fair in Jerusalem. Dozens of survivors offered
me their manuscripts. Each individual's story is a tragedy. Sometimes the people break into tears, but mostly they are very composed. It's hard to say, No thanks, the market's saturated."[11]
Koralnik lives body and soul, night and day, for her books and
authors; she takes a lively interest in the fate of other people.
One can imagine how difficult such a refusal must be for her.

But after reading Wilkomirski's manuscript, she was not
faced with such a dilemma for a single moment. She had known
him superficially as a musician for several years, she says. "The
fact that I knew the person and now such a horrible world about
which I had no idea suddenly opened up may have made it especially moving." But she was impressed not merely by that but
also, and above all, by the unusual form his memories took—
their fragmentary nature and at the same time the fully rounded
composition of the whole. She asked Wilkomirski how he had
been able to put such painful memories on paper. He replied
that his therapist had been of considerable help. It hadn't been
enough for her simply to read the texts; he had had to read
them aloud to her, which had been difficult. The manuscript,
however, was not the crude detritus of therapy sessions, but
was instead perfectly shaped throughout. Koralnik asked Wilkomirski what certain gaps with ellipses meant. He replied that
he had put down only the things he remembered, nothing else.

Eva Koralnik began looking for a publisher. And now something happened that she had never seen in her thirty years in
the business. Whereas she had had to for search six years, for
example, to find a publisher for Ida Fink's masterly stories about
the Holocaust, it all went surprisingly quickly with Wilkomirski. Almost every international publisher to whom she showed
the manuscript—including the most prestigious—immediately
wanted it. At the end of July 1994, she turned to Suhrkamp
Verlag. Thomas Sparr, editor in chief of the Jüdischer Verlag
at Suhrkamp, replied at once. These memories had greatly im-

pressed not just him but his colleagues and friends as well. The firm's publisher, Dr. Siegfried Unseld, promptly decided to put the book on the Jüdischer Verlag's list for the coming spring, if possible. Sparr suggested that the book be called *Bruchstücke. Aus einer Kindheit 1939–1948* (Fragments: From a childhood 1939–1948). He considered the text ready for publication and had only a few minor changes in syntax to suggest.[12]

Wilkomirski invited friends and acquaintances to a party at his home at the end of January 1995, the fiftieth anniversary of the liberation of Auschwitz. He says he saw the day as a substitute birthday for his real one, whose date he did not know. There was music, and he read from the manuscript, already in production at Suhrkamp.

"A VERY TICKLISH MATTER" — HELBLING'S DOUBTS

"I was on a ski vacation, in the middle of February 1995, when I received an alarming phone call from Thomas Sparr," Eva Koralnik recalls. "Our agency's reputation was at risk. I had never sold a manuscript about which there were any doubts whatever." Siegfried Unseld had received a letter from Hanno Helbling, the former head of the feuilleton of the *Neue Zürcher Zeitung*. It read:

> Dear Herr Unseld,
> While here in Rome, where the final phase of my more or less journalistic activity has landed me, I've happened to hear something I am passing on to you on the presumption that it might be new to you in some way.
> A fifty-year-old musician who has or has had a very difficult life—I don't know his name—has found his "identity" with the help of a psychotherapist. Just as it used to be a good thing to know that one was secretly descended from

royalty, he has been able to persuade himself that he is a surviving victim of Auschwitz. On the basis of this assumption or certainty—perhaps not created out of thin air, but at any rate incompatible with reality—he has written a book that is ostensibly about his "concentration-camp memories" and is to be published by the Jüdischer Verlag. It also appears that certain Jewish circles have encouraged him in this.

Everything depends, then, on how such a publication is presented: as an "Auschwitz novel," to which the author has given the literary form of a first-person narrative (thus leaving obscure that he himself actually believes the book to be remembered); or as "genuine" memoirs that sooner or later may be identified as fiction; or as what it is: a psychological rarity, testifying to the Holocaust's ability to radiate into new mythic shapes. . . .

In any case, a very ticklish matter and, given the right circumstances, dangerous as well, in the sense that a legend about Auschwitz might be welcomed by those who endeavor to explain Auschwitz as a "legend."

It's quite possible I'm telling you in a general way something you already know in detail—if so, please forget this signal, or merely take it as a sign of life.

With warmest regards, your

Hanno Helbling[13]

The partial vagueness of these statements—"I don't know his name"—are in stark contrast to the certainty with which they are presented. One could choose to be either worried or outraged by the letter, but the writer needed to be taken seriously. Koralnik says that she immediately phoned Wilkomirski. He broke down and said it was starting all over again. These were the same rumors that were always coming from the world of musicians and from his ex-wife. It was all about his documents, about his not having a real birth certificate but only a summary of one, since his adoption meant he wasn't allowed to see his own files;

THE ORIGINS OF *FRAGMENTS*

it was all so wrapped up in mystery that only with great difficulty had he been able to get the official documents he needed
for his marriage. This news came as a shock to Eva Koralnik.
Wilkomirski had never spoken previously of any lack of clarity
in regard to his documents. She now began to question him
about those documents and about his own memory. She also
called Verena Piller to the phone; Piller said that Bruno always
started to tremble when he heard mention of or saw a film about
the Holocaust. All his memories came welling up then, she said.
Koralnik demanded that Wilkomirski provide her with all the
relevant arguments and papers that supported his memories.
Since he apparently had a phobia about bureaucratic offices, she
insisted that he hire a lawyer and that together they search for
his documents so she could then show them to his publisher.

Koralnik says that at the time she also discussed this matter
at home, at some length. If he was not who he said he was, how
could he make up such an outrageous story? But if he had been
through all this and his past was now being called into question,
that was horrible, too. What an upside-down world, in which a
victim of the Shoah had to prove his story; what a dreadful
humiliation for the man. "I was in a very difficult position," she
says, "for I knew the most improbable cases of children who had
been hidden in monasteries, among peasants, and so forth, and
were then confronted with their real identities only much later,
but had no documents, only shadowy memories."

In response to my question, Koralnik says she continued to
believe in the authenticity of the memoirs even after Helbling's
letter. I asked if she had not found it unsettling.

"His answers all sounded so convincing and so congruent,"
Koralnik replies. "I proceeded from the assumption that it was
all true." Since she herself had fled from Nazi persecution as a
child, at about the same age as Wilkomirski, she could, in contrast to someone untouched by those events, put more objective
and critical questions to him based on her own experience.
"What language did you speak? Who brought you to Switzer-

land? Where were you registered?" Wilkomirski had an answer
for everything and promised to produce the documents in a very
short time. "He was searching, desperately, feverishly, for documents to give to me or Suhrkamp. Everything was always *en
suspens* with him; we kept thinking we'd have something tomorrow. He told us where he would be going, where there were still
lists, that there was yet another orphanage where his name
might show up, and so forth."

Thomas Sparr wrote Wilkomirski that, given the accusations
that had been made, the Jüdischer Verlag had "stopped delivery
of the book, which is almost ready. I beg you to provide me with
your birth certificate, your adoption papers, some document
about the transport of children to Switzerland, your naturaliza-
tion papers, as well as any other documents that show your identity or nonidentity. I am also asking you to obtain an opinion by
experts at Yad Vashem as to how they regard your status."[14]

Elitsur Bernstein says his friend was in terrible shape at the
time. Wilkomirski thought of withdrawing the book himself,
because he felt defeated, not because he doubted its truth. Both
Bernstein and Verena Piller opposed this idea: he had started
something, had invested a great deal, emotionally as well as
otherwise, and he must not give up like this. It wasn't a matter
of bringing out the book come hell or high water, but he must
respond to the accusations.[15]

No sooner had Sparr mailed his request to Wilkomirski than
he received a letter from the latter's psychotherapist.[16] On the
basis of twenty years of clinical experience with childhood and
infant trauma, Monika Matta writes, she can clearly distinguish
between her clients' authentic and their "allegedly real" experiences. Wilkomirski has spent two and a half years working
through his childhood with her, and has been able to make traumatic memories accessible again to his own experience. She has
shared in the experience at close proximity while, by frequent
repetition, he recalled all the scenes of this book and many other

situations as well, down to the most minute detail, at the same time reawakening all the physical and psychic symptoms—for her there could be no doubt as to their authenticity. One could regard his book *Fragments* as the result of this thoroughly painful and debilitating process. Wilkomirski has never tried to hide the existence of his birth certificate, she goes on, but has always insisted that it was not his own. He would be unable psychologically and physically to undertake long years of legal challenges to these documents, especially in light of the fact that encounters with civil authorities trigger panic attacks in him (a familiar problem among survivors of concentration camps). She therefore requests that Sparr explore every other avenue available in order to take the wind out of his opponents' sails—for example, some other form of publication. She notes that she has found Wilkomirski to be a highly gifted, open, and honest man, who is equipped with an extraordinarily precisely functioning memory and who has been profoundly shaped by his childhood experience. She can attest with certainty to his identity and hopes that these absurd doubts can be dispelled and declared null and void. She notes that the publication of this book is very important for Wilkomirski, and says it is her wish that fate not overtake him in such a perfidious way, demonstrating to him yet again that he is a "nobody."

Only days later her fellow psychologist Elitsur Bernstein chimed in, though not in his professional capacity, but as Wilkomirski's close friend. His clinical viewpoint is nevertheless evident in his letter to Sparr:

I have known Bruno D. W. [Dössekker-Wilkomirski] since October 1979, when I applied to him for clarinet lessons without knowing anything of his origins and/or his past. To be sure, I had the "suspicion" even then that Bruno's origins might be Jewish, primarily because there were several books about Jewish issues in his library and because I noticed several Jewish objects (a Torah pointer, a Torah breastplate, pictures) in his apartment. This was, however, not yet a topic of conversation between us.

My first confrontation with Bruno's past occurred in December 1981, when he fell seriously ill for the first time and I visited him unannounced at his hospital in Samedan. On his table I found a Yiddish-German dictionary, as well as a book in Yiddish (*Sholem Aleichem*). This prompted me to ask direct questions. From then on our friendly relations developed into a sincere friendship, which has since deepened to the point where we are very attached to each other. In 1982, I returned to my family in Israel, but we continue to see each other several times a year.

He goes on to say that he thinks he knows Bruno as well as he would his own brother. On the basis of his own training he has tried to test his observations in psychological terms, but he has never acted as Wilkomirski's therapist. Since 1981 he has accompanied him "on his 'search' for his past and identity"—in countless conversations, on trips to Poland and Riga, in contacts with Yad Vashem as well as with the group "Children Without Identity." He adds that Lea Balint, "a historian who works at Yad Vashem" and uses lists from archives to reconstruct the origin and identity of child survivors, is "convinced of his Jewish identity and his stay in a children's home in Kraków." Bernstein notes:

I was able to observe Bruno during our trips to Poland and Riga. Long before the trips, he prepared drawings and maps on the basis of his memories and dreams (and/or nightmares), especially of Majdanek and Birkenau, talked about details that had resurfaced in his memory, and was extremely caught up in it all, sometimes as if in a trance. This pattern was repeated more clearly once we were there. The way in which he ran about among the barracks at Majdanek and

Birkenau revealed a unique mixture of shock, despondency, and a goal-oriented search. He seemed to me to be led by so-called body memories. I was present, both in Poland and in Riga, when he spoke with knowledgeable persons, historians or those who themselves had been caught up in these events, and I noticed that whenever he spoke with Jewish or non-Jewish persons, his German, which is normally oriented toward correct syntax and vocabulary, was transformed and took on a Yiddish color. Moreover, he was at times so agitated and engrossed that he would stutter severely. He could not find the appropriate words and used a very limited, childish form of speech. Hours would pass before the phenomenon would fade, until he found his way back to his usual correct mode of expression in German. Something similar occurred in the summer of 1994, when Wilkomirski searched the lists of names at Yad Vashem for the living or dead Wilkomirskis registered there. He did this upon the advice of Frau Lea Balint, who was able to induce Israeli television to produce a program on "lost children." I was present during the filming in Israel and saw how Bruno was asked many extremely difficult, at times even unsparingly provocative, questions. In one instance Herr Julius Löwinger of Petah Tiqua (Israel), who as an adolescent was himself in the orphanage in Kraków, was very hard in his interrogation. He showed Bruno photographs of various buildings and demanded that he recognize the orphanage in question from among them. Then he asked him to describe in detail both the interior of the children's home and its environs. Finally Herr Löwinger said, "You were there, there can be no doubt about that." The film was broadcast on 22 November 1994 on Israeli television as a feature on *Mabat Sheni* (comparable to the BBC's *Panorama*). Had anyone doubted Bruno's basic assertions during the filming itself, Israeli television would not have got any further than its own internal censorship mechanism.

Bernstein explains that he was exposed to Bruno's manuscript
from the beginning "as a reader," and that he has "listened to
hundreds" of reports of survivors at home in Israel.

> In reading Bruno's manuscript I never had any doubt as to
> its so-called "authenticity." I shall take the liberty of saying
> that in my judgment only someone who has experienced
> such things can write about them in such a way. To be sure,
> I have no knowledge as to what extent particulars are accu-
> rate down to the last detail. But the spirit that moved me as
> a reader was the same one that I encounter working with
> someone who has been through these things and that is the
> hallmark of the stories told by a great number of those who
> were children at the time. . . .
>   As a very close friend and as a clinical psychologist I
> assert that every charge that, for whatever reason, seeks to
> expose Bruno as a pathological liar cannot be true in any
> sense. It fills me with great sadness, making even my anger
> superfluous.[17]

Wilkomirski also faxed Sparr that same day. He had been
trying to reach him by telephone to no avail, and was writing
simply to inform him that he had an appointment with the
authorities for the next day to gather information. He would
then supply a report as soon as possible, both by telephone and
in writing.[18] Two days later Wilkomirski faxed a long letter.

> Dear Herr Dr. Sparr,
> Since yesterday afternoon I have tried in vain to reach you to
> tell you that this letter would be coming. Friday morning I
> went to Zurich, where I had an appointment at the office
> where adoption papers are kept. I went alone, afraid that I
> would stutter and be unable to make myself understood and
> that I would be put off as always before with a few gruff,
> curt words that told me nothing. The problem was that I

recall the date of my adoption only within a range of several years and possess no document myself. . . . The notary who received me actually found an entry and was prepared to show it to me and give me a photocopy of it. The entry is the official "decision to adopt," dated March/April 1957. Otherwise there was nothing new, nothing I didn't already know. Here, too, only the name of a mother was entered and her place of residence in the Jura near the French border. (I would ask that for now, the copies I am sending you by mail, and not by fax, not be shown to third parties without my consent. I will also include a copy of the "abridged birth certificate"—it is the only document to which I have legal access.)

After that I did something I have never dared do with a civil servant. I told the notary that I was certain that there was something wrong here, that I doubted [the document's] accuracy, that I could say with one hundred percent certainty that my personal memories could not in any sense be made compatible with the official record of a mother in the Jura. I also said that I had studied history, that I was well versed in how to deal with official records, and that I knew what importance such records have—and nonetheless I had to insist on what I was saying. I waited for the usual snigger or some other nasty response. I was surprised when nothing of the sort occurred! The lady simply said, "Just a moment," and fetched her supervisor, an older gentleman. I explained to them that the son named in the records of the lady from the Jura is presumably someone, that I, too, am someone, but that it is not possible for these two things to match. I said that it is my memory alone that stands, stands immovable, in opposition to an official paper. The incredible thing was that both civil servants listened calmly, took what I said seriously, and did not treat me like some "deluded mental patient" or "crazy crank." They explained to me how all data based on some original document are simply passed on, relayed, until they arrive where people can no longer check their accuracy, where such a check never takes place. They consulted with each other, began to ask me questions. By way of example I described in brief the events at the train station in Basel, where I was told over and over that no one knew who I was, that I was not on the list, that there was no place for me. Then they asked whether what I had in mind was some confusion, some intentional or unintentional exchange. I said yes, that was the variant explanation on which I had insisted since childhood, but to no avail, since no one had ever taken me seriously. To which they responded that an unintentional exchange of children was of course not provable by official documents, but that an intentional exchange could certainly not have been accomplished so deftly as to leave no traces behind. They regretted not being able to help me in the matter. I said that such a case must sound terribly absurd to the ears of civil servants. They said that they did not find it absurd, merely unusual, and that they had never encountered a case like it before in their office. They concluded by saying a friendly goodbye. I made a point of turning around one last time—and indeed no one was laughing, no one was tapping his forehead behind my back.

I am telling you all this in such detail, Herr Sparr, because it was such an important step for me. The news of Herr Helbling's objections came as a sudden blow that cast me back into the old childhood situation of total impotence and helplessness. It is a difficult battle not to fall back into the old pattern of response, into chronic resignation, and to realize that I am now in the position of an adult and am not a defenseless child.

The process of writing down my memories was extraordinarily painful, and it was an attempt to stand fast by my memories, and by my share of guilt as well. Suddenly it has become clear to me that this "processing" and my book itself are incomplete. It would be extraordinarily important to me if I could add a final chapter—or an afterword, or whatever it might be called—in which I describe the contradiction with which I have had to live since childhood. The contradiction between my own and my documented identity.

Wilkomirski continues his letter by saying that he cannot sleep, that night and day his thoughts keep circling around important events he would like to tell about. He tells how his foster family made his adoption a taboo, denied his past, and forbade him any contact with his Jewish schoolmates. He also describes in detail Dr. Jadassohn, who had a hand in the exchange of the two children. Finally he comes back to his sole source of truth:

Given the pointlessness of "battling authority," I began during the years of my illness to investigate and verify my memories with the acquired methods of the historian. I have drawn plans, detailed and general sketches from memory, and consulted countless experts, asking them to check my assertions. I have traveled up and down Eastern Europe, have asked experts there, and listened to their advice; friends accompanied me there, performing a "control function," and I have learned, and it has been confirmed: My memory functions correctly, I can depend on it. All this while well aware of necessary limitations. A small child's memory can be authentic, but one may not read unconditionally from it a historical/juridical authenticity in terms of the events contained within it. For a child's memory orders events differently; sometimes it builds bridges between events where there are none, in order to hold on better to individual images. The child's memory does not order things chronologically, but usually in terms of intensity. The sense of time is different. Something that expands in a child's memory over several years can in actuality have taken place within six months.

My illness showed me that it was time for me to write it all down for myself, just as it was held in my memory, to trace every hint all the way back. My life partner, friends, and a special therapist have helped me do that. No one knew that a book would ever come from it.

And with that I have explained, as best I can, my situation at the moment, have said what I know. And yes, I would also like for the book to be published.[19]

In the wake of Helbling's letter, Eva Koralnik assured Siegfried Unseld that she had "never had a shadow of a doubt as to the authenticity" of Wilkomirski's story. "That doubts have arisen among third parties came as total shock to me, and we must get to the bottom of the matter. I will be happy to join Thomas Sparr in Jerusalem, to visit Yad Vashem with him and see if we can find any documentary evidence."[20]

In early March, only a few days later, Sparr and Koralnik were both at the Jerusalem Book Fair and took this opportunity to speak with several people about Wilkomirski. Sparr met with Julius Löwinger, who had been a resident of the orphanage at 1 Augustiańska Boczna, Kraków, from 1946 to 1950, and who also supplied a written statement: "After I met with Bruno Dösseker-Wilkomirski in my home in September 1994, and he described to me the entrance to the building, the common room, and the playground, I did not doubt for a minute that he had in fact been with us in Kraków at the time." Bruno had also described in detail the routes down to the Vistula River and the place where they swam. Furthermore, he had identified in a photograph Frau Misia Leibel, the head attendant of the orphanage. "In light of this I am convinced beyond doubt that the child Bruno . . . was with us, although because of the difference in our ages he was not in close contact with me."[21]

Koralnik, Sparr, Bernstein, and Lea Balint met for a discussion at the King David Hotel in Jerusalem.[22] Balint likewise put her convictions in writing: "I am a historian, my studies concern the Shoah of Polish Jewry, and my speciality in particular is the issue of 'children without identity.' Within the framework of my research, I have thus far been able to trace the identities of seventeen people—date of birth, place of birth, names of parents, as well as the course of their lives during the war—all of which were previously unknown." Bruno had told her that his name was probably Binjamin Wilkomirski, though he was not certain of that, and also about his stay in two children's homes on Długa Street and Augustiańska Street in Kraków after 1945. For her "the most important information" he gave was Karola's name. "In June 1994, I had the opportunity to be at the Jewish Historical Archives in Warsaw, and there I photocopied every possible piece of material from the orphanage in Kraków, especially the lists of names of those children who presumably resided at that institution between 1946 and 1949. Due to a lack of time, I did not study these lists at once, hoping that I could do that in Israel. On the way back to Israel, I stopped over in Switzerland and left the lists with Bruno for a day. . . . When I returned that same evening, Bruno fell weeping into my arms and told me that he had found Karola on one of the lists. For me this was absolute proof that Bruno had been in the orphanage in Kraków."

Balint concluded by telling about the making of the film *Wanda's List* in Kraków in September 1994, when Bruno identified the children's home on Długa Street but could not find the second orphanage.[23] In her discussion with Sparr, Koralnik, and Bernstein, Balint cited the examples of two women about whom she had had her doubts as to whether they had ever really been in concentration camps. But she was certain about him: "Wilkomirski is real. I'm a hundred percent convinced he is real." Balint's statements were what convinced them, Koralnik says: Balint was a woman with a great deal of experience, she was familiar with the archive materials, and she had tried unselfishly to help Wilkomirski find his papers.[24]

Wilkomirski had meanwhile induced yet another acquaintance to take a position: the man who since 1969 had served as his translator on his trips to Poland. "I, Sylwester Marx, residing in Bochum, declare that I served as an interpreter in a conversation between Herr Bruno Dössekker and Frau Dr. Ewa Kurek-Lesik in Lublin on 19 October 1993. Frau Dr. Kurek-Lesik studied at the University of Lublin and wrote her dissertation on 'The Fate of Jewish Children During the Nazi Period.'" Marx quotes what the historian had said on that occasion: "She knows cases where through bribery and/or corruption children were moved from Field 5 and placed among Polish children in Field 3." Further, she was said to have claimed that "after seeing his mother, who gave him some bread, [Wilkomirski] was brought to Field 3, since no one who was in Field 5 survived the concentration camp at Majdanek."[25] And with that Wilkomirski offered a statement by an expert in the field about a remembered scene that had occupied his mind every day since childhood.

"LEGAL STEPS TO HAVE THIS IMPOSED IDENTITY ANNULLED" — THE BOOK IS PUBLISHED WITH AN ADDED AFTERWORD

Finally Wilkomirski asked Rolf Sandberg, the lawyer he had hired in the meantime, for a legal statement. In a letter to Sparr, Sandberg identifies two difficulties: "The first problem appears in connection with the birth certificates of adopted children, and thus with that of Herr Bruno Dössekker-Wilkomirski. Without considerable difficulty, i.e., without a suit brought against the registry office, it is impossible to obtain more than an abbreviated birth certificate, like the one that Herr Bruno Dössekker-Wilkomirski has presented to you."

Wilkomirski had asked Sandberg to confirm the fact that as an adopted child he had "no right to a full and complete review" of his files.[26] The lawyer was evidently not willing to be tied down to such an explicit statement—it would have made any further research among Swiss documents appear pointless—and so wrote somewhat more cautiously:

> A common difficulty is found in being granted the right to review old files, particularly if the government office—whether justly or not—feels called upon to protect the privacy of some third party. An attempt could also be made to break the blockade in this regard, but it would require a major expenditure of effort. . . .
>
> Nor can the possibility be fully excluded that an exchange—intentional or unintentional—was made at the time. Even if such a thing appears rather improbable and would in all probability be disputed and/or excluded by the authorities, general circumstances of the period must be taken into consideration. [Sandberg—at Wilkomirski's instigation—here alludes to the drama of Gypsy children who were taken from their parents during this same period, ostensibly in order to make them proper and respectable members of Swiss society.] These children banded together some ten or fifteen years ago in an attempt to shed light on their dark past, but without notable success: despite protracted lawsuits, registries and files remained closed to them for the most part. . . .
>
> Herr Bruno Dössekker-Wilkomirski would not shrink from attempting to determine the "official truth" by means of a lawsuit, either, but he must ask himself whether this burden should be placed on him and regarded as commensurate with circumstances, if it were to be done only in relation to publication of his report. [Wilkomirski's own attempts to deal with this problem over many years would appear to render such a strategy] practically hopeless.[27]

The head of Suhrkamp, Siegfried Unseld, stated in his reply to Sandberg that while he "personally [had] no doubt as to the correctness of these memories," it was nevertheless necessary for the firm to react to these charges, "if we do not want to be guilty of playing into the 'lie of Auschwitz.' One thing in your letter I do not understand: you write that Herr Dössekker-Wilkomirski asks himself if he should be burdened with taking legal action 'if it were to be done only in relation to publication of his report.' If in the course of publication a controversy ensues, Herr Dössekker-Wilkomirski can always point to the fact that he has initiated such a suit; it is not his fault if it lasts forever and is 'practically hopeless.' I have also consulted with Herr Ignatz Bubis, chairman of the Central Council of Jews in Germany, who urgently advises that such legal action be initiated." Unseld closes with the remark that he would be very happy to meet with Wilkomirski.[28]

Wilkomirski forwarded to Sparr confirmation from the philosophical faculty of the University of Ostrava that in the near future he would be delivering "lectures on methods for researching the Holocaust," and sent along a letter from Yad Vashem. Without expressing any opinion of its own, this institution in Jerusalem confirmed that he had done a video interview for them and had searched for his parents. No one at Yad Vashem, the most important institute for remembrance in Israel, highly regarded by Jews and non-Jews alike, would have frivolously filed his testimony there.[29] All these statements, confirmations, and testimonies on Wilkomirski's behalf were enough to allay whatever budding doubts the Jüdischer Verlag may have had. In May 1995, Wilkomirski relayed to his lawyer the statement of the firm's editor in chief that "he wants to publish my book as quickly as possible and is of the opinion that they have done everything possible to counter whatever charges Herr Helbling of the *Neue Zürcher Zeitung* may make." Sparr had made no further mention of the pending petition to inspect the files of the Biel Guardianship Authorities. He did, however, want "a fore/afterword for the book" by Wilkomirski himself, "which should 'take the wind out of the sails' of any objections on Herr Helbling's part." Moreover, it was important, Sparr said, that Wilkomirski make the personal acquaintance of Unseld.[30]

A few weeks later Wilkomirski wrote to his lawyer about the meeting in Frankfurt: "The conversation was very positive and has settled the matter for the publishing house to the point where Herr Dr. Unseld gave orders for my book to be published at the end of August 1995 with only an afterword." Unseld had evidently had another "definitive conversation" with Ignatz Bubis, who told him that, in Wilkomirski's words,

> a case like mine was not all that unusual in his circle; there was a very similar case right in his own family—a relative of his wife, whom he had only chanced to meet for the first time in Paris recently. This relative has been living there for decades as a French citizen with nongenuine 'genuine' papers—I wanted to ask you if anything else has turned up for me, or if the matter can be settled (for now?). I have only one more request, which I made to you on my first visit: What is the possibility that my name 'Binjamin Wilkomirski' can be legally protected, at least as a pseudonym—perhaps in the same way as a registered trademark?[31]

In August 1995, *Fragments* was published with Wilkomirski's afterword, in which he refers to the fate of "children without identity" who lack any certainty about their origins, live under false names, often with false papers as well. "As a child, I also received a new identity, another name, another date and place of birth. The document I hold in my hands—a makeshift summary, no actual birth certificate—gives the date of my birth as February 12, 1941. But this date has nothing to do with either the history of this century or my personal history. I have now taken legal steps to have this imposed identity annulled."[32]

I ask Eva Koralnik if all doubts were then dispelled. Not entirely, she says, but she simply could not conceive that anyone could invent such a story. And so the decision was made *in dubio pro reo,* and additional trust placed in the legal action that Wilkomirski said he would initiate.[33]

A GLOBAL LITERARY EVENT

The first review of the book appeared in the Swiss weekly
Weltwoche at the end of August 1995. The reviewer, Klara
Obermüller, visited the author at his home filled with Shoah
literature and archival materials. As an acquaintance of Eva
Koralnik, she knew of Helbling's doubts.[1] Her review mentions
the contradiction between Wilkomirski's official documents
that say he was born in Biel and his Shoah memories, and hints
at other ambiguities at several points. Obermüller describes
doubt as a painful experience that Wilkomirski himself had to
go through, as well as a possible critical position, though one
that she herself never explicitly takes. "The man knows what
there is to know; but each time he holds something like proof in
his hand, that proof can also be interpreted as something that
speaks against him. The image of a Kraków synagogue, his
entering the camp at Majdanek—he alone knows whether he
was really there, and at times the line between authenticity and
suggestion blurs for him as well."[2] Obermüller neutralizes her
reservations by letting Wilkomirski report his own version
without any distancing of language. In reference to the ambigu-
ity of the name Wilkomirski, she says, "It is his name, and the
name stands for decades of searching, in the course of which he
succeeded in verifying the details of his story, giving a place to
the images he bore within him, and finding people who con-

firmed for him what he already knew without being able to prove it." The indicative mood of the verbs show her strong sympathy for this man struggling to reclaim his own identity— a sympathy that perhaps came easily to Obermüller since she herself had had some experience with adoption. She emphasizes Wilkomirski's search for his past and his "gradual arrival at himself," and also allows that the advice of his psychotherapist to write everything down "was a great help. . . . Wilkomirski took the advice. He discovered not only that his anxieties abated but also that what can be put into words on paper becomes more real." The therapeutic need to express oneself does not make one a writer, Obermüller notes, but Wilkomirski has "presented us with a work whose literary distinction cannot be doubted." At the end of her review she returns to the problem of the documents, asserting that it was only by becoming himself that Wilkomirski was saved from death. "In his book Binjamin Wilkomirski has put the truth of his life up against the officially documented facts. That truth freed him, healed him. And it took from him the burden of having to prove what for him no longer needs proving." Aware of Helbling's letter, the reviewer has made those doubts the subliminal leitmotif of her review— not as an objective problem with which the public must concern itself, but as Wilkomirski's personal anguish, which has been inflicted upon him by external circumstance and for which he must find his own solution. She leaves the reader with the reassuring knowledge that one man has found the truth that frees and heals, that saves him from suffocating under lies.

The same reviewer made a few introductory remarks at the publishing party that took place a few days later. At even greater length and more explicitly than in her newspaper article, she describes Wilkomirski's situation. She emphasizes the purely subjective character of his memory and in doing so repeatedly suggests her own uncertainty—but, once again, without taking any position. In her closing words, she bolts the door to any pos- sibility of critical questions: "It took decades before Binjamin

Wilkomirski found the courage to stand by the truth of his life, before the world and before himself. How vulnerable that truth is, how fragile his certainty still is, can be read from every line of the text. And so I wish for him and his book readers who treat it as gently as it deserves, given its origins. It is first and foremost a piece of literature—good, very good literature—but it is also the recovery of a lost identity. Anyone who wishes to meddle with that needs to be clear about just what he is doing."[3] At the party an actor read from the book and the author himself played the clarinet. The audience was very moved—except for Emmanuel Hurwitz, a Jewish psychiatrist and psychoanalyst, who approached Klara Obermüller that same evening and, remarkably immune to the general rush of emotion, said that he didn't believe one word the author had written.[4]

In later reviews such doubts would disappear entirely. The contradiction suggested in Wilkomirski's afterword appeared to vex reviewers not at all. Only Eva-Elisabeth Fischer in the *Süddeutsche Zeitung* seems to have slight reservations, writing: "The descriptions of excessive cruelty . . . have the effect of a traumatized patient reconstructing his nightmares on a psychoanalyst's couch. The worst fears and guilt feelings take the shape of deep-hued descriptions in order, it seems, to be free of them."[5] She does not doubt, however, that the author is telling "his authentic story," only whether real events are reproduced with factual accuracy. But factuality is not her criterion. "Fragments—the record of a therapeutic analysis, arranged strictly by motifs. The facts that make up these motifs play a subordinate role. Because these fragments of memory are Binjamin Wilkomirski's truth."

The subjective perspective, which suffices as truth for Fischer, takes on the authority of fact for other critics. For the *Neue Zürcher Zeitung*—the former head of whose feuilleton had, only nine months before, urgently relayed his reservations to Suhrkamp—this slender volume carries "the weight of this century. The stony, photographic precision of a defenseless child's eyes and the spare words spoken in a low voice make it one of the most essential witnesses to the death camps. There are images here that can sear the bones. Without laying claim to being literature, with its density, irrevocability, and the power of its images, it nevertheless meets all the criteria of literature—if that were to be one's measure. But shame forbids that."[6]

The reviewer for the Swiss *Wochenzeitung* was no less impressed: "It is the view from far below, from very early on—that is, the child's perspective—that upsets, outrages, shames us."[7] And a critic writing in the American magazine *The Nation* finally drops to his knees in reverence before the author: "This stunning and austerely written work is so profoundly moving, so morally important, and so free from literary artifice of any kind at all that I wonder if I even have the right to try to offer praise."[8] In *The Guardian*, Anne Karpf, herself a second-generation Shoah victim, calls *Fragments* "one of the great works about the Holocaust" and raises Wilkomirski to the level of a Primo Levi. Another article in the same issue places the author in the ranks of Elie Wiesel, Anne Frank, Louis Begley, Paul Celan, Claude Lanzmann, and others who have created impressive works on the topic.[9]

After such enthusiastic critical praise in almost countless reviews from all around the world, honors were not long in coming. By the end of 1995, the celebrated author had already been honored by the city of Zurich—no major prize to be sure, since Wilkomirski was only one of many singled out, but he accepted it nonetheless as "a sort of rehabilitation through the Swiss government."[10] This was only the preamble. A year later in New York, he received the National Jewish Book Award for autobiography and memoirs (among his predecessors were Elie Wiesel and Alfred Kazin); in the spring of 1997, the English magazine *Jewish Quarterly* awarded him its prize for nonfiction; and that same spring the *Fondation du Judaïsme Français* presented him with its Prix Mémoire de la Shoah.

If the critics' enthusiasm was unanimous, these awards went equally unchallenged. To be sure, the president of the Zurich

Literature Committee—once again Klara Obermüller—offered gentle demurrals in her speech honoring the same work that she herself had so energetically promoted. But her criticism took a form that contravened itself, since she said that Wilkomirski's fragmentary memories were "too few for reconstructing a trustworthy biography, but enough for a book whose higher literary significance silences every doubt as to its authenticity."[11] Only Gary Mokotoff, a member of the board of the Jewish Book Council, was out of step. A few days after Wilkomirski received the National Jewish Book Award, Mokotoff wrote the chairman of the jury a letter in which he said that he considered the book to be a work of fiction. He presented his argument point by point. Among other things, he found it unbelievable that a three- or four-year-old child would have survived for more than a few days in a camp and that he would have been moved from Majdanek to Auschwitz. At the same time, he offered an explanation as to where Wilkomirski's memories had come from if not from his own experience: "If you take each of the events he describes, they seem to be the sum of the experience of all survivors." No one acknowledged Mokotoff's misgivings.[12]

The presentation of the award for the Prix Mémoire de la Shoah was an especially remarkable occasion. Wilkomirski received the French prize along with Jean-François Forges, for his book *Éduquer contre Auschwitz*. In this finely differentiated pedagogical work—noteworthy as well for the author's commitment to his topic—Forges notes among other things that the real danger lies not only in the Shoah's being denied but also in its being sacralized. Even in the narratives of the deportees, he suggests, there are many errors and exaggerations, and it is imperative to distinguish between factual and symbolic truth in their testimony.[13] Originally the jury had wanted to award the prize only to Forges. One has the impression that it may have seemed too bold a move to present it solely to a high-school teacher who was not a Shoah survivor himself, and whose thesis was rather ticklish besides, and that in choosing Wilkomirski they considered they were offering a counterbalance that represented the validity of personal experience.

The celebrated author was now often away on tour, giving readings, above all in Germany and France. The presentations all followed a similar dramaturgy. They began with Wilkomirski, dressed in a shawl reminiscent of a tallith, the Jewish prayer shawl, playing on his clarinet the *Kol Nidre* of Max Bruch, a touching melody sung on the eve of the high holiday of Yom Kippur. As a rule he himself did not do the actual reading; instead it was usually done by an actor. In Frankfurt, Thomas Sparr, editor in chief of his publishing house, took over this duty. To conclude, there was a klezmer piece, "Shalom Binjamin," composed for Wilkomirski. "Only many, many minutes later came the hesitant, very soft sound of people standing up in a slow trickle, as if everyone feared [making] the smallest noise—no one wanted to leave. No words. Silence," one woman wrote about one of these events.[14] A teacher who had attended one of Wilkomirski's many presentations at schools thanked him for the "shattering encounter." "To see you, to experience it and to know: this is a man to whom people have done unimaginable things; he was a child (and still has the child in him!) who was so inhumanly, so incredibly and cruelly, so pointlessly tortured: it simply left me weeping uncontrollably." The students were usually no less moved.[15]

Even those who were specialists in the field were impressed. The political scientist Daniel Goldhagen, author of the controversial bestseller *Hitler's Willing Executioners,* called *Fragments* a "small masterpiece [that] conveys the shattering effects of the Holocaust upon one child's life, human relations, and capacity to use language. Even those conversant with the literature of the Holocaust will be educated by this arresting book. All will be deeply moved." In the German weekly *Die Zeit,* Wolfgang Benz, director of the Berlin Center for Anti-Semitic Research, certified that the book had "not only authenticity, but also literary importance"; it was "a presentation that like no other document gives readers insights that allow them to trace this complex tragedy within themselves." James Edward Young, who has made an international name for himself in various publications about the way in which the Shoah is represented, declared the work to be "a wonderful witness."[16] *Fragments* quickly appeared as a topic on university lecture lists and was recommended by pedagogical journals for reading in school.

Wilkomirski made personal appearances at various universities, though in Europe only at the University of Grenoble in France, which invited him to several events and held out the prospect of a cooperative project researching the language of the camps. There was greater academic interest in the United States, where among other appearances Wilkomirski took part in a Holocaust symposium at Notre Dame University in South Bend, Indiana, in the spring of 1998, presenting his therapeutic concept and protesting the "academic arrogance" displayed by historians in their dealings with child survivors.[17] Present on that occasion were both Raul Hilberg and Lawrence L. Langer, two internationally recognized specialists in the Holocaust. Hilberg was known for his multivolume work, *Destruction of the European Jews,* and Langer had published several studies of how the Holocaust has been presented in literature. Outside the symposium itself, both experts spoke personally with Wilkomirski. Hilberg asked him if the book was fiction. The answer was an emphatic no—it was a memoir. Hilberg continued to have his doubts, but he wanted to study the German edition before going public with them. Langer, who even before the conference had described *Fragments* to Hilberg as a "powerful novel," thought it too soon to confront the author with his skepticism.[18]

Wilkomirski's public profile was not limited to reviews, interviews, newspaper articles, and radio presentations. Along with his readings in Europe, he undertook a fund-raising tour of American cities for the Holocaust Memorial Museum in Washington, D.C., where he gave a long video interview—as he did for Yad Vashem and the Survivors of the Shoah, founded by the movie director Steven Spielberg. Finally, in 1997, he was the portrait subject of two longer documentary films. *Fremd geboren* (Born a stranger), by Esther van Messel, documents his story and his search for his identity; Eric Bergkraut's film *Das gute Leben ist nur eine Falle* (The good life is only a trap) is a visual essay on the book. Both films proceed from the same consistent aesthetic of facticity, and neither even so much as hints at the contradiction between Wilkomirski's memories and his official documents, although both filmmakers were aware of it.[19]

"Your story broke my heart—I could only read a few pages at a time, as I was overwhelmed with tears at every word," one reader wrote to Wilkomirski. "I barely know how to put into words the sadness I felt at your lost childhood, but the respect and admiration I have are without bounds. Your story will be with me forever, and I can only say thank you for your courage."[20] Countless other letters—primarily from Switzerland, Germany, the United States, Great Britain, and France—confessed to the author the deep emotions his book had unleashed. A majority of these letter writers were women, from a variety of backgrounds; some were acquaintances or friends who had suddenly come to know a totally different person from the Bruno Dössekker they had known previously; some were students or teachers thanking him for stirring hours spent in school; some were Swiss women who found their own criticism of Swiss society's blindness toward its own history confirmed by his book; some were first- or second-generation Shoah survivors who found their own experiences articulated in his work. There was also a Paul Celan translator—and a reincarnated Anne Frank.

Most of them confessed that they had read some things about the Holocaust but had never been so shocked and stirred by a book. Many admitted they had at first postponed reading it, and then had hardly been able to bear it and wept a great deal. Others expressed gratitude to the author for opening their eyes to this horrible world. Most striking, however, is the empathy of these readers, who give their emotions free rein. Many express the hope that, despite his disrupted childhood, the author may come to know happiness and love. "It was as if I had to take this little child in my arms and tear away all that had happened to him," says one letter from Switzerland. And the sympathy is not just for the child of long ago: "I want to put my arms around you (I know I could never take away your pain), but just to show my feelings to welcome you to life, again, and honor you," a woman writes from England, and she is only one of many who felt this same need.[21] Some people see their own sufferings confirmed and thank the author for giving them courage or hope. One reader, referring to the afterword, writes: "Your final sentence, 'They should know that they are not alone,' brought a flood of tears, bound up with the thought that if you have survived such cruelty, I must surely also find the strength to make it through my own problems, so much smaller in comparison to yours."[22]

The book was translated into a total of nine languages and published by the most eminent houses. The enthusiastic reviews, the awards, Wilkomirski's countless public appearances, and the effusive letters from his readers all might give the impression that the book was a huge hit and that the author, his literary agency, and his publishers made piles of money. That is not the case. The most copies, 32,800, were sold of the version in English—not really all that many when one considers the huge market: the United States, Canada, Great Britain, and the rest of the British Commonwealth; it was a long way from being a bestseller. Amazingly, the German version sold only 13,000 copies over four years. The Italian version, with 8,100 copies sold, came in third. Of the French translation 6,000 copies were sold, and none of the other translations had larger sales than that. No one got rich on the book; it was more a media event than a sales smash.[23]

WORDS FOR THE UNSPEAKABLE —
CHILD SURVIVORS FIND A VOICE

It was through the publication of his book, Wilkomirski says,
that he came into contact with Shoah survivors his own age for
the first time. They write to him after reading the book; he meets
them at readings; groups of Swiss with similar experiences get
together to speak of the past for the first time, and Wilkomirski
joins them. From our conversations I can tell how much these
meetings mean to him. The distance he usually maintains gives
way to an emotional directness and openness, as if he felt that in
this context he is finally being understood and recognized for the
person he is. I ask him if in writing his book he was trying to pre-
serve a long-buried love as hope, and in reply he talks about the
child survivors: "What they experience for the first time is a kind
of totally self-evident, unconditional solidarity and love for one
another. They live in a world where they usually still feel surrounded by the perpetrators." His book gives them "a tiny bit"
of help in experiencing solidarity and finding hope.[24]

In Eric Bergkraut's film we see Wilkomirski opening a door
and entering a room where a group of survivors have gathered.
Wilkomirski says, "What makes this meeting so important is
that for years we were in a situation where we couldn't even
mourn what happened. Now that we're together we find moments when at least some initial mourning is possible, because
there's also joy at each new person who comes to the door. Somebody else has made it."[25]

Among those present is the artist Stefan Schwartz, who survived Auschwitz. The filmmaker asks him if he knew Wilkomirski before the publication of his book.

"I hadn't heard before. This book opened my eyes, opened my
heart. And I feel the whole thing once again," he says in broken
German.

"Did you have a story similar to Herr Wilkomirski's, Herr Schwartz?"

"No, no, certainly not. There is not another one, I don't think, there's not one like it. I have heard many tragic stories about young boys. I was seventeen at the time, he was much younger. That is the one and only story."

Miriam M., from Berlin, is another survivor who became aware of Wilkomirski through his book and met him after a reading. In the film by Esther van Messel, we learn that she was at Birkenau as a small child. "He lived more or less behind my back," she says, while a moved and concurring Wilkomirski listens. "But this is the first time—and that is actually the decisive and healing part about it—the first time that I've met anyone who has reestablished a kind of continuum in my life, simply by the fact that he's here."[26] And it is not just his presence: Wilkomirski has also helped her understand some memory fragments that have long been baffling her. "Binjamin knew that those were laundry barracks and that children were hidden there, and suddenly the whole thing made sense. Yes, I mean, I remembered it before, but it was so inexplicable why certain things were the way they were. And I never understood why things took the course they did; it was simply odd. And then suddenly it made sense. It was the missing piece of the puzzle, simply the fact of what had happened there, which he knew. And then it was clear."

Wilkomirski adds, "Yes, it's often so, that we have memories like images, like movies, but the logical thread is missing, you can't explain how it all hangs together, you simply know that you've seen it in a certain sequence, but the logic behind it is gone. And sometimes some tiny detail puts it all together, and only then do you realize what the logic of the events was. It's simply very important for our identity and the sense of our own identity that we be able to explain such minor details. And that's what has such a healing effect, because we don't have an identity strongly tied to growing up in an intact family or the like, where you can secure your identity, and also have it confirmed day in, day out, over the years. We don't have that. Our identity, in fact, is put together out of a small child's memories, and if we can verify them in some way, then that's also a verification of our own identity. And I think that's what has a certain calming effect for us."

Wilkomirski apparently had the same calming effect on a Swiss woman who asked him for his help in December 1997. She lives in the Emmen Valley, in the canton of Bern, and he calls her Sabina Rapaport, though at the time she knew nothing of this name and even now still introduces herself as K.M. She had always kept her story to herself, until she read about Wilkomirski in two different newspaper articles and finally found the courage to break her silence and write him through his publisher. He contacted her immediately. Shortly thereafter she wrote to the president of a Jewish congregation:

> Up to that point, and even then it was only in the last couple of years, only two people knew a tiny portion of my story. I had mentioned only in passing to my husband (who died in '82) and my four children that I was Jewish. . . . They simply registered the fact, and that was fine with me. Since I've become a widow and the children are gone, I've consciously become aware again of the most dreadful images of horror. The feeling that I had no identity, no roots, became more and more of a burden. I racked my brain, was tortured by guilt feelings, and almost lost my mind, until Wilkomirski *crossed my path* and saved me. Since then my children have been informed, I am seeing a psychotherapist and have joined a group of Holocaust survivors (in Zurich), and there I am *encouraged* to tell my experiences, and above all, people *believe* me and I am understood.[27]

When she first became acquainted with Wilkomirski, all she knew of her own story was that she had spent part of her early childhood in Theresienstadt. She then discovered that prior to that she had been in a French camp at Rivesaltes and at the end of the war had found her way to an orphanage in Kraków. "I came to Switzerland in 1946 and was supplied with *false genuine* documents that said I was the birth child of my adoptive parents, born on 18 May 1942 in the hospital at S.—where there isn't even a hospital! My age was determined from a superficial medical examination, presumably three or four years too young. My *official* name, K., was that of a deceased child of my adoptive parents. I always *knew* that these were not my parents but kept silent under threat of punishment." In Wilkomirski she at last found someone whom she could tell about all this. A friendship developed between the two of them, and they saw each other whenever the survivors' group met in Zurich.[28]

Reactions to his book came from abroad as well, Wilkomirski says. "I also received many invitations to America, to speak to organizations of survivors. We heard over and over how they thanked us and said, 'Finally, someone who speaks our language and has the courage to say this.' In America, too, they called me their spokesman, because they remember in exactly the same way I remember, sometimes the very same things."[29] It was thanks to one such invitation that he met Laura Grabowski, who now lives in California.

Grabowski's memories are similar in many ways to Wilkomirski's. She was likewise at Birkenau, at about age four, and later grew up as an adopted child in a non-Jewish household "where I was never allowed to use the words *Poland* or *Jewish*," she says. She hid her Shoah past and tried to find comfort in music. She, too, had been the victim of medical experiments, but the perpetrator in her case was Dr. Josef Mengele himself, who left her infertile. She also remembers the crematorium and seeing corpses disappear into it and come out the chimney as ashes. Just as Wilkomirski remembers Jankl, she has never forgotten her friend Ana, with whom she wandered the barracks hand in hand and whom she lost in the camp.[30] In July 1997, she participated for the first time in a meeting of a Holocaust Child Survivors Group. She had first learned of the group's existence two months before, and she wrote to her hosts after taking part: "I have not had the courage to attend any of the regional meetings as I have remained silent about being a child survivor for over fifty years. But now that I have tested the waters, so to speak, and have found that I truly feel safe, I hopefully will find the courage to attend the meetings. I suppose in a way that coming to your home was my 'coming out of the closet' and breaking my silence."[31] That same year, Grabowski read *Fragments* and was deeply touched. She established contact with the author and told him that she had had the same experiences as those related in his book. How surprised and thrilled she was, then, when he told her that he remembered her from Birkenau! And since she had also been in the same Kraków orphanage as he, he sent her a photograph in which they were both pictured.[32]

Wilkomirski says that Laura Grabowski is "very weak" now and her "health terribly precarious. She was a 'guinea pig' and since then has suffered from a blood disease similar to the one that I've had for years." When he and Grabowski speak, most of what they say ends with question marks. "We remember something, but then simply can't explain what it might be. For example, there's the factual observation that all our coccyx bones were broken." He remembers being struck by Grabowski's paleblond, almost white hair. "That suggests," he proposes, "that we must have been among the so-called depot prisoners, who were not registered, whose heads were not shaved, and who were not given numbers."[33]

He mentioned this fact on another occasion, at his first meeting with Grabowski, in Los Angeles in the spring of 1998. She picked him up at the airport so they could spend the weekend preparing for a concert, to be given on 19 April, National Holocaust Remembrance Day. The proceedings, parts of which were filmed by the BBC, were organized by the Holocaust Child Survivors Group Los Angeles, of which Grabowski was a member, and took place in a synagogue in Beverly Hills. Leon Stabinsky, the co-chairman of the group at the time, still recalls the opening very well. It began with Wilkomirski playing *Kol Nidre* on his clarinet, stirring up a great deal of emotion. Then Grabowski, walking with difficulty and leaning on a cane, came forward and embraced him. After a few introductory words by a moderator, Grabowski sat down at the piano and played first a solo and then a duet with Wilkomirski.[34]

Wilkomirski next began to explain to the audience—a great many of whom were Jews and Jewish survivors—"how my biography at a certain moment crossed the biography of Laura." He told how his family had fled from Riga but never arrived at their goal of Lemberg, how he had hidden with his brothers, been arrested, and been sent first to Majdanek and then at the end of 1944 to Birkenau, where he had remained until 22 January 1945.

And just there we were in a special group of children. First, it was a very large group. I at that time did not understand what really happened and just saw that by and by people came and selected children, took them away, never brought them back. Our group became smaller and smaller. And one day we were only maybe five or six children left, and that was the moment when I the first time really realized Laura: I saw that someone was brought back to the barrack, I was sitting in the mud, and then I thought I was the last of the children. And then I was very happy when I saw that the door of our barrack opened and two girls of our group came out holding hands. And I looked at them and that's why I kept it in my memory. I was very much astonished, I thought: Why had one girl's hair turned white? The other girl was normal blond. Then there I saw Laura again, but at that time with all the experiences I was terribly afraid to have contact with anybody who had the same experiences.

This second meeting with Grabowski, Wilkomirski indicated, had occurred in an orphanage in Kraków. He then went on to explain how in 1947 he had been taken by a Jewish organization from Kraków first to France and from there to Switzerland, where he was assigned foster parents. At this point he left his personal story and began to speak about the Shoah in the style of a formal lecture. In particular he spoke at length about the depot prisoners, who had no tattooed numbers, about medical experiments, and about the phenomenal capacity of traumatized children to recall their past. One adult, who had been just a year-old baby at the time, was nonetheless able to sketch out and relate his memories, and a later visit to the camp confirmed it all in detail. After another musical interlude, Wilkomirski talked about how the book had come to be and answered questions. One of his listeners asked about his relationship with his foster parents. He replied that it had been asking a lot to expect them to take care of a traumatized child, and he spoke of their making a taboo of his past and of his foster father's lack of interest in children. But the man had been an excellent doctor, he conceded, and had a medical interest in getting a boy like himself through it all. "He did a wonderful job as a doctor; he saved me really at that moment."

After the final applause, Grabowski and Wilkomirski did an interview for the BBC. Grabowski, who had been silent until then, spoke a few words. The two companions who had found each other again stood side by side and looked directly into the camera. Grabowski has short gray hair, sharp facial features, and thin lips.

"Did you recognize each other?" the woman doing the interview asks.

"Yes, from the picture," Wilkomirski says.

"No, when you saw each other?" the interviewer says more precisely.

"Yes," Wilkomirski says eagerly. "The same skull, the same form of the face." He gestures with his hands and sketches in the air, outlining and almost touching Grabowski's head.

"I didn't recognize him," Grabowski says. "I did remember one of the names he was called. I think I now have the permission to say that." She laughs.

"A certain time they called me Andrzej," Wilkomirski says twice.

"I feel very guilty," Grabowski confesses, "but he recognized my name and I did not recognize his. I felt bad. Once his wife was talking and said 'Andrzej.' I said, 'Andrzej, I know that name!' And he said, 'That was me.'"

Wilkomirski explains that as Jewish children they had changed their names often as a way of protecting themselves. When asked about their seeing each other again in Kraków, Wilkomirski can say little about it, since at that point in his childhood he had lost his voice and was afraid of all human contact. The interviewer asks Grabowski how Wilkomirski has changed physically since then.

"He is my Binje, that's all I know." Grabowski laughs and nestles against his neck. "He has my heart and soul and I have his heart and soul."

The local Jewish newspaper—there are some 500,000 Jews in Los Angeles—makes the occasion its cover story:

When the survivors finally met in person in Los Angeles last week, they cried and embraced like long-lost siblings. "Meeting Binjamin has been the dream of my life," says Laura, who composed an "Ode to the Little Ones" that she performed with Wilkomirski at the April 19 event. "It has been very healing, just finding someone who can say, 'I know.'" Wilkomirski, who is continuing to help Laura reconstruct her memories, says that complete healing is impossible. "If your arm has been cut off, it never grows back," says the author, who held Laura's hand as she cried during a recent interview. "My book hasn't lessened my personal pain, but it has helped me to reclaim my history. I am no longer afraid to tell people who I am, and that is a big relief."[35]

THE PLUNGE INTO THE ABYSS —
AUTOBIOGRAPHY OR FAKE?

"NEVER CONFINED TO A CONCENTRATION CAMP"

The charge could not have been more explosive: "Binjamin Wilkomirski, alias Bruno Dössekker . . . knows Auschwitz and Majdanek only as a tourist," was the conclusion of a two-page article that the writer Daniel Ganzfried published in the Swiss weekly *Die Weltwoche* on 27 August 1998.[1] Ganzfried surmises that *Fragments* is "an internalized collection of images by a man whose imagination has run away with him." The author was born not in Riga, but rather as the illegitimate child of one Yvonne Grosjean in Biel, on 12 February 1941, was later placed temporarily in a children's home in Adelboden, was put up for adoption in 1945, and was finally placed with the Dössekkers in Zurich. Contrary to his claim of having first arrived in Switzerland in 1948, he can be seen posing for a photo "as early as the summer of 1946, merry as can be and surrounded by his family outside their villa in Zürichberg," where he entered the primary school in April 1947. Still living is his mother's brother, who at the time had tried in vain to take the child in; and even Bruno's father can be traced as well, since he continued to pay child support until the adoption was finalized, in 1957. After the death of Bruno's mother, Yvonne Rohr née Grosjean, her estate had fallen to him, and he had "presumably laid claim to the small inheritance." In short, "although his new identity is written on the nameplate beside his door, 'Binjamin Wilkomirski' is a pseudonym, and its bearer was never confined in a concentration camp."

But Ganzfried does not leave matters there, after these disclosures; he also explores the reason for the book's "phenomenal success." The "need to sympathize" with another individual's fate, he argues, releases one from the onerous task of analyzing what is incomprehensible. Wilkomirski thus "relieves us of the task of thinking and the dreadful realization that our human understanding fails us when confronted with the fact of Auschwitz. We use the experience of the other person to keep from having to make good on something beyond our power to conceive. Lost in mindless sympathy, we find in the victim the hero with whom we can fraternize on the side of morality: Binjamin Wilkomirski."

Wilkomirski was in a bad state after this article attacking him was published. His girlfriend, Verena Piller, was afraid he would go crazy: "That was the worst ever, I've never seen him like that. He sat upstairs and screamed for Jankl and for bread in Russian." Wilkomirski sat there petrified, totally removed. Piller wanted to take him in her arms. Fortunately, Eli Bernstein was visiting them at the time, and "he knelt down in front of him and began talking to him as if they were there together. I wasn't allowed to touch him; he would wince and say, 'Go away!' And he didn't even notice that it was me sitting beside him. It was simply awful; I did not want to lose him to the mental hospital because of this campaign against him. He just shouted 'Khleb, khleb.' His mind was somewhere else entirely and understood nothing at all. Only because Eli was there, talking with him so calmly, holding him, and walking there with him once again, did he gradually calm down. It was a horror show."[2]

Three days later he was well enough to give an interview to Peer Teuwsen of the *Zürcher Tages-Anzeiger,* a journalist who had portrayed him with total empathy three years previously. When asked about Ganzfried's charges, Wilkomirski says, "Every reader can see from the afterword in my book that my papers do not correspond to my memories. My memories are all I can put up against a seamless Swiss identity. That was clear from the start. These charges are nothing new. The reader was always free to regard my book as literature or as a personal document. The contradiction was addressed at length by Klara Obermüller in *Die Weltwoche* at the time of publication and at the party celebrating it. But it is most certainly false if this journalist wants to give the impression that I covered that up. Also untrue is the charge that I never attempted to locate the documents: I had extensive conversations with the authorities thirty years ago."[3] Wilkomirski denies having anything in common with Yvonne Grosjean, but can give "no truly conclusive answer" for the discrepancy between his official documents and his memories. He cites the example of other child survivors, who had likewise been supplied with another identity for their own protection. Finally, he alludes to the story about the exchange of children in which Dr. Jadassohn is said to have been involved, but without naming him or explicitly indicating just what happened. Teuwsen notes in summary that Wilkomirski's statements have not put an end to all doubts. "Yes, I know that," the author responds. "No one has to believe me. I have pointed out the contradiction again and again, but I am not prepared to deny my memories because of outside pressure."

After Thomas Sparr, the editor in chief of the Jüdischer Verlag at Suhrkamp, took the same position—"There was nothing in Ganzfried's article that we did not know before; it is all mentioned in the afterword"—Daniel Ganzfried replied in the next issue of *Die Weltwoche*: "When [Wilkomirski] and those close to him claim that there is nothing new in our charges, since they were all included in doubts first expressed far too gently by Klara Obermüller in *Die Weltwoche* of 31 August 1995, then one must counter that no mention whatever was made of his biological mother, biological father, or uncle, of an orphanage in Adelboden or his residence in Zurich since 1945. Indeed, any such doubts gave way to total belief once the book proved so success-ful." That belief, however, was the real problem:

> Whispered doubts as to [the book's] authenticity are heard, but no one wants to dirty his or her hands or sully a reputa-tion. And so it remains: a masterwork, to be mentioned along with Paul Celan and Primo Levi. We know that within ten years perhaps no one will be left who is able to recall and tell us from personal experience about the reality of the concentration camp and the gulag, the only places where the attempt at total control ever became reality. How that remembrance is constituted is of primary importance for coming generations. Our responsibility, then, is all the greater in regard to the published results of that remem-brance. In fateful concert the publisher, feuilletons, televi-sion, and radio have brutally abused that responsibility in the case of Wilkomirski and have assisted in deceiving the public. Their bunglings, along with the almost total lack of civil courage shown in the cultural establishment of our day, have helped turn Auschwitz once again into a matter of faith, while the fact itself is left to erode under our hands.[4]

In a press release Siegfried Unseld, the head of Suhrkamp, referred to the measures his house had taken up to that point:

> In February 1995, we received information suggesting that Binjamin Wilkomirski's memoirs were a matter of fiction. We immediately stopped production of the previously an-nounced book. I asked Dr. Thomas Sparr, editor in chief of the Jüdischer Verlag, to conduct extensive conversations with historians in Israel, including Frau Lea Balint, who evaluated Binjamin Wilkomirski's story in Yad Vashem, the Institute for Remembrance and Research of the Shoah in Jerusalem. Dr. Balint studied Binjamin Wilkomirski's life story in detail and found his remembered identity credible.

She expressly confirmed this on 12 March 1995 and again a few days ago. The Polish historian Frau Professor Kurek-Lesik, who has researched the children's and women's fields at Majdanek concentration camp, stated her position in regard to certain details remembered by Binjamin Wilkomirski, as did Julius Löwinger, who as a boy of fifteen lived at the same Kraków orphanage that plays a role in the account. We requested and received confirmation from Yad Vashem that they had, without any objection, accepted and placed Binjamin Wilkomirski's life story on file, along with a request that a search be made for his parents. It is not the task of the publishing house to resolve this contradiction [referring to the book's afterword, in which Wilkomirski acknowledges the existence of documents that contradict his own memories]. It is, however, the task of the publishing house to point out the contradiction between the remembered and the legally recognized identity of the author. Which we did.[5]

Balint is mistakenly awarded a doctorate in this release, the text of which seems also to indicate that she is an employee of Yad Vashem, which likewise is not the case. The reference to Kurek-Lesik is based only on secondhand testimony by Wilkomirski's friend Sylwester Marx concerning Wilkomirski's meeting with the historian in 1993. Kurek-Lesik herself never prepared a statement for Suhrkamp; her research dealt, moreover, with Jewish children, but not in the narrower scope of Majdanek, and as an expert in the field she is unknown to the research department there. She does have a doctorate but does not hold a professorship. All this drastically reduces the authority of her testimony. Yad Vashem confirms solely that Wilkomirski requested a search for his parents and gave them a video interview; it has nothing to say about the authenticity of his memories. According to its director, Yehuda Bauer, this Israeli institution does not check any of the testimony it receives unless it is used for publication.[6] Whoever wrote the Suhrkamp press release—it was probably not Unseld himself—was presumably inspired by a desire to continue to believe Wilkomirski and defend his story authoritatively, while presenting the house's earlier explanations as sufficient. The errors are hardly explicable otherwise.

The most important reference for Suhrkamp was no doubt Lea Balint, who in essence repeated her arguments from 1995, and furnished one additional anecdote. She had once shown Wilkomirski a newspaper article about a former resident of the home on Augustiańska Street, and he had excitedly pointed to the photo and said, "That's the entrance to my orphanage."[7] For Balint it was further proof of the veracity of his memory. She wrote out her statement only a few days after Ganzfried's attack; it is obvious that she wanted to help Wilkomirski. She later tried to mobilize Laura Grabowski to act as a witness, but Grabowski had little to offer. "Our reunion was the most meaningful thing in my life," she wrote Balint. "We cried together and hugged each other and shared things about little kids in the barracks. He remembers my Ana and that we were always holding hands. He described me as having blond hair, almost snow-white, before he ever saw a photo of me. These are the things I have to offer. Not names and dates and places and the hows and whys and whos and whens. I don't think too many four-year-olds can do that."[8]

Ganzfried's article created a public uproar, above all in Switzerland and Germany, but in English- and French-speaking countries, too, countless reports began to appear in the media. They all appealed to Ganzfried and appropriated his arguments, frequently without mentioning their origin, and a great many of them—noticeably more so in Germany than in Switzerland—presented his disclosures as fact. For now, the media were conducting no independent research.

In a long article in *Die Zeit,* Jörg Lau followed Ganzfried's lead in judging the way reviewers had failed in their critical task by identifying with the victim: "Automatically accepting every text with touched reverence has nothing to do with showing respect for the survivors of the Holocaust. To put it more polemically, one might pose the question whether the reflexive wave of emotion that greeted Wilkomirski was not actually a subtle mechanism of defense."[9] This journalist was also the first to examine Bernstein and Wilkomirski's joint therapy proposal, which led him to the insight that it was here that the book's origins lay: "It was written in the spirit of a presumptuous psychotherapy that believes it can provide meaning in life, indeed an 'identity,' by accepting, supporting, and authenticating as 'historical reality' anything the client may choose to offer." Lau also gave a hearing to the views of the historian Raul Hilberg. This renowned pioneer in Shoah research had himself considerable reservations about the book, and criticized several passages that to him "seemed improbable or totally impossible." These included, among other things, the description of the partisan bands and German tanks in Poland, as well as of Wilkomirski's being transported from Majdanek to Auschwitz. "How could this book make its way through several publishing houses as an autobiography?" Hilberg asked. "How could Wilkomirski receive invitations from the Holocaust Museum in the United States as well as from prestigious universities?" Hilberg's position of authority emboldened several newspapers to pick up on the doubts he voiced in *Die Zeit*.[10]

Jörg Lau also addressed the fear expressed by various people that confirmation of Ganzfried's disclosures might encourage those who deny the Holocaust: "Those who deny Auschwitz did not need to wait for Wilkomirski to nurse their mad ideas, and if *Fragments* should prove to be a mere victimization fantasy, then the witness, the poems and novels, of real victims will not be discredited by that. Permanent damage can arise only if the status of this text remains uncertain, which is what its author wants. That everyone is free to believe or not to believe in the authenticity of reports about the Holocaust is precisely the cynically laid-back position of the modern revisionists, who have taken a lesson from postmodern epistomology."

The Jewish weeklies in German-speaking Switzerland saw the matter very differently. The editor in chief of the *Israelitisches Wochenblatt* took issue on principle with Ganzfried's basic question as to whether the book was authentic or invented: "A biography like the one described by the author of *Fragments* occurred a hundred, a thousand times in World War II. . . . And thus Ganzfried's 'revelation,' however honestly it may have been intended, finally and really serves only those who dismiss in general the industrialized slaying of Jews by the Nazis as an 'invention.' " The *Jüdische Rundschau* sang the same tune: "If Wilkomirski's book turns out to be a novel instead of a memoir, those who deny Auschwitz can rejoice. . . . Not a few people, Jews and non-Jews alike, take offense at the *Weltwoche*'s having published a report that adds grist to the mills of those who deny the Holocaust, but that itself sounds like fiction and not like cleanly documented research."[11]

In the same issue, Esther van Messel, who had offered a portrait of Wilkomirski in her 1997 film *Fremd geboren,* declared that she was "outraged" by Ganzfried's attack, though she did not address the biographical contradictions. "The report is destructive," she told the paper. "It offers no proof, and even if it had been offered, I would have found it hard to believe." There is not only one truth, she said, and she supported her opinion with examples drawn from her own family: her father and his brothers and sisters, who had all fled before the Nazis, all told different versions of the same story. Even if Ganzfried could offer documented proof, it would not mean that Wilkomirski was lying, the filmmaker pointed out, for many Shoah survivors had contradictory birth certificates, or none at all.

Eric Bergkraut, who had made a similarly uncritical film about Wilkomirski and taken a drubbing for it in Ganzfried's article, published a statement in *Die Weltwoche* itself. He accused Ganzfried of taking at times "a sneering tone" that served no

good purpose, and of having conducted biased research. Ganzfried, he charged, has simply proceeded from the assumption
that the book is a hoax, instead of carefully checking Wilkomirski's memory "against possible truth." "All the 'proofs' provided by Ganzfried (birth certificate, first registry at school)
prove only that there is a seamless official Swiss account for a
Bruno Grosjean, born in Biel in 1941. But they do not refute
that from some particular moment on, for example with the
(possible) death of Bruno Grosjean in a children's home, there
might have been a child of the camps who continued to live
under that name." After referring to the "historical expertise" of
Lea Balint, Bergkraut justified his own work: "Wilkomirski's
book stands at the center of my film *Das gute Leben is mur eine
Falle* [The good life is only a trap]. It is not a research film. My
presumption was that his story was 'valid' insofar as I was dealing with a man who had been in the camps as a child. I
depended, among other things, on the aforementioned expert
opinions gathered by the publisher before the book went into
print. Yes, I believed Wilkomirski, as did with many other
people—including survivors of the camps, in whose company I
experienced and also filmed him. I am now open to attack
because of that 'belief'; I may have been mistaken." But one
must first consider "the hypothesis of the 'conferral' of a false
identity that left no traces . . . , before one sets out to judge Binjamin Wilkomirski in public."[12]

A particularly lively defense of Wilkomirski was mounted by
a group of Jews of the second generation, who called themselves
by the awkward name Contact Point for Children of Survivors
of the Persecution of Jews by the Nazi Regime, Switzerland.
According to their spokesperson, Samuel Althof, the group
regarded Ganzfried's article as irresponsible and horribly dam-
aging to all survivors, including the second generation. Contact
Point members wrote letters to the media, which were printed
in various forms and occasionally found their way into editorial
pieces. By their reckoning, the man "who presumes he is a seri-

ous writer" and who wanted to unmask Wilkomirski as "a liar and a fraud" was himself "an author with out-of-control rage and appears to us to be a man who has not mastered his own problems of identity." He had "discovered nothing new" but merely "engaged in an outrageously aggressive public dissemination" of materials that Wilkomirski had already researched himself. As proof of the authenticity of Wilkomirski's memory, Contact Point also pointed to the testimony of Julius Löwinger.[13]

"I WILL NOT BE BLACKMAILED" — WILKOMIRSKI'S REACTION

In a statement released to the media on 16 September 1998, Wilkomirski appealed to the Bergier Commission, an independent panel of historians established by the Swiss government to research Switzerland's role during the Third Reich. "I am asking the Bergier Commission," Wilkomirski declared, "which is examining Switzerland's relationship with Jews in the 1940's, also to research my early years within the general context of the history of refugee children, including 'Yenish people' (gypsies) in Switzerland. I will give the commission all the information I have, and grant it exclusive and unconditional access to all available documents, including those of the research institute Children Without Identity in Jerusalem. I am asking the Bergier Commission to contact me."[14] The man making this request clearly had a very good idea of how such research should properly be done: first in cooperation with Lea Balint, and second by expanding it to include the history of those Gypsy children who had been robbed of their families by the Swiss relief agency Children of the Road. Wilkomirski had already used the Gypsy analogy in defending himself to Suhrkamp against Helbling's charges. He had been bolstered in this position by a letter he had received in early September 1998, in which a Yenish woman explained to him that they shared the same fate, that like him she also lived with two identities, and like him could never prove what had happened to her. "I wish you much energy, much courage, and at some point you will find a pheasant feather that I have put in your mailbox. Gypsies regard pheasants as the bravest of all ground-breeding birds, which is what we all are in some way," she wrote. The commission, however, rejected Wilkomirski's research proposal, saying it fell outside the scope of its assignment.[15]

Having been declared ill by his physician, Wilkomirski, along with his girlfriend, Verena Piller, and Georges Wieland, a fellow teacher and friend who had acted as the first editor of *Fragments,* traveled to Horgen, on Lake Zurich, on 20 September. On the suggestion of Samuel Althof, they visited Max Grosjean, who according to Ganzfried had confirmed that the child of his sister Yvonne had been given up for adoption in 1945. Wilkomirski looked "terrible" during this visit and sat there with his head lowered the entire visit, Trauti Grosjean tells me. "He was trembling like an old man," her husband adds. They showed their visitors photographs of little Bruno Grosjean. Wilkomirski took the old snapshots to the window, photographed them, and said that they bore no resemblance to him.[16]

Wilkomirski's literary agent, Eva Koralnik, says that after the appearance of Ganzfried's article, her office was paralyzed by the affair for weeks. Day and night "there were calls from around the world asking questions. We had to provide answers and kept telling the whole story over and over."[17] Now that Ganzfried had "brought some things to light," she kept telling Wilkomirski, "if it isn't all true, you have to provide counterarguments." She presumed that a real survivor would be "at least offended or angry. . . . He would always say, 'When the right time comes, I'll say what I have to say.' " He would not let the press blackmail him.

I point out to Koralnik that one important witness, Lea Balint, did not act like an independent expert and kept no distance at all between herself and Wilkomirski. "I was impressed by her work, her commitment to Children Without Identity," Koralnik replies. She herself believed absolutely in Wilkomirski's story from the start, which was why she later "wished very much that he was right, that these really were his memories." It is so awful for her now—the possibility that she may have played into the hands of those who deny the Holocaust. How awful for the survivors, too, if their memoirs are now to be called into question.

With Wilkomirski alluding to new leads that he still had to investigate, and Koralnik waiting in vain for proof, the people at the agency considered suggesting a DNA test to him. Inquiries made at the Institute for Forensic Medicine at the University of Zurich revealed that a test could help clarify matters, and so in the middle of September, Koralnik approached Wilkomirski with the idea—though for various reasons she did not find it easy to do so. He refused, even though only a few years previously he had undergone just such a procedure for the sake of his alleged father, Yakov Maroko. DNA tests did not provide unequivocal proof, he argued. He would repeat his refusal later on when the same suggestion was made by the Biel Guardianship Authorities and by his own lawyer, Rolf Sandberg, who had learned that Bruno Grosjean's birth father was still alive and that the test would therefore yield definitive results.[18]

After Ganzfried published a third article in *Die Weltwoche*, demanding, without success, that the publisher withdraw the book temporarily while the facts were clarified—and having made no progress herself—Koralnik asked Wilkomirski at least to issue a public statement. Both Suhrkamp and her agency were being "subjected daily to the familiar charges and have to provide answers. Your publishers worldwide, especially in the U.S., England, France, and Scandinavia, demand an explanation; Jewish commissions that have awarded you prizes must be informed. Till now we have stood behind you, but the accusations are now so grave that you yourself must reply. We can no longer do it in your stead." The Frankfurt Book Fair, where Koralnik would meet with all of Wilkomirski's publishers, was only days away, and she expected him to produce an explanation by that date. "You must offer new evidence and deal conclusively with particular issues regarding your identity and past. I fear your silence only makes the situation more difficult. . . . It is also insulting to let yourself be branded publicly as a liar. You ought to take legal action. I advise you to secure a lawyer at once."[19]

Wilkomirski faxed the demanded explanation directly to the Book Fair, responding to individual points. Bruno Grosjean's documents were indeed genuine, he conceded: he had had them examined, and his suspicion that an exchange had taken place was directed not against the civil service, but against other persons; he would research the matter further. The civil authorities had denied him access to his papers thirty years before, claiming there was no birth certificate that he could see. To this day he possessed instead of the original only an "abridged birth certificate" presented to him "for the first time in 1995 after repeated requests, after decades of its being denied me." On a visit to Yvonne Grosjean's brother, he had seen photographs of his "alleged mother" and the baby Bruno Grosjean but had found no resemblance to himself. He also expressly refuted "having ever been in a children's home in Adelboden." He protested most strenuously against critical historians, whose competence he questioned and whom he termed the representatives of the first generation of historians, "for whom the 'children of the Shoah' were never an explicit subject of research." He named no names, but it was clear that he meant Raul Hilberg and Yehuda Bauer of Yad Vashem, who had both expressed skepticism about his memoir. These historians treated his book as the "historical and factual report of an expert adult witness," whereas the issue here was one of images explicitly designated as "those that remained in a young child's memory, without the critical and ordering logic of adults." The debate, moreover, had excluded with "distasteful stubbornness" the real central problem: the fact that, after the war, thousands of children had been left without any documents or certain identity. Wilkomirski closed his statement by observing, "The present discussion has bolstered me in my personal memories—they are a steadfast part of my biography." In the introduction to his statement, he had declared that given the poisonous climate in the media, he did not intend to make any further comment beyond these explanations.[20]

SUPPORT FROM SURVIVORS

Wilkomirski received countless letters—none from opponents, he says, only from people who gave him encouragement.[21] Many had experienced the Shoah themselves. One woman, who had been in Theresienstadt as a little girl and was now on the board of the Zurich survivor organization, let him know that the publicity had brought their association to the public's attention: "As a result of your book several members who had until then repressed their past or even their true identity found their way to us." One reader thanked him, in English, for the enormous help his book had been in "our battles" against such crimes and in the effort to ensure that children and their memories were taken seriously. The campaign against him was not a sign of defeat; on the contrary, "It is a sign of to have HIT VERY HARD." Another woman, who had been hidden among Christians as a small child, wrote, "No one has the rights and power to steal your memories! You are who you remember that you are. I hope you will be strong and keep your memories like a precious treasure."[22]

Several sympathizers became active in other ways. Especially tireless was Guta Benezra, a friend of Laura Grabowski's, who herself had written a book about the Shoah.[23] At the end of

October 1998, she learned that the bookstore of the Holocaust Museum in Washington had withdrawn Wilkomirski's book from sale. She wrote a letter to the Shoah specialist Lawrence Langer, asking for his help: Since she belonged to the group of youngest survivors, this controversy was of the utmost importance to her and others. They asked his assistance in bringing a close to the discussion. When Langer did not respond, she intervened herself and persuaded the museum to put the book back on the shelf. In the numerous letters that she wrote to the media and to survivors, Benezra stressed that many child survivors had experienced stories similar to Wilkomirski's. But the media and general public understood nothing of the unbelievable conditions under which most of the Jewish orphans from Eastern Europe have survived. Moreover, they ignored the fact that no Jewish child could have stayed alive without a false identity, meaning that false or non-existent papers were the norm for them, not the exception. Those whose families were murdered still needed false papers after the war. That was the only way in which the survivors could cope with the bureaucratic constraints in the normality of Western countries where they ended up. The charge of fraud was familiar to those children who managed to escape the Nazis' hell. Benezra wrote that this was particularly true of the handful who survived the same region as Wilkomirski. Few of them were able to find out their real name even if they remembered one as such, as in Wilkomirski's case. They were just as uncertain of their language because at the age of between three and six they mostly had to keep silent or they mumbled a mixture of languages, which was just enough to survive. Witnesses who could confirm their muddled memories were scarce. Benezra admits that naturally Wilkomirski could have simply discovered the facts about the camps from books. Yet his voice is so true, so comparable to her own innermost voice of horror and sorrow that it is beyond doubt. It is the voice of a child survivor of the Nazis' camp; a voice that overcomes a barrier of fear and judgment. A voice that had remained deeply buried since no one wanted to believe or recognize it. Now that the voice of this child is being heard in a wonderful book the survivors must not turn away and let it be silenced again by a hateful denial. Daniel Ganzfried's fable is being treated as fact by the public because he himself is a second generation Holocaust survivor. His alliance with superficial, sensationalistic press coverage, along with the rumors and the customary indifference, do not only damage Wilkomirski, but all the survivors and their memories.[24]

In November 1998, the American television network CBS prepared a report on the Wilkomirski affair for its newsmagazine 60 *Minutes,* which reaches a vast audience every Sunday evening. Pressured by American survivor organizations, which expected some statement on his part, Wilkomirski at last declared that he was prepared to be interviewed. His agreement went against the wishes of the Swiss Contact Point for Children of Survivors, his most important champion in Europe, which dropped his cause at that point. In e-mails sounding the alarm, however, the group's spokesperson, Samuel Althof, continued to urge Wilkomirski to act. On 6 December 1998, he begged him to hire a lawyer to research the "precise details" of his story: "That is the only possibility, if there still is one, of limiting the IMMENSE DAMAGE. THE FUSE IS BURNING! ALL THAT WILL BE LEFT IS ASHES!" Two days later he was back again: "I am certain that if you do not take things in hand, SERIOUS CLAIMS (COMPENSATION, FRAUD, ETC.) WILL BE MADE AGAINST YOU, AND AGAINST ELI AS WELL. You simply cannot withdraw and do nothing and wait till it is all over. YOUR FOES ARE AT WORK; I KNOW IT!"[25]

Also alarmed by receiving such letters from Althof was Laura Grabowski. As early as November 1998, she had written to Lea Balint that she and Wilkomirski were being accused of fraud, of inventing their finding each other again after fifty years; older survivors were demanding from younger ones proof that they did not have. Early in 1999, Grabowski wrote to Wilkomirski:

"Now I am really frightened—for you, dear Binje, and for me. What to do I don't know. I will do nothing unless there is something you ask for me to do. I wish I could protect you. I could take you and Verena to some desert island in the Pacific. Let's go!"[26]

DANIEL GANZFRIED AND
THE BACKGROUND OF HIS DISCLOSURES

Daniel Ganzfried, who started this avalanche, was born in Israel in 1958, the son of a Hungarian who had survived Auschwitz. When he was two, he was sent to Switzerland, where he was raised by his maternal grandparents. His attitude toward Judaism appears to have been critical or at best indifferent before he began to research his father's life story in the early 1990s. But his struggle to understand his father brought about a marked change in his relationship with his own origins and became the basis for his first novel, *Der Absender* (The sender of the letter), published in 1995. The novel met with critical applause and was reprinted three years later as a paperback.[27]

In September 1999, I meet with Daniel Ganzfried at his office.[28] In response to my question about what had inspired his investigation, Ganzfried replies that he read Wilkomirski's book in 1995 because it appeared at almost the same time as his own novel and he was often asked to comment about it at his public readings. He quickly noticed that something was wrong: that was not how you write if your purpose was to present the memories of a three-year-old. The pathos had irritated him—for instance, when the child watches his father die and thinks, I'll have to manage without you now. And the bits of pseudo-wisdom, such as "If you don't know where you came from, you don't know where you're going." But for Ganzfried the decisive factor was a conversation with Klara Obermüller, who had first reviewed *Fragments* and who delivered the honorary address when Ganzfried received a prize for his novel. On that occasion, Ganzfried says she told him that Wilkomirski had probably been born in Switzerland and later adopted.

In mid-May 1998, Pro Helvetia asked Ganzfried if he would write a profile of Wilkomirski for its magazine, *Passagen.* The most important state-supported cultural foundation in Switzerland, Pro Helvetia had subsidized the French translation of *Fragments.*[29] The inquiry came via Obermüller, who had already turned down the assignment. Ganzfried told Michael Guggenheimer, the editor in charge, about his doubts. Guggenheimer had recently heard Obermüller state her reservations as well. It was agreed that Ganzfried would receive an additional fee to conduct the research and that *Die Weltwoche* would act as a partner.

Ganzfried says that Obermüller at first supported him in his investigation because she was outraged that in all the reviews, and in both documentary films, every doubt had vanished in the face of categorical acceptance. But she did not believe that unambiguous proof could be found, and only wanted things to return to their original state, when doubt and belief still hung in the balance. The more facts and proof Ganzfried found, the more hesitant she became. When he published his article, she angrily distanced herself from him. Publication was preceded by massive pressure, Ganzfried says: the Contact Point for Children of Survivors tried to intervene with Pro Helvetia, and Wilkomirski personally wrote to Guggenheimer on 24 June 1998: "Please keep in mind that I survived Auschwitz as a child and that my health has been considerably impaired by Herr Ganzfried's actions, which others likewise regard as offensive." Three weeks later Rolf Sandberg, Wilkomirski's lawyer, told Ganzfried that his client would not permit his name or his book to be mentioned in connection with Frau Grosjean. In the end the editors of *Passagen* were pressured by their own board of directors to reject the article, so Ganzfried could publish it only in *Die Weltwoche.*[30]

Ganzfried says that several people reacted by accusing him of making his disclosures out of malice. Some claimed that he begrudged the author of *Fragments* his success; others, that he was driven by some pathological obsession. Wilkomirski himself, along with Samuel Althof, came up with the theory that Ganzfried wanted to slay Wilkomirski in lieu of his own, now deceased, father. In response to my question about his actual motives, Ganzfried says his concern is for people to think about the Holocaust in rational categories. Rather than coming to terms with it analytically, we just read teary autobiographies of its survivors. It has become unclear whether Auschwitz was a concrete place, bound up with equally concrete events, or is merely a metaphor.

He does not believe that remembrance of the Shoah is seriously endangered by an isolated fraud. Apparently the facts are no longer important, however, but only a "frame of mind. Suddenly it's the inner mood that takes the place of the well-researched subject. I do find that state of affairs alarming." Particularly, he says, since Wilkomirski's book is very badly written.

In his article Ganzfried poses a question about memory and the complex relationship between fact and fiction, an issue that also plays a central role in his own novel. As if in contradiction to Wilkomirski's basic position, the novel deals with the impossibility of authentically reconstructing a memory or a life story. I ask Ganzfried whether the experience of writing his own book had been important for his investigation. Yes, he says. In long conversations with his father he noticed that he told a very different version of Auschwitz or Buna than, for example, Primo Levi, who was in the same camp. Since it was not Ganzfried's task to ferret out the truth, he had to make his own narrative position clear. He had not been there himself and could not bridge the deep chasm that separated him from his father's experience. "I can't pretend that my father told me about the Holocaust. He understood it least of all, for he was its victim and not a historian, a young man who ended up in its death machinery. The victims could understand what was happening to them least of all."

I also meet with Klara Obermüller[31] and ask her what her motives were for turning down Pro Helvetia's request. She gives two reasons. First, the editor Guggenheimer had come to her with the idea of writing a portrait of Wilkomirski as a two-fold talent—a musician who also writes—but in her opinion that was not an accurate description. She told him that Wilkomirski would never write another book, that he had said what he had to say in the process of working through his memories and his trauma. He is a musician, not a writer. Second, she expressed to him her massive doubts about Wilkomirski's story, which had only grown since her review of the book; she simply felt incapable of writing a further text. When I ask why she had distanced herself from Ganzfried's investigation, she explains that first of all, it was out of fear of people who deny the Holocaust, for whom the disclosure would be a mouth-watering treat, and second, because she was "dreadfully" afraid for Wilkomirski. "I always had the feeling that I was pulling the rug out from under someone, and I didn't want to be guilty of that." When Ganzfried told her about the progress of his investigation—with "eerie passion and a kind of gloating"—she tried to stop the article and advised Pro Helvetia and *Die Weltwoche* not to publish it.

RESEARCH SINCE GANZFRIED

On 7 February 1999, CBS broadcast its story. The reporters followed the lead of Ganzfried, with whom they had also worked. Ganzfried's earliest proof of contact between the Dössekkers and Wilkomirski was a photograph from the summer of 1946. As a new argument, *60 Minutes* showed a letter sent to Ganzfried by the archivist of the city of Zurich, declaring that Bruno

Grosjean was already registered as the Dössekker's foster child on 13 October 1945.[32] Wilkomirski's previous assertion that he had first entered Switzerland in 1947 or 1948 was thus impossible—presuming that the child so registered was identical with him. Otherwise the report offered no new facts. It was based on photographic material, including an amateur film of the Dössekker family, and above all on the expertise of Raul Hilberg. In his opinion, children in concentration camps were either murdered or died of privation; Wilkomirski's story hovered between "the highly unlikely and the utterly impossible." Besides, he criticized the "cult of testimony." Although he had little that was substantial to offer about the concrete facts, his appearance was important, since his statements formed the dramaturgical framework at both start and finish, lending the report additional seriousness.

Wilkomirski reacted in a vehement response in English, aimed primarily at statements Hilberg had made during the 60 *Minutes* broadcast and in *Die Zeit* months before. He accuses the historian of "intellectual dishonesty" and more or less dismisses all his arguments. Referring to the literature, he explains that contrary to Hilberg's claim, children had indeed been transported from Majdanek to Birkenau. Moreover, he notes, he himself had never spoken of a direct transport to a different camp, since for the period in question there was a gap in his memory. He rebuts the historian's examples of the fictional character of the book—descriptions of "partisans" and "tanks" in Poland—by pointing out that he had never used those terms. Finally, he adamantly rejects Hilberg's judgment of "very unlikely": "He forgets that the SURVIVAL OF EVERY SURVIVOR is linked to many very 'unlikely' happenings, ways, tricks and coincidences. Because it was not the rule to survive. ARGUING LIKE THAT WOULD MEAN TO DENY EVERY SURVIVOR'S EXPERIENCES!" Sharpening his criticism, he accuses Hilberg of the kind of captious argumentation that reminds him of times past: "It is the same tactic, used in the fifties and sixties, by former Nazi-judges in Nazi wartime trials towards Jewish witnesses and victims by catching them in endless discussions, whether a uniform of a culprit was grey-green or green-grey—just to make the witness' memory insecure and to demonstrate that the witness is not reliable! This is a real FASCIST TECHNIQUE OF ARGUMENTATION. I can even hear the noise of Mr. Goebbels's dances and shouts of joy in hell!"[33]

After CBS, the Biel Guardianship Authorities put in a word as well. As early as December 1998, officials entrusted with the Bruno Grosjean files had invited Wilkomirski and his lawyer to meet with them. Since Ganzfried's article, the media had been hounding officials there for information, and as a result they wished to speak with the "*Geheimnisherr*" [master of secrets], as Wilkomirski was called in their official jargon, about their policies on sharing information. They and Wilkomirski had agreed on a statement for the press that, owing to the discovery of additional files in their archives, was not released until after the CBS broadcast. Among other things, it said that the "routine supervision" of Bruno Grosjean had been "documented and can be reconstructed on the basis of summaries contained in the files. On the other hand, a biography of the child with no gaps in it cannot be constructed solely on the basis of these files. . . . That also means that the whereabouts of the boy Bruno Grosjean cannot be determined beyond any doubt day by day. Conversely, on the basis of these same files the Guardianship Authorities have no reason to assume any exchange of children."[34]

Three months later, the first detailed and independent research into the case since Ganzfried appeared. At the end of May 1999, the English literary magazine *Granta* published "The Man with Two Heads," an extensive study, almost sixty pages long, by the writer Elena Lappin.[35] She had become acquainted with Wilkomirski in 1997, when the English magazine *Jewish Quarterly,* of which she was editor at the time, awarded him its prize for nonfiction. In the course of her research, her views of the book changed, and she came to believe that *Fragments* was fiction. Since his own Swiss story had nothing anywhere near so dramatic to offer, she speculated, Bruno Dössekker had made use of the Holocaust to explain where he came from and who he was. She found support for her chief arguments in favor of a theory of fabrication by examining the passages about Kraków, where she came across numerous contradictions in Wilkomirski's story. But if Lappin's work was simply a diligent and meticulous gathering of facts that turned a life in the context of the Shoah into the fate of one Swiss citizen, but did not discuss the larger implications of the case, a second, even longer article that appeared in the prestigious American magazine *The New Yorker* looked at the case from a very different angle.

The article was written by the journalist Philip Gourevitch, who had made a name for himself with a book about the genocide in Rwanda. As is apparent from his title, "The Memory Thief," Gourevitch too had become convinced that *Fragments* was a hoax, but he was also interested in core questions about how we deal with the past. On the factual level he has little new to offer; more important for him are the psychological issues, and not just in regard to Wilkomirski the individual but also in relation to his immediate world and to society at large. He addresses the issue of the suggestive power of psychotherapists, a frequent topic of discussion in the United States, and reviews Elitsur Bernstein's role at some length. According to Gourevitch, Bernstein's position—ultimately, that the decision of historical truth should be left to the individual—turns the Shoah into a matter of faith. In his critique of those who use the Holocaust for their own purposes, Gourevitch quotes Norman Manea, a Jewish writer from Romania: "It's a huge event, the Holocaust, so trivialization, commercialization, false memory, and impostors are inevitably going to arise. But one must impose standards." Gourevitch himself is more concerned about what the phenomenon of a Wilkomirski says about how society deals with the past: "After more than six months of studying the mischief that has followed from Wilkomirski's fantasies and obfuscation, I am more fearful for and depressed by the culture that received him as an apostle of memory than I am for the man himself, who-ever he thinks he is."[36]

Before Wilkomirski's story came under fire, the BBC had worked on a film portrait of him. In the spring of 1999, they had also begun to investigate newly arisen doubts. With their film *Child of the Death Camps: Truth and Lies*, they were to come to conclusions similar to my own, if not as comprehensive.

LEA BALINT'S UNCONDITIONAL FAITH

In the wake of Gourevitch's article, Lea Balint wrote a letter to *The New Yorker* in which she defended Wilkomirski and accused the media of playing fast and loose with the truth. She repeated her familiar arguments; new, however, was a reference to "the survivor of Auschwitz who identified Wilkomirski with certainty as a child who was with her in Dr. Mengele's medical-experiment block." Although Balint named no names, this could only be Laura Grabowski, who had been in hiding ever since CBS did its investigation. Balint also charged the media with instilling a fear of similar attacks in those survivors who might otherwise speak in Wilkomirski's favor, driving them to silence and into hiding. She closed her letter as follows:

> Even if there is only a slight chance that Wilkomirski's story is true, we have a moral obligation not to allow him to experience a second Holocaust and not to give him the feeling that threads his memoir, that enormous powers which he cannot understand are working in his life. The careless, ugly, and inhuman treatment he has received must stop. He needs to be given the benefit of the doubt until additional evidence can be uncovered to verify his story. It may be possible that

at some point in his life, he will remember his real name, which could lead to a renewed archival search as has happened to other child survivors without identity. Or maybe, like Dreyfus in his time, an Émile Zola of the twentieth century will come forward and bring his innocence to light.[37]

Lea Balint is the most committed of the defenders who have stuck by Wilkomirski, and one of the few who still publicly speak out for him. As she noted in her statement to Suhrkamp only a few days after Ganzfried's first article, she has been concerned with child survivors since 1991 and is the director in Israel of the Children Without Identity division established within the Ghetto-Fighters House in January 1995. "As part of my work for the division I have set up a data bank containing information on 2,400 orphans found by various Jewish relief agencies after the war. It is the only data bank in the world designed to help survivors who cannot remember their past because they were children during the war and lost their parents."[38]

Many survivors can begin to talk about their experience only now, fifty years later, Balint emphasizes when I meet her for conversation in Zurich in July 1999. She tells me, in English: "I always said, all the unbelievable what happened there you have to believe. Even Professor Friedländer says, 'Every testimony is history.' Every testimony. Because those people who were there, there is no reason to lie."[39] Balint studied history and literature and has a master's degree, but she, too, kept the Holocaust at a distance for a long time. Not until 1991—about the same time as Wilkomirski, she says—did she begin her research. She also still runs the office of her deceased husband, which deals with reparations for Holocaust survivors.

She became acquainted with Wilkomirski as a result of her historical research. At the end of November 1993, she went to Moschaw Ein Iron to attend a meeting of survivors who had lived in a Zionist children's home in Lodz after the war. A bearded man showed up, accompanied by a rather confused-

looking man who spoke no Hebrew, and asked those gathered
there if they could help his friend Bruno, who had been in a children's home in Kraków. Balint went over to them and explained
that they were in the wrong place: these people here had all been
cared for by Zionists, whereas the home in Kraków had been run
by a Communist organization.

A little later Balint agreed to work with Vered Berman of
Israeli Television, and out of their cooperation came *Wanda's
List*. Before going to Poland to research the project, she asked
Wilkomirski, "Do you want to join us and to be in the film,
because maybe somebody will find you in the film?' He said,
'Yes, I would like to expose myself for the first time; maybe
somebody will recognize me in Israel.' " Not long after that,
Balint began to work in the Jewish Historical Institute in War-
saw and discovered in the historical files there traces of stories
she had already heard from Wilkomirski: the addresses on
Miodowa, Długa, and Augustiańska streets, as well as the name
Karola.

Balint says that she herself has never looked for proof of
Wilkomirski's story because she has always believed it. I ask her
if she did any further research after her conversation with Sparr
and Koralnik in 1995. She answers, again in English, "If it was,
it was only coincidentally. When I started to do it, it was now,
because now when Ganzfried denied this question, I was interested: How it's possible, did I make a mistake? It's impossible,
for me it was impossible. You know, all [Wilkomirski's] psychological reactions are exactly the reactions of children with a lost
identity: this anxiety that he has, the suspicions that he has of
people that they are like the Nazis, you know, the searching, you
know, he wants to know and then gets frightened, and then
there are months that he is doing nothing and then he tries
again to find—exactly the same as the others."

"Could you describe," I ask, "how you could have this feeling,
that it's so clear?"

"It is not a feeling," she corrects me. "There are facts."

"What are the facts for your security?"

"That he came for example to the Lodz meeting instead to Kraków. When he was a historian he could know exactly that he has not to come to this place, it was very far. Everything, you know, everything before what happened to him was so clear that I never had a suspicion. He never said, 'I remember this person.' Never. And his reaction to the name Karola and the picture in the newspaper was so true." She once asked him to show her the film of his visit to Majdanek. "I was in the kitchen and he put the film inside and I wanted . . . and he started—he didn't see me—he started trembling like this when he looked at the place he was." She heard him say, " 'When I came back to my home-land it is like for me to come back to my childhood.' He was alone, and I was in the back in my kitchen. And I saw him, he was trembling. I went to bring him water. And I brought him the water and he was like this trembling." (She imitates his trembling.)

"If I understand exactly," I ask, "it was Wilkomirski's reaction that made you so sure?"

"One of the things that made me sure was his behavior."

Balint complains about the journalists who are so certain that Wilkomirski is lying. "You know what a suffer[ing] such a person could have passed. And now he is in another Holocaust. We are dealing with somebody's life. After, maybe he will make a suicide. I don't know. Maybe like Primo Levi and all the others, because those people are so fragile." She asks me to picture the situation of a man who first enjoys the respect of everyone and whose past and future are assured; then, all of a sudden, he is reduced to a nobody, everyone is against him, and no documents, no memories, no witnesses speak for him.

I am impressed by how unconditionally convinced she still is of the truth of Wilkomirski's story, and by the almost boundless empathy with which she defends him. At the end she advises me to be careful. So long as there is no DNA, she says, one can find an objection to every answer. Sometime after our meeting,

Balint sends me a letter that concludes as follows: "A few weeks ago I met with Herr Wilkomirski, Dr. Bernstein, and the historian Dr. Nachum Bogner. To our great surprise we found in the lists in Herr Bogner's possession the name of a child named Andrzej. As early as 1945 the child knew only this name, not even his last name. Herr Wilkomirski—and I believe Laura as well—have believed since 1945 that this is his name. This is the first time that I have seen this name on the lists of children rescued from Poland. Herr Wilkomirski received a copy of the document. I hope that your sense of justice and caution will guide you in your work. Ultimately you and I are only searching for the truth, and we will not find it in historical documents, but only in a medical laboratory. I will no longer concern myself with the Wilkomirski case."[40]

AGAINST THE MAELSTROM OF DISBELIEF—
THE ORTHO PRIZE

Unambiguous and publicly accessible proofs were still lacking, but Ganzfried's disclosures seemed plausible to many people, and following the CBS report of February 1999, statements on Wilkomirski's behalf became rare. All the more astounding to the general public, then, was an action taken at the annual meeting of the American Orthopsychiatric Association (ORTHO), an interdisciplinary organization for professionals dedicated to the psychological health of children and adults. On 10 April 1999, at its convention in Arlington, Virginia, ORTHO presented its seventh Hayman Award for Holocaust and Genocide Study to Binjamin Wilkomirski, "in recognition of his writings and collaborations with clinicians, which have furthered the understanding of genocide and the Holocaust."[41]

With his wife, Tsipora, Harvey Peskin was one of three people who proposed this nomination to the board of ORTHO. A psychoanalyst and professor emeritus at the University of California at Berkeley and a member of the ORTHO board, Peskin had defended Wilkomirski repeatedly in private and in public, and so high was his regard for him that he spoke of him in the same breath with Jean Améry, Paul Celan, and Primo Levi.[42] Shortly before the award was to be presented, he wrote a long letter to Carol Brown Janeway, the translator of *Fragments* into English, in which he took up the cudgels for the beleaguered author. His text, in a slightly different form, was eventually published in *The Nation*. It is not the official speech honoring the awardee, but it contains a representative selection of the most important arguments that Wilkomirski's defenders have put forward.[43]

Peskin repeats many of the familiar arguments and assertions others have advanced (primarily the testimonies of Balint, Löwinger, and Genislav; the allegedly comparable exchange of Gypsy children by the relief agency Pro Juventute; and so on). But Peskin also—and this is his chief concern—views the critical treatment to which Wilkomirski has been subjected by the media as a repetition of a familiar experience of Holocaust children. "Wilkomirski's failure to prove irrefutably his own innocence replays the tragedy of many child survivors . . . whose legal claims for compensation are denied because they fail to present incontrovertible proof of Holocaust suffering." Noting the damage done to a survivor when he or she is not believed, Peskin goes on to say that a lack of witnesses only exacerbates this injustice. "Rather than risk the even higher cost of not being believed, the child survivor often closets and dismisses the memory of the suffering itself. Nowhere else has Hitler's plan to leave no witnesses of the Holocaust come closer to being realized than in separating the very young from their own experience."

Peskin sees the award primarily as a demonstration against the "maelstrom of disbelief" that drives survivors to fearful silence. "To be disbelieved is to be hunted again," he writes; in such a situation, the ORTHO prize sends a signal: "The ORTHO Hayman award, in honoring the very uncertainty of a child survivor's identity, acknowledges the unfinished memory of many. And where the usual stakes of fragmented, hidden, and lonely memory have favored forgetting, that is an important truth to remember." The award is also intended to honor Wilkomirski for "promoting interest in traumatic memory. . . . Specifically, the award also honors Wilkomirski as an historian in his work with Dr. Elitsur Bernstein, an Israeli clinical psychologist, for their innovative conceptualizations in helping young child survivors recover a sense of personal identity through historical verification of their fragmented memories. . . . The ORTHO award honors, then, the memorist and the healer and his journey from one to the other."

Before awarding the prize, the director of ORTHO telephoned Lawrence Langer to discuss with him the organization's intention of honoring Wilkomirski. The literature professor advised strongly against such a plan, for he had regarded *Fragments* as fiction from the start. One reason for his skepticism was that the book had immediately reminded him of Jerzy Kosinski's novel *The Painted Bird,* a book he had studied carefully. In a 1968 interview, Kosinski had told him that "what happened to him during the war was even worse than what happened to the boy in *The Painted Bird.* As it turned out, he was lying. Kosinski was in hiding in Poland with his parents throughout the war. He also told several people, including Eli Wiesel, that he was not Jewish—another lie. So when I read Wilkomirski's text, it never occurred to me that it might be anything but fiction." But Langer's critique was based on more than just the fact that the book reminded him of Kosinski. He had spoken with many survivors, researched hundreds of video interviews with eyewitnesses, and written a book about Holocaust testimony. "No one who was a young child at the time had any but a few scattered memories, none as vivid as the ones Wilkomirski presents. Many episodes in *Fragments* have an impact as imagined experience, but not as history." Despite Langer's substantiated doubts, ORTHO could not be dissuaded from its plans.[44]

The presentation of the award at Arlington was Wilkomirski's first public appearance in the United States since Ganzfried's attack. To protect him, the organizers denied television teams access to the hotel ballroom where the ceremony took place. The speakers, however, did not wish to ignore the worldwide discussions, nor could they. In his introduction Richard Ruth, who had joined the Peskins as the third person to nominate Wilkomirski for the award, compared *Fragments* to "the slave narratives of an earlier time, the truth they revealed and the controversies and criticisms they evoked." The awardee himself read to the assembly a congratulatory e-mail from Lea Balint: "You deserve this award, particularly in the face of attacks and denigration of which the sole aim is to silence those who as children suffered in the Holocaust."[45]

In his acceptance speech, Wilkomirski makes some general comments about the connections between "memory, speech, and identity."[46] Since we can only put words to those things that occur in our collective memory, he said, speech is always memory-work. "A language which reproduces our common experience and memories permits us to develop our sense of identity as individuals, as a people or nation, and as a sociocultural community." After emphasizing the importance to each collective of recognizing its own identity, he explains the individual's analogous situation: his or her identity is rooted in the experience of a commonly shared language in the family and in society.

But there are people who have not been able to develop a recognized individual identity nor a feeling of belonging to a greater social community in their childhood. This happens when little children are brutally eradicated from their sociocultural milieu. They grow up with experiences and, consequently, with memories that are totally strange to the consciousness and horizon of the society where they happen to live later on. [This prompts in these people a permanent feeling that their identity and existence are endangered.] Most of them feel that their only chance to survive in this hostile world is to suppress, disguise, and hide their memories. . . . They are condemned to silence by a society that does not recognize and acknowledge their language. I am saying this with particular reference to persons who, as very small children, were thrown into the death machinery of the Shoah and miraculously survived. Not accepting and recognizing the language of child survivors means denying their true personality and, in the long term, annihilating their identity. But annihilating one's identity means also destruction of one's personality, and that is a direct threat to their psychological and physical existence.

In closing, as if to give his abstract discussion of the disastrous results of denied recognition a human face, as it were, Wilkomirski describes for his audience the story of Sabina Rapaport, who had asked him for help two years before. He explains how the official Swiss documents of another child were given to her, how her memories were then forbidden to her and she was told that she was dreaming, lying, crazy—"all because she had had regular and irrefutably good legal Swiss papers." Not until decades later did a psychologist bring her to the point of trusting her memories. "He was also able to create an atmosphere of safety and security that allowed her to say out loud what she had always known but always had to hide."

Wilkomirski tells how she came to him looking for help, how she was able to recall the name Theresienstadt and Zizi, the nickname by which she had once been called, and also that she had had a sister named Rivka, five or six years older than she. But she knew neither her last name nor her native country, and was not even certain of her mother tongue. He describes how she finally discovered what it was. In their first telephone conversation, Sabina spoke of a recurrent nightmare:

> She was standing in the middle of a street in a camp and saw many children coming toward her. The children walking in front were holding up a kind of banner on which the initials EEM were written. When she saw it, she started crying, then she woke up. Sabina told me that her first thought was: "These initials stand for the French words *Elle Est Morte*, meaning 'she is dead.' " And to her it meant, "My mother is dead!" I suggested that she should ask somebody familiar with several languages to say to her, in all these languages, the sentence "She is dead." And she should listen with her eyes closed. I thought that perhaps she would recognize the sound of a language. As it turned out, this sentence, spoken in every Eastern European language, had not the slightest effect on her, but whenever it was said in French, her pulse went up and she started perspiring. This caused us to extend our attention to French-speaking countries when looking for historical events that might match what she remembered.

Even before that, Wilkomirski says, he had checked her memories of Theresienstadt. She recalled the sign L414 posted at the entrance of the building where she lived. With the help of a projector, Wilkomirski shows the audience in Arlington a plan of Theresienstadt and tells them what he discovered: L4 designated a particular street, and number 14 was the girls' dormitory. Next he presents visual evidence of his further investigatory steps. Sabina had made drawings of her memories: white buildings with exceptionally small doors and posts between the buildings. Between the buildings she wrote, "Thirst. Hot! Dry, sandy ground, lots of wind." These were obviously not memories from Theresienstadt, with its moist, cold climate. After a six-month search, they found a photograph of Rivesaltes, a camp

in southern France, which Wilkomirski also shows. It reveals
white buildings with small, high entrance doors and telephone
poles in front. He places Sabina's drawing next to the photograph. The sandy ground, the tile roofs, the windows, even the
alignment of the buildings are all the same. Sabina had been in
Rivesaltes.

He discovered her family name thanks to a memory she had
of schooldays, Wilkomirski says. Whenever she was unhappy or
in difficulty, she would repeat rapidly to herself the syllables,
"rababorababorababor" and would promptly feel better. "You
know," he told her, "Rapaport is a well-known Jewish name! If
this word gave you a good feeling, even a feeling of security, it
might be your real name, maybe you have found your family
name!" Since Sabina recalled being transported from Rivesaltes
at the hottest time of the year, he looked in the Klarsfeld lists,
which contain the names of all deportees. On the list that he presents to the audience there are twelve Rapaports, one below the
other, with the number 72 next to each. It was a very large family that was deported on transport 72 in the early summer of
1944. Among the names, Wilkomirski found a Sabina Rapaport,
born in 1939; this could be Zizi. She now knew her real first
name and her place of birth: Bielitz in Poland. On the same list
he also found a Rivka Rapaport, six years older than Sabina—the
older sister whom Zizi remembered.

Now I was convinced that we found substantial traces of her
family and that Rapaport was her real family name. It is
interesting to see how a child's memory works: at that time
it was dangerous to tell a child that it was Jewish but nevertheless it was necessary to somehow remember the original name. So this child just remembered it as a "magic
word." As such, the child would never be tempted to reveal
it as her name to a possible enemy. . . . Today, Sabina is a
very balanced, realistically thinking and speaking person.
And for the first time, she feels to be centered in herself.

She asked me to stop investigations at this point. She now just wants to enjoy the feeling of her reassured identity. . . . The award you have given me today is encouraging me to continue collaborating with therapists to help people like Sabina despite all the obstacles I have met in the last few months.

The audience responded to this story of healing with a standing ovation.[47]

When Peskin wrote his letter to Carol Brown Janeway, Wilkomirski's translator, he was already aware that a historian was to be hired to clarify the matter. He expressed his concern that the debate over Wilkomirski's guilt had been dominated by historians, and had not involved experts in trauma and traumatic memory. He felt that this reinforced the bias toward documentation, whereas Wilkomirski, like many child survivors, was laboring under the difficulty of falsified documents and a lack of witnesses to verify his memories. To have a review conducted on documents alone would result in the marginalization of memory, and the publisher would be placed at a disadvantage if the historian did not have the input of trauma experts. Peskin therefore suggests in his letter that the method developed by Wilkomirski and Bernstein and commended in the ORTHO award be adapted for use on its own creator.

As a historian who has long been involved with the Shoah, I of course know that trauma in both its individual and collective senses lies at the very core of our century's great crime. Meetings with traumatized people are among my own most unforgettable experiences. I consider the most essential mark of individual trauma to be the fact that a past experience occupies a person's present as if it were not something already past.[48] It is a speechless terror that overwhelms everyday life with images, emotions, and sensations, that defies being sequenced into a narrative with a beginning, middle, and end. What is not understood, what is indeed incomprehensible, is the true fundamental characteristic of trauma. In the moment of its happening an experience vanishes and continues to elude the victim's understanding from then on, revealing itself to us only in its symptoms, for which there is no language. To deal with the symptoms of a traumatization is to confront what is inaccessible and incomprehensible in an experience. There is a fundamental difference between interpreting the symptom of a past event as the faithful representation of that event and seeing it as the expression of a subjective failure to comprehend the event. Taking traumatic memories seriously means understanding what is evoked as the memory of something steadily drawing further away, and certainly not as some easy-to-read facsimile of the past. Authentic remembrance of a trauma is a story that cannot be told. Presuming that Wilkomirski does have traumatic memories (and this will become my working hypothesis in my research), I can do only one thing as a historian: investigate the circumstances that so traumatized him that he in fact does not understand them and cannot fully relate them even today. In which case a historian's work is assisted not only by documents—as Peskin would have it in his simple dichotomy of documents and memory—but also by both the present and the missing memories of contemporary witnesses, including those of Wilkomirski himself.

TRACKING DOWN THE TRUTH—
THE HISTORICAL RESEARCH

THE BOATMAN FROM RIGA

In lectures and personal conversations Wilkomirski tells about
how on his visit to Latvia with Frau Piller and Herr Bernstein in
August 1994, his story about fleeing Riga was confirmed for
him in its essentials by the historian Margers Vestermanis. In
May 1999, I establish a correspondence with Vestermanis. He
replies that he "condemns most emphatically the campaign
against the author of a good book," and that "as an interested
reader and survivor" he congratulates Wilkomirski on his work.
"I am of the opinion that every author has the right to use the
first-person form, even if it is a mystification of his own identity." At the same time, however, he concedes that "a few details
of his Riga memories are not quite precise."[1]

Vestermanis recalls that in the mid-1990s two gentlemen
paid him a call. "The one was tall, said that he was a psychiatrist
from Israel, but he spoke German without an accent. The other
said little, seemed somehow shy and uncertain. The first question was whether I believed that a two- or three-year-old child
could recall his past in the ghetto and a concentration camp. I
said I did: one cannot remember things in context, but individual episodes remain in the memory as fragments, visions, 'flash
photos,' even when they are buried under later experiences. The
psychiatrist then said that this was the case for my second visitor. I found this interesting, and my original reserve gave way to
a relaxed conversational tone."

They talked for a long while, among other things about how Wilkomirski had fled from Riga. Vestermanis noted:

A rescue by ship is very implausible, though of course it cannot be excluded entirely. Where would you have gone by ship in the winter of '41? The passage down the Daugava into the Gulf of Riga was hermetically sealed. Theoretically you could have sailed upstream, but all the cities in Latvian territory were already "free of Jews." Farther upstream you would arrive in Belorussia, at the cities of Polotsk and Vitebsk, where there were still Jews in ghettos. For such a long journey you would need not only Aryan documents, but also various "permits" issued by the German occupation authorities. From Belorussia the Wilkomirskis (if they looked Aryan and had very good documents) could have made it to Poland, to Kraków. In terms of my own Holocaust research and my current work on a book about stories of rescue in which the most fantastic things did happen, it's not impossible, but this variant is hard to believe.

As evidence for the believability of his flight, Wilkomirski in his talks mentions the historically documented example of a boatman who brought people to safety across the Daugava. "This version of a rescue operation by a Latvian fisherman is an absolute misunderstanding," Vestermanis explains. "I remember exactly that I told the story of Žanis Lipke, a *former harbor worker,* who saved the lives of over fifty Jews—but by hiding them in Riga or in the countryside near Dobele." When Wilkomirski and Bernstein had nevertheless insisted on the former's flight by boat, he had related how the Gestapo had deceived people on several occasions by releasing information that it was possible to flee to Sweden by boat. "But once lured to the harbor, those people were all arrested there."[2]

Wilkomirski has passed on Vestermanis's alleged supposition that little Binjamin got wet that night because of a snowfall, which also accounts for his having been been so cold at the harbor. Vestermanis denies, however, having said anything about snow: "It was below freezing, but a sunshiny day. Other survivors from the Riga ghetto will confirm this."[3]

Wilkomirski's family was fleeing as the result of a police sweep, and Wilkomirski recalls hearing the shout, "Watch it: Latvian militia!" But the historian Raul Hilberg considers this memory historically impossible. That "the term 'Latvian militia' was never used among us" is likewise confirmed in the letter from Vestermanis, the historian and eyewitness from Riga: "The term 'militia' first came into broader use after 1940, when the Soviets marched into Latvia, and was the term for the Soviet police: policeman = militia man. Raul Hilberg is one hundred percent correct—the Latvian collaborators were generally called 'auxiliary police,' or 'Bendeldikke,' from the armbands on their prewar military uniforms."

In 1994, Wilkomirski not only again found the house on Iela Katolu, in which—or so he quotes Vestermanis as saying—there was once a Jewish charitable organization, but also recalled the church steeples and a library with a clock that, at the age of three at most, he could see from there. The Latvian historian, however, knows nothing about such a Jewish organization: the claim is "absolute nonsense." It is correct, he allows, that several church steeples could be seen along Iela Katolu—"Catholic and Russian Orthodox. There was, of course, no library with a clock (!!), nor would a three-year-old child have paid any attention to a library."[4]

Wilkomirski is, though, correct in saying that Vestermanis showed his visitors that day an address book containing an entry for the family of one Avraam Wilkomirski, residing in the vicinity of Iela Katolu. Vestermanis himself can no longer recall this, but the episode is included in Bernstein's tape recording of the day's events. Moreover, in researching the state archives of Riga, I, too, found an Avraam who wrote his name Wolkomirski and lived in the city until July 1941.[5]

168 THE WILKOMIRSKI AFFAIR

THE RATS AT MAJDANEK

Wilkomirski says that his memories are in part physical and emotional—for example, when he feels the bump on the back of his head, he connects it with a kick by a Nazi guard. Likewise, emotional reminiscences can turn into panic when he is questioned by bureaucrats or traffic police. He describes one such panic attack that he experienced in the company of his partner:

A while back we had just returned from Israel and wanted to board a train at the Kloten airport. We had cut it fairly close and had to hurry. My wife said to me, "Come quick." And I just lost it. I had a huge panic attack, was completely beside myself. I had the feeling I was the last one. And I thought I saw a whole lot of people all around me, but I was alone, felt so small, surrounded by legs that were almost trampling me to death. They were all pushing and shoving onto the train, but the ramp was way too high for me. Suddenly I had a moment of physical memory that told me I had to take a ten-step running start and make a pirouette so I could swing up and in. So I threw both my bags, which I really couldn't carry all by myself, onto the train and then landed on board on my belly. I had gone totally to pieces. My wife told me later that the train platform was completely empty.[6]

Wilkomirski also describes states that remind him of the bug plagues in the camps. "There were times when I would get skin rashes that itched horribly. I would scratch all night long and feel like I was being chewed up by insects, with lice everywhere, bugs everywhere. I had to take pills to control it. The worst was in the months before and during the tour for the Holocaust Museum. I constantly felt lice everywhere, crawling into my nose, my eyes, my ears."[7] Verena Piller has explained how external circumstances can put him into such states: "Last spring we kept finding these triangular beetles that came out of the wooden beams; it's normal for this house. They always come in the spring and make a really funny noise, banging against the windowpanes and buzzing. And he goes into absolute panic and leaves the room, shouting. He's shouting for help." This is not the case with all insects, she says; just with beetles that remind him of the dog kennels at Majdanek. "And he can't even get close to them. I have to come and take the insects away." It doesn't help for her to reassure him that they're harmless.

As a result of the plague of rats at the camp, Wilkomirski still always moves his feet at night, Piller says. "I asked him, 'Why do you do that? You're always so nervous.' He said you didn't dare fall into such a deep sleep that you could no longer keep your feet moving, otherwise the rats would gnaw on them. Other child survivors have said the same thing. They talked about the rats, how they were everywhere, and how the little children especially were terrified of them. It's awfully hard to wake him sometimes, to make him stop it, because he's usually in a very deep sleep."[8]

Verena Piller tells me about the rats and the insects when I ask her what, for her, is the most persuasive confirmation of Wilkomirski's memories. "Those are things that are simply always present; you can't simulate them, you can't play-act at it."

For Wilkomirski these experiences at Majdanek were the cause of his rat phobia. But according to Tomasz Kranz, who heads the research department of the Majdanek museum, while there were indeed lice and fleas in the camp, there were no rats. One cannot exclude the possibility of individual rats, but in contrast to Birkenau, there is no evidence of a plague of rats at Majdanek. Wilkomirski, Kranz says, has perhaps confused the two camps. Such a confusion is out of the question, however, since Wilkomirski has frequently recalled in detail how it was his friend Jankl who taught him to keep the rats away by moving his feet. And according to *Fragments,* Jankl was only at Majdanek, where he died before Wilkomirski's eyes.[9]

Wilkomirski likewise talks about his current eye and blood problems, as well as his fractured coccyx, all of which he traces to medical experiments performed on him by doctors named Fischer and König, after his arrival in Birkenau toward the end of 1944. Dr. Hans Wilhelm König, however, worked at Birkenau only until September 1944, and Dr. Horst Fischer only until November 1943.

Incidentally, one of Wilkomirski's sons also has a bump on the back of his head.[10]

KRAKÓW

After being liberated from Birkenau, Wilkomirski says he lived in various orphanages in Kraków. He speaks of people whom he can remember or whom he met again later, and also of a pogrom that was the immediate cause of his flight to Switzerland. Elena Lappin has already researched parts of this portion of his narrative.[11]

Conditions in Kraków immediately after the war were chaotic, but they are well documented all the same. Whoever wishes to gain some idea of what life was like for Jewish children in the city during this period can, for example, visit the Jewish Historical Institute of Warsaw, which has collected a great many documents from those days, or read accounts by the children themselves, some of which have been published in books. But above all there are many survivors who supply information by word of mouth.

As early as 1946, Maria Hochberg-Mariańska published the testimony of children which she had begun to gather in early 1945. During the German occupation of Kraków, Hochberg had helped hide children for the Jewish resistance movement, Żegota. At war's end, she looked after Jewish children who had returned to the city but were now homeless and abandoned. Hochberg's organization was the Communist Centralny Komitet Żydowski (C.K.Ż.P.), to which the homes on both Długa and Augustiańska streets belonged. Such children were also looked after by the Zionist Koordynacja and the religious organization Kongregacja, which ran a home on Miodowa Street.[12]

The first to return were the children from the camps, Hochberg says, then those who had been in hiding, and finally those who had been protected by "Aryan" papers. They came like moles out of their holes, looked at the world with new eyes, were like old people and newborns at the same time. They saw everyday objects for the first time and had to learn how to use them: "Some of them were afraid of a bed, a cupboard, a chair, a plate, a spoon. It was difficult to find words to explain the change that so terrified them. Deafened and blinded by their new surroundings, they often cried helplessly and pulled away from arms that brought them caresses. They did not understand all this and wanted to go back to their hiding places." Over time a lot of this became normalized. There were moving scenes of children being discovered by mothers returning from the camps. Others, though, guessed that no one would come for them. "Hope died anew in the eyes of those children. More and more frequently, in bouts of depression one would hear: 'Why couldn't I have died with mama?' "[13]

The first children that Hochberg met after the liberation were boys and girls of four and older who came from Birkenau at the end of January 1945. In listening to their stories of suffering and terror, Hochberg writes, she felt all her own experiences in the resistance fade to meaninglessness, as if they were not worth wasting words on. Some of these children were taken to an orphanage on Długa Street. "Over the next three months still more groups arrived; the children were kept here temporarily and then sent to their 'home regions.' " Among them were sets of twins, "who had been kept at Birkenau for scientific purposes. That was according to the wishes of the executioner in chief, Dr. Mengele. During this period a total of perhaps two hundred children found refuge in the house on Długa Street. Twenty were left behind; they were the unhappiest of all, those who could find no relatives whatever."[14]

In their first few months on Długa Street, the children lived under very inadequate conditions. They wore rags, slept on the floor in damp rooms, and had to eat horsemeat—butter and sugar were luxuries.[15] Material conditions soon improved, however, especially thanks to support provided to various Jewish orphanages by philanthropic organizations in the United States.

Misia Leibel, who met Wilkomirski during the filming of *Wanda's List,* can likewise report about the situation at the children's home. At the end of April 1946, she and her twelve-year-old daughter returned from Russia, where they had spent the war years. Misia had lost both her parents and her husband. Until 1951, she worked as a home attendant in Kraków.[16] It was a very important time for her, and she can still recall it down to the smallest detail.

When she began to work as an attendant at Długa Street in May 1946, the home was set up temporarily in an apartment with three or four rooms, two of which were reserved for sick children. At the time, a total of twenty-five to thirty children lived there. In June 1946, Frau Leibel went to the train station to meet more than a hundred children returning from Russia. There was an urgent need to arrange other quarters for these children, and a suitable place was found on Augustiańska Street. The large, four-story building had been constructed before the war as an old folks' home, but in 1939 the Germans had turned it into a hotel—or perhaps a bordello, as rumor had it. There was a terrace and a view of the mountains, a garden, and even a playground.

As one can read in a letter written by Maria Hochberg, the move from Długa Street to Augustiańska Street took place in August 1946. Hochberg was on the staff at Długa Street, and after the move to Augustiańska Street was a regular visitor there. In one of her letters she includes a list of all the orphans living on Długa Street. No child who might have been Wilkomirski is among them.[17]

Unfortunately, I was unable to question Hochberg myself, since she died a few years ago. Through the good agency of Lea Balint, however, Wilkomirski met with her in Israel, where she was then living under the name Peleg (a Hebrewized form of Hochberg). After their conversation, an annoyed Hochberg telephoned Balint to ask that she be left in peace in her old age. She had apparently been unable to connect the visitor from Switzerland with her own past. After so many years she could not remember those children from bygone days, who had long since become adults. As Balint tells it, Peleg later apologized and said she did recall a Binjamin, but he had gone to France, not to Switzerland.[18]

In speaking of his visit with Misia Leibel in 1994, Wilkomirski says that she did not wish to be reminded of her past as an attendant at the Augustiańska Street home and did not recognize him. Only later did he learn indirectly that she in fact had remembered him.[19] Frau Leibel is very friendly when I call, and not for a moment do I have the impression that she no longer wants to talk about those times now long past. She can remember very well her meeting in 1994 with Wilkomirski, who introduced himself as Bruno. She is absolutely certain that he was neither on Długa nor on Augustiańska Street. "Here in this apartment where I'm sitting, he told me that he was in our children's home, but that he had been unable to speak. If he had been different from all the others, it's impossible that I would forget him." Leibel can provide the names of many children who stood out for one reason or another, because they limped, were blind, sickly, or whatever. There was never a mute boy among them. She stresses that she does not want to be unfair to Wilkomirski; just to make sure, she even made inquiries with several other of her "wards" with whom she still maintains regular contact. No one from Długa or Augustiańska Street can recall a child matching Wilkomirski's description.

Telephone conversations with various other former residents of these homes confirm Leibel's statement.[20] This seems all the more remarkable because those I question remember the names of other children whom I have found listed in archives. One witness, who had been among the first on Długa Street, does remember Wilkomirski—but not from the time he spent in the home. He says that Wilkomirski contacted him some four years previously, and later they met during the filming of *Wanda's List*.[21] The question is, Had Wilkomirski used this contact in order to research his own story?

There is a scene in *Wanda's List* showing Wilkomirski in conversation with Julius Löwinger. He convinces the former resident of the home on Augustiańska Street by answering a number of questions to his satisfaction. Among other things, Wilkomirski describes a playground with exercise bars. Elena Lappin later discovered that Löwinger had been mistaken on this point—during the period in question, no such equipment had yet been installed.[22] I telephone Löwinger and ask him if Wilkomirski might not have come by his knowledge by some other means. Löwinger tells me not to ask him this. "Bruno answered several of my questions [and] about these questions I came to the reality, my reality. He was in Kraków. What time, in what year, I don't know. Maybe I met him, maybe not. But not more, I'm not sure. I can swear about the questions, not more."[23]

A remarkable incident took place during the filming, which the film's director, Vered Berman, described to me as follows: as

Wilkomirski and Löwinger looked at photographs, they were watched out of camera range by other former residents of the Augustiańska Street home. Wilkomirski suddenly pointed to one picture and cried, "Oh, that's Karola!" But all the who were people standing around knew the girl only as Marta. Wilkomirski was the only one who did not know the name by which she had been called back then.[24] In the files of the home, to be sure, the girl is listed under the name Karola. What had so impressed Balint when she discovered these lists was that Wilkomirski pointed out in them the same name he had previously talked about.

I would very much have liked to speak with Karola/Marta about this strange discrepancy in names. Wilkomirski, however, is not prepared to put me in contact with her. Leibel and the other residents remember the girl very well—a beautiful, tall, blond girl, they are all unanimous about that—but no one knows her current address. When I ask Bernstein about her, he tells me that he himself has seen the woman only once, at the memorial celebration at Wilkomirski's home in January 1995. "She was very moved and it was difficult to talk with her, she hardly said a word. To me she said, 'I know you are his best friend and it's important that you're his friend, for he is my brother, he was always my brother.' She implied that she knew him from days past. The whole story about Karola is very complicated, because Bruno is not prepared to give anyone any identifying details about her. For various reasons he prefers that contact not be made with her. . . . Her husband has forbidden her to speak about it, and she has always felt under pressure from him." I tell Bernstein how sorry I am that that is the case, since Karola might finally be able to provide evidence for Wilkomirski's story.[25]

In *Fragments,* Wilkomirski also tells about how he begged in Kraków. In interviews he even explains that beggars had certain territories they defended, depending on which group they belonged to (Jews, Christians, or Gypsies), and how the mem-

bers of each group were identifiable by the way they held out
their hands to beg. When he was in Kraków in 1993 with his
friend Bernstein, he even discovered in the Podgórze Quarter a
street corner where he had once begged.[26] When asked, Leibel
and all the former orphanage residents strongly deny that the
children from Długa or Augustiańska Street ever begged.
Instead, in voices warm with gratitude, they describe how well
they were cared for; one former attendant recalls that the staff
even went directly to farmers to buy food. Wilkomirski, however, says that he had to beg because he had run away from the
home. Moreover, he claims that other former residents of the
home on Długa Street have told him that older children sometimes got younger ones to beg for money.[27]

The pogrom that sparked Wilkomirski's flight to Switzerland presents various puzzles. To be sure, the defeat of the Nazis
did not mean that anti-Semitism had vanished from Kraków.
There were disturbances in the old Jewish quarter of Kazimierz
as early as 11 August 1945.[28] That Sabbath morning, while a
service was being held in the synagogue on Miodowa Street,
about sixty rowdies gathered outside the doors and threw stones
at the building. One of the young stone-throwers was beaten up
by Jewish soldiers and ran off screaming that the Jews were trying to kill him. That sufficed to whip the crowd into a frenzy.
They insulted and assaulted Jews in the neighborhood, demolished their apartments, and robbed them. The violence ended
toward evening, but the city remained tense for several days.
There were similar riots in other towns, including Rabka. Especially dreadful was the pogrom in Kielce the following year,
when a frenzied mob murdered forty-one Jews.[29]

Wilkomirski first dated the pogrom that led to his flight
to 1947. Since he had never read anything different, he says,
he must have thought it was connected with the pogrom in
Kielce—though those riots occurred in 1946. After it became
known that he was already registered in Zurich by October

1945 and was attending primary school there by April 1947, he moved the pogrom's date to two years earlier. In the summer of 1998, Lea Balint told him that there had been violence against Jewish orphanages as early as 15 August 1945 (this was presumably a reference to the historically documented pogrom of 11 August of that year). Wilkomirski has always said that he experienced this violence either on Długa or on Augustiańska Street, but both of those lie outside the Jewish quarter, where the events actually occurred. Leibel and other residents affirm that no violence of this sort ever took place on Długa or Augustiańska streets. Moreover, the home on Augustiańska Street did not even come into existence until the summer of 1946.

The only possible setting for these events, then, is Miodowa Street, which was indeed the focal point of the riots. And in fact there was a refuge there for Jews who had come from the camps (which could also fit with Wilkomirski's description of his arrival in Kraków).[30] On the same street, according to Lea Balint, there was also a home run by Sara Stern Katan, whom Balint cites as a witness. Balint asked Stern about the pogrom reported by Wilkomirski. She would never forget it, Stern replied, and told the exact same story as Wilkomirski. He had described to Balint how he had been taken from Miodowa Street to Długa Street, perhaps because the former was no longer safe. Stern is of the opinion that the children in her home were eight or nine years old, and thus older than Wilkomirski. She does not recall any Binjamin.[31]

There is the added difficulty that the Miodowa orphanage belonged to a different organization than was running the homes on Długa and Augustiańska streets; it is hard to imagine why Wilkomirski would be switched from one organization to the other. But there is something that is even more puzzling: Wilkomirski says he resided on different occasions in the homes on Długa and Augustiańska streets, with occasional periods of living on the street and at least one excursion to Rabka or

Zakopane. He arrived in Kraków sometime after the liberation of Auschwitz, on 22 January 1945. After the pogrom, which he now claims he experienced in August 1945, he left for Switzerland. It appears rather improbable that during this span of time he could have arrived at Miodowa Street, made a tour of his various stopping places, returned to Miodowa in time for the pogrom, and then gone back to Augustiańska Street, whence he was brought to Switzerland. Not to mention the contradiction of his being fetched in 1945 from a home that was not to open until a year later.

I send Leibel a copy of *Fragments*. After reading it, she writes me a letter in which she confirms what she has already said on the telephone. She adds that Olga is described in Wilkomirski's book as if her job was the same as Leibel's,[32] when in reality she was a fourteen-year-old girl. Although Leibel has consistently denied that Wilkomirski could have been in either of her two children's homes, she nonetheless finds the book itself "cruelly true." She knows nothing, she says, of its wider circumstances: "Someone could have told him about those cruel deeds—but his description of fear seems very honest to me." People in Kraków, she informs me, are very interested in the controversy that has arisen around the book in Europe and Israel. "The concentration-camp theme has been used so many times, in books of varying literary quality. I must admit I found this book especially touching—quite apart from whether it's a true biography of Wilkomirski." The book is going to be read aloud to groups of eyewitnesses, she says; she will let me know about their reactions.[33]

When I call to thank her for her letter, her response is strangely cool. I have the impression she regrets having said such positive things about the book. Some trouble seems to be brewing in Kraków: the next day the telephone rings; an anonymous female voice says that she is calling from Kraków, but then she falls silent and hangs up.

ARRIVAL IN SWITZERLAND

Fragments tells how after the war Wilkomirski was sent from Kraków to Basel, where he was smuggled in as part of a group of French children on vacation. Alone and with a blank label around his neck, he was retrieved from a waiting room in the Basel train station, taken to a children's home, and ultimately exchanged for a Christian child. Various questions arise: Could a child enter Switzerland after the war in the way described? What would happen to him upon being received by a relief agency? Would a change of identity afterward be plausible?

I have studied Swiss policy toward aliens for many years now and have come across the most improbable stories of how refugees found their way into Switzerland during the period of the Shoah—whether secretly or legally, with falsified or real documents—but I have never heard a story like the one Wilkomirski tells. In order to carefully check all possibilities, I research the pertinent Swiss archives and also interview the eyewitness Liselotte Hilb, who worked for the Swiss Committee for Emigrated Children (SHEK) from 1940 to 1948. She knows the conditions of the time from personal experience and can best provide information about the sort of illegal actions that are often inadequately noted in the files—since it was not in the interest of those involved to leave any trace of what they did.

Around the time of Wilkomirski's entry into Switzerland, Hilb confirms, the Swiss Red Cross (SRK) was indeed bringing in many children to spend a vacation with families there.[34] Trains arrived week after week, and in fact the number of transports increased once the war was over. In 1945 around 28,000 children, half of them from neighboring France, traveled to Switzerland. A committee from each local Red Cross chapter selected the neediest children, but those who were so psychologically ill that they could not be helped within three months' time were excluded. Immediately before their departure, all the children underwent medical examinations, ending in the final decision that allowed them entry. So-called *convoyeuses* then accompanied the trains to Switzerland. As the annual report for 1945 explains:

> Volunteers who receive no compensation, these women have been providing this service for years and quietly accept all the rigors familiar only to those who know what it means to keep children quiet and occupied for days on end on often unheated trains, to play mother and hold heads in cases of motion sickness so common among children, to take care of all those who are used to having buttons unbuttoned by mothers at home, to cook and make sandwiches, to keep lists in order, to clean lavatories—and then, after an exhausting day, to watch over the sleeping children and comfort them in the homesickness that inevitably comes with nightfall.

In Switzerland other volunteers waited at four locations—of which Basel, where Wilkomirski claims to have arrived, was one—to receive the children and distribute them among the families.

Along with these vacationing children, who came to Switzerland by normal means, the Red Cross also took care of those arriving illegally, sharing this task with the Swiss Committee for Emigrated Children. Who are these children, the Red Cross report asks: "They have not been cast upon our borders in great waves nor do they come in well-organized trains and with name tags around their necks. They have wandered on foot across the mountains by secret paths, arriving illegally, sometimes with parents or relatives, often in small groups, often quite alone— little lost leaves borne by the wind across our borders—without parents, without a home, sometimes even without a name." During the war, countless children entered Switzerland illegally—there were 4,000 just seven years old or younger, the age group to which Wilkomirski would have belonged. It was primarily Jewish refugee organizations that helped them in their flight, although a smaller number were also assisted by the staff of the Red Cross.[35]

The children came across the border illegally because Switzerland, the only island of freedom in Nazi-occupied Europe, barred Jews from entering by legal means. This little nation liked to think of itself as an asylum for the persecuted and a bulwark of humanity, but it had long followed a policy of anti-Semitism. Heinrich Rothmund, who had built a Federal Police for Foreigners after World War I and was its head till the mid-1950s, once summarized the policy as follows: "Since the beginnings of the Federal Police for Foreigners we have held to a clear position. Along with other foreigners, Jews were considered a factor for an excessive foreign influence. Until now we have succeeded by systematic and careful procedures in preventing Switzerland from being Judaized."[36] Even after the Nazis began their systematic murder of Jews, Swiss authorities held fast to their goals and turned back at the border countless numbers of people seeking asylum, a rejection that for most of them amounted to a death sentence.

These anti-Semitic immigration policies continued after the end of World War II, so that even those Jews who had found shelter in Switzerland were eventually forced to leave the country. This was also true of Jewish orphans: by the estimate of Police Chief Rothmund there were only fifty or so who should remain in Switzerland and be granted citizenship. He could count on wide public support for his position, even within the relief agencies themselves, as he noted with satisfaction: "Frau Dr. Sutro, the outstanding head of the Swiss Committee for Emigrated Children, has shown truly excellent understanding of her task. Free of any useless humanitarian nonsense and aware of her great responsibility in regard to these children, she quickly determined that Switzerland is not soil in which these pitiful creatures could freely develop their personalities. She therefore put all her energies to work to send these children to countries where such conditions exist."[37] As for the "fifty well-assimilated children who remain," Rothmund shared Sutro's view that they should retain Swiss citizenship; he would gladly endorse the idea.

What happened, then, to Wilkomirski upon his arrival in Switzerland during this period? Since, according to his story, he did not cross the border secretly but very publicly and indeed caused some commotion, his advent would have to have left various traces. In the canton of Basel, the names of all persons who entered without having their documents in order were recorded in a special journal, but neither there nor in the files of the canton's Fremdenpolizei (Police for Foreigners) could I find any corroboration. Wilkomirski says that women took care of him; those who might have been involved would be women working for the Swiss Red Cross and especially for the SHEK, which after June 1945 were in charge of all children who entered irregularly. I found not a trace in these organization's archives, either.[38]

Relief agencies at the time worked closely with the civil authorities and would most certainly have registered the boy with the federal Police for Foreigners. All of that bureau's personal files are now part of the data bank in the Swiss Federal Archives. I request a systematic search of these data banks according to all possible variations of specific attributes: for a Wilkomirski under every conceivable spelling, for all the first names he himself has mentioned, and finally for an unnamed boy with an approximate date of birth who arrived without parents, at all possible places of entry. All in vain.[39] Wilkomirski says he came from Kraków with a Swiss woman who was returning home; but a search of the files for Swiss citizens returning from abroad turns up nothing.[40]

And so I turn to Liselotte Hilb, who immediately begins to speak with fire and intelligence about the problems and psychology of children, as if she were still caught up in her work for

SHEK. Quite by chance, she says, she had seen Wilkomirski at a event before Ganzfried's article ever appeared. "Strange," she had thought, "I've never heard of the case before. Thank heaven it wasn't our Children's Relief that put the boy in that stupid family. And then I thought to myself, But then I don't have to know everything." In the end, impressed by Wilkomirski's presentation, she had believed his story. But when Ganzfried's article appeared, her initial uneasiness was confirmed. On the basis of her own experience, she now considers Wilkomirski's description of his entry implausible.[41]

Hilb had worked at the central office of SHEK and had thus been in close contract with the authorities, had even known Police Chief Heinrich Rothmund personally—he who had espoused the cause of allowing the fifty children to stay but was otherwise an ambivalent character. Of course, she had also dealt with individual children who entered the country and needed looking after. During the war she had been in Zurich and had helped smuggle refugee children onto children's vacation trains entering Switzerland. After the war, she had accompanied two such vacation trains herself.

Those trains, she says, were very tightly organized. Every child had to have papers allowing entry into Switzerland before he or she could even be placed on the list. At every border crossing, at every stop, papers were checked. A child who wasn't on the list and didn't belong with the group, like Wilkomirski, would have been quickly discovered. A child first acquired a name tag only after other formalities had been taken care of at the point of departure. And it wouldn't have been left blank, either, but rather would have borne a fictitious name (presumably that of Bruno Grosjean in this case) and the name of the Swiss vacation family.[42] "Wilkomirski made a mistake in his story," Hilb says. "He would have had to arrive before the end of the war. Until then chaos ruled; it was a mess, people being smuggled in and everything else."

After the war's end, hardly any illegal children arrived, since entries could be easily supervised. If Wilkomirski had in fact gotten off alone at the train station in Basel, Hilb says, he would have been handed over to the care of the Swiss Red Cross, SHEK, or perhaps the Pro Juventute. He would immediately have been reported to the federal police. An identity sheet would have been prepared with his fingerprints, photo, and personal data, and on that basis a blue refugee card would have been issued. It seems only logical to Hilb that I have been unable to find any trace of our new arrival in the files of any of those institutions. "The story definitely doesn't square," she confirms.

She is further convinced of this because, she says, now and then there were children whose origins had to be clarified, and the relief agency involved would have done everything conceivable to do so in this case as well. "Like a detective, you put all the machinery in motion to find brothers and sisters or other relatives." Data and photographs were sent to other countries, other offices, whereby for other countries, the Swiss branch of the International Social Service, the Aid for Refugees, Geneva, took over the research. Sometimes a child knew very little; maybe there would be only a name sewn into his or her coat. She cited as an example a child named Jacques, who had arrived illegally in Switzerland during the war and was in such bad shape that he would not eat or speak. Finally he was shown a photograph from Belgium. His response was to eat it—he had found his brother again.

Neither can Hilb understand why a child would have needed false documents to be brought to Switzerland after the war, where no one was in danger anymore. I protest that the authorities wouldn't have wanted to keep Jews after the war, either. Hilb agrees and adds that the relief agencies also thought it best that such children continue on to somewhere else. But she believes that a child could have stayed if he or she really wanted to. The relief agency would have fought for that and won, "in every case." Although she offers examples of this, I recall the minuscule number of those who were allowed to stay and am not truly convinced. Might she not be overestimating the options available to her back then, on account of the unconditional commitment to the children that is still discernible in her every word?

During the war the Swiss authorities, with bureaucratic closed-mindedness, had torn apart those families who, remarkably, had gained entry. Men and women were placed in separate camps, and children were given to relief agencies, who then placed them with families, in children's homes, or in youth camps. By far the largest number of these children were Jewish, and indeed it was impossible to find Jewish foster homes for all of them. The Jewish community in Switzerland was much too small for that, numbering only 18,000. Among some Jewish groups, however, placing these children with Christians reactivated the old fear of proselytization, and they warned against their progeny's being lost to them by baptism. In response, the relief agencies agreed to set up religious training—the children would either visit religious schools or be taught by traveling Jewish teachers.

Once the war was over, a fierce argument was waged in Europe about what to do with the young survivors. The Jewish community had been horribly decimated and did not want to lose a single one of its rescued children. In Poland, Lea Balint says,[43] Jewish organizations even kidnapped children from the Christian families who had hidden them during the Nazi terror. In many countries the emissaries of Zionism were working to bring orphaned children to Palestine; everywhere they found neglected children who had had hardly any Jewish upbringing and had been assimilated into a Christian milieu, some even secretly baptized.

At war's end the great majority of orphans and abandoned children left Switzerland, and then interest was redirected toward the good hundred or so who still remained. Orthodox Jewish circles pleaded that these children not be forced to wait for their planned departure, but that they instead be removed at once from their Christian families. This was opposed by the Swiss Federation of Jewish Communities and the relief agencies, who insisted that the children should not be uprooted yet again, and right before they were due to emigrate in any case. Their Orthodox opponents warned them that the "Jewish world" would brand "their position as an unforgivable Jewish assassination of every abandoned Jewish child." But despite this vast difference of opinion, the various parties all agreed that the children should remain part of the Jewish community. I first heard of an "ideology of despair," arguing for a radical assimilation of Jewish children, in Wilkomirski's description of Jadassohn, but I have never run across it in the historical debate.[44]

I ask Liselotte Hilb if she thought it probable that a Jewish organization would have even considered smuggling Wilkomirski into Switzerland after the war. "No, not at all. They would have kept him, they were happy for every child they could rescue." When I tell her Wilkomirski's story about Jadassohn, she considers it implausible for the same reason: a Jewish organization never would have supplied a child with a Christian identity. Jadassohn would have had to be acting solely on his own. Hilb also made inquiries among her Jewish acquaintances, and they could not see any sense in an exchange of children, either. If Jadassohn arranged such an exchange, he was a fool. "It would have been quite unthinkable to attach a different faith to a child. It's unethical; no one would have done it." Two days after our conversation, I receive two letters at once from my fidgety source. In one she quotes Nettie Sutro, the Jewish director of the Children's Relief Agency, on how a child's religious needs were looked after:

> Every child was raised in the tradition of its parents; if they were no longer present, we felt we were their trustees and tried faithfully to realize their views, to the extent that we knew them. That was and remained our basic principle. . . . Anyone who has ever been involved in issues of religious

pedagogy, and not just with them but also with the profound effect of a genuine religious milieu, knows how easily children can be influenced, and thus converted, even if that is neither the intention nor the wish. . . . In a very few cases we monitored very closely any desire for a change of faith and attempted to make the circumstances more difficult. For ultimately we knew that young people who are on their own have made no permanent decision, even in choosing baptism, unless they can remain in this newly acquired religious world.

Frau Hilb added that my investigation had put me in a difficult position and that perhaps she should send me some results of her own research as to Jadassohn. This she did in her second letter. Among other things she confirmed that a physician by that name had taught at the University of Geneva, beginning in 1946.[45] The meeting in Geneva at which Jadassohn revealed to Wilkomirski his motive for the exchange thus could have taken place, at least in terms of physical circumstance.

The final item to be checked, then, is whether a change of identities could possibly be connected with the practices of the relief agency Pro Juventute. Wilkomirski and his lawyer have repeatedly pointed out that Pro Juventute exchanged the identities of Gypsy children in a similar fashion. Moreover, Wilkomirski says, his foster father maintained special and intense contact with that agency and its director, Alfred Siegfried. I had previous knowledge that this same Siegfried had also assumed functions in the children's relief work of the Swiss Red Cross and SHEK.[46]

In 1926, Pro Juventute founded the Relief Agency for Children of the Road as part of its own institution. In an attempt to end so-called vagrancy—the wanderings of whole families and clans—this agency systematically took children from Yenish (Gypsy) families and placed them in children's homes and with foster families. This practice continued into the early 1970s.

Such measures had their roots in the mid-nineteenth century, when in an effort to establish its own bourgeois order, the nascent modern state opposed and disciplined anything on its margins. From that point on, the demand was repeatedly voiced to "clean up this plague of Gypsies" and to make these nomadic peoples settle down. When Swiss society was racked by social conflict during the period World War I and the call for order and discipline became ever louder, the Relief Agency for Children of the Road set out purposefully to destroy Yenish culture. It was a private institution, but one with such strong state underpinnings that it could act as if it were an official agency. It was not by chance that those who supported it were often the same men who led the state crusade against all things foreign and Jewish.

Siegfried, the agency's fanatical director, took Yenish children from their parents and erased every trace of their former life. He forced parents not only to give written consent for the unconditional seizure of their children, for possible changes of name, and for later adoption, but also to promise in writing never to search for the children. The unutterable suffering and injustice the agency inflicted on hundreds of Gypsies first became a public scandal in 1972, and both officialdom and the agency are still having trouble today redressing their crimes.[47]

A comparison of this story with Wilkomirski's presentation indeed reveals several parallels, but one difference is telling: Wilkomirski was given the identity of Bruno Grosjean, a boy who must have existed, for there are extensive files on him from the period before the alleged exchange. When Siegfried took a child away, however, he did not give him or her the identity of another, already existing child, but simply used the name and the documents of the new family. In fact, he would have had a considerable problem following the procedure à la Wilkomirski: what would he do with the children for whom he had an official biography but for whose actual existence he had no use? He could have made them disappear, but that would not have been all that easy. In any case, thus far there is no plausible explanation as to where the "real" Bruno Grosjean spent the years between the time of the exchange and his emigration to America at age seventeen.

Despite the alleged contact between his foster father and Siegfried, there is no mention of Wilkomirski in the files of the Relief Agency for Children of the Road.[48]

BRUNO BERTI REMEMBERS AN UNEXPECTED EVENT

Bruno Berti lives in a small house at the foot of the slopes of Zürichberg. Despite his advanced age—he is seventy-eight—he continues to work as an architect.[49] Having been informed of my intentions, he has meticulously assembled various documents, postcards, and photographs showing that from 1942 on, he was in regular contact with the people who would later become Wilkomirski's foster parents. He came to know them through his future wife, who as Rosie Baumann was Dr. Dössekker's medical assistant from 1938 to 1957.

Since Rosie was not all that well paid, at Christmas she was given an annual bonus, presented to her at the villa by Frau Dössekker. From 1942 on, she was accompanied to the Dössekkers' by Herr Berti: "It became the usual thing for us to go up there every year, bring a little present, wish them a merry Christmas and a happy New Year." One Christmas, much to their surprise, Frau Dössekker had her arm around a five-year-old boy. "That memory is as clear as a photograph," Berti says. "You see, in those social circles that sort of thing naturally caused a sensation. People whispered, 'Have you heard, Frau Doctor Dössekker has taken in a child?' and so on." He and Rosie had never imagined that the wealthy Dössekkers would take in a foster child. "Several members of their family grew up at Castle Wetzikon; at one time they would have been called country gentry." Berti shows me lists of relatives teeming with the names of important industrialists; to them Kurt and Martha Dössekker were probably "poor cousins." But things at the villa were very elegant, Berti recalls. "The parlor was 'Don't touch me!' You almost didn't dare use the elegant chairs, just sat on the front edge. Given the furniture and the meticulous housekeeping, you couldn't even imagine a child romping around in there."

I ask Berti if it was his impression that Christmas that Bruno had only just arrived.

"Yes, absolutely. Something else started happening shortly thereafter. Whenever Frau Dössekker went into town, she'd leave Bruno with my wife at her husband's office. My wife would have to take care of him. She'd tell me each time on our way home that Bruno had been with her again, that it'd been so nice." This happened frequently.

I ask Berti if the boy who was at the Dössekkers' that day was definitely Binjamin Wilkomirski.

"Yes, there was no other boy in 1945."

"You saw him regularly?"

"Yes." And his wife saw him even more often. "She would have known about any exchange."

I ask the follow-up question: "Assuming that in 1945 some boy had arrived in the family who presented difficulties, and another had then come six months later, would your wife have noticed?"

"Yes, with one hundred percent certainty. My wife and Herr Dössekker told each other everything. He even read her love letters; she told him everything about me. Let me tell you something: of course Herr Doctor Dössekker couldn't pay much attention to the child; he was a physician through and through, and a good one. But I'm certain he made very precise inquiries about Bruno."

Berti remembers Bruno as a quiet, modest, and satisfied boy who was always well dressed. He does not pretend to hide his outrage at Wilkomirski's recent conduct, and at his book.

"What he writes at the end about his hard-hearted foster parents
is a mean thing to do to the Dössekkers. I'd tell him that to his
face. Frau Dössekker, who was so fond of him and spoiled him
so! Believe me, even after his divorce they stood by him." Berti
provides examples of how the Dössekkers spoiled Bruno and
later supported him financially. If Berti's wife were still alive,
she'd be very upset and would call Bruno to account.

Berti's view is that Bruno was already at the Dössekkers' at
Christmas 1945. On this point, Wilkomirski's story and Berti's
statement are obviously contradictory. If Berti is correct,
Wilkomirski never could have lived at the children's home on
Augustiańska Street, which first opened in the summer of 1946.

WILLIAM TELL AND OTHER LEGENDS

On 22 April 1947, Wilkomirski entered first grade at the
Fluntern School in Zurich.[50] The date is surprising, since in
interviews he occasionally says he started school in the spring of
1948. He is registered in the school records as Bruno Dössekker.

In May 1999 I look up Ruth Akert-Giger, who was Wilkomirski's teacher for his first year and a half of schooling.[51] My
hostess, now over eighty years old, begins to speak with lively
enthusiasm about the school. "Bruno Dössekker came to me
with his so-called mother. But he told me very soon that she was
not his real mother. . . . He seemed a little fidgety and edgy to
me—an excitable little boy who couldn't find anything to hold
fast to. He had no particular friends, no particular preference for
children who went to school with him. He was fairly isolated,
but not intentionally." Frau Dössekker would pick him up from
school now and then, "but he was not as tied to his mother as the
other children who were picked up by their mothers and wanted
me to see and greet them. I never saw a really affectionate relationship between the two. I thought, Ah well, she's just a rela-

tively old mother. She was over forty and of course made no jokes, never had fun with the boy, but simply took him by the hand and left."

His attitude toward Ruth Akert remained somewhat distant and shy. Other children "hugged me when I came into the classroom. That never happened with him." But he was not a problem child. "There was no shadow of sadness hanging over the boy." His speech was normal, though he stuttered. She remembers him as being an average student. We look at the school records together; they show that in his first year Bruno was among the best students.

I ask her about the school excursion Wilkomirski remembers taking to a folk fair, where he caused a scene by begging.

"I know nothing about that. I also know nothing about my ever having taken children to a fair with booths and stalls. Visiting a fair is a struggle for a teacher, what with little children fluttering off in every direction." Akert is certain that she never took any first-graders on such an excursion. I read her the passage in question from *Fragments,* describing an episode that is supposed to have taken place during the first days of school in the spring. We are agreed that of all Zurich's festivals only the traditional *Knabenschiessen* (Prize Shooting for Boys) would fit; but that event always takes place in the fall. For Akert, Wilkomirski's episode reads as "pure fantasy."

I ask whether he begged somewhere else, then. Akert has no recollection of it and instead mentions his appearance: "He looked very proper, was always dressed tip-top, clean, no mended clothes, always spiffy, neat as a pin."

We turn to the William Tell story. Akert says she never told her pupils legends about heroes, only fairy tales. They were too small for sagas, and the Swiss myth about Tell wasn't in the first-grade curriculum. Nor had she ever used a picture of William Tell in her classroom. I read to her from *Fragments,* about how as a confused little boy Wilkomirski turns the hero of Swiss liberty into an SS man, his uncomprehending teacher into a raging block warden, and the class into a horde of savages. Wilkomirski has told me which teacher he was describing here; it was Frau Akert,[52] and I fear I may have angered her by reading her this text.

"He writes well," is her spontaneous reaction. "And a lot of it probably has to do with his experience with his schoolmates. But I can't recall his ever coming to me and saying, 'The other children deserted me, laughed at me, mocked me.' " Akert believes she would have noticed conflicts of that sort and done something about them.

I ask her if she would have reacted like the teacher in Wilkomirski's account. "No. I would have tried to find out what that was all about with the SS man. I would have asked the boy whether he'd ever heard of an SS man, ever met one." Would it have been possible for one of her classrooms to react as described in the book? "No, we had a cozy classroom"—she laughs—"with no screeching children. That's all part of the context he describes, of course."

Before leaving, I lend her Wilkomirski's book. Three weeks later I ask her for any additional impressions. She seems amazed at the whole media circus: "The whole thing seems terribly irrelevant to me. I still wonder what all these investigations are good for."

WILKOMIRSKA

Wilkomirski says he first became acquainted with Sylwester Marx on a train trip to Warsaw. From then on there were occasions when Sylwester and Christine Marx put him up or accompanied him on his travels in Poland. At one time they lived in Katowice, but now they reside in Bochum, Germany. I telephone them there.[53] Sylwester, however, says that he met Wilkomirski in a Zurich restaurant and there learned of his desire to travel to Poland to search for traces of things from his past. Sylwester extended him an invitation, since in those days under the Communist regime it was not easy for foreigners to gain entry. Wilkomirski came that same year to Katowice, visited towns in the area and presumably—Sylwester cannot be certain of his memory here—Auschwitz as well.

Wilkomirski came a second time in March 1972, Sylwester says. (Wilkomirski dates the trip to 1973.) They visited the Auschwitz Museum but could not enter the block of Jewish martyrdom—entry was forbidden. They also took an excursion to Kraków. "He was very quiet and didn't say that he was looking for anything in particular. He only said he knew the area around Miodowa Street from earlier, but otherwise offered no information, and just wanted to see the city." People told him where the orphanage had once stood but explained that the site had changed completely since then. He did not speak with any former residents of the orphanage who were still living in Kraków.

On his way back to Switzerland with Sylwester, Wilkomirski did in fact end up being checked by the militia. Since he had not registered daily with the authorities as required, the officers told him that "he had better not show his face in Poland for the next twenty years." Sylwester confirms to me that Wilkomirski's next trip to Poland, in the company of the Marxes, did not in fact take place until 1993; his description of their two trips together that year corresponds to Wilkomirski's own account.

Sylwester's wife, Christine, recalls the visit that Bruno Dössekker, as he called himself at the time, paid them in Katowice in 1972. By chance the famous violinist Wanda Wilkomirska was in town at the same time for a concert at the philharmonic. Professor Stanislaw Mamin, the director of the music school and an acquaintance of the Marx family, got tickets for them all. There were large posters of the artist displayed at the philharmonic, the music school, and the theater. Professor Mamin looked at the picture of Wilkomirska, then at Dössekker, and cried, "For heaven's sake, he must be a relative or a brother!"

That's how similar the two looked. Dössekker was surprised and quite delighted, Christine says. He was determined to speak with Wilkomirska and ask her about her memories. But she refused any conversation, as if afraid that contacts with the West might have negative effects. Dössekker was despondent and desperate. Professor Mamin tried to console him: perhaps things would change someday and they would still have that conversation. At any rate, Dössekker should now research his entire story and write down where he came from and who he was. Wanda Wilkomirska gave a second concert, this time at the conservatory, which they also attended, accompanied on this occasion by Lengowski, the director of another music school. Again Bruno got nowhere in his attempt to speak with the violinist.

"At the time, when you and Herr Dössekker met Herr Mamin, did you know his name was Wilkomirski?" I ask.

"No," Christine replied, "I didn't know that yet, only after the professor called our attention to it. Looking at Bruno, he said he had to be from the Wilkomirski family."

"So one could say that Herr Wilkomirski came to his name by way of this professor?"

"Yes, precisely," Christine confirmed.

Sylwester adds that Wilkomirski has always known he came from a family of Polish musicians. The woman who brought him to Switzerland as a child had impressed upon him that he should never forget that.

Once he was back in Zurich, Dössekker hung a poster of Wilkomirska in his second residence (he had another apartment that he shared with his first wife and children) and later would occasionally show a photograph of her. He told those around him that he had met his sister or half sister: her name was Wanda Wilkomirska and she was a violinist. Another sister was living with Gypsies, he said, somewhere on Lake Baikal, but the rest of the family had been killed—his mother and his five brothers in concentration camps, his father by Polish partisans.[54]

When asked about Wanda Wilkomirska, Wilkomirski says,

"I simply refuse to give the same information over and over again about things that have nothing to do with the story and only serve to blow some secondary story out of proportion. The only thing I can tell you is, we have very warm, very close, very good contact with each other today."[55]

AN OUTRAGED PHONE CALL — KAROLA

The telephone rings one August morning. I have looked for her around the world and finally had a message passed on to her by a roundabout route that she should contact me, but by now I hardly expect any answer. And now she phones me from Kraków: Karola.[56]

Wilkomirski is not telling the truth, she says right off and with undisguised outrage. She met him decades ago; he interrogated her, and then wrote false things about her. She had only been telling him about her life, opening her heart to him as a friend, and he had abused her trust, done violence to her biography. She emphasizes that I must not write about her or use her name, no matter what: "I don't want to cross out my life!"

She is understandably mistrustful in dealing with me: What are the views and intentions of this Swiss historian? Is he perhaps a Wilkomirski partisan? Is he independent of the agency that commissioned him? I inform her that I am interested solely in the truth and want to be fair to everyone involved. I promise not to betray her name in my report and to reveal as little as possible about her story.

At last she tells how she first met Wilkomirski, in about 1971. It was on a train from Zurich to Paris, and she was on her way home to visit her mother. At the time he did not yet have his curly hairdo, but straight hair. He began asking her about her past: "He took over my whole life, all my memories, and the lives of all those who were deported." She says that she grew up in Lemberg and that she and her mother were arrested there by the Germans during the war. "We were never separated. We were deported together and came back from deportation together. But Wilkomirski claims we lost each other." At war's end, she had traveled with her mother directly to Kraków, where they lived together in a collective apartment. They went to the house on Długa Street to eat, then later to the one on Augustiańska. Therefore, there is no basis whatever for Wilkomirski's writing that the girl had walked the streets of Kraków asking about her father and mother.[57]

We come around to talking about various details in Wilkomirski's story. I first ask about the years in Kraków. "I didn't know him in Kraków, he wasn't there back then, only later, to search for lies. I was in the orphanage, not he." And what of his claim that he met her again on Augustiańska Street? "He says that, but it's not true. It's one big lie. He says that I was with him at Auschwitz. I was never there, I was in a concentration camp in Germany." *Fragments* also tells of how an SS man saved her and her mother. "That's true," she confirms.

"He had this story from you, then?" I ask.

"He simply used it. He didn't have the right to do that, he should have asked me, it was told in confidence."

At least on that point Wilkomirski appears to have stuck to the truth, I thought. But something is annoying me. Is it the fact that the narrator, who the rest of the time remains totally trapped in his child's perspective, here provides the experiential world of other people, in detail and truthfully? Is it the fully developed composition of the narrative that matches poorly with real experience? Or is it the all-too-miraculous escape itself? I prick up my ears at another remark my witness makes:

"We were let go because my mother looked like the wife of a Nazi and I looked like his daughter. That story is correct. And when we left the place I said to my mother, 'We don't dare, they'll come and take us back right away.' "

"But he tells a different story in the book," I object.

"What story?" she asks.

It turns out that, fearing the book to be full of lies, she has never really read it to this day. She also refused to let me read to her from it. So I briefly summarize Wilkomirski's presentation, in which she and her mother were thrown on a pile of corpses by an SS man and then crept back among the living later that night. "No, that isn't true," she protests. "The man told us, 'Get out, go!' "

"You were blond?" I ask.

"That was the reason we were spared: my mother was a red-head and I'm blond. They didn't throw us on the corpses. Wilkomirski invented that, it's not true." And it hadn't happened in the camp, as Wilkomirski wrote, but before that, in the Lemberg ghetto. The SS man had let them go during a sweep of the ghetto to round up deportees. They had gone to the camp only later, and finally were liberated by the Americans.

She cannot agree with Wilkomirski's description of how, despite being liberated from the camp, he had the feeling in Kraków of being on the wrong side or of being deceived by the adults. That's nonsense, she says: "No one felt like that at all, we were being helped."

There is a simple explanation for the strange story about the name Marta, which all the former orphanage residents except Wilkomirski recognized. My informant is indeed named Karola, but during the war, by way of self-defense, she took the Christian name, a pseudonym that she kept in the Augustiańska home. She had never told Wilkomirski anything about that, however.

Karola says Wilkomirski never met her in Poland. Nevertheless, she and many of her former way stations in life—Lemberg, a concentration camp, Kraków, Długa Street, Augustiańska Street—appear in his autobiographical text. She is convinced that he was inspired by what she told him and that it was through her that he got the idea of his several trips to Kraków. "I was his memory; he appropriated it."

Wilkomirski had also told her that he came from a family of Polish musicians. At one point he had showed her a piano in his apartment and explained that it had belonged to his parents in Poland. In the early 1970s, he came back from a trip to Katowice and announced that he had met his sister, that her name was Wanda Wilkomirska, and that she was a well-known violinist. She was so beautiful, he said, that he had fallen in love with her and had dared not stay there—she was his sister, after all.

Finally, Karola tells me how at the end of January 1995, on the fiftieth anniversary of the liberation of Auschwitz, she was invited to Wilkomirski's home. It was a party for his book, which was soon to be published. "Everyone wanted something from me," she said, "as if I had been the pivotal point of the story. People sensed that I was in fact just that. He wouldn't have known anything about Kraków without me." Several psychotherapists were present and tried, in an obtrusive way, to engage her in conversation. The wife of Georges Wieland, who had done the initial editing of the manuscript, was determined to maintain contact with her and telephoned several times afterward. Wilkomirski's psychotherapist told her how good she looked in her black dress. Referring to her past, Bernstein called her a poor child. The mother of Wilkomirski's girlfriend asked her how she and Binjamin had met. In order not to lie, she evaded answering by leaving the room. My witness remembers the party as a poorly staged event, where no one believed any of it and even the musical performances were bad. "It was awful. You could feel the phoniness." By that time she had already skimmed through the manuscript. "I felt sorry for him but didn't know everything yet. Only later did I discover that it wasn't to be taken seriously."

We speak at length on the phone several times over the next few months. She tells me that since the war she hasn't trusted people and has developed a reliable instinct for inconsistencies. So I am all the more impressed by her openness with me. After many conversations, she at last gives me permission to use her real name in my report. The Wilkomirski affair has been troubling her the whole time, Karola explains. She is especially angered by his falsifying her story. "And now the journalists are accepting the falsifications, or adding others to them—for instance, Elena Lappin has told the whole world that I was never in a concentration camp. Do you think that's right, for my story to be misused in front of everyone? After those horrible years, I've been able to put together a modest life. Suddenly this nitwit shows up and upends everything. I asked him to send me his book; he said I could buy it at a bookshop. And here he is using my life for it."[58]

Spurred on by our conversations—and despite her own anger and outrage—she has called Wilkomirski several times during the period of my research. She doesn't want to retract the things she has said that incriminate her old friend, but at the same time she can sense his distress and that he is increasingly in danger of losing his last sense of reality. Full of sympathy, she can only watch helplessly as he becomes less and less like the man she remembers and more and more a victim of a past that he has created for himself.

She is especially angry at Bernstein; she claims he got Wilkomirski in his power and instigated him to present himself under a false identity. "He led him on to ask me all those questions when I was living in Zurich." When I inquire further about this, she replies that it's only a guess on her part; she has no proof of it.

One day the mood of her call is pensive and melancholy. "I had a relative I lost at Auschwitz. I think he was born in 1939. For years I thought he was Wilkomirski. So now you understand why I let myself get caught up in this story." The idea had not presented itself to her at the start; "only over time, he looked a little like him. You see, when you've lost someone, you create

your own illusions. That contributed to my affection for Wilkomirski when I first got to know him."

"Did you tell him this story about your relative?"

"Of course, but I don't know if he really accepted it, since he
knew it certainly didn't concern him."

I ask if I may mention this in my report.

"I'll think about that. I think you can write that I was uncon-
sciously looking for something at the time. You yourself are
involved with the Holocaust and know all that—how there are
so many people who have sought other people for decades now.
I thought he was my lost relative, that's how it was." At the
time, she gave Wilkomirski a photograph of the boy. A few days
later she sends me a copy: a pretty three-year-old boy, blond,
with a big wave in his hair as was fashionable then, but there's a
look of horror in his eyes, as if he can see his future.

My informant also called Daniel Ganzfried in the summer of
1999. In early November of the same year, he wrote about that
telephone conversation in an article for *Die Weltwoche:* "She vehemently denied ever having met Dössekker in the Kraków
orphanage and emphasized that before the manuscript was ever
printed, she informed the literary agent Eva Koralnik to that
effect."[59] This is a serious accusation, and if it is true, the agency
must be charged at least with gross negligence. I am annoyed,
since Karola had never told me of any such warning. Moreover,
my own research of the files and my conversations with Koralnik have convinced me that both the publishing house and the
agency published the book in good faith. Although a clarification of the responsibility for publishing the book is not part of
my commission, I ask Koralnik to make a statement. She is outraged by Ganzfried's claim and denies ever having heard anything of the sort.[60]

When I ask Karola about this quotation in *Die Weltwoche,* she
explains that she has met Koralnik only once—at Wilkomirski's
party in January 1995.[61] That was only two weeks before Helb-

ling's letter to Suhrkamp, as I reconstruct it; Koralnik had not yet been warned. But in hindsight that party must have had special meaning for all those present. I ask Karola whether she spoke with the literary agent that evening. "Yes, after the reading. She asked me what I did. Wilkomirski had told her I wrote poetry. Frau Koralnik asked how I had survived the war."

"Did she ask about your shared past with Wilkomirski in Kraków and in the camps?" I want to know.

"No."

And when I ask if she had warned Koralnik and if Ganzfried's quote is accurate, she declares, "No, I cannot have said that." After skimming through Wilkomirski's story, she had sensed that it was "a parody or fiction," and "tossed [the manuscript] in the wastebasket right away. And at the party I wasn't feeling well and didn't stay long." In her brief conversation with Koralnik, she had mentioned nothing of this.[62]

Despite various long conversations with my witness, I had never understood exactly why she hadn't felt well and what had happened to her that night. I ask her to describe the course of the evening's events for me once more. She says that first Wilkomirski gave a speech, in which, among other things, he thanked her for coming all that way just for the party. Then Georges Wieland read from the text. What was the passage he read about? I ask.

"Why, about me!" she exclaims in outrage.

"About your shared days in Kraków?" I ask, taken aback.

"No, I would have shouted out loud in that case. He read about the meeting between me and Wilkomirski in the seventies, in Zurich. And I think the story about how my mother and I were liberated."

"But that story is told wrong, you should have protested," I object.

"It was in German; I didn't understand it very well."

So he had introduced Karola with her concentration-camp history to his audience, and then disclosed their common past by his choice of texts, thus increasing the credibility of his story as a memory from the camps. "I felt I'd been put on show and misused," Karola recalls. "Everyone wanted to latch on to my story."

"The story of your meeting in the postwar period has a certain truth," I observe. "After all, you did in fact meet. He has them read something you cannot protest against and presents you as his star witness, as material proof of his story."

"Yes, that was the reason he invited me. I didn't want to come to the party, but he begged and begged until I gave in."

I send Karola those passages from my report in which she is mentioned. She agrees with my presentation. In addition, she corrects Bernstein's claim that her husband has forbidden her to speak about her story or pressured her in that regard. "This is absolutely not true. My past is no secret. Everyone knows about it, including my husband, of course."[63]

I had, incidentally, come across the conjecture that Bernstein had massively influenced Wilkomirski before, not just in my conversations with Karola. When asked to respond, Bernstein "denies this assertion in all its forms." He never "directly or indirectly, instructed, led, encouraged, and most certainly never manipulated any memories, let alone the design or concoction of an entire biography. . . . All claims that I invented [Wilkomirski's] *gestalt* or that I may have been the driving force behind his actions are absurd and untrue." Since September 1998 (that is, after the publication of Ganzfried's article), Bernstein says he has pondered whether he could have been led by "subconscious motives." Thus far he is unaware of any. Of essential importance as well is the fact that he had "received no material gain" through Wilkomirski. "On the contrary. Not only have I spent my own money and an enormous amount of time on his behalf, but my entire family has been very involved emotionally. Moreover, at present almost all my professional duties in Switzerland have been canceled. I mention this not in any way as a complaint or accusation. . . . I can reproach myself with having made mistakes, but I had absolutely no manipulative motives."[64]

A TERRIBLE VICTIM — LAURA GRABOWSKI'S PAST

During our conversation, Bernstein told me about a revealing episode that he himself had witnessed even before Wilkomirski's memories came under public fire. He and Wilkomirski and their wives had been invited out. Also present was Aharon Appelfeld, a well-known Israeli writer of Romanian origin who as an eight-year-old had lost his mother to the Germans, had been deported, had managed to escape from the concentration camp. He had then spent three years hiding in forests before being found, at age eleven, by Soviet soldiers, who took him along with them as a kitchen boy. Appelfeld recounted to the group how in the early years of his career he had published a totally fictional story in a literary magazine. It was about a trip to a rabbi's court and everything that happened there—the Hassidim who came and went, their customs and rites, and so on. Upon its publication, several people called to praise him for his precise descriptions—they had been there, too.

Everyone laughed at the anecdote. On the way home, Bernstein's wife asked, "Why do you suppose Appelfeld told that story?" Only then did Bernstein realize that the writer was perhaps using this story as a way of signaling to Wilkomirski that he doubted his tale.[65]

I would have liked to repeat this episode to Laura Grabowski, the woman who had appeared with Wilkomirski at an event in Los Angeles, because she shared his memories of Birkenau. On that occasion, Wilkomirski had told about how he first met Grabowski at the camp and then later in a Kraków orphanage. Now that Karola has refuted his memories, Grabowski remains the only witness who might speak in his favor. But any contact with her has become impossible. Bernstein tells me that after the CBS 60 Minutes broadcast, she went underground because she was "being followed by a journalist who claimed that she was lying and that her story was untrue." Balint explains the

woman is ill and that remembering is so horrible for her that she
would never say anything; Wilkomirski describes her condition
as so bad that she is no longer available for interviews. Then,
too, there are Wilkomirski's general qualms about contacting
child survivors. More than once he has lambasted the "lack of
respect and the vile treatment given by the media to the problems of the youngest child survivors." The people in question
were so shocked and frightened that they even stopped speaking
to their psychological caretakers. "If persons who have some sort
of relationship to my biography are prepared to say something,"
he once wrote to Elena Lappin, "they will contact you on their
own. But I will never demand or even ask them to do so. That
would burden me with a responsibility I am unable to bear."[66]

Leon Stabinsky, whom I met through Ganzfried and the
BBC, was able to speak personally with Laura Grabowski before
her disappearance.[67] He was the cochair of the Survivors Group
of Los Angeles that organized the event with Grabowski and
Wilkomirski in 1998. Like other members of that group, he
originally had reservations about this woman who suddenly
came out of nowhere in the summer of 1997 and outed herself as
a survivor, but always wept if anyone spoke to her about her
past, and never said anything substantial. Wilkomirski's story
had also aroused Stabinsky's skepticism. To him and to other
survivors it seemed impossible that such a young child could
have survived for years in concentration camps. (Doubts already
circulating in Los Angeles about his story were perhaps the reason why Wilkomirski explained in his speech there that it was
only toward the end of 1944—that is, only weeks before its liberation—that he arrived at Birkenau. To my knowledge, he had
never previously specified his arrival date at Birkenau.)

Stabinsky broke a taboo among the survivors and challenged
Grabowski's Shoah story. This was a primary reason for a split in
the group in the autumn of 1998. Stabinsky found the first tan-
gible lead suggesting that something was wrong with her
concentration-camp biography in a letter that was passed on to

him, written by Grabowski and dated 20 July 1997. She had signed her name as Lauren Grabowski-Stratford, but was unable to offer any satisfactory explanation for the use of this double name. The second last name vanished again later, and Lauren became Laura. Stabinsky's misgivings grew. A search of the Internet for the vanished name yielded an incredible result: "Satan's Sideshow: The Real Story of Lauren Stratford"[68] was the title of an exposé that Stabinsky downloaded from the Web site of the small Evangelical magazine *Cornerstone.*

"Step right up! It's Satan's Underground! A hundred thousand copies in print! Featured on radio and TV, from *Geraldo* to the 700 *Club!* Stories of satanic rituals, snuff films, and human sacrifice! Author Lauren Stratford survived to tell us all about it! Now judge for yourself.—This article is the extraordinary chronicle of how one woman's gruesome fantasy was twisted into seeming fact. . . . The hard evidence we have uncovered and which we present here speaks for itself. The story of *Satan's Underground* is not true."

Together with Jon Trott, the journalists Bob and Gretchen Passantino had very carefully researched and documented how a confused woman named Laurel Rose Willson had become the bestselling author Lauren Stratford. Since her youth the woman had been fabricating terrible stories in widely diverging variations, but always with herself in the role of victim. In the mid-1980s, when cases of allegedly widespread satanic ritual abuse (SRA) of children became a subject of public concern in the United States, she took elements from her horror stories to create a biography that was unsurpassed in its ghastly cruelties but that had no connection to reality. Within three years it had sold 140,000 copies, and the author was given a prominent place in the media, where she appeared as a victim of satanism who had recovered her memory through therapy to become an expert on such cults.[69]

In her "autobiography,"[70] Stratford describes how she was born an illegitimate child and adopted by well-to-do parents;

that was almost the only element of truth in her story. She goes on to tell how her mother handed her over as a six-year-old to be raped by men for weeks and months on end, and how two years later she was used for pornography, including sodomy. Although the child sought help from various adults, she was always greeted by disbelief. Lauren was introduced by her mother to a group of pornographers, in whose clutches she remained through her youth and into adulthood. She was the love slave of Victor, the boss of a cartel that made its money off porno films, prostitution, drugs, and the sexual abuse of children. He forced her to take part in satanic rituals, during which she was regularly raped by him and others. Eventually he demanded that she take part in the ritual sacrifice of babies. She refused, was held prisoner for weeks in a crate full of snakes, then in a metal barrel. Each week a dead and skinned baby would be thrown into her cage, until at last her will was broken and she assisted in a sacrifice. Finally she had to give birth to three children whose fate was already determined. The first two were murdered in snuff films shortly after birth; the third child, Joey, was slain by the satanists in a bloody ritual before her eyes. "As the flames began to consume the sacrifice, I yelled, 'Satan, you didn't get Joey! Joey went to be with Jesus. He fooled you all. You may have gotten his heart, but you didn't get his soul!' "[71]

Was it possible that the author of this totally fabricated "autobiography," who had meanwhile found her way to Jesus, was Laura Grabowski, the Jewish woman with whom Wilkomirski had shared the hell of Auschwitz? The best proof was a matching Social Security number. Stabinsky sat on the advisory board of the Swiss Fund for Needy Victims of the Holocaust/Shoah. He discovered that Grabowski—who in the meantime had used her autobiography as a Jewish victim of the camps to obtain money from various sources—had also asked the Swiss fund for financial support and had received around five hundred dollars.[72] To get the money she had had to provide her Social Security number: it was identical to that of Laurel Willson, alias

Lauren Stratford. The chain of proof was forged: the victim of satanism had indeed mutated into a victim of Nazism. The woman had exchanged her cross for the Star of David. She was no longer tormented by Victor the satanist but by Mengele the Nazi doctor; the fruit of her body was no longer being ripped from her, she was being made infertile; her horrified eyes beheld not the flames of sacrifice but the acrid smoke of the crematorium. Her current physical ailments were the result not of abuse and rape but of ghastly medical experiments.

The woman who would later appropriate both these autobiographies was in reality born in a hospital in Tacoma, Washington, on 18 August 1941. Forty-four days later, the baby girl was taken in by Mr. and Mrs. Willson, who adopted her in February 1942. While Laurel's adoptive parents were devout Presbyterians, her maternal grandparents were Polish Catholics, named Grabowski.[73] As she grew, the girl proved to be very talented musically and was given lessons in voice, piano, clarinet, and flute. As an adolescent she told stories about sexual harassment that were not true and made her first suicide attempt. As an adult she also told a great many fabricated stories in which she was the victim and made several more attempts to harm herself. In 1989, a year after her satanic autobiography came out, she published *I Know You're Hurting,* a book of psychological advice dedicated to Jesus, an effusive tract full of platitudes for suffering souls. This was followed in 1993 by *Stripped Naked,* yet another "autobiographical" text, in which she described herself as having multiple personalities, but said that with the help of a therapist she was now meeting her various egos.[74]

In this last opus, her rising interest in the role of a Shoah victim already glimmers through at several points. Referring to the historian Raul Hilberg, who has documented how Jews were stigmatized in the Middle Ages, excluded from society in later centuries, and then liquidated under the Nazis, she compares the victims of satanism to those of the Shoah: "We, who are the victims and survivors, had to remain silent for too long. We finally braved the outside world and broke our silence in cautious whispers. Now, some of you are listening to us, and some of you are believing us. But there are many who do not listen, and there are many who do not believe. There are a few of you who do not even believe that we exist! This is a tragedy."[75]

The similarities in content between *Satan's Underground* and *Fragments*—between life stories as told by Stratford and Wilkomirski—are striking. Both "autobiographies" tell the story of a child adopted by an affluent middle-class family. Both children are innocent victims of the most horrible crimes but can find no one who will listen, and learn only much later to stand by their past and their suffering. *Fragments* was written from a therapeutically inspired perspective and developed within the framework of therapy. The situation is much the same with *Satan's Underground*. Stratford quotes her therapist's explanation "that writing down my feelings would act as a catharsis, cleansing the wounds of my emotions. In time, she said, I would come to regard the journal as my friend. I questioned that, but after many tear-filled writing sessions I began to see that my writing did have a healing effect."[76] One could list a great many other parallels between the contents of these texts.

Much more interesting, however, are their structural similarities, which I likewise only can sketch briefly here. Both texts make uninhibited use of a rhetoric of violence. These "pages are full of pain, suffering, abuse, and yes even the horrors of hell itself," Stratford writes. "We should be horrified. We should be asking ourselves why and how such evil can thrive in our midst." Both texts are extremely vague in terms of facts. "For my own protection, but . . . also . . . to remind you that what I've endured is not restricted to one city or region"—this is Stratford's explanation why she can provide no definite place names. As with Wilkomirski, the rhetoric of fact is supposed to convince the reader of the truth of the story. "This is not fiction," Stratford claims. But her memory has so many gaps that she can "only recall that dreadful scene" of rape "in fragmented images, like a collage of black and white pictures in a war documentary."[77]

Both texts proceed from a simple division of the world into victims and villains, and the reader has no choice but to identify with the victim. The alternative is to be one of the villains, one of those who have never listened to the victims. By identifying himself or herself with the victim, the reader also wins, for as a victim he or she can also find consolation. "If it weren't for you—the thousands of you who are out there alone, hurting, and desperately looking for a way out—I wouldn't be writing this book," Stratford tells her readers. Victims should know, she says at another point, that "they are not alone." Wilkomirski's book ends with the similar sentence "They should know that they are not alone."[78]

Having mutated to a victim of Dr. Mengele, Stratford did not remain alone in her suffering, either. In 1998, out of deep sympathy and moral duty, a German woman gave her over a thousand dollars to cure her blood disease and fly to join Wilkomirski.[79]

THE PAINTED BIRD—THE TRUTH OF A NOVEL

Wilkomirski says that nothing shocked him as much as the book *The Painted Bird,* by Jerzy Kosinksi,[80] which he read in the 1960s. The first-person narrator tells of his horrible experiences as a boy in Poland during the period of the Nazi occupation. He is separated from his parents at age six and placed with a foster mother in a remote village. But the old woman's death two months after his arrival leaves the child entirely on his own and marks the beginning of years of wandering from village to village. Sometimes he finds a refuge, but usually he is met with violence, hate, and humiliation, for his hair, skin, and eyes are dark, and the peasants take him for a Gypsy or a Jew, both of whom they despise and persecute. He experiences this world as a nightmare, where in episode after episode unutterable violence, repulsive sexuality, and superstition reign. A miller puts out the eyes of his wife's would-be lover. Girls are brutally raped. A father abuses his daughter, forcing her into sodomy. A carpenter is eaten alive by rats. Peasants toss the protagonist into a cesspool, and he is so terrified by the experience that he loses his voice for years. Passing trains, from which babies are thrown, proclaim the horrors of deportation. But though constantly in danger of his life, the narrator survives the war and arrives in an orphanage where his parents find him again. Later he also recovers his voice.

The original American edition of Kosinski's book appeared in October 1965 and was greeted with enthusiastic reviews. Peter Prescott compared it to the diary of Anne Frank and called it "a testament not only to the atrocities of war, but to the failing of human nature." Elie Wiesel, who had been told by the author that the book was autobiographical, paid tribute to it as an authentic testimony of the Holocaust. "It is as a chronicle that *The Painted Bird . . .* achieves its unusual power," Wiesel wrote. "Written with deep sincerity and sensitivity, this poignant first-person account transcends confession and attains in parts the haunting quality and tone of a quasi-surrealistic tale. One cannot read it without fear, shame and sadness." Wiesel stressed that the boy's suffering was caused by his obviously dark appearance: "it could have happened to anybody, anywhere. If we ever needed proof that Auschwitz was more a concept than a name, it is given to us here with shattering eloquence in *The Painted Bird,* a moving but frightening tale in which man is indicted and proved guilty, with no extenuating circumstances." Wiesel's judgment was typical of reviews that saw the book as an authentic witness and historical document. It was translated into all major languages. In Germany it became a bestseller, and in France it received the prize for the best foreign book. It appeared on university syllabi, and Lawrence Langer did a detailed analysis of it in his study *The Holocaust and the Literary Imagination.*

Langer would later doubt Wilkomirski's *Fragments* precisely
because it reminded him of *The Painted Bird,* but at the time he
read Kosinski's book as an impressive allegorical presentation of
the *univers concentrationnaire.* The book, he said, shows men
reduced to beasts—"the descent of man from the pedestal of civilization into the mire of brutish endurance," forcing readers to
revise their understanding of human nature.[81]

The deep impression Kosinski's book made on Wilkomirski
was, presumably, not without its consequences. In any case,
there are many obvious parallels to *Fragments*: the protagonist
in both books is a young boy left totally on his own and subjected to the horrendous violence of Poland during the Nazi
terror—a frail child, and yet a superhero who miraculously survives. The perpetrators of the violence are also similar. In *Fragments* the Nazis play a central role, and Kosinski's primitive
peasants reappear in the person of the frightening farmer's wife
who hides little Binjamin. In *The Painted Bird,* the farmers are
the chief villains; Germans sometimes appear as well, but for the
most part they remain as a threat in the background. The world
in which the children find themselves is dominated by brutal,
primitive cruelty. Here, human nature knows neither rational-
ity, love, nor care—the crass antithesis of any civilization. Both
children are subjected to such a violent world devoid of norms
that they must constantly struggle for their identity and finally
lose their ability to speak. In Kosinski's book the metaphor for
this fractured identity is the painted bird, which is sacrificed
because of the disguise imposed upon it. Wilkomirski's memories are of playing with a glider, an act of the imagination that
saves him in the midst of the horror and appears to be the bird's
positive antitype. Both texts tell of a stay in an orphanage after
the war, but whereas Kosinski's protagonist is fetched by his
parents, for Wilkomirski it is a Frau Grosz who promises to take
him to Switzerland as her purported son. Additional parallels
may be seen in the deadly danger of a plague of rats and, finally,
immoderate episodes dealing with excrement. Kosinski's hero

almost drowns in a latrine, while Binjamin's feet sink into human feces. In formal terms as well, Kosinski's work seems to be the inspirational model for *Fragments*. Both texts break up into disconnected episodes told from a child's perspective. This increases the reader's identification with the innocent victim, who is helplessly handed over to a world of villains. The style is simple, but the descriptions of acts of violence are as drastic as anything one has ever read.

Wilkomirski says that Kosinski came to Switzerland after the war; evidently he sees parallels with his own life. But he goes further still and compares the current attacks on him to Kosinski's own experiences. Because Kosinski "mercilessly put into words what it meant to be a Gypsy or Jewish 'child between two fronts' in wartime Poland," he was persecuted. People jumped on Kosinski, slandered and cursed him "like a criminal, without sympathy or understanding for the confusion of a battered child." And thus they at last drove him to his death. That experience, Wilkomirski says, is one reason why he will not provide addresses of other child survivors who might testify on his behalf.[82]

What happened to Kosinski? In June 1982, the author—by then a famous writer, one even regarded as a possible Nobel Prize winner—came under massive attack. The New York newspaper *The Village Voice* accused him of having been a liar all his life. Among other things, he told contradictory versions of leaving Poland to emigrate to the United States. (He left his country of origin in 1957 and did not go to Switzerland after the war, as Wilkomirski believes.) Especially grave consequences resulted from the accusation that he made excessive and unacknowledged use of the services of translators and editors for his books, including *The Painted Bird*. The article set off an earthquake in the literary world and for the most part destroyed Kosinski's credibility. He took his own life in 1991.

The main criticism was directed at how he dealt with the facts of his own life story. As is shown in the biography by James

Park Sloan, Kosinski kept blurring the border between invention and fact throughout his career. Whatever he invented seemed to become part of his life, and his narrated life was unmasked as invention. This problem played a role in the publication of *The Painted Bird:* Kosinski was able to awaken the enthusiasm of the woman who would become its publisher by suggesting that it was autobiographical. He made a similar impression on his reviewers: "I thought it was fiction," Elie Wiesel says, "and when he told me it was autobiography I tore up my review and wrote one a thousand times better."[83]

In fact, the author's biographical reality had little in common with the descriptions in his book.[84] Kosinski was born in 1933 in the Polish city of Lodz, the son of a Jewish couple named Lewinkopf. To escape the Germans, the family left the city soon after the outbreak of war and went to Sandomierz, where they assumed the non-Jewish name Kosinski. Thanks to their wealth and the help of local citizens, they were able to live in relatively good circumstances and, under false identities, to survive the reign of terror in various villages. The son was never separated from his parents and never lost his voice. Most of the events Kosinski describes are invented. It is certainly true, however, that living for years under a false identity must have been a terrible ordeal for the little boy, who as an adult tried to express what he had felt. He constructed a novel out of his inner images. The plot was invented, but the pain was genuine and rooted in early childhood. Might this also be the case for his admirer Wilkomirski?

MAROKO AND WILKOMIRSKI — A COMFORTING TALE

It was because of the film *Wanda's List* that Yakov Maroko happened upon Binjamin Wilkomirski, whom he regarded as the lost son he had now found again. What conclusions can we draw about Wilkomirski's biography from this constellation of events? Before he died in 1998, Maroko wrote an autobiography of his own that focused solely on this meeting, to which he devotes an entire chapter. "Exceptional events of this sort are not within the realm of nature," he writes. "They have always belonged among the mysteries of life. One can come to grips with such a situation only by believing in miracles." Those words provide the general perspective. The ultra-Orthodox author—Maroko belonged to the community of the Gerer Hassidim—interpreted his meeting with his ostensible son as a miracle, as proof that God's deeds have meaning. The tone of his writing is visionary, almost ecstatic, the style baroque and extravagant, the argumentation cloudy, with little regard for facts.[85] But if the book is read along with other source materials, its subjective narrative of events is quite revealing all the same.

Maroko describes how in early 1995 he was suddenly reminded of Sara Lerner, the sister of his first wife, whom he had lost at Majdanek. He did not know where these memories had suddenly come from. "The voices in my heart never left me, I feared for my reason, and I felt I had to search for my sister-in-law and speak with her."[86] She also lived in Israel but had lost contact with Maroko's family, and it took him three days to find her telephone number. Despite decades having passed without any contact between them, she did not appear the least bit surprised by his call. He had surely called her because of the television show, she said by way of greeting. For religious reasons, Maroko did not watch television, and he knew nothing about it. Lerner began to talk "like a waterfall" about a Bruno Wilkomirski whom she had seen in a film, a man who had been looking for his roots for years. "Yakov!" she pleaded with him, "this man reminded me at first sight of my dead sister! Of your first wife!! The facial traits . . . the eyes, the hair color, his whole appearance. I am almost certain that this is your murdered son Binjamin whom you have mourned for so long."[87] Tears came to Maroko's eyes, his body began to tremble uncontrollably, and he feared he was having a heart attack. "God has taken mercy on a Jewish soul despairing over the loss of its own roots," he thought. "Surely the hour is come in which a lost child finds his father again." His sister-in-law told him that she had sought additional information and that the TV station had given her the address of a doctor of psychology named Elitsur Bernstein.[88]

Maroko telephoned Bernstein and asked for details about this man who might be his son and whom he had believed dead now for decades. He barraged the psychologist with questions, without coherence or logic; he did not know what was happening to him. "Circles spun before my eyes. My Michael Binjamin was alive!" He asked for the man's telephone number, but Bernstein insisted he first wanted to talk with Maroko at greater length.[89] So Yakov Maroko and his second wife, Guta, went to see Bernstein, with whom they had a long conversation. When the psychologist showed them the film footage of Wilkomirski, Maroko was overwhelmed with emotion. "That figure kept appearing before my eyes," he writes. "My heart kept saying over and over: He's the one! I held my tears back, but a hard lump stayed in my throat." Memories resurfaced of being arrested in the Warsaw ghetto, of marching in icy cold weather, of arriving at Majdanek with his wife and children. He began to relate all this to Bernstein, who wanted to know the smallest details. From the reactions of Bernstein and Bernstein's wife, he concluded, "The two stories match! I begged my host for a Swiss telephone book. But Dr. Bernstein refused. My emotions were quite clear to him, but he still hesitated to draw the ultimate conclusion. . . . There was nothing left for me to do but yield. I spent sleepless nights. Dr. Bernstein was traveling abroad, and until his return there was nothing more I could do."[90]

Today Bernstein explains that his hesitation at the time was due to "my concern for them both. I wanted above all to prevent severe disappointment, and my concern was to carefully prepare the way on both sides for this contact, and in particular to first set it in motion with Binjamin's approval." With their consent, then, he made a videotape of a portion of the conversation with

Yakov and Guta Maroko and took this ten-minute tape—along with two photographs of Maroko's first wife—to Wilkomirski during a visit to Switzerland in early February 1995, so that he could carefully observe his friend's reaction. First he gave him the photographs. After about two minutes he told him of Frau Lerner's belief that he must be her nephew. Wilkomirski's reaction was, "Maybe there's something to it, I don't know." Bernstein then described his conversation with Yakov and Guta. When he showed him the videotape, Wilkomirski was visibly touched but continued to express his doubts about any possible familial connection. "At which point I brought forward Frau Lerner's suggestion of having a DNA test performed. Binjamin asked for time to think about this, but agreed to it two days later. In the second or third week of February 1995, I flew back to Israel, bringing with me a sample of Binjamin's blood for the genetic laboratory of Assutta Hospital in Tel Aviv."[91]

Maroko was finally given the telephone number he so desired. He called Wilkomirski: "This is Maroko!" At first he couldn't utter another word, then he began to weep. "I never stopped loving you since I lost you at Majdanek. This love burns in me to this very day."

"I have never before experienced such love, not even from my adoptive parents, not once," Wilkomirski said.

Asked if it disturbed him that Maroko was a *haredi,* a keeper of tradition, Wilkomirski replied, "I am very fond of the *haredim.*" Maroko could hear the "honesty in his voice."[92] The very next day he received a letter:

Sunday, 12 February 1995

My dear
I don't even know how I ought to address you. I don't even really know what I should say—my emotions are so indescribable! You can surely imagine how confused and at the same time how happy I was yesterday after your phone call.

I have lived without parents for over fifty years and now—can it be that I have found you, my father? Has "HE" performed a miracle? And just think: today is February 12, the anniversary of my arrival in Switzerland, and that day was made my official birthday. Is that not a gift?

Whatever the scientific blood and tissue tests show is not so important to me—there are too many connections here, as Elitsur Bernstein has told me. You were also at Majdanek. I have lists of over a thousand Jewish children from Poland who either survived in camps or in hiding, and the name Benjamin does not occur even once. It seems to have been a very rare name in Poland at the time. It is thus very unlikely that there could have been two different Benjamins at Majdanek in 1943. And some things that you told Elitsur match my own memories as well! I will quickly find out if it's possible for me to visit you in Israel before Pesach. I can hardly wait to embrace you.

Until then, with all my love
Benjamin.[93]

By April 1995 everything was in place. Maroko and his family were waiting in the arrival hall at Ben Gurion Airport at Lod. In the same voluble, exaggerated way that he tells his entire story, he describes his feelings: "A drama was unfolding before my eyes: a great many people, hundreds, even thousands . . . from all levels of society! Among them many reporters from the local and international press. Many photographers . . . not a one was missing! Who had made this whole private story public? I do not know even today who the source of that indiscretion was. What I do know is this glorious sight. I saw a huge, curious audience filling every inch of the waiting room." Wilkomirski arrived. "My son, my son!!" Maroko cried. "My child, my child! How do you feel?" Maroko's heart, he writes, was overflowing with love. "The hearts of everyone there were beating wildly with excitement, they were touched. Even hard-nosed policemen hid their faces trying to conceal their unwanted tears. Even the officials, who demanded information about everything, softened, and excitement seized them when at the high point my Benjamin fell into my outstretched arms and embraced me warmly for a long time."[94]

Maroko remembers the "huge echo" unleashed by

> the unique meeting between me and my lost son. . . . All over the world thousands of people read the newspaper article about our story. I was swamped by countless letters and overwhelmed for days by telephone calls. There were congratulations from people I did not know but whose hearts had been warmed by this event. Others, however, saw me as a magician whose eyes could restore lost sons. . . . I was asked to release them from their terrible suffering, to help them with my miracles, and to find those members of their families who had been lost during those horrible years and about whom they knew nothing. Although over fifty years had passed, they had not given up hope.[95]

Wilkomirski, however, had found what he sought. After his arrival, Maroko's entire family gathered at the vacation village of Yad Habanim, where they celebrated Pesach and the return of their lost son. "And he—the famous speaker, who had given lecture series around the world—sat there with his mouth shut," Maroko notes with his usual dramatic overstatement. Finally Wilkomirski's tongue was loosened: " 'I am happy for this day and I thank my family for taking me to their hearts like this.' "[96]

Three mechanisms fundamental to Wilkomirski's own story are evident in this "miraculous" reunion of father and son: facts are unimportant in the face of the need to belong; a sense of belonging arises out of a common past; the story of a son who is found again fills painful gaps in both individual and collective narratives and symbolically restores what had been irretrievably lost.

As for the insignificance of the facts: Bernstein says that Sara Lerner, who herself was a nurse, first suggested the blood test and indeed insisted on it. Wilkomirski was not enthusiastic about the idea, but he, Bernstein, talked him into it. In his first letter to Maroko, written before they received the results, Wilkomirski downplays the importance of the test. Instead he lists the arguments that nourish the old and totally confused man in his belief in a miraculous providence.[97] The DNA test turned out negative. Wilkomirski is well aware of that fact, but as he puts it in *Wanda's List*, the decisive factor is "the very strong feeling to belong together"; for him, "the biological thing is in the background." Maroko, however, appears to ignore the test and does not even mention it in his book. His arguments are of another sort: "It is enough to look into his face and at his hair, which is like that of his dead mother. It is enough to compare his hands with mine to know that he's my son." Maroko says a blessing and then goes on: "We call in help from Dr. Liebermann, an expert at comparing identities. Pictures of my son and his mother . . . proved beyond doubt that any further clarification of traces was unnecessary. But to tell the truth, I didn't need any more proof." After all, he had his faith, which was confirmed for him by various rabbis. How permanent his faith was is less certain. Bernstein says that four weeks prior to his death, and in the presence of his wife and daughter, Maroko made it clear that he knew there was no blood relation. "I've found a lost son, Bruno a lost father, that's what counts."[98]

Belonging arises out of a common past.[99] In his initial letter, Wilkomirski asks Maroko if he has indeed found his father in him. He implies a positive answer by claiming the same memories and a common past at Majdanek. According to Maroko's narrative, the past played an important role in the rabbis' judgment as well. The two found each other because they both claimed a common story. Sara Lerner's motives are interesting in this context. According to Bernstein, she was a secular Jew who after her divorce had lost contact with the Orthodox Maroko family. The discovery of the "lost son" gave her the chance to restore the connection; thus she found an alleged piece of a common past and belonged to the family again.[100]

In order to arrive at this past, Wilkomirski had to give up everything to which he really belonged. In his letter to Maroko he claimed that the day of his arrival in Switzerland, 12 February, was his official birthday. The illogic of the claim is obvious, since Wilkomirski has always insisted that he was exchanged for the boy Bruno Grosjean, who actually existed, while at the same time conceding that his own papers are genuine. How can there be a plausible explanation, then, for the entry of a falsified date of birth on Bruno's papers based on Binjamin's date of arrival, 12 February 1941?[101] It would be more reasonable to understand Wilkomirski's stories as a permanent attempt to turn his birth into an arrival so that he could belong somewhere else and find a coherent history.

What gaps did this staged story of a rediscovered son help to fill? Bernstein believes that Sara Lerner had remained very much the captive of her own horrible past in the camps. The return of a nephew long believed dead became a piece of the present that could help soften an irrevocable pain. We can only surmise in Maroko's case that he could not have contemplated both the loss of his family in the camps and his own survival without a sense of guilt. By bringing a son back into his family, he would become a figure of hope to many who shared his suffering, one to whom a miracle was restored after half a century of desperate longing and searching. Wilkomirski, on the other hand, lacks any memory of his father, or more precisely, as he himself has stated, he failed even to recognize his lack of a father and always searched only for his mother. In Maroko, for the first time, he finds a father he can accept. In this light, the story of Maroko and Wilkomirski appears to be an impressive attempt to transform what cannot be told—and yet constantly needs to be told—into a story of consolation, and then to stage it as a living reality.

"STOPPED AT ONCE"—LEGAL STEPS

In an effort to clarify his own story, Wilkomirski has conducted extensive research in Poland, Latvia, and Israel. Remarkably enough, he has devoted far less attention to the documents in Switzerland, even though that was where the turning point in his life—the alleged exchange of children—took place. He has repeatedly claimed that "almost thirty years ago" he "tried to gain access" to his documents "from the officials in charge." This access, however, was denied him; his new identity eludes "any possibility of legal proof, given the failure of several such attempts to proceed according to current law."[102]

By way of example, Wilkomirski frequently mentions his attempts to find information about his birth. "Like all adopted children in Switzerland I have been given only a substitute, an 'abridged birth certificate,' listing merely the place of birth, the mother's name, and the community of record as 'hometown.' The difference is that Swiss adopted children receive this 'substitute document' at birth or shortly thereafter. My 'abridged birth certificate' was denied me for many years and was first presented to me, after repeated requests, in 1995. The date of record on my document ('Abridged Birth Certificate') is given as February 1995 (!)."[103]

Wilkomirski's argument proceeds from several false assumptions. First, the birth certificates of adopted and nonadopted children do not reveal the differences he suggests. The "abbreviated birth certificate" for adopted children—that was the rather misleading formulation according to previous law—is in no way any less complete. No one in Switzerland receives a document with more detailed information, other than excerpts from the family register. Wilkomirski's own register excerpts, however, were surrendered without any hesitation to his lawyer, Rolf Sandberg, who was proceeding from false assumptions himself when he told Suhrkamp in 1995 that they would have to take the authorities to court in order to get anything more. Second, there is no uniform regulation by which a child, adopted or not, is automatically given a birth certificate; in some localities it must first be requested. Third, every person has a right to see the summarized material in question; any infringement of that right is grounds for a lawsuit. There is no indication whatever that the registry office in Biel refused to comply, as Wilkomirski claims.[104]

In 1995, Wilkomirski contended that "as an adopted child under the old law" he had "no right to a full and complete review of my files." His lawyer, Sandberg, was somewhat more cautious and emphasized to Suhrkamp that only a major effort could "break the blockade." Indeed there are cases in which considerable barriers have to be overcome, typically when the child's interests might conflict with those of the birth father. Sandberg's statement, however, was not based on experience as regarded the Wilkomirski case, for until that point he had never requested access to the files from the civil authorities in question, nor could he possibly have known whether or not the specific interests of Bruno Grosjean's father stood in conflict with that access. Even in this hypothetical case, it was in no way certain that the authorities would not have decided in the child's favor.[105]

In April 1995, Siegfried Unseld, the head of Suhrkamp, insisted to Sandberg that Wilkomirski take legal action. On his own initiative—and not at Wilkomirski's behest—the lawyer requested that the Biel Guardianship Authorities open their files to him for a complete review. To do this, the office in Biel first had to ask permission from the birth father. Since the story lay decades in the past and the authorities did not have the father's address, clarification of the matter was delayed, prompting Sandberg to write two letters of admonishment.[106]

In the middle of October 1995, Sandberg was informed by the Biel Guardianship Authorities that Bruno Grosjean's father had been located, and thereafter he received a letter (altered to render it anonymous) in which the father asked for the "motives" that had led to this "search request. . . . I am prepared to offer a hand if this is a matter of a humane request. My wife and my daughter are of the same opinion." Two weeks later a letter arrived from the man's daughter: "Dear Solicitor X: I would like to become acquainted with my half-brother. Could you please clarify whether there is also such an interest on his part?"[107]

Sandberg forwarded the requests to Wilkomirski, who promptly faxed back: "I have carefully read through all the official materials provided thus far and see that in pursuing this route no explanation can be found of when and how it happened that my own person was declared identical with a 'Grosjean son.' If in the course of such researches, members of that family have been alerted and thus possibly entertain certain false hopes, that is simply going too far for me (especially emotionally). I therefore wish that no further steps be taken and that the search via this route be concluded for good and all." By way of clarification, he repeated for Sandberg the story about the exchanged children, about the young man he had seen again shortly before the latter's emigration to the United States, about his foster parents' systematic attempts to keep his guardian, Stauffer, at a distance. "I also recall," he added, "an overheard conversation between my foster parents after the guardian's final visit, when I came of age. They expressed great relief that it was 'finally all over,' that they could 'breath a sigh of relief,' and that this 'snoop' would never come to their home again."[108]

Uncertain whether his message had gotten through, Wilkomirski backed it up with a certified letter. He asked his lawyer, "How does it happen, in fact, that the family of the so-called 'biological father' has been informed of this research? I am not searching for just anybody so that I may come into contact with them. Was it absolutely necessary to upset these people? The question was merely that of checking on the basis of available documents whether there was some break in them, some incompleteness, that might explain how it happened that I became equated with a 'Grosjean son.' Aware that these documents offer nothing in this regard and that I may well be able to pursue other sources, I ask that for now no other legal steps be taken and that the matter be brought to a close at once. I want this portion of my research concluded before the end of 1995."[109]

On 30 July 1996, nine months after the father's and daughter's inquiries had been forwarded to Sandberg, the Biel authorities asked him why they had received no reply, given that he had previously been in such a hurry. Three months later the Biel authorities also made inquiries in a phone call to Wilkomirski, and were told that he was no longer interested, that his lawyer had misunderstood the intent of his request. Sandberg himself did not reply until a year later: although he had no "clear understanding" of the reasons, he said, his client had lost "interest in pursuing this trail." He must accede to his wishes.[110]

Now, of all times—when Bruno Grosjean's biological father had signaled his cooperation and nothing stood in the way of full disclosure of the files of the Biel authorities—Wilkomirski called a halt to his lawyer's attempts. From the start, then, Wilkomirski waived his right to see the very documents that were most likely to throw better light on the alleged exchange of children. Wilkomirski is hiding these facts when he claims: "In 1995, I had a lawyer examine all the documents to which the authorities gave me access at that time, in order to discover whether those documents were genuine or if the authorities had discernibly manipulated them. The result: the documents are the genuine documents of a 'Bruno Grosjean'; in terms of those documents and on the basis of what we know today, no charges can be leveled against the authorities. My suspicion (of some manipulation and exchange of documents) is directed against other persons who were involved, but are no longer alive."[111]

The "legal steps to have this imposed identity annulled" that

Wilkomirski mentions in the afterword to his book consisted, first, in his allowing his lawyer to search the official files for a few months and, second, in his inquiring of him whether the name Binjamin Wilkomirski could be protected in the same way as a registered trademark. His lawyer first examined the files of the Biel Guardianship Authorities in April 1999; he wanted to have a look at the dossier himself before permitting his client to let me examine them. Wilkomirski, who claims to have been searching for gaps in his documents "without pause for years," took his first look at the dossier at the end of April 1999.[112] A few days previously, I had likewise gone through his records; in doing so I had picked up the trail of a man who would, in a very surprising way, turn out to be the most important witness in the course of my research.

THE POLISH FARM IN SWITZERLAND

Before being sent to the children's home in Adelboden, little Bruno Grosjean had been a foster child to the Aeberhard family in Nidau, Switzerland, from June 1944 until March 1945. In early June 1999, I met with René Aeberhard, the son of the family, in his old hometown. In the course of that meeting I showed him a series of old photographs of various children of the same age, including one of Wilkomirski. Aeberhard positively identified one of the boys as Bruno Grosjean; it was the picture of Wilkomirski. At that moment, I had no doubt that Wilkomirski and Grosjean were one and the same person.

All the same, I wonder if Aeberhard will find a photograph of little Bruno when he returns to the United States. I call him there on 10 June 1999.[113]

Aeberhard at once surprises me with some exciting information. He has read Bruno's book in the meantime, and says that what is described there is memories of Nidau! On page twenty-six Bruno writes about a farmstead with an empty stable, and two pages later about a canal: "A canal ran past the farmstead. We had to cross a small footbridge over a weir to get to a meadow where we were sometimes allowed to play. There was only one rail and it was too high for me, and I was afraid of the deep whirlpool under my feet." But that, says René Aeberhard, was exactly the way it was at home, on Grasgarten Street, where his family lived at the time. There was a canal there, the Nidau-Büren Canal, a weir with a footbridge, and on the far side of the canal the vacant meadow where they played and where his daughter's house now stands. There was a crossing at the locks. "Both there and on the footbridge was a railing, but the rail was too high for him." I ask Aeberhard whether there were frightening whirlpools under the Nidau footbridge. "Oh yes, were there ever! The water plunges two or three meters, and there's a whirlpool. You hear an incredible roar."

Bruno describes it all precisely, Aeberhard says, just the way things looked there. "Our house was actually a farmhouse; it had a hay barn and a little stall for two, three cows. It was empty, too, just like in the book. We weren't farmers, we just had rabbits." And Motti, who in the book makes a glider out of paper and sticks, sounds familiar as well. "I made gliders, too. Even a little motorized plane, with a little Dino diesel engine, a Swiss patent. I made a model Rietstern plane. I think Bruno has turned me into his older brother Motti. It would have worked in terms of age, too. I was maybe fourteen, fifteen years older than he was." He quotes Binjamin's memories of Motti, "who's in a sunny field throwing his handmade airplane" into the air. "But that's me," Aeberhard says, "flying my glider in the meadow behind our house."

"And Bruno was with you, and it was fun for him?" I want to know.

"Oh yes, and how! He'd jump around and do somersaults." Aeberhard says that he flew the plane not only behind the house but also—again like Motti in *Fragments*—on the meadow at the edge of the wood. "Yes, that's up the hill, the Hueb—from there

you can get a beautiful sail out of a glider." The correspondences
are so fascinating that I decide to make a systematic check of all
the details.

I remind Aeberhard of little Binjamin's fear of the farmer's
wife, of "her dark and angry look." That's understandable, he
says; his mother had an incredible temper, you could see the fire
in her eyes. "A child would definitely have been terribly intimidated. You could never forget that look in her eyes." In René
Aeberhard's view, Wilkomirski's description of the farmer's wife
so exactly matches Frau Aeberhard that he sees no need even to
explain his assumption, let alone to back it up. Wilkomirski's
farmer's wife simply explodes and sends everybody away; Aeberhard recalls his mother the same way. She would get into a
dreadful state, screaming hysterically, ripping her clothes, and
banging her head against the wall. There was hell to pay then,
and you were happy to escape.

"Did she punish in the same way as the farmer's wife, did she
lock Bruno in the cellar?" I ask.

She would grab the boy by the arm and shake him, he says,
but she never turned violent, "at least not so there were any consequences afterward. It's possible she locked him in the cellar—
anything was possible at such moments. If he had got her mad,
she would just throw him in the cellar and say, 'All right, into
the cellar with you!' And he'd have to stay there. But from the
window in the wash-kitchen cellar he could look out and see
everything that was going on."

In the book, Binjamin runs into soldiers several times at the
farm. And Aeberhard has an explanation for that as well: it was
wartime, and the neighboring farmer, who lived about a hundred or two hundred meters away, always had soldiers quartered
with him. Wilkomirski's text tells how he learned at the farm
that there was a war on—actually a rather late discovery, when
one thinks of what had happened before that in Riga. But given
this information about the farmstead in Nidau, this timing now
makes sense. It was probably there that Bruno saw soldiers for

the first time and heard that there was a war going on. I wonder if those soldiers might also explain the gunfire Binjamin hears. No, that was more likely the military auxiliary, Aeberhard says. "Every Saturday and Sunday the local guard would march past our house. There was a rifle range about a kilometer away where they went to shoot. You could hear them, of course. They wore uniforms like soldiers, but they had an armband as well. I was in the local guard, too. We'd shoot away like crazy, and only stopped during mass." He cannot, however, remember a drunken soldier bursting into the kitchen and demolishing everything, the way Wilkomirski tells it. It couldn't have been his older brother, who served as a corporal in the military. But it is conceivable that some experiences of Bruno's with Frau Aeberhard were behind this. She sometimes threw things, so that there were just smithereens left; all hell broke lose at their house now and then.

I find the details that emerge from this long conversation with René Aeberhard very impressive: the farm near Zamość was actually in the Swiss Jura, the canal there was the Aare canal; Motti's glider was Aeberhard's; the frightening wife of the Polish farmer was Bruno's mentally ill foster mother in the canton of Bern; the *soldateska* were the Helvetian militia; and the gunfire came from the rifle range at Nidau. I had not counted on so much authenticity. Wilkomirski-Grosjean did not have two heads; he had not led two lives. Instead, his book tells his own life, the life of Bruno Grosjean—but with breathtaking alienation.

Aeberhard moves between sympathy for little Bruno and outrage at the grown-up Dössekker, who stands every fact on its head. He regrets not having learned more about the matter while he was still in Europe. "If I could only visit him now. Where does he live now, our Bruno? I'd speak my mind, I'd give him a piece of it. He'd be shocked to the core. I'm one hundred percent certain he lived with us; it all fits together. I'd show him photographs of our parents, that would jog his memory.

Wouldn't it be marvelous to hear what he had to say?" In any case, he promised to keep looking for photographs of Grosjean.

Over the next few weeks, we make further discoveries.[114] I send Aeberhard plans and sketches that Wilkomirski drew of his hiding place near Zamość, along with sequences from the video interviews in which he explains them and talks about his experiences on the farm in Poland. In Aeberhard's opinion, Wilkomirski's drawings and interview statements match the conditions on Grasgarten Strasse. According with Wilkomirski's description, the Aeberhard house had a cellar with small windows and fruit racks; there had also been a horse cart no longer in use, a nearby building that looked like a granary, a bridge, and a weir with a hill nearby. Wilkomirski had even correctly indicated the position of the rising sun. His accurate memory—the boy was only three, four years old at the time—amazes us both.

Aeberhard does not know what to make of Wilkomirski's other descriptions of the farmstead, however; nor of his stories about Jonah and the whale, the soup ladled out in the little house in the snow-covered woods, the vehicle that slams into the house; nor of his description of the outhouse. But—like Wilkomirski and his brothers—the Aeberhard family had eaten a lot of porridge, either oatmeal or a mixture of apples and potatoes.

Wilkomirski uses details from Nidau for other parts of his story besides the stay on the Polish farm. He places his Swiss children's home somewhere on the slopes of the Jura, on the shores of Neuenburger Lake or Lake Biel, on which Nidau is also located. Likewise, his memories of happy sled rides on the frozen city moat through a silver tunnel of trees—all brought to an abrupt end by dark events—probably belong to Nidau. Ice skating, Aeberhard says, had also been possible in Nidau because every winter the water froze where the lake emptied into the canal. They had skated under the alder trees there, and they would have taken Bruno along on the sled every time.

We could not definitively localize two stories of Wilkomirski's, but they too could belong to that fateful year in Nidau: in several different interviews, he mentions the visit by a very important lady. Her presence had been *the* grand event; it had made him happy and meant that he was at last able to leave the house and roll in the grass on the other side of the river. Aeberhard is certain that the visitor was Bruno's mother. "She came almost every weekend. She was really an elegant lady, nicely dressed. Bruno was truly happy whenever she came. And our mother was very different then, too, I'm sure. She could be raging with anger, but as soon as a visitor arrived, she was completely transformed." It seems plausible to me that Yvonne's visits would have had a positive effect, much like the one Wilkomirski describes in his meeting with the lady; Bruno would have felt his mother close by and been protected at the same time from the unbearable side of his foster mother.

In both Wilkomirski's written and oral narratives, the meeting with his mother serves as a leitmotif, though he says he saw her only once at Majdanek concentration camp when he was four years old.[115] A block warden wearing the same uniform as the woman who took him away from the farm shouts for him and indicates that he is to see his mother, but she tells him to not to say a word about it and to keep his distance from her—or at least that is how he understands the alien word *dahle.* The warden leads him past rows of bunks full of dying women, to a woman who looks at him with large eyes from under dark hair. Not daring to get any closer (which he says he regrets deeply to this day), he is finally given a signal from the door that his visit is over; the woman waves him nearer, and he steps up to her, gazes into her face wet with tears, and from her hand, which is hot and damp as it touches his, takes a piece of bread. Then he turns away and walks toward the wide-open door.

This poignant scene recalls another, involving Yvonne Grosjean, when, as she lay fighting for her life in the Biel district hospital, her four-year-old son was taken away from her for good. Particularly since Wilkomirski describes the block warden—the woman with little Binjamin—as someone who might correspond with Bruno's perception at the time of his foster mother. The block warden—normally an evil woman who reminds him of being captured at the farmstead by another woman in the same uniform—suddenly does something good. I ask René Aeberhard if Bruno had visited his mother in the hospital in the company of Frau Aeberhard, and if she might have used the world *dahle*. From his own experience in the same hospital, he recalls that in those days you had to be very quiet when visiting: "You only whispered, never spoke out loud." When I remark about the large number of women in the book, he says the hospital rooms were larger back then, usually holding four to six patients. But he knows nothing concrete about a visit, and *dahle* doesn't ring a bell, either.

Aeberhard has been looking everywhere for photographs that include Bruno Grosjean, but none has yet surfaced. But a few days later, his son-in-law discovers something in the attic at Nidau, under cobwebs and a thick layer of dust: two model airplanes. One is the Rietstern model with which Bruno had played. Made of pine, it has plywood ribs only a few millimeters thick and wings covered with tissue paper. It is painted with enamel. Only the little motor is missing; otherwise this bird could fly.

THE MOTHER'S INHERITANCE—
THE FATHER'S NIGHTMARE

After leaving Biel, Yvonne Grosjean lived in Bern. In 1951 she married Walter Max Rohr, a charming but unlucky man—or so I am told by his sister, who lives in French Switzerland. He had been sickly even as a small child.[116] Walter Rohr died in 1978 and left Yvonne a small estate. She set about putting her affairs in order. Through a third party, she found out about the circumstances of her only child, Bruno, with whom she had been forced to break off all contact when he was taken to Adelboden and then placed with the Dössekkers. Yvonne Rohr-Grosjean died in Bern on 25 September 1981.

One day Wilkomirski got a telephone call from a lawyer, he says, explaining that he would inherit his so-called mother's modest estate. There was no legal will as such; the dead woman had merely written a letter asking that the inheritance be shared between her son and two of her women friends. "And of course I told him that I did not accept her as my mother." The lawyer replied that he didn't "give a hoot" about that; it was simply that the law automatically took Wilkomirski into account as the officially documented son.

Wilkomirski says that at the time he presumed that Yvonne Grosjean was the woman who had accompanied him to Switzerland and had then suddenly vanished without a trace. Moreover, he was not doing well just then. He had recently had a spleen operation, for which he had to make a large deposit of money, and he didn't know how he was going to get his family through it all. Although the inheritance was a matter of "only a few thousand francs"—and he insisted that the money be shared with the two women—he finally accepted it, Wilkomirski says.[117]

I decide to pursue the matter of Yvonne Grosjean's inheritance, and find a will that she herself wrote on 16 September 1979. In it she says, "I have been informed that my son, Bruno Dössekker, whom I gave up for adoption shortly after his birth, has rights to a portion of my estate. And yet I hope that Bruno Dössekker will not take advantage of these legal rights, inasmuch as he has put together his own life today and no personal connection exists." She therefore names the two sisters of her deceased husband as her heirs.[118] In its execution of current law, the testamentary office of the chancellery in Bern notified Wilkomirski that the deceased woman had not named him as a beneficiary. But on the same occasion they doubtless also informed him that as a birth son, he had a legal claim to a portion of the estate.

On 3 November 1981, Wilkomirski wrote a letter to the testamentary office in which he referred to "the final will and testament of Frau Yvonne Berthe Rohr-Grosjean, my *birth mother.*" He wished, he said to "contest said will and testament by claiming my legal rights to a portion of the estate." He held a strong hand, since as the birth son he was legally entitled to three quarters of the estate. He settled out of court with Yvonne's sisters-in-law by sharing the estate equally with them. On 10 November 1981, Wilkomirski and the two women met in Bern, at the dead woman's apartment. A civil official removed the seals from the door, and the executor of the will took an inventory. There was an estate of 90,000 francs free and clear. Wilkomirski received a third of it.[119]

I tell Wilkomirski's ex-wife, who has been divorced from him for a long time, this story about the inheritance.[120] To protect her from any suspicion that she has been involved in the accusations against Wilkomirski, or perhaps even initiated them, I contact her only after having completed my basic research and reached a definitive conclusion of my own. She is totally surprised, since she knew nothing about his contesting the will. She also says that at the time she could make nothing of Wilkomirski's claim that Yvonne Grosjean had been the woman who brought him to Switzerland. He could give her no satisfactory explanation as to why a strange woman should seek him out to make him the heir of her savings. Eventually, he admitted to her that Yvonne Grosjean was in fact his mother, and said that she came from a Jewish family. It was not difficult, however, to determine that hers was not a Jewish name.

People we don't know but whom we've arranged to meet in a public place are usually first recognizable by the way they stand there waiting and searching. But it's different with Rudolf Z.: I recognize him at once from his face, particularly the eyes, which remind me of his son's, and from the chin that was probably nicely chiseled in youth but is now rather shapeless in the case of both men. In the course of our conversation, other similarities become apparent, for instance, that they are both adept with their hands and gifted musically. But Bruno has his mother to thank that he is a good dancer.[121]

Rudolf Z. says that he had had to pay child support until Bruno's adoption in 1957, after which he had been relieved of all responsibility. He had never had any personal contact with his son—his first name was all he knew about him. All the more unexpected, then, was the letter from the authorities in Biel in 1995, informing him that his son's lawyer wanted to look at the files. During a conference in Biel he was advised to agree in principle but first to ask about the motives. Even after several letters were sent by the youth office to the lawyer, there was no response. Not until two years later did a letter come back: "The person making the request has lost interest"—without any reason given.

Rudolf Z. tells how his daughter came across the name Yvonne Grosjean in media reports that followed Ganzfried's disclosures and believed she had finally reached the end of her search. "She came home beaming with joy and said, 'I've traced my brother. His name is Bruno.'—'Yes, we know that.'—'And he lives in Zurich and is a writer. I'm going to get his address.'" But in the end, it was denied to her, and she is still disappointed by Bruno's refusal to have any contact—and by all the other things she's heard about him.

"And how is it for you as a father when you hear about your son's biography?" I ask.

"It's hard to explain, but I haven't slept well ever since, and I constantly have dreams I never had before, terrible dreams, where I'm always in the wrong. I always have to defend myself, to fight with somebody, but I'm always in the weaker position." I remark that this reminds me of his powerless situation in 1941, when his parents didn't want him to have any contact with Yvonne. "Yes. As I said, I'll be happy when it's all over." He tells me about the serious operations he's had, then has to leave for a doctor's appointment. As he says good-bye, he stresses yet again how happy he'll be when everything "vanishes completely."

METAMORPHOSES OF MEMORIES

Wilkomirski says that he always remembered his present story in the same way and even wrote it down for the first time at age ten. These early "memoirs" cannot be found and remain no more than an assertion on his part. And so I am interested in learning how those around Wilkomirski recall his life and his earlier stories. I ask questions of several people and evaluate statements made by others elsewhere.

Upon being asked, almost everyone who knew the Dössekkers expresses outrage that Wilkomirski presented such a negative description of his foster parents. Some of them admit that the couple were very conservative and quite possibly overwhelmed by the demands of raising a child. Some indication of Bruno's distress as a child can be seen in the suicide attempts mentioned by various sources, and in the fact that the housemaid Hermine Egloff was his only confidante. Annie Singer, Wilkomirski's girlfriend from his youth, asserts, however, that he has "much to thank his adoptive parents for. He was pampered and loved. As he grew older he had a great deal of freedom for those days, could attend large parties, come home late, go on vacation with friends, attend private schools, study at the university."[122]

Singer recalls Bruno as a very charming, strikingly handsome young man who was an excellent dancer. He was religious and took his confirmation classes very seriously. She never noticed anything Jewish about him. He possessed a robust imagination, which made him very attractive but also enticed him to tell a good many stories that bore no relation to reality. This evaluation is echoed by many of those I question, including several former classmates. Singer believes that his panic attack at the ski lift was a fabrication, since she knew him to be a passionate, confident skier. Similar doubts were expressed by others who had seen him engage in winter sports.[123]

I find no witnesses who can recall his ever having claimed during primary school that he was a survivor of the Shoah.[124] While attending high school, however, he did tell people he was a refugee child who had fled from the Baltic to Switzerland. Not until the mid-1960s did he begin to manifest a Jewish heritage, wearing a necklace with the Star of David, donning a yarmulke at home, and mounting a mezuzah on his apartment door.[125] At the time his ex-wife says he claimed his name was Nils Raiskin (or something similar). Not until 1972 did he use the name Wilkomirski and assert that he had had two sisters and five brothers and that his brothers and mother had died in a concentration camp—either Mauthausen or Treblinka. But even then he did not see himself as a camp survivor; at least his wife, whom he married in 1964, never heard anything of the kind from him. In rebuttal, Wilkomirski says that her weeping prevented him from talking about his past. His former wife—they separated in 1982—vehemently protests this claim. Nor during their marriage did she ever notice the symptoms that Wilkomirski now traces to the horrors of the camps.

Wilkomirski's story about his difficulties with the documents for his wedding is disputed by his bride of that day. It may have taken a while to get them, but only because in Wilkomirski's hometown a volunteer organization was in charge of these matters. At the wedding, his former wife says, the name of Yvonne Grosjean was also mentioned. At first Wilkomirski described her as a stranger who had brought him to Switzerland, but later he said she was his Jewish mother.[126]

In the early 1980s a period of crisis began for Wilkomirski. His marriage fell apart, and he was often seriously ill. He told his acquaintances that he had cancer or leukemia and might die any day. In reality, he suffered from a low white-blood-cell count and other illnesses that were certainly a great burden but apparently put him in no danger of death. And yet those around him were under the impression that they were dealing with a terminally ill man.[127] "It almost knocked me off my feet when his book appeared so many years later. I'd assumed he had died long ago," Peter Indergand tells me in June 1999. In 1983 he had been chosen as the cameraman for a film about Wilkomirski. Before the actual start of the production (which was never realized), they had filmed the ailing man giving a concert, fearing there might be no chance to do so later. The brothers Rolando and Fernando Colla, who initiated the project, have firm recollections of a man in anguish and fated to die.[128]

The young filmmakers were no less impressed at the time by the way their host entertained them, introducing them to Jewish rites and customs. For them he had stood at no distance from his Jewish identity, but lived it out with a perfection that reminded Indergand of a model pupil. As non-Jewish visitors, they had simply acquiesced, even though his behavior was somewhat alienating, raising their anxiety levels. Their impression was apparently very different from that of Bernstein, who only two years previously had judged Wilkomirski ignorant of such matters, though harboring a slumbering potential. The filmmakers did not, however, have any sense that their subject was staging this and so, Rolando Colla emphasizes, had not doubted his story for a moment.

Their film script—which Wilkomirski did not provide me, so that I had to go through other channels—is very informative, for its sole subject is his past and present life.[129] It was based on the many conversations that the Collas had with him and contains a great deal of personal information that must have come from him as well. It seems reasonable to assume that the script prepared by the filmmakers was authorized by Wilkomirski and accords with the story that he himself was telling at the time. The film was intended to present Wilkomirski as an maker of instruments, a musician, and a survivor of the camps. The script suggests locations including Geneva, Zurich, Vienna, a concentration camp, and a Polish town, with the atmosphere of each place corresponding to the way Wilkomirski had experienced them. A voice-over commentary would site the audience fully within Wilkomirski's perspective, for it was to be the subject himself reading diarylike entries about his own life.

For example, the script describes an almost empty Vienna train station at night, a train with cars from various nations, a few people saying their good-byes. In the voice-over for this scene, Wilkomirski was to talk about his "trip to Poland for the purpose of historical research and of searching for traces of my childhood. The problem of one's own identity, the difficulty of integrating oneself later into a normal life." Another sequence was to show a poor, deserted "farm after a thunderstorm. Thunder rolls in the distance." The voice-over was to be Wilkomirski talking about how he "felt totally abandoned and helpless. During World War II he lived as a foster child on a farm. He was in the cellar as German soldiers forced their way into the house and deported his five brothers and his foster parents to a camp that knows no survivors." Yet another scene was set in a concentration camp: "A school class is visiting. Binjamin steps through the entrance gate, watches the rather lighthearted school class. He strolls along the barracks and then enters a broad, deserted square. A boy, who has evidently slipped away from his class, looks at him from the far side of the square. His eyes are warm and calm. From the viewpoint of the clarinet builder, we see the boy standing against the wall. After a while the boy turns away and vanishes behind the barracks." Wilkomirski, in voice-over, tells of his "emotions in the camp: angst, distrust, the imperative of total subjugation." Then he talks about the "only meeting with his birth mother." This central memory, which corresponds in all essentials to his later stories about it, will be picked up again later, in another scene, this time presented by actors.

The film was planned to end in "almost painfully bright" images of the Israeli desert, with Wilkomirski reading a three-stanza poem of farewell. Written to the Adagio by Albinoni, it has as themes "approaching death" and "the pain of being deserted by a girlfriend in that condition."[130] It ends: "With you I have / now given all away, / all the hope I ever had. / And death alone will save / me from this life. / Oh grant to me / like some secret spring: / Memory, / the power of death / as one such path / into my / great eternal / freedom."

The script includes a list of the most important stations in his life: "Presumably born in German-occupied territory, 1940–41. / Earliest memories of five older brothers. / Only survivor of a sweep for deportees, short time in one of Majdanek's auxiliary camps. Liberated by advancing Russians. / At war's end in a Jewish orphanage in Kraków. / Journey through war-ravaged Germany to Switzerland. / Stay at various children's homes and with foster families." Elsewhere appears the additional note: "At the age of eight he came to Switzerland, after losing parents, brothers, and sisters in a concentration camp in Poland."

By the early 1980s Wilkomirski's biography had definitely become a Shoah story, of which the film scripts are the most extensive version. Witnesses from the period have reported hearing similar, if not so detailed, stories from his own mouth.[131] A comparison of the script with earlier versions reveals that Wanda Wilkomirski, the alleged sister, has now vanished.

Even more numerous are the variations between the script and the later narrative of *Fragments* and the interviews of the 1990s.[132] In the script Wilkomirski dates his birth in 1940–41; later he would push it back to 1938–39. Here he points to the murder of his parents in a Polish concentration camp, where he meets his mother; later he names Majdanek as the camp where the meeting took place and says nothing more about his father's being in a camp (he has only vague memories of him, perhaps of witnessing his murder in Riga). The foster parents on the farm later become the farmer's wife, living by herself. Here he says that his five brothers and his foster parents were murdered in a concentration camp; in later versions the brothers and the farmer's wife vanish from the farm without his saying anything more about them. Here he is placed in a camp that is an auxiliary to Majdanek, where he is liberated by Russians; later he is first brought to the main camp at Majdanek and then taken from there to Birkenau, where he experiences the disbandment of the camp and walks away. Here he lives in only one orphanage in Kraków; later there are several. Here he journeys to Switzerland at age eight, which given what he then claimed was his year of birth would have been in 1948 or 1949; nowadays he dates his entry into the country to the winter of 1945. Here he was placed with various Swiss foster families (which corresponds to the story of Bruno Grosjean); in *Fragments* and afterward, he speaks of only one such family, the Dössekkers.

The first version of the script had the film ending with Wilkomirski's speaking about the "necessity of being able to experience and understand oneself (with the help of writing, making music, filming)." He already had the medium of music at his disposal as a means of finding himself. Film was proving, at least for the moment, to be an impossibility, since the Collas' project remained unrealized. That left writing.

With *Fragments,* written in the early 1990s, Wilkomirski's story assumed the same form as it retains today. After the book's publication, he added only a few details that did not change the story, and made one modification that was forced upon him. That modification essentially had to do with the pogrom in Kraków and his arrival in Switzerland, whose date he moved back once it became clear through Ganzfried's disclosure that his original facts stood in contradiction to documented events. There was, however, nothing that needed correction in the actual text of *Fragments,* since he supplied dates only in interviews. After writing the manuscript, Wilkomirski supplemented his presentation with two more elements. First, he added—presumably for the first time in early 1995, when he needed to reply to Helbling's doubts—a vague story about an exchange of children. Second, he began to indicate in interviews that he had been the subject of medical experiments. Apart from this, his biography as he told it underwent its final metamorphosis in the ten years that lay between the writing of the Colla film script and the drafting of *Fragments*. His memories of his early childhood were now more concrete and complete than ever. A refugee child from the Baltic became a victim of Nazi death camps, whose biography was one of incomparable terrors. The question arises as to just how he came by such discoveries.

His transformations were evidently inspired by meetings with people such as Karola, who told him about her days in Kraków, or with the professor who turned him into a Wilkomirski. Presumably books and films also had an influence; there are, for example, astounding parallels in both content and structure with Jerzy Kosinski's *The Painted Bird*. It is possible that in this case the influence went further still—even to Kosinski's method of "remembering" itself, with which Wilkomirski was familiar. He owns a German edition of the book with an afterword in which Kosinski offers a theory on the literary treatment of memory and the relation between fact and fiction. For a writer "objective reality acquires . . . a secondary importance," Kosinski declares. A writer "makes use of it only to the extent to which it is already accommodated in the universe created by his imagination. *It might be said the writer takes from outside himself only what he is capable of creating in his imagination.*"[133] To support his "own thinking and identifying "a person creates his own personal pattern out of his memories. These patterns are our individual little fictions. For we fit experiences into molds which simplify, shape and give them an acceptable emotional clarity. *The remembered event becomes a fiction, a structure made to accommodate certain feelings.*" To remember is "the automatic process of editing. . . . One cannot say that memory is either literal or exact; if memories have a truth, it is more an emotional than an actual one." As a result Kosinski considers it "not easily justified" that his book should be called "nonfiction"—it is "not an examination, or a revisitation of childhood," but rather a "vision." "The locale and the setting are likewise metaphorical, for the whole journey could actually have taken place in the mind. Just as the setting is metaphorical, so do the characters become archetypes." This story is not simply the product of facts and memory, but "rather the result of the slow unfreezing of an mind long gripped by fear." "*The Painted Bird* can be considered as fairy tales *experienced* by the child, rather than *told* to him."

Kosinski asserts that memory is fiction, a subjective reality that one can turn into a fairy tale to conquer fear. With that Wilkomirski would never agree—after all, he still insists that his narrative has the quality of a photographic copy. And yet Kosinski probably describes fairly accurately the process by which Wilkomirski's inner images may have become "memories."

Another source of inspiration was presumably Eberhard Fechner's documentary film on the Düsseldorf trial of fifteen guards from Majdanek, which was broadcast in 1984 and had an enduring influence on Wilkomirski.[134] Verena Piller tells how emotionally he responded to it, and he himself says that it was in this film that he first saw historic photographs of the camp. During the four-and-half-hour documentary, extensive statements are made by judges, defense lawyers, prosecutors, defendants, and witnesses—above all, former prisoners, as well as a few of their guards. Particularly unusual for a Nazi trial was the fact that in Düsseldorf a good many female guards were sitting in the dock. It is quite conceivable that the presence of these obtuse women, so lacking in insight, may have inspired Wilkomirski to accentuate the female perpetrators in his book. The film mentions a good number of other details that Wilkomirski would later describe in his oral and written narratives: the miserable water supply, the dog kennels, the plague of lice, the crematorium with its iron dampers, the women's barracks, the "children's quarantine" on Field 5. Some experiences and events are mentioned that also occur in Wilkomirski's stories: prisoners

were whipped, the children had no toilets and had to relieve
themselves wherever they happened to be, children were led
away in round-ups, the camp personnel were corrupt, and so on.
There is a very detailed presentation of the "Harvest Festival
Action" of 3 November 1943, in which all Jewish internees,
about 18,000 in all, were murdered. We hear twice about transports from Majdanek to Auschwitz; one prosecutor even suggests these represented the only possibility of survival. This
latter statement may have inspired Wilkomirski to describe the
same sort of transfer in his own story—a description one of his
critics, the historian Raul Hilberg, would later count against
him. Still other details would reemerge in Wilkomirski's account, but he could have found most of his information in other
ways—through literature or archival research or by questioning
survivors.

Wilkomirski may very well have let another film inspire his
story of experiencing a panic attack while on a skiing trip. He
explains his reaction as due to the ski lift's being equipped with
the same kind of Saurer motor once used in gassing vans at Majdanek. There is, however, no evidence in the research division at
Majdanek that either such vans or Saurer motors were ever used
there. Both, though, are known to have been employed at
Chelmno. In one of the most impressive scenes in Claude Lanzmann's ten-hour documentary film, *Shoah,* a van is seen slowly
approaching on an autobahn somewhere in the Ruhr region. In
a voice-over, Lanzmann reads from the report of SS Lieutenant
Colonel Rauff about the technical improvements made on vans
sent to Chelmno. Just as the van gets close enough for us to
make out the word *Saurer* on its fender, we learn from the narrator what the company's engineers actually do: they perfect
equipment for gassing human beings in the loading well. We
see only harmless goods being transported, and the noxious
exhaust from the passing vans, but the presence of the past could
not be more unbearable. The scene has the same structure and
some of the same content as Wilkomirski's panic attack on the

ski slope. It would be very strange indeed if the author of *Fragments* had never seen Lanzmann's work, a milestone in the history of films dealing with the Shoah.[135]

To be sure, Wilkomirski's stories also contain many elements that can be assigned to his own world of experience. In video interviews he says, for instance, that after fleeing from Riga, he was taken to a town where he was dragged from address to address, while a place was sought for him to no avail. This search bears striking similarities to the story of little Bruno Grosjean, who in his early years frequently had to change addresses and foster homes, at first with his mother and then without her. There are likewise parallels between Binjamin's and Bruno's stays at the children's homes in Kraków and Adelboden. Binjamin comes from the concentration camp and ends up in Kraków, among people with fat faces and fine clothes who live in stone houses instead of barracks; he feels alien, on the wrong side, and asks himself whether it might not be better to return to the barracks. In Switzerland, Bruno Grosjean leaves Nidau, where his foster mother had at times made his life a hell, and arrives in Adelboden, a private home for recovering children, where he encounters unaccustomed luxury, tidy rooms, and children who at least in part come from the upper social classes. Did he not perhaps long for the simple farmstead at Nidau sometimes? A third noticeable element is the metaphor of illegal entry. Binjamin arrives in Switzerland without documents and suddenly cannot find Frau Grosz, who has promised to pass him off as her son; he is given a false identity and is constantly afraid that his illicit presence will be noticed and he will have to leave again. If Frau Grosz is replaced with Frau Grosjean[136] and order-loving Swiss society with the Dösseker family, one has the story of Bruno, the illegitimate, proletarian child deserted by his mother and set down in the bourgeois milieu of the Dössekkers, where some family relatives see him as something of an intruder who, without actually belonging to the family—and thus, as they see it, illicitly—will come into a large inheritance.

I have already pointed out in greater detail the parallels between the farm in Nidau and the one near Zamość: similarities between the houses and their surroundings, between Frau Aeberhard and the farmer's wife, between visits by Yvonne Grosjean and by the "lady," between a possible visit to the hospital to see Frau Grosjean and Binjamin's encounter with his mother in the concentration camp. Motti, who protects Binjamin in the literary fabrication, corresponds in biographical reality to René Aeberhard, one of the family's sons. Both the invented brother and the historically real foster brother play in the meadow with model airplanes. The narrative reserves a prominent place for this idyllic scene. It represents the importance of friendship with someone older, a safe counterpart to Binjamin's terrible experiences with the farmer's wife, or Bruno's with his foster mother. At the same time, it is a basic metaphor of Wilkomirski's life and narrative: the flight into fantasy. When reality becomes unbearable—when, for instance, his schoolmates fight with him because of his reaction to William Tell—Binjamin flees in his thoughts to the clouds, where Motti throws his airplane into the air. The tragic counterpart to this escape and rescue can be seen in the metaphor of the book that had affected Wilkomirski so deeply decades ago: the bird with the painted feathers is hurled into the air; it climbs high above its fellow birds, who, failing to recognize it in its disguise, reject and kill it. Who could not be reminded of Wilkomirski himself—of his phenomenal ascent, his veritable apotheosis in the guise of a concentration-camp victim, and then his exposure as a hoax and his plunge into the abyss?

FINDING LOST MEMORIES — THEORY AND TECHNIQUE

On the second page of *Fragments,* Wilkomirski writes that his earliest childhood memories are "planted, first and foremost, in exact snapshots of my photographic memory and in the feelings imprinted in them." These memories are "a rubble field of isolated images and events. Shards of memory with hard knife-sharp edges, which still cut flesh if touched today. Mostly a chaotic jumble, with very little chronological fit; shards that keep surfacing against the orderly grain of grown-up life and escaping the laws of logic." He attempts "to use words to draw as exactly as possible" what has been preserved in his memory.[137] In conversation he goes on to explain that his main task has been to find appropriate language for these images. He could put his experiences—some of which had occurred when he was mute—to paper only "in the way" he had "imagined language to be" at the time. It had to be a child's language, but one that "an adult can understand today, otherwise the translation would have been pointless."[138]

This process of unearthing and translating can be precisely reconstructed, for both his lecture on his theory of memory and the therapy concept he developed with Bernstein—and then used as an "experiment on himself"—offer examples exclusively from his own memory.[139] In the autumn of 1995, he delivers a lecture at the University of Ostrava, "Childhood Memory as a Historical Source," in which he deals with the "reactivation of lost memories"—thus admitting that they can become lost. He discusses four techniques:

1. Concentration exercises should be done on as regular a basis as possible, just before sleep over a longer period of time.

2. Whenever possible, the witness should visit the original sites involved. Confronting the place of the event often brings back memories believed lost.

3. It can be of great help if the witness first tries to draw his memories on paper, perhaps to make plans and maps. The smallest details of such drawings can be decisive for identifying a scene or an event.

4. Conversing with people who have been dealt a similar fate can give the witness courage and often make it easier to put into words what are still just unclear, apparently "illogical" memories. It helps him overcome the fear of attracting unqualified criticism and of looking ridiculous because of his imperfect memories.[140]

It was thanks to these techniques, for instance, that Wilkomirski arrived at his current story about Riga. By means of "concentration exercises" conducted under therapeutic guidance (technique 1), "vague recollections" became detailed knowledge that enabled him, after hours of marching about in a strange, large city, to find the house in which he had stayed as a three-year-old. His trips to the East (Kraków, Majdanek, Birkenau, Riga) corresponded to technique 2. On these trips he also depended on technique 3 (drawings), as when he used previously sketched church steeples to confirm that the house on Iela Katolu was his, or when a hydrant he had drawn proved that he had been in Birkenau. He had made this latter discovery, however, only because he also employed technique number 4: conversations he had with survivors when he visited these places and on other occasions as well.

According to Wilkomirski's presentation, these techniques assist in the recovery of lost memories. In his case, however, they also served to furnish his story with factual credibility in the eyes of those around him and of his larger audience. The trips to the historical sites and the conversations with eyewitnesses—along with a study of the relevant literature—may very well have helped him to produce his memories in the first place. One example of this was his feat of reconstruction in Riga after some fifty years—made all the more remarkable by the fact that in 1941 he had been carried away from the house at night by a woman making a run for the distant harbor,[141] whereas he was now making his way in the opposite direction and thus assuming a perspective he could not possibly have had as a small child. It seems probable that he may have accomplished this not only by means of concentration exercises but also with the help of preliminary research on the town.

Further clues to the genesis of Wilkomirski's memories may be found in his description of the various problems that emerge when "dealing with a child's memory"—for example, that of "fractionalized memory": "If a traumatic childhood experience is too complicated or distressing to be preserved in the memory as a whole, this may result in its being divided into various partial images, which as individual images (individual memories) reduce the whole to a bearable mass. It can be of significance, then, to gather and list the smallest individual memories of any one witness. This gives rise to the possibility that the historian, the psychologist, or the person himself can find an inner, reasonable connection among the individual images and by employing concentration exercises may perhaps even retrieve the entire event."

Wilkomirski's own efforts at remembering his obscure transfer from Majdanek to Birkenau might be read as an example of this phenomenon:

A client [i.e., Wilkomirski himself] remembers that one evening after some kind of massacre he and a few other survivors flee and begin a long march on foot, following train tracks. He remembers exactly how he had to turn his head to the left because on his right was the setting sun, shining directly into his ulcerated and inflamed eyes, which resulted in severe pain. Thus he could not see very well where he was walking and fell several times. The historian [again, Wilkomirski himself] would consider: if the sun was setting on his right, then the client was following train tracks toward the south. The next step: the historian searches old railroad maps to see if in that region there is a railroad line that, for a longer or even shorter distance, is laid due south. Given the sparse network of railroads in prewar Eastern Europe, this is an easy task.[142]

The second difficulty Wilkomirski mentions in his lecture is that of nightmares, which increased when the witness "is intensively involved with his childhood past" and also, perhaps at bedtime, engages in the appropriate concentration exercises. Such nightmares are to be "subjected to especially careful analysis," since they might be able to offer "extremely clear, precise, and real memories that can often be held up to proof." They often exhibit a "clarity of detail that the witness would be unable to provide in a purely waking state." In conversation, Wilkomirski expresses the supposition that such nightmares are intensified by "repressing" the past. They become particularly unbearable then because the majority of them enter "directly into the body" and cannot be pushed aside like normal thoughts. "You lie on the plank bed in your nightmare fighting off insects. And it's always no use, you can't stop it, there are no boundaries."[143]

Wilkomirski also postulates in his lecture that one should "investigate every traumatic memory to whatever extent possible to see if it is about the original traumatization. It has been observed that an unbearably painful memory will later be covered over with a less onerous memory that apparently cannot be penetrated. This only happens when both memories are bound together in some thematic or emotional way. The hermetic layering of a traumatic memory by a second, less onerous memory is an especially common self-defense mechanism of children (screen memory)."

Denial can also inhibit the reconstruction of the memories, Wilkomirski declares in Ostrava: "In cases of the most severe traumatic memories, often accompanied by strong feelings of shame and guilt, the witness can develop a tendency to trivialize his memory, can refuse to recognize it as his own or even deny it entirely and not accept it as true. Just as small children sometimes declare what they have dreamed to be truth and reality, traumatized children are ready to do the opposite and are happy to declare unbearable truth and reality to be fantasy, a dream, and in that way to find some escape and relieve themselves of their burden." Hearing, or reading, such a description, one automatically thinks of Wilkomirski's claim that he spent years fighting off the idea of his ever having been in Birkenau concentration camp, out of shame at having been subjected to medical experiments.

In his lecture and his and Bernstein's therapy concept, therefore, Wilkomirski explicitly proceeds from the notion that photographically exact images in memory that have been rendered inaccessible by psychological processes—repression, denial, fragmentation, screen memories—can be returned to the conscious mind by certain methods.[144] In his own case as well, he speaks of having reversed such repression. Only after fifty years, sensing an incipient self-destruction, had he carefully lifted the "lid" on his childhood, even though "the remembered images I called up caused acute anxiety."[145]

Wilkomirski was given therapeutic support in this process by Monika Matt, who, as she told Suhrkamp, helped him work through his memories by frequent repetition, thus making his experience accessible to him again. Just as his therapist regards *Fragments* as the result of a quite painful and debilitating process, Wilkomirski himself describes his memories as the product of concentration exercises.[146] Today, however, he vehemently denies—as do Bernstein and Piller—that the book is to be understood as recovered memory. "Never in my life have I forgotten what I wrote in my book," Wilkomirski insists. "I had NOTHING TO RE-DISCOVER again!—Some of the memories have been, and are still now, present every single day!!"[147]

For several years now, recovered-memory therapy has been met with the most vigorous criticism, in the United States in particular. To my knowledge, the journalist Mark Pendergrast was the first to place *Fragments* in this context.[148] In the spring of 1998, he grew wary when he read the jacket copy for the British edition of *Fragments,* where it is said of Wilkomirski, "Only in adulthood did he find a way to recover his memories."[149] Recovery therapists proceed from a twofold presupposition. First, traumas from childhood are repressed but continue to have a subconscious effect and create specific psychological symptoms. These vanish when the repressed memory is made conscious and worked through. Second, the traumatic situation is retained as a photographic copy, so to speak, in the subconscious; memory thus corresponds to a past reality. In the afterword to the first book by Lauren Stratford, alias Laura Grabowski, three clinical psychologists and advocates of this therapy write: "When children or adults are faced with inescapable pain beyond their ability to endure, they dissociate or withdraw inside their minds. They cut off awareness of their abuse from their conscious life and bury the memories. The more severe the trauma, the greater the degree of dissociation that is likely to occur. Sustained abuses are buried layer by layer in the mind and can stay hidden for many years. The recovery of memories is also a layer-by-layer process, like peeling an onion. Dissociated memories cannot simply be retrieved at will."[150]

Opponents of such therapies charge that so-called recovered memories are in reality nothing more than the inventions of patients and therapists. The "myth of repression," they believe, produces people who imagine themselves to be victims of sexual abuse, and can discredit innocent people as sexual criminals. This is not the place to trace this bitter debate, which is carried on like a religious war.[151] One cannot help but notice, however, how much Wilkomirski has appropriated from the two basic principles of recovered-memory therapy. Particularly noteworthy is the assumption that past experiences leave behind photographic traces, so to speak, that can remain unchanged up to the present. If there is any consensus in the broad field of memory research, it concerns the abandonment of a memory model that proceeds from a storing of engrams or representations. The schools of both cognitive research and psychoanalysis have long regarded memory as a construction subject to the influences of the present.[152] At dispute is not whether memories have a connection to the past, but whether their interpretation is a faithful copy of the past. Several studies have shown, in fact, that it is possible by means of hypnosis or suggestion to create in individuals memories of events that never occurred. The psychologist Elizabeth Loftus, one of the sharpest critics of recovered-memory therapy, writes: "Once a person adopts a reconstructed memory, he or she tends to believe in it as strongly as in genuine memories, even replacing earlier recollections with the new, invented facts."[153]

I have found no evidence to date that traumatic memories can be implemented with no relation whatever to reality.[154] But even some scientists who are convinced that repressed traumas can be recalled to consciousness assume that such memories may be greatly falsified. Among the proponents of this view—but certainly not one of the terrible simplifiers of the recovered-memory movement, who fully misinterpret Freud's theories—is the trauma researcher Bessel A. van der Kolk, for whom the problem lies in the nature of trauma itself. A traumatic event is first experienced as fragments of its sensory components and is stored as such on a nonverbal level without being admitted into one's personal narrative. The first memory of the trauma surfaces, accordingly, as a flashback of physical sensation—that is, as a picture, odor, sound, movement, or feeling. Patients regularly testify that their perceptions are exact representations of their feelings and sensations at the time.[155]

Traumatized people attempt to integrate this speechless, dissociated, and fragmented experience and to translate it into a narrative that will explain what once happened to them. And it is precisely this need to find words for a nameless horror that opens the door to confabulations. According to Kolk, "Although trauma may leave an indelible imprint, once people start talking about these sensations and try to make meaning of them, they are transcribed into ordinary memories—and, like all ordinary memories, they are then prone to distortion. People seem to be unable to accept experiences that have no meaning; they will try to make sense of what they are feeling. . . . Once people become conscious of intrusive elements of the trauma, they are likely to try to fill in the blanks and complete the picture."[156]

The dangers become even greater with traumas in childhood, for children have less mental capacity for constructing a coherent narrative out of a traumatic event. Van der Kolk writes, "It is likely that their autobiographical memory gaps and their continued reliance on dissociation make it very hard for these patients to reconstruct a precise account of both their past and their current reality. The combination of a lack of autobiographical memory, continued dissociation, and meaning schemes that include victimization, helplessness, and betrayal is likely to make these individuals vulnerable to suggestion and to construction of explanations for their trauma-related affects that may bear little relationship to the actual realities of their lives."[157]

Events in the first years of Wilkomirski's life, above all his stay with the severely mentally ill Frau Aeberhard, leave hardly any doubt that he bears traumatic scars from that period. This may in part explain the powerful effect of his texts, for they gain authenticity by appearing to articulate a nightmare. Without doubt these experiences left traumatic gaps in his memory, which later needed to be filled with some sense of meaning. He himself has explained how that happened, using the example of his being apprehended at the farm near Zamość, an event that he recalls with ever-increasing accuracy:

A client tells how as a small child he was apprehended at his residence by men in uniform. He *recalls only vaguely* the name of the place—three similar-sounding place names are possible—and the historian does not know in what archives he should search for the client's family. *The therapist can induce the client to increasingly detailed accounts of the circumstances of his arrest.* After telling the narrative *several times,* the client suddenly mentions the bright green color of the uniforms and a shiny belt buckle at eye level. The historian now knows that his client was arrested not by the SS, the Gestapo, or the military, but by a unit from a battalion of reserve police. These were the only units in noticeably green uniforms serving behind the front lines—meaning, in most cases, hunting for Jews. But there were several such battalions deployed in various areas. *The therapist is able to persuade the client* to make a sketch of the belt buckle, even when the client is *reluctant* and says he cannot remember such details, only that there was "something like this" on the buckle— and in annoyance and irritation he draws some strangely looped lines. The historian consults a military historian, a specialist in uniforms.

It proves possible to ascertain which unit wore belt buckles with a design similar to that in the drawing; the same unit was deployed in the area where the client suspects he was apprehended.[158]

If Wilkomirski has faithfully described this therapeutic event, the therapist's contribution to his fabrication of pseudo-memories was considerable. She had him repeat his story several times and even make detailed sketches, against his opposition. In the end, vague memories of a possible place-name became certain knowledge of the scene and circumstances of his apprehension[159]—including a detailed drawing of a belt buckle, which in turn helped locate the exact region.

The question is whether others who have undergone therapy based on Wilkomirski's and Bernstein's concept had memories that occurred in this same way. Operating from Wilkomirski's theory of memory, the authors postulate that "psychotherapeutic work with these 'children of the Holocaust' has to take very different paths from those followed by various schools thus far." The therapist's basic position "should be one of acceptance of the memories related by his client; he should regard them as an indication of the client's past 'external reality' and support him in his further memory work. For the client, the psychotherapist's position is first evidenced by the inclusion of the historian in the process. Meanwhile the therapist's constant encouragement must confirm for the client that his memories are being heard and accepted as parts of a historical reality. . . . The 'setting' is very different from usual. In such a therapy the meaning of 'boundaries' takes on a totally different dimension. Moreover, there must be an enabling of transitions from verbal to nonverbal modalities." Here the authors mention—while stressing the "immeasurable importance" of "body memories"—such things as drawings and movement.[160]

In his Ostrava lecture, Wilkomirski had already formulated the posture to be assumed by the historian called in to assist in such therapy: "The historian should never expect merely to receive confirmation of his previous knowledge from such a witness—on the contrary. The historian should never offer a snap-judgment contradiction of what a witness tells him by saying: 'It wasn't that way, otherwise I would know about it as an expert.' Let the historian never forget: Not he but the witness was present at the event—the witness always has a head start in knowledge!"[161] It is, of course, part of the historian's elementary handiwork that he or she should take what a witness says seriously—while always remaining aware, to be sure, that memories are unreliable as a rule. Wilkomirski's demand here is tantamount to doubling the therapist's affirmative stance. Only the client, it would appear, has at his disposal the criteria by which to judge the truth of historical facts. Since in his own case studies Wilkomirski himself is not only the client but—though he never finished his degree in history—usually the consulted historian as well, his postulated division of labor does not de facto exist. He verifies memories that he himself has constructed on the basis of his own historical research.

This therapeutic concept is dubious not only because of its contrived empirical basis. The authors have also created a therapy for people who by definition—since they have no secure identity—have suffered severe trauma. It is well known that therapy for such people is among the greatest challenges a therapist can face and that the countertransference problems involved are often very complex. The vaguely outlined "setting"—if it can be considered that—is, moreover, an open invitation to ambiguous entanglements among all those involved. My doubts only increase when Bernstein says that he has already used it—in cooperation with the self-help organizations ESRA and AMCHA—with over fifty patients.[162]

Wilkomirski himself presumably has not been active as a therapist. In interviews he relates, however, that, along with his music, doing research on behalf of people without a secure identity has become his chief occupation. One senses his passion in his repeated statements of how he has helped to win for child survivors and their memories the recognition which in his view has long been denied them.[163] In his acceptance speech for the ORTHO award, for example, he describes how he allegedly helped one such woman find her identity. I have researched the matter, though only to the extent that it has any connection with Wilkomirski—meaning that I have examined the construction, but not the truth, of her story, which I wish to respect as her private affair.[164]

The woman whom Wilkomirski calls Sabina Rapaport introduces herself to me as K.M.; I shall therefore call her that in the account that follows. K. is a Christian first name, but the woman says she is Jewish and has known this since childhood, when she accidentally picked up this information from a conversation between her adoptive parents. She realized only later that she must have been at Theresienstadt—in a documentary film or in photographs she discovered the house corner where a cobbler named Klein had worked, whom she remembered. In 1995, she read a book that confirmed her recollection of the spot. "In reading a book by Ruth Klüger," she says, "I also then learned what the letter L and the numbers 4 and 1 meant. These were the designations for the girls' dormitories. Block L 4 and L 14 in Theresienstadt!"[165] In his ORTHO speech, Wilkomirski claims this discovery for himself.[166] Moreover, he asserts that K.M. had remembered the name Theresienstadt, whereas she herself maintains that she later reconstructed the place name on the basis of pictures.

She became acquainted with Wilkomirski in early December 1997. Soon afterward, she learned that before Theresienstadt she had lived in the French camp Rivesaltes; she found this answer in a newspaper photograph of the camp. Likewise during that first week of friendship with Wilkomirski, she made another discovery:

> The story had not been in my conscious mind until 29 December 1997. After a week of trying to reanimate images just before falling asleep, but without exactly knowing what it was I wanted to see, I suddenly woke up at two in the morning because I heard something ringing in my mind. Three words. I heard them very clearly and it was my own childish voice that was screaming. I could hear the sound, but did not understand the words. I just kept screaming these three words. I was bathed in sweat and my heart was fluttering. The screams were connected with something, with something dreadful that I had seen. Bit by bit the images that belonged to the screaming emerged. I got up and wrote it all down. Could something like that have actually happened? The images were so clear, the colors so true, the emotions so strong, that it must have been so.

The scene that K.M. wrote down bears the title "The Dead Girl" and describes how a young girl is abused. About this scene,

K.M. comments: "In the meantime I've come to know what I was screaming. I've heard it again: *Elle est morte, elle est morte!* Because I have proof that I was in the camp at Rivesaltes near Perpignan before going to Theresienstadt, I of course know that in my panic I spoke French." K.M. gave Wilkomirski her outline of the scene. He turns it into a fully different story for his ORTHO speech, taking only the sentence *"Elle est morte"* from the original and inventing a banner with the letters EEM. Moreover, he describes the scene as a nightmare, when for K.M. it was a memory. According to Wilkomirski, she took the scream *"Elle est morte"* to mean that her mother was dead. But she says, "I never claimed this story had anything to do with the death of my mother. I know absolutely nothing about that."

After writing down another memory of abuse, she had noted, "I don't know what I should do. I cannot sleep anymore and don't know if I'll ever eat again. I've been doubly blocked by the story of the girl who fell over dead because someone stuffed something in her mouth. When is this going to stop? I can't go on. I don't want to raise any more images. I can't bear this any longer!" Alerted by remarks of this sort, I ask her what techniques she had used for remembering. She had bought a book on "self-hypnosis," she explains.

From her file I learn that after being at Rivesaltes and Theresienstadt, she went to Kraków. I find this amazing, particularly because she presumed she had been in the home on Augustiańska Street. When I ask her about this, she explains she only vaguely recalled a building, whereupon Wilkomirski suggested to her the names Kraków and Augustiańska Street.

In January 1998, she was paging through a Jewish magazine and found a word that filled her with a sense of security: Rapaport. She had established a connection with what might have been her last name. In his ORTHO speech, however, Wilkomirski ascribes this feat to himself. Toward the end of March 1998, she recalled the name of an older sister: Rivka. This led her to write a hopeful letter to her daughter: "Assuming that my last name is Rapaport, it might be possible to find a list containing that name. I only have to search for such a list! Whether I'll ever find it is another question, but I'm beginning to know the little girl from Theresienstadt, there's a skin I can slip into, and that feels good." Only two days later, it happened: "25 March 98. A call from Binjamin. A list with a Rapaport family. A Rivka Rapaport, born in 1929. A transport of children from Rivesaltes on 29 April 44. Ma Rivka as I remember her about 15 years old. The question of my father. The pain in my stomach is getting worse, unbearable. I decide to try self-hypnosis once again." Entitling it *"Mon Papa,"* she now wrote a description that evoked images of her father and her sister Rivka. She concluded:

> It took half an hour and I'm exhausted! I intentionally let the film run a thousand times. It's all very clear, the voices distinct, the colors intense. The sun is shining through a window, and I can see trees, their leaves are yellow, brown, and reddish. Autumn colors! I'm wearing a dark-blue dress with long sleeves, Rifka a yellow knit pullover and a brownish beige skirt. She has brown, shoulder-length hair, with a bit of curl. Papa has black hair, wears a green-checked shirt and beige cloth trousers. I have to learn more, but later. I'm drained and overwhelmed. These are the first images of my father to find their way into my conscious mind. My stomach still hurts, I feel uneasy and afraid. I take a sleeping pill and go to bed.

K.M. studied the list with the Rapaports; the list bore the number 72 and came from a book compiled by the Nazi hunter Serge Klarfeld about deportations from France. The age of her sister Rivka was right. "But where am I? No date of birth on this list can match my age." She spoke with Wilkomirski. "Binjamin suggested that I might be on list 72 after all. A Sabina

Rapaport, born in Bielize on 11 June 38, might possibly work. But I have absolutely no memory of anything Polish." She tried "to put things in order": "I read again all the stories I've written, paying close attention to sensations of warmth and cold, to the colors of trees, whether they have leaves or are bare. Result: I could have been born around April 1940." Feeling that she still hadn't done enough research, she contacted the Nazi hunter Serge Klarsfeld, who replied that her story was impossible: there had been no Jewish children in Switzerland without documents.

In his ORTHO speech of April 1999, Wilkomirski declares that Sabina Rapaport now feels she is herself for the first time, that she has found peace of mind and is enjoying her restored identity. He thanks ORTHO for giving him the courage to go on helping people like Sabina. K.M. had never received a copy of the speech Wilkomirski gave about her, and asks me to send one to her. No sooner has she read it than she telephones me. She is furious with Wilkomirski, is disappointed, feels her trust has been horribly abused. It angers her that in his speech he had turned himself into her therapist. She had acquired these techniques all on her own; all of her memories had already been there before. He has taken credit, she says, for things she did herself. Most of all she is angry at him for claiming that she is Sabina Rapaport. She has never believed that herself, so where does he get that from? It has never been proved and it would be almost a pure accident if it were. She simply doesn't know who she is.[167]

In the face of the statements and files of K.M., little remains of Wilkomirski's case study, of his "reconstruction" of Sabina's identity. K.M. acquired her memories on her own, partly through self-hypnosis. His acrobatic construction contradicts not only historical probability but also K.M.'s own memories and feelings.

To my knowledge, Wilkomirski's own story and the manner in which he dealt with K.M.'s past were the only applications of the therapy concept he developed with Bernstein. The concept itself is highly questionable, and the two documented applications do not withstand scrutiny. What, one might well ask, has Bernstein done with his fifty clients?

In reply to my inquiry in this regard, Bernstein declares that though he is of the opinion that his concept could be empirically tested and modified, he himself has not worked with it since September 1998. The number fifty had been a "major mistake," he concedes; he has used the technique with a total of six clients, three of whom withdrew after just a few hours of therapy, and the others after the doubts about Wilkomirski became public.[168]

THE TRUTH OF THE BIOGRAPHY

In regard to the particulars of Wilkomirski's story, my research has essentially yielded the following results:

1. Wilkomirski says that the historian Marǵers Vestermanis, himself a survivor of Riga, has confirmed several important elements in what he remembers, including a historically documented rescue action by a boatman. In point of fact, the contrary is true. In response to my inquiry, Vestermanis explains that Wilkomirski has totally misunderstood the story of a harbor worker named Lipke, who saved people by hiding them in Riga and in the countryside (but not by ferrying them away by boat!). A rescue by boat is "very implausible." Nor is it true that it snowed during the liquidation of the Riga ghetto or that one might have heard the cry "Latvian militia!"

2. Wilkomirski claims that after this, he and his brothers were hidden on a farmstead near the town of Zamość. In 1944 and 1945, Bruno Grosjean also lived on a farmstead in Nidau, Switzerland, where he was cared for by a foster family named Aeberhard. René Aeberhard, a son of that family and eighteen years old at the time, remembers the boy well and believes that Bruno and Wilkomirski are the same person. In reading *Fragments,* Aeberhard was struck by a great many parallels between the scenes on the Polish farm and Bruno's stay at his parent's home. The maps of Poland that

Wilkomirski sketched from memory also show great similarities to the topographical features in Nidau.

3. Wilkomirski explains that he moves his feet in his
sleep because he had to do this as a child to protect himself
from the rats at Majdanek. The bump on the back of his
head, he says, also comes from that period—it is, he alleges,
the result of mistreatment. According to the research department at Majdanek, there was no plague of rats in the
camp. Moreover, Wilkomirski's eldest son also has a prominent bump on his head.

4. After arriving at Birkenau at the end of 1944, Wilkomirski says that he was the victim of Drs. Fischer and
König. Both had left the camp, however, by the date of his
alleged arrival. Wilkomirski remembers Laura Grabowski
as being one of the few other children left alive in the camp.
In truth, Laura Grabowski is an American citizen of the
Christian faith who since her youth has assigned to herself
the role of victim in fabricated stories, including sexual violation and satanic abuse.

5. Wilkomirski claims to have first heard the name Wilkomirski in Kraków in 1945. In reality, it appears he did
not come by the name until 1972, when attending a concert
by the violinist Wanda Wilkomirska and an acquaintance
noted that he looked so much like this woman that they
must be related.

6. Wilkomirski says that he lived in several orphanages
in Kraków. Numerous former residents of those homes
can recall other children without difficulty, but not one
of them has any recollection of Wilkomirski. He claims to
have fled to Switzerland after a pogrom that he says he witnessed on Długa or Augustiańska Street. Historical evidence
for such excesses, however, exists only for Miodowa Street in
August 1945. The orphanage on Augustiańska Street was
not opened until the summer of 1946. The witness Bruno
Berti is certain that he saw Wilkomirski at the home of his

foster parents in Switzerland at Christmas in 1945 at the latest. Wilkomirski therefore can never have been in that particular Polish orphanage.

7. Wilkomirski claims to have known Karola both in the children's home in Kraków and before then (implying that they were in the concentration camp). In fact, Karola says they first met at the beginning of the 1970s. Karola's story as told in *Fragments,* recounting how she and her mother were saved from the concentration camp and also how they were later separated, is false. Moreover, Wilkomirski did not know the alias under which Karola is still known today by former residents of the Augustiańska children's home.

8. Wilkomirski mentioned the name Karola to Frau Balint, the chief witness for Suhrkamp and the Liepman Agency, before she found the name in the files of the Jewish Historical Archives, Warsaw. Since Wilkomirski came by the particulars from Karola herself, what Balint considers to be the best evidence of the truth of his story turns out to be a deception.

9. In 1945—he had previously said 1947 or 1948— Wilkomirski says, he was brought by train to Basel as part of a group of vacationing French children, of whom he alone had a blank name tag around his neck. Even in cases of illegal entry, this would have been impossible. He could not have entered on a Red Cross transport with his name tag left blank, nor could he have obtained such a tag without papers—either genuine or false.

10. Wilkomirski relates how he was received in Basel by women who made a great fuss over the lost child. The relief agencies that cared for children entering the country worked in close cooperation with the civil authorities, with whom they also registered their wards. Any such case, then, would have been documented. Systematic analysis of all pertinent data in Swiss archives has yielded nothing whatever.

11. Shortly after his arrival at his foster parents' home, Wilkomirski says, he discovered that another child had been there before him. He claims to have known this boy from his short stay in a Swiss children's home and later to have learned of his imminent emigration to the United States. In the files of Bruno Grosjean, however, who was registered as the foster child of the Dössekkers after October 1945, there is no suggestion of an exchange of children. Witnesses from the period, who surely would have noticed such an event—especially since the boy's arrival in the family had already created a stir—have no memories compatible with such an event. Moreover, there is no plausible motive for the foster parents' having attempted such an illegal and difficult act, nor any explanation of how the "predecessor" could have vanished without a trace once his official documents had been transferred to Wilkomirski. (Where was Bruno Grosjean until he allegedly emigrated at age seventeen?) Another incongruity stems from the encounter Wilkomirski claims they had in the children's home in Adelboden. Bruno Grosjean was there from March to October 1945. Wilkomirski therefore must have arrived in Switzerland by October 1945 at the latest, yet he claims to have lived at the Augustiańska Street home in Kraków, which did not exist until the summer of 1946.

12. By means of such an exchange, the Jewish boy Binjamin Wilkomirski is supposed to have received the documents of the Christian child Bruno Grosjean. A crucial role in this exchange is said to have been played by a Dr. Jadassohn. It is difficult to imagine, however, why a Jewish organization—or even one Jewish man acting on his own—would voluntarily have given a Jewish child a Christian identity *after* the war, since by then intensive efforts were under way to recover all surviving children and return them to the Jewish community.

13. Wilkomirski tries to lend his story plausibility by pointing to similar experiences of Jewish children who were given other documents for their protection; he also cites the abduction of Swiss Gypsy children by a semigovernmental relief agency. Neither Jewish children nor Gypsy children, though, received the papers of existing persons—which is what Wilkomirski claims happened to him, as he tries to explain away the extensive files that bear the name Bruno Grosjean and that even he admits are genuine.

14. His teacher and all those schoolmates of his who were reached for questioning agree that neither the William Tell nor the beggar-boy incidents ever took place. The teacher in question never told the Tell saga and never led an excursion like the one where Wilkomirski claims he begged. Several of Wilkomirski's close acquaintances remember him as an accomplished, indeed a passionate, skier. They have no recollection of the episode he describes with the ski lift and consider it improbable.

15. Wilkomirski has conducted virtually no serious research into his past in Switzerland—which is indeed amazing in light of his claim of an exchange of children on Swiss soil. Not until 1999 did he personally examine the very important files of the Biel Guardianship Authorities *for the first time.* His claim in the afterword to his book to have "taken legal steps to have this imposed identity annulled" can be considered true only if the most charitable interpretation is given to his contacts with his lawyer in the wake of the letter written by Hanno Helbling. In fact, attempts to review the important Biel files were made solely on the initiative of his lawyer. Wilkomirski gave him no instructions to do so; on the contrary, he pulled back from such a review out of fear that it would open the floodgates. Wilkomirski tried to make his story more credible by speaking of an abbreviated birth certificate—of which he had received only

a makeshift summary—and of other difficulties with Swiss documents. In reality, the abbreviated birth certificate is a complete document, and there are no indications of any irregularities in this regard—that he was denied a copy or the like. It is also improbable that he would have met with serious difficulties if, in reaction to Helbling's charges, he had demanded to see his files, particularly since both his birth father, who might have hindered him in his attempts, and the man's daughter tried to establish contact with him in October 1995. He, however, blocked their attempts. A comparison of photographs of the nineteen-year-old Wilkomirski and of Bruno Grosjean's father at the same age reveals a striking resemblance—one that remains visible for the most part even today.

16. Wilkomirski claims to have nothing in common with Yvonne Grosjean. Yet in 1981 he contested her will— *"my birth mother"*—in a letter to the chancellery of the city of Bern and demanded his "legal portion of the estate." There was an out-of-court settlement, in which he received a third of the estate.

In summary, it may be said that the elements of Wilkomirski's story are full of contradictions both in their particulars and in regard to historical reality. Above all, however, they are incompatible with his own biographical reality. There is not the least doubt that Binjamin Wilkomirski is identical with Bruno Grosjean, and that the story he wrote in *Fragments* and has told elsewhere took place solely within the world of his thoughts and emotions.

THE REASONS

It is not a historian's task to describe in detail by what motives or psychological processes Wilkomirski came to his stories. But three basic principles are clear. First, Wilkomirski's memories do not build a continuous narrative. Second, they are closely related to his biographical experiences. Third, in their present form they are largely the product of a specific therapeutic position and of his interaction with the people closest to him.

It is evident how contradictory and poorly grounded in history his story is. It is thus out of the question that "we are dealing with a coldly calculating man systematically executing a fraud," as Daniel Ganzfried has claimed.[1] Wilkomirski did not one day decide to carefully construct a character and devise a story with which to deceive the world. His present-day identity arose, rather, over the course of four decades, unplanned and improvised, with new experiences and necessities constantly woven into it and contradictions arising from a lack of any plan smoothed over, though over time with less and less success.

The genesis of his stories is bound up with traumatic experiences which—at least until he read this report—we may assume had scarcely found their way into his autobiographical knowledge. The experiences from his early years have the dimensions of a cumulative trauma that eludes all understanding and yet is all the more determinative since it occurred during the phase when the child was developing an ability to speak, to think symbolically, and, finally, to shape experiences into stories. *Fragments* is the attempt of the adult Bruno Grosjean to assemble elements taken from humanity's remembrance of the Shoah in order to find a means of expressing experiences that were not verbally retrievable either when they occurred or later, and which for that very reason cried out for a narrative that would give them meaning. This same unnarratability coalesces in the fragmented nature of the text and in the metaphor of falling mute.

After Bruno was taken in by the Dössekker family, his need to find a story for something incomprehensible can only have grown worse, for Wilkomirski's story is a cautionary tale of how certain adoptions are doomed to failure.[2] His birth mother is literally coerced by the civil authorities to give up her child. Before he is finally taken in by his foster parents in Zurich, the boy has already changed foster homes several times and has a series of dreadful experiences behind him. The authorities have provided no professional support for or supervision of the various foster parents, and the Dössekkers themselves have clearly not reflected on their reasons for adoption in ways that could fairly meet the boy's needs; in fact, their wish to continue a medical dynasty is already a constraint on the child's development. Some of the couple's relatives are hostile toward the child because of issues of inheritance. His past is made taboo by the parents, so that he is practically forced to fantasize about his origins. Contact with his birth mother is officially denied him, and certain legal barriers erected to make it even more difficult as he grows older, both of which actions may have negative effects on the formation of his sense of identity. He is taken in by the Dössekkers at age five, but his adoption is not finalized until *twelve years later,* so that he not only finds a real family much too late, but also lives in uncertainty for a very long time. Wilkomirski experienced the worst conceivable conditions for successfully coming to terms with his adoption. It seems obvious to me that all these difficulties only aggravated the original trauma and reinforced his need to flee into fantasy.

Presumably Wilkomirski tried for a long time to fill the gaps in his memory on his own. In the 1980s, however, and then, in an almost explosive fashion, during the 1990s, his fantasies of victimization were radicalized with the help of those around him. As far back as the 1920s, Maurice Halbwachs had demonstrated in his pioneering studies that social conditions are essential for each individual's memory. But the French sociologist was not interested in traumatic memories that are characterized by the fact that they cannot be recovered verbally, are not communicable, and thus lie outside the social realm. In certain cases, however, this paradoxically makes them especially sensitive to social influences. The need to translate memories that consist of fragments and gaps into a meaningful narrative opens the way for suggestion and for those images that society offers and accepts for the narration of horrible experiences: for Grabowski it was sexual abuse by satanists; for Wilkomirski it was Nazi terror.[3]

In Wilkomirski's case, memory with this disposition resulted in devastating productivity. During the entire period in which he radicalized his biography into a tale of the most awful victimization, he was accompanied by Elitsur Bernstein and Verena Piller. But Bernstein—and perhaps Piller as well—held a position that granted privileged status to subjective memory, as was evident in the therapy concept he developed with Wilkomirski. Particularly in the case of traumatic memories, such privilege opens the door to misinterpretations that can balloon into fantasies. This process is merely aggravated by the sort of writing therapy that Piller urged Wilkomirski to undergo and that Bernstein encouraged. Piller challenged Wilkomirski to take his memories seriously and to write them down, because otherwise, she warned, he would destroy himself. Wilkomirski has said that in his therapy with the psychologist Monika Matta, the point was to tie "an existent memory . . . to its appropriate emotions." Everyone who was involved thus turns out to be an adherent of a well-established therapeutic philosophy that promises healing through the integration, abreaction, or working through of dissociated experiences.[4] This catharsis or integration model—far more differentiated in Freudian thought, from which it is taken, than I am able to present here—might be useful in many cases. For Wilkomirski, though, it was a catastrophe. It only made the sufferings from which he was to be freed that much worse—and gave birth to countless new ones.

Each member of the Wilkomirski-Piller-Bernstein constellation had his or her role to play. Piller and Bernstein responded sympathetically to Wilkomirski's victimization fantasies. Their empathy and active participation in his reconstruction journeys, which at times took on the character of bizarre staged events, allowed Wilkomirski to drift ever further into his fantasies. Some of the luster in which the victim was bathed also fell upon his steadfast helpers, as with great courage and selflessness they assisted in establishing the validity of ostensibly forbidden memories. Wilkomirski's psychological gains were at least equally great. As a victim who could not have been more innocent and more ill treated, he was met with worldwide solidarity and boundless sympathy. As a person who had never felt he belonged, he now found entry into a community of victims who held him on occasion in the highest esteem. What was more, his whims or blunders in concrete, everyday life were now obviously excused by his former suffering. The most important gain, however, was that he had found a meaningful story for an inexplicable and inaccessible past. The dark side of his metamorphosis was that he lost himself in the role written for him. In that sense he was indeed horribly victimized. This disastrous mechanism was strengthened by therapy; without it and without the therapeutic position that proceeded from it, Wilkomirski's tragic aberration would be unthinkable.

In his first article, Daniel Ganzfried compares Wilkomirski's book to the novels of a Karl May, which likewise had contributed to the "uplifting" of their readers. But, he goes on, "with his chief of the Apaches, with his Kara Ben Nemsi, and all the rest of them, Karl May created literary figures that are instantly recognizable as such." The difference between fiction and fact in the works of Karl May is, however, not nearly as unambiguous as Ganzfried suggests. Even as a young adult, May blurred the border between imagination and reality. He went through phases in which he was a pathological liar and would put on the masks of a confidence man, including, among others, those of a doctor, a police lieutenant, and a secret-police agent. At the zenith of his literary renown he asserted that he himself had lived out the adventures of Kara Ben Nemsi and Old Shatterhand. He had his picture taken in appropriate costumes and bared his chest to reveal the scars of battle. His rifle, "Bear

Killer," hung in his study, along with countless hunting trophies and a doeskin blanket, said to have been a gift from Winnetou's sister. He could so captivate his listeners that they would respond with frenetic enthusiasm. Some contemporary critics likewise believed his travel novels to be autobiographical. The stories sometimes even overwhelmed the storyteller: when Karl May described Winnetou's death to his audience, he would fall silent in mourning for long intervals and break into tears.[5]

The emotion-laden interaction between May and his audience is startlingly reminiscent of the present case. Videotapes and eyewitness reports of Wilkomirski's presentations give the impression of a man made euphoric by his own narrative. He truly blossomed in his role as a concentration-camp victim, for it was in it that he finally found himself. There is every indication that Wilkomirski found his own narrative true and authentic because it unleashed such stunned silence, such waves of sympathy. Perhaps he did not really believe his story, but he did believe his own telling of it. Anything that had such an effect on listeners must be true. The glow in their eyes lent him a living, coherent identity—that of the greatest of all victims—and gave his story overwhelming authenticity. Without an audience, there would be no Wilkomirski.

THE TRUTH OF THE FICTION

There are two parts to the public phenomenon of Binjamin
Wilkomirski, both of which require analysis and reflection.
First, there is the book's success and Wilkomirski's equally successful embodiment of the concentration-camp victim. Second,
there is the sequence of events set in motion by the disclosure
of his true identity. The core element of this phenomenon is
the interaction between the author and the audience that he
deceived with his fabricated autobiography. The effect that
Wilkomirski produced was based on many mechanisms that
are constitutive for dealing with the memoirs of survivors but
that have become visible only with his unmasking. What has
become questionable in his case is not necessarily questionable
in regard to real survivors—but that is a discussion that I cannot pursue in the following analysis.

The book's exceptional success and the effect Wilkomirski
had on the public were reflected far less in the number of copies
printed than in the enthusiastic reviews, the awards, the audience's reaction whenever he appeared in public, and the letters
sent him by readers. How does one explain this success? Why
did everyone believe Wilkomirski? The answers are to be found
in the text itself, both in Wilkomirski's staging of his own character and in the assumptions and needs of the public.

WHY WAS THE BOOK SUCCESSFUL? — STRATEGIES IN THE TEXT

When we write a story, or listen to or read a narrative, one principle always plays a decisive role—Professor of Literature Peter von Matt has called it the "moral pact."[1] As I see it, his exposition also applies to autobiographical literature, even if it is invented, as in Wilkomirski's case. Whoever reads a text, von Matt writes, is presented with a value system. The reader cannot do with it just as he or she pleases; rather, "all the delights and pleasures offered by the text can be had only if the reader says 'yes' to its context of norms. The moral pact is thus an important ingredient in experiencing the text, and is called a 'pact' because it consists of equally active input by both the text and the reader."

Let us turn now to the first pages of *Fragments*:

I have no mother tongue, nor a father tongue either. My language has its roots in the Yiddish of my eldest brother, Mordechai, overlaid with the Babel-babble of an assortment of children's barracks in the Nazis' death camps in Poland.

It was a small vocabulary; it reduced itself to the bare essentials required to say and to understand whatever would ensure survival. At some point during this time, speech left me altogether and it was a long time before I found it again.

. . . But the languages I learned later on were never mine, at bottom. They were only imitations of other people's speech.

My early childhood memories are planted, first and foremost, in exact snapshots of my photographic memory and in the feelings imprinted in them, and the physical sensations.

. . . If I'm going to write about it, I have to give up on the ordering logic of grown-ups; it would only distort what happened.

I survived; quite a lot of other children did too. The plan was for us to die, not survive. According to the logic of the plan, and the orderly rules they devised to carry it out, we should have been dead.

But we're alive. We're the living contradiction to logic and order.

I'm not a poet or a writer. I can only try to use words to draw as exactly as possible what happened, what I saw; exactly the way my child's memory has held on to it; with no benefit of perspective or vanishing point.[2]

The pact Wilkomirski implicitly demands of his readers is as follows: You must read my text as a photographically exact copy of my remembered experience. I am no poet inventing stories. You will come to know the truth if you learn to read between the lines and surmise what is not said, for language is not my real mode of expression and I lack words for what is most essential. All the same, I address you today in the reduced child's language that allowed me to survive back then and that I had to struggle to recover later. Treat my text with respect, with consideration, and do not measure it by false standards. Never forget: I come from a world divided into victims and villains, and I am among the most innocent of all victims, whose remembered origins are not a father and mother but a barrack in a death camp. If you want to understand my story, you must give up your adult's ordering logic and assume my child's perspective. If you choose order, you are on the side of the villains who planned to murder me and those like me. That is, readers must commit themselves. Once they have established the pact, they must read *all* of the text on those terms. They have to know who is good and who is evil, know whom they are to fear and condemn and with whom they are to share fear and suffering. Only then can the total reading potential of the text be fully exploited. Both the nature of that potential and what the reader makes of it will be explored in greater detail later.

In presenting itself to the reader, this moral system has yet another fundamental trait. For the reader's obligation to identify with the author is reinforced by a motif woven through the text: the mute victim and the deaf, dismissive world around him. "I grew up and became an adult in a time and in a society that didn't want to listen, or perhaps was incapable of listening," Wilkomirski writes in his afterword. It wanted to erase his memories, to silence him. "So for decades I was silent, but my memory could not be wiped clean."[3] Wilkomirski seems to be speaking here of the same kinds of painful experiences that we know from what many other survivors have told us, from Gerhard L. Durlacher in *Stripes in the Sky* to Sarah Kofman in *Smothered Words*. And so he joins the chorus of voices, the witnesses of the death camps who have seen their testimony as a moral duty or even the sole reason to survive. The implicit context increases this text's authority, reiterates the demand that the voice of this victim be taken seriously, and intensifies the strict division of the world into victims and villains. In concrete terms, the narrator describes a society in which traumatic memory is never given its due, or even a hearing, because it encounters anti-Semites who don't want to deal with the past. He demonstrates this in greatest detail with his own Swiss foster family, who forbid him any contact with Jews, declare the history of World War II and the Nazi regime taboo, and reinterpret his memories as a bad dream to be forgotten.

Many critics have remarked on the book's emotional and brutal aesthetic of violence; some have even spoken of a pornography of violence. The writers of numerous letters addressed to Wilkomirski admit that at first they could not read the book, but that after overcoming their resistance they had read it through in one sitting, and now, weeks or months later, are still haunted almost daily by some of its images. I assume that for many, Wilkomirski's book has created this sort of resonance because in a certain sense he does relate authentic facts—that is, his own nightmares. He puts into words events he has created by self-hypnosis and possibly by other techniques, experiencing them so intensely that he possibly considers them true memories. His book is true in the emotionality it evokes, in the density of its horrors; that is perhaps also why so many genuine survivors have found their experiences expressed therein.

Wilkomirski's particular feat is to have found a unique translation for the part of his experience that he has been unable to present, and which he takes to be his memory. Because even the most personal memories are always prestructured by society,[4] Wilkomirski fell back on collective memory in order to articulate his own memories, and chose images that had no direct connection with what had happened to him but that seemed to express the quality of his experience. He made use of the Shoah as the source of his metaphors. Wilkomirski, an outsider to his own society, became a Jew, the prototypical outsider in the modern world. Wilkomirski, who carried with him a past as tormenting as it was incomprehensible, became the victim of unutterable horror. A fabricated narrative about a concentration-camp victim has the advantage of being understood and accepted everywhere, because the remembrance of the Shoah has established itself as collective knowledge beyond its German-Jewish context, and in the last decades, memoir literature has grown ever more extensive. The chances for unconditional acceptance of such a narrative are far greater than they would be for the story of an unhappy, illegitimate, adopted working-class child.

In reaching back, for his narrative, to the cultural memory of the Shoah and its aftermath, Wilkomirski makes use of many familiar elements: the guards' unpredictability, plagues of rats, children hidden in laundry barracks, experiments by doctors (mentioned only orally), obsessive hoarding of food by children after their liberation, the survivors' sense of guilt, the returnees' painful experience of finding no one who will listen, and so on. Thus readers find in Wilkomirski's text essential historical facts that are already known or sound plausible. They automatically locate the story within the realm of reality. The context and the individual facts scattered within it lend the narrative the authority of fact.

Wilkomirski likewise pursues a formal approach of his own: written from the viewpoint of a dreadfully overwhelmed child, his narrative leaves a great many things vague and ambiguous. It neither explains nor establishes historical connections, provides no dates and hardly any place names, and follows no simple chronology—it is told as fragments. The rigorous adoption of a child's perspective as a means to reflect the overpowering terror of a Nazi regime beyond all subjective understanding is in fact a common strategy in works of fiction,[5] but it is extraordinary for an allegedly autobiographical work. One important, a priori effect of this artifice is that the reader does not expect historical precision—after all, it's only a small child speaking. Historical imprecisions or contradictions do not impair credibility; on the contrary, they underscore the authenticity of a childlike perception. This assumed perspective suggests that the child's world of experience is directly present within the text, that what is being told is an unadulterated version of what has happened—experience writes itself, as it were. This posture conceals the fact that every word is written in the present and that the author surely shapes his memories with the conscious, knowing mind of an adult.

To do so requires a manifest understanding of how traumatized memory functions. In assuming a child's perspective, Wilkomirski is imitating patients who often say that they recall a traumatic experience with the same intensity as if it were immediately present. This fragmentary form also allows the author to make use of a hallmark of authentic memories of Shoah survivors: they cannot give what happened a meaning, cannot put the disparate pieces together into a coherent narrative so that what they have suffered may loosen its hold over their present life and become the past. These formal characteristics turn *Fragments* into what is apparently a textbook case of traumatic memory. The psychologist Sarah Traister-Moskovitz writes in Wilkomirski's defense:

> I have been listening to child survivors' memories for over 21 years and have heard close to 300 individual accounts. Binjamin Wilkomirski's book is consistent with the way young children's memories for traumatic events are sensed, stored, and related, consistent with the struggle to make sense of a chaotic, horrific world during the Holocaust and in the aftermath. The struggle to piece the fragments of self and world together also ring true, as do the young child's doubts, confusions, and mistrust about who certain people were.[6]

In shaping his narrative, Wilkomirski magnifies a mechanism that plays a role in all reading: every text has ambiguities and gaps that readers must fill in for themselves. Wilkomirski's text explicitly offers many such lacunae. The moral pact leaves readers scarcely any choice but to fill these lacunae with their own sedimentary knowledge of the Shoah and to read the text as the genuine story of a survivor. The elements of survivor literature are well known, and it is not by chance that many of his readers begin their letters to Wilkomirski with the remark that they have read a great deal on the topic, but never anything comparable to *Fragments*. How heavily the text relies on lacunae that are intended to be filled was not evident until Ganzfried's disclosure that the author was never in a concentration camp. Ruth Klüger, who herself wrote one of the most moving narratives of a childhood spent under the power of the Shoah, responded: "A passage is shocking perhaps precisely because of its naive directness when read as the expression of endured suffering; but when it is revealed as a lie, as a presentation of invented suffering, it deteriorates to kitsch. It is indeed a hallmark of kitsch that it is plausible, all too plausible, and that one rejects it only if one recognizes its pseudoplausibility."[7] Once the professed interrelationships between the first-person narrator, the death-camp story he narrates, and historical reality are proved palpably false, what was a masterpiece becomes kitsch. Lacunae previously filled by readers with some knowledge of what is unutterably horrible are suddenly left empty. The text, which in its artificiality has previously circled an empty core assumed to envelop something nameless, is mercilessly reduced to its sheer material value. What remains is childish speech. The book is no longer an incarnation of horror. Its silences have no content; it merely means what it says.

We read a book presented to us as fiction differently from one that we regard as an autobiography, Ruth Klüger suggests.

There is no absolute value judgment, and literature is always dependent on some sort of extraliterary context. The context in which this book is presented to us is one of a particular life within the framework of familiar historical facts. And however valid it may be that much of this may have happened to other children, with the falling away of the authentic autobiographical aspect and without the guarantee of a living first-person narrator identical with the author, it merely becomes a dramatization that offers no illumination. The original readers have nothing to feel embarrassed about. A few weeks ago they had a very different book in their hands from the one they have now, even though the text has remained the same. We shall continue to have to read those books that claim to be history differently from those that merely contain stories. And it is not our fault if that task is made more difficult by fraudulent facts.[8]

The decisive factor, it must be noted, is that Wilkomirski did not choose just any historical context, but the Shoah. Read as autobiography, the text is enlarged by the Shoah; but read as fiction, it is no match for the especially high demands of that subject. What previously carried with it the weight of the century now founders under the burden of its subject and seems merely banal.

When there are breaks or contradictions between the interior and exterior worlds portrayed, we find a literary work stimulating, fascinating, and rich. This is the source of a special kind of credibility, meaning, and truth. As soon as the author tries to make these interior and exterior realities congruent, however— as by immediately duplicating an internal emotion or threat with an external one—we sense it to be a one-dimensional world, that is, kitsch. That is exactly what happens in *Fragments*. As long as readers can assume the authenticity of memory, they do not perceive this one-dimensionality. It automatically puts them into the context of familiar historical events, so that the childish inner world is dialectically connected with the objective horrors of the Shoah. But once this assumption of authenticity falls away, the interior and exterior worlds of *Fragments* merge seamlessly into one, and all that is left is the world of trivialities. That is, unless we read the text as a description of a different reality, as that of the traumatized little Bruno Grosjean.

HOW DID WILKOMIRSKI CONVINCE HIS AUDIENCE?

In the wake of Ganzfried's vilification, Wilkomirski said that no one had to believe him. But even my brief analysis of the text shows that it is precisely this freedom of choice that he denies his readers, forcing them to read what he has written as authentic autobiography. Moreover, all his public appearances were powerful staged performances of this ostensible identity between author and first-person narrator. He never left room for the least doubt that he had once been a concentration-camp victim. He lived—presumably down to the most intimate parts of his private life—the life of the person whose biography he had described.

Strong effects and emotions were part of the spectacle of his readings. As a rule he did not read his text himself (the exceptions were primarily English-language events), but had an actor present it. This would not in itself have been unusual for a reading, were it not for other added elements. By restricting himself to playing musical melodies charged with emotion, he staged his own muteness in the face of unutterable suffering and at the same time dramatized those lacunae in his text that embraced what could not be spoken. In an extended sense, his seat on the stage remained empty. His audience could automatically imagine itself in his place and immerse itself in his world, for in holding himself back, he let his person fill the entire room. His wearing a shawl reminiscent of a tallith gave him the additional aura of a religious Jew and lent the event a sacral dignity. That all this came very close to a cliché—one might say, echoing Ruth Klüger—only made it the more plausible. It would have required an exceptionally skeptical mind to have responded with critical questions.

Many of his appearances took place within the context of established institutions. No one, of course, would think of doubting the authenticity of a life story when the author steps before a class of students, engages in fund-raising for a renowned Holocaust museum, or testifies as a historical witness at a university. Without question, such institutional settings presume a documentary reading.

The appearances he made with actual survivors were especially convincing. His joining other Shoah survivors to search for his traces in the film *Wanda's List* automatically made him one of them in the public's eye; with that, he had achieved public authority as a death-camp survivor. This ascription was all the more effective since documentary films provide far more of the self-evident authority of factuality than do mere texts. The same effect was achieved in the films by Bergkraut and van Messel, who, in keeping no distance from their subject, assume Wilkomirski's perspective and show him in the context of other survivors. All three films, by the way, use scenes from his own videos of visits to Poland and Riga, whose very amateurishness lends them an aura of authenticity. The credibility is further reinforced by scenes of witnesses from the period who believe they share a common past with him, particularly in van Messel's film when the survivor Miriam declares that, thanks to Wilkomirski, she now better understands her own stay in the laundry barrack at Birkenau. The peculiar power of a documentary film can be explained in part by the fact that it provides an especially strong connection between the narrator and the narrated material—an essential connection if what is narrated is to be understood as autobiographical. The narrator, says the literary expert James Edward Young, embodies the presentation, and vice versa. "Rather than becoming separated from his words, the speaker reinvests them with his presence, his authority, and the link between a survivor and his story is sustained in video as it cannot be in literary narrative."[9] The image also communicates what words cannot—that which can be shown only in gestures, body language, and facial expressions. Those scenes appear especially genuine, then, in which Wilkomirski shows emotion and thus becomes the total embodiment of his autobiography. This is much more the case, by the way, in the scenes of his travels in Eastern Europe and his visits to concentration camps than in the video interviews, where he seems much more like an overacting performer who doesn't trust his own stage presence for a single moment.

The aforementioned scene where Miriam describes the laundry barracks is an example of Wilkomirski's technique of "amalgamation." He takes a historical fact (here, that children were hidden in laundry barracks) and ties it in with his own fantasy— "I was hidden there, too"—so that what is merely fantasized gains in turn the status of fact. The most effective illustration of this technique is the way he handles the photograph from the Augustiańska Street orphanage, in which he recognizes himself as one of the residents pictured there. There are numerous such examples, since his entire story is larded with references to historical facts, from the Deskur files to the photograph of the low supporting wall at Majdanek. Perhaps even more striking is his instrumentation of other people. A whole series of witnesses— among them Vestermanis, Löwinger, Janowski, and Karola— were entangled in his staged performances so that their contributions would lend credibility to his story.

With equal effect, Wilkomirski and his associates employ an argument that gains its powers of persuasion from a core problem of the Shoah and its aftermath: the fundamental contradiction that is inherent in the unique relationship between the Shoah's factuality and the very fact that it is beyond belief. On the one hand, the Nazis performed the singular feat of transforming their grisly phantasmagoria into reality, exterminating an entire people with industrial efficiency. What they made true was unthinkable until then, a thing so horrible that people at the time had enormous difficulty believing it even when they knew about it. More than a half century later, we still find ourselves overwhelmed when grappling cognitively and emotionally with that crime in its full dimensions. Dealing with the Shoah means first of all having to account for something beyond belief. On the other hand, we know from the reports of many of those who were saved that they have a concatenation of lucky and improbable circumstances to thank for their survival. Where being murdered was normal, every escape was a grand exception. Wilkomirski's story profited from both these characteristics: the unbelievable as fact, survival as improbability. He tells how the most unbelievable things happened to him and how he survived in the most improbable fashion—and is believed in both instances. Given the unquestioned acceptance of the premise that his story was authentic, almost no one proved capable of distinguishing between improbability and impossibility. One of the few exceptions was Gary Mokotoff, who expressed his critical arguments to the Jewish Book Council when they awarded Wilkomirski a prize for his book.

WHAT DID THE PUBLIC FIND IN THE TEXT?

The public, however, is not simply the victim of Wilkomirski's staging and narrating. The moral pact can be complete only if readers play an active role—that is, if they *construe* the text's complex of norms on the basis of their *own* presumptions. "The moral content of a literary text," von Matt writes, "is not a static entity," but rather "what I, in my *enjoyment of the text,* consider to be correct."[10]

The enjoyment that the public gained from *Fragments* is evident from the letters written to Wilkomirski and from the book reviews. One reader, who is evidently someone from his larger circle of acquaintance and whose letter I shall use throughout the following pages by way of example, wrote him in the autumn of 1995:

> Shocked, shamed, and full of sympathy, I stand before the violated child that you once were and that speaks for millions of fellow sufferers. All my words sound empty amid so many absurd and horrible facts. Sad and silent, I thus join the circle of your friends, your readers, who gather around you in spirit and can do no more than bow low before such pain. Before you, who despite all the horror and violence of your early years, still have such inner strength to turn your life into something good, something creative. A miracle that comforts us all.[11]

For this reader, Wilkomirski speaks as the representative of "millions of fellow sufferers." She automatically reads his text as one of many Shoah memoirs. Following the definition of the aesthetics of reception, she reaches for the standard images available to her and creates her own subjective picture. If people are to read the text as an authentic account, they need previous knowledge of the Shoah. In order to complete the image in their own minds, they must have some idea of what might be contained in such a memoir. Paradoxically, the automatic belief in the authenticity of these narrated memories—and the ability to make them one's own—ultimately rest on a collective memory that has established itself in the Western world and simultaneously separated itself from the individuals who are the bearers of memory. And that is why a memory that is incongruent with biographical truth can circulate as historical truth. Even after Ganzfried's disclosures, there were voices like this one in the *St. Galler Tagblatt* that insisted: "The horror that Wilkomirski describes through the eyes of an uncomprehending child still retains its collective and historical, albeit not its biographical, truth."[12]

Many readers—and it was primarily women who wrote to Wilkomirski—revealed their shock, agitation, and confusion. The moment they embarked on such a text, they evidently experienced from close up and with unbearable intensity the scenes and feelings that once overwhelmed the child and now the author. The text offered them images removed from rational discourse and evocative of a traumatized child's world of sensitivities. The same helplessness, violence, and fragmentation that threatened to destroy the narrative "I" thus acted upon the readers themselves. Countless readers reacted, then, with the spontaneous wish to take this abused child into their arms, to comfort and protect him.

Empathy or identification generally plays an important role in every act of reading, whether the text is fictional or documentary. This is also true for the literature of Shoah survivors. Empathetic reading can make possible emotional experiences that prevent how we deal with the Shoah from degenerating into a pointless ritual with no meaning for our present reality.

This is especially true for succeeding generations in the societies that committed these crimes. It would be akin to a perpetuation of the Nuremberg racial laws if such empathetic reactions toward its victims were to be forbidden rather than welcomed. The reception of *Fragments,* however, reveals that this ability to empathize does not automatically lead to more differentiated reactions to the past. Not a few readers—and the letter quoted above is not an exceptional case—gathered "sad and silent in spirit" around Wilkomirski and could do no more "than bow low before such pain." That kind of reaction takes one aback; it is obvious that sympathy displayed in this fashion has little to do with the needs of the victim. First, it is lovely to be moved by one's own sense of humanity, to relish one's own sensibilities, to watch oneself responding—"pseudo-overcoming of the past" is what Ruth Klüger calls it when the focus is shifted away from those who suffered. Second, one can share this sympathy with others, thereby joining a larger symbolic group. Third, it is possible to take narcissistic possession of another person's suffering and so find comfort in one's own woes. In his afterword, Wilkomirski explicitly tells "people in the same situation . . . that there really are people today who will take them seriously, and who want to listen and to understand. They should know that they are not alone."[13]

The public's reverent pose is one of the most striking hallmarks of the book's reception. What looks like approval and affection on a superficial level may in fact turn out to be a subtle form of rejection. "As with objects of disgust, one keeps one's distance from objects of reverence,"[14] Ruth Klüger asserts. What victims deserve, however, is a respect that sees them for what they are. The almost religious zeal that set Wilkomirski the victim on a pedestal, above all standards of measurement, may also explain the astounding evaluation of the work as great literature. Even if Wilkomirski had been in the camps, that would not automatically mean that he had to write a good book. Literary exceptions like Primo Levi, Elie Wiesel, Imre Kertész, or Jean Améry should not blind us to the fact that, like many other memoirs, autobiographical texts by concentration-camp survivors are usually rather clumsy as literature.[15] This in no way detracts from their importance. But the general reaction of wishing to bow in reverence before Wilkomirski and to elevate his work to a literary Olympus could also be motivated by a resistance to dealing seriously with the Shoah.

Our reader stands "shamed and full of sympathy . . . before the violated child" that Wilkomirski once was. She wrote him this letter in 1995 and is a resident of Switzerland, which since around that date has begun to come to grips with unprecedented intensity with the fact that anti-Semitism was a decisive factor in its refusal to provide life-saving asylum to countless refugees during World War II. Feelings of shame are an appropriate response to deeds for which a previous generation was responsible. But one can also interpret the shame evident in so many of these reactions as the expression of a sense of guilt. And of course that is all the more applicable to analogous reactions in Germany. Such a reading is embedded in the text itself, teeming as it does with the motifs of silence and deafness. Switzerland is presented as the cliché of a society that is blind to history, that makes a taboo of the past. Especially effective in this regard is the scene in which a panicked Binjamin confuses William Tell with an SS man, while the teacher reacts with a total failure to understand and dismisses the boy's confused stammerings about the murder of children as "drivel"—a word that is then read as the epitome of how Switzerland has repressed the historical reality of these mass crimes and its own involvement in them. One critic wrote: "The word *drivel* says that the story and the place to which it refers, a German death camp, are simply nonexistent, turning any words about it—the gas, the fire, the shootings—into confused speech, 'useless, stupid babbling' without any point of reference or logical context."[16] Public discussion of the dark sides of a past that Swiss citizens had in large part long repressed resulted in criticism, within Jewish and American circles in particular, of the scandalous way in which Swiss banks had handled the funds of Nazi victims. In the second half of the 1990s, this critique reached levels previously unknown, but quickly deteriorated into a cliché-ridden ritual that tended more to squelch true critical discourse than to foster it. Wilkomirski's book offered a comfortable way for readers to identify with the victims in this debate and to take the moral high ground without having to reflect on their own connection to events at their doorstep—an opportunity that, under different sets of historical conditions, also surely holds true for Germany, France, and other countries.

If we look more closely at this kind of identification, we see that for a part of Wilkomirski's audience—that is, the children of villains or bystanders in the past—it provides a twofold reward. First, they can take issue with their parents, accusing them of being directly or indirectly responsible for these crimes. At the same time, they can fantasize that they themselves are victims and can join the ranks of their community. These are wishful fantasies, which negate both their own real position in society and the deeds of their parents. In deceiving themselves that they are critics of the past, they in truth avoid the question of how they should deal with the responsibility or guilt of their parents.

Finally, there is another special attraction of reading as identification: the text has all the elements of a fairy tale about a small child who strays into the clutches of evil, but survives. The most innocent and fragile of victims overcomes humanity's most horrible crimes. He suffers unutterable torments. He loses the power of speech, which distinguishes man from the animals, and yet maintains his humanity and his fearlessness, so that in his outrage at the slaying of another child he bites deep into the arm of a uniformed villain. He survives not only this rash act but also a massacre that spares no one else, and especially not the children. Even the traumatizing blindness of postwar society cannot touch his innermost core. This child hero is indestructible, and once he has grown up, he makes of his life, as our letter-writing reader says, "something good, something creative." Generations of readers have been moved by Anne Frank's diary because they know what the girl herself only suspected and would never be able to describe: her end in a death camp.[17] At the point where Anne Frank left us, we take up the path and go farther with Binjamin. He goes through horrors, but survives and returns. The story really does have a happy ending. The woman who wrote Wilkomirski in the belief that she was the reincarnation of Anne Frank wrote the right man. Wilkomirski's life story, as our reader says, is "a miracle that comforts us all."

My observations are based on the situation in Germany and Switzerland; but of course the book's reception must be more precisely differentiated according to its readership. Conditions in the land of the chief perpetrators are far different from those in the United States, which historically had comparatively less to do with the Holocaust, and even that in an opposing role. But this only increases the need for clarification as to why the largest number of copies of Fragments were sold there. Wilkomirski appears to have profited from the fact that since the 1970s the Holocaust has become a core element in the collective identity of American Jews, in the form of a story of incomparable victimization. In this special sense, the reception of the Holocaust moved beyond the borders of the Jewish community and was awarded a position of central value in American culture as a whole. The television miniseries Holocaust (1978), the Hollywood film Schindler's List (1993), and the Oscar-winning film Life Is Beautiful (1999) are significant phenomena in this development.[18] As the most innocent of all victims and one who knew how to tell an emotional and shocking story, Wilkomirski was the figure the public had been all but waiting for. In addition, he is not only a victim; at the same time he is also a hero, and as such he was able to satisfy the fundamental American need for success stories.

The biographical preconditions for the book's reception are also worth noting. Many of the people involved with Wilkomirski's book or in the various films produced about him felt close to him on the basis of their own stories and thus found it especially easy to identify with him. His therapist Monika Malta and the filmmakers Esther van Messel and Eric Bergkraut belong to the second generation of survivors; van Messel was also—like Wilkomirski's first reviewer, Klara Obermüller—an adopted child. Finally, special consideration needs to be given to the book's reception by Shoah survivors. They are not a homogeneous group. On the one hand, they include Leon Stabinsky, who had his doubts about Wilkomirski early on and showed unwavering good sense in uncovering the false identity of Laura Grabowski, the self-proclaimed victim of Dr. Mengele. Also in this gathering is Daniel Ganzfried, the son of an Auschwitz survivor. On the other hand, many of Wilkomirski's most committed supporters also experienced the Shoah, a remarkably large number of them being so-called child survivors—Balint, Benezra, Peskin—whose endorsements contributed much to Wilkomirski's credibility. What I have said about the rewards of a reading that identifies with the author does not apply to them. As the survivors themselves have told us, Wilkomirski's book moved them because in it they rediscovered their own experience—especially feelings of fear, helplessness, and horror. This holds true not just for experiences in the camps, but for what came afterward as well. Wilkomirski's literary agent, Eva Koralnik, who was spared the worst of it by being rescued from Nazi terror and brought to Switzerland as a little girl, told how she was particularly agitated by the scenes in which Wilkomirski describes being excluded by his schoolmates.

It seems that many survivors found in Wilkomirski a spokesman who made the impossible possible. He remembered precisely what they could recall only dimly. He gave his memories a form for which they had struggled fruitlessly, and for their scream of pain he created a hearing they had sought in vain. Even more than they themselves, Wilkomirski was the true witness who, though younger than most, had seen the ovens of the crematoriums and, unlike almost all the others who had been there, returned to tell the world about it. In meeting Yakov Maroko he went even further—his very person brought back a piece of the story that had been lost forever. For these people Wilkomirski embodied the deceptive hope that the wounds of Auschwitz might heal and that a narrative might transform those experiences into a story with meaning. But the only authentic autobiographical story of Auschwitz is the one that marks the impossibility of its authenticity in the text.

THE TURMOIL FOLLOWING GANZFRIED'S DISCLOSURES— A FINAL OBSERVATION

Ganzfried's disclosures and what happened in their wake have all the typical ingredients of a scandal, and like every scandal, this one also has brought certain social processes into focus. What norms and values were violated in the Wilkomirski case? What social mechanisms became visible through his transgressions? What societal order was strengthened by the processes and ritual of disclosure, by research and perhaps even punishment? Analysis shows that the process which denounced the Wilkomirski phenomenon as a scandal can be understood as the struggle over (correct) memory. But before I turn to this central, and final, aspect, I shall address some questions that emerge in regard to the most important figures and entities involved: Wilkomirski and his sympathizers; publishing houses, archives, and museums; readers; the critical media.

Wilkomirski and His Sympathizers The author of *Fragments* would not have unleashed such outrage if he had simply thought up any given biography. The crucial factors were his personal appropriation of a Shoah story and the public success that followed. There is nothing new about the Shoah being used for various purposes with no direct relation to the historical events themselves.[19] Writers and politicians have applied it as a metaphor to the Gulag, to Palestinian refugees, to the transatlantic slave trade, to their own personal suffering, to endangered nature. Many such transferrals have aroused opposition and controversy—perhaps the best-known example being *Ariel,* a volume of poetry by Sylvia Plath, who was not a victim of the Nazis but who nevertheless presented her emotional world in the character of a Holocaust Jew.[20] What is new with Wilkomirski is that he represented the experience of the Shoah as his own, although he himself had an entirely different past and no Jewish roots at all. Why did he choose these particular images? Quite possibly his affinity for them was based in standard understandings of the Jewish concentration-camp victim as an educated and cultivated individual, as the man next door who is abruptly wrenched from his bourgeois life. A European (or American) can find herself or himself more easily in such an understanding— which like every such representation differs from historical reality—than in images of other groups of victims who stand at a greater cultural or social distance.[21] For Wilkomirski, moreover, there was the fact that his story of a Jewish refugee child entering Switzerland could be easily fused with the irrevocable facts of his actual biography.

Even at a time when the book was not yet a matter of dispute, Wilkomirski used the prophylactic argument of the additional pain inflicted on the victims because their stories were not believed. To critics who doubted that anyone could remember the events of early childhood, he replied, "Each time it's as if someone wanted to kill us because they are taking away our identity."[22] His argumentation was primarily psychological and

founded on his knowledge of work done with traumatized people. Among other works on this topic, Wilkomirski has in his
library a book by the psychoanalyst Hans Keilson,[23] who developed the theory of sequential traumatization while investigating Jewish orphans who had either been hidden during the Nazi
era or had survived the camps. Keilson shows that during the
postwar years, the earlier damage done to these children continued, and was sometimes even exacerbated, when the world
around them did not react appropriately—for instance, by not
allowing them to grieve, by denying the past or ignoring the
injustice they had suffered. One has the impression that Wilkomirski applies such psychological research on a one-to-one
basis to his own story, especially when telling about his Swiss
foster parents.

In attempting to defend the book after Ganzfried's disclosures, his supporters (and Wilkomirski himself) reverted to these
arguments. The strategy was especially effective because it was
based on the worst experiences that those once persecuted had
had to undergo in so-called reparation proceedings.[24] The problem in such suits was that people became objects for the bureaucrats and doctors processing them, and if a claim was rejected,
the burden of proof fell upon the victim—a situation reminiscent of past persecution and so devastating for those involved
that some never even filed a claim. Recalling these precedents,
Wilkomirski's defenders argued that to put the burden of proof
on him was to repeat past injustice and traumatize him again.
Mincing no words, they spoke of renewed persecution, of a second Shoah. As early as Helbling's warning letter, Wilkomirski's
therapist, too, had told Suhrkamp-Verlag that not to publish his
manuscript (thus indicating they did not believe him) would
make a nonperson of him.[25] These reactions revealed that the
field of participants—reflecting the Manichaeism of *Fragments*
itself—was structured as victims and villains. For anyone involved in the controversy, the only choice was between being a
savior and being a persecutor.

Publishing Houses, Archives, and Museums The public success
of the man and his book was due in part to the platform provided Wilkomirski by prestigious publishers and museums. In
hindsight, Suhrkamp and the Liepman Agency made a mistake
in not calling in competent and independent experts the moment the first doubts surfaced. Moreover, the author's afterword
has merely the effect of authorizing his point of view. It is not by
chance that the contradiction he refers to between his version
and the official documents was never mentioned in any reviews
of the book and was discussed only at greater length by Klara
Obermüller, who had her information not from the book itself
but through personal contacts. The affair's drama was only
enhanced when Wilkomirski's publishers and literary agency
did not decide to withdraw the book at once after Ganzfried had
presented his very serious new arguments. A provisional with-
drawal until the questions raised could be resolved would have
obviated misleading speculations—for example, that the book
was being kept on the list purely for the sake of profit.

Readers Wilkomirski offered the public—journalists, historians, and literary specialists included—an "autobiographical
pact" (in Philippe Lejeune's phrase), that is, the assurance that
he was identical with the first-person narrator and that what he
was telling corresponded to his own experience.[26] Thus he made
use of social conventions—for instance, the programmatic for-
mula "I am not a poet or writer"—that vouched for the autobiographical nature of his story. Ganzfried accused reviewers of
being "incapable of forming a judgment" and of having "lost the
courage of their own judgment."[27] In reality, the problem lay
not in a lack of courage, since that presumes a personal opinion
that diverges from the common consensus, but rather in their
inability to free themselves from those conventions that structure every reader's perceptions.

It would be interesting to investigate this context and inquire about the social function of *Fragments*. One look at the reception of both the book and the man reveals its fetishistic character. In its traditional ethnological meaning, a fetish is an object invested with magical or spiritual powers, or in an extended sense, one met with excessive trust or reverence or obsessively believed to be a source of libidinous fulfillment. A fetish fulfills certain functions in a social collective. When it vanishes, the question arises as to what has changed in the society to make it superfluous or useless. Let us take the example of Switzerland.

The German-language version of *Fragments* appeared in the summer of 1995 and by chance met with very unusual conditions for its reception. Shortly after the book's publication, and on a scale previously unknown in Swiss society, there developed, mainly as a result of pressure from other countries, a critical discussion concerning the involvement of Switzerland in the crimes of the National Socialist regime. At first, it was primarily the Swiss banks that stood at the center of the criticism leveled by Jewish organizations—with the World Jewish Congress at their head—and other parties in America. The banks were accused of unscrupulous cooperation with Nazi Germany and in the postwar period of insensitive, indeed cynical, treatment of legitimate (Jewish) claimants to dormant accounts. Another criticism concerned the anti-Semitic rejection by civil authorities of people seeking refuge in Switzerland during the war. The controversy came to a head in the fall of 1996, when, in a class-action lawsuit, Holocaust survivors sued the banks for billions of francs, and the Swiss government then felt compelled to set up an Independent Commission of Experts: Switzerland–Second World War—soon to be called the Bergier Commission, after its chairman. This agency was to investigate, on an unheard-of scale, the role Switzerland had played at the time. The Holocaust Fund that Laura Grabowski milked was a direct result of that debate; it was conceived as a goodwill gesture by the major

banks now under fire. In February 1997, together with the Swiss
National Bank and various segments of the Swiss economy, they
established a fund of 190 million dollars, which was then dispersed worldwide to Holocaust survivors. In August 1998, the
class-action litigants came to a compromise agreement with the
major banks, who pledged to pay 1.25 billion dollars.[28]

Ganzfried's article appeared only two weeks later. By that
point, public opinion had already turned around. Provoked by
what was in part superficial and indiscriminate criticism, many
Swiss, especially older and more conservative citizens, felt dis-
concerted and deeply wounded in their patriotism. These people
were weary of hearing the critical discussion about their past and
increasingly demonstrated anti-Semitic and anti-American ten-
dencies. This discontent found its political expression in the slo-
gans of the right-wing populist Swiss People's Party (SVP),
which showed no restraint in playing off resentments against foreigners and in proclaiming its isolationist viewpoint. The unof-
ficial head of this protest party was the industrialist Christoph
Blocher, who had always vehemently opposed any demands from
Jewish blocs and who even compared a threatened boycott of
Swiss banks to the Nazi boycott of Jewish businesses. This tribune of the people did not shrink from praising a potboiler by a
notorious denier of the Holocaust, Jürgen Graf, who had already
been condemned in Germany and Switzerland for his lies and did
not miss the chance to use Wilkomirski's exposure to his own
rhetorical advantage on the Internet. Blocher's scandalous praise
became known to a wider audience shortly before parliamentary
elections in October 1999, and this may well have helped mobilize right-wing conservatives for the People's Party. The number
of voters for Blocher's party increased by more than half, making
it the largest single party and resulting in the greatest shift in the
balance of power in the Swiss parliament in eighty years.[29]

Ten days after this political avalanche, Ganzfried accused
Wilkomirski of effecting a "coldly planned swindle" and called

for an official investigation of the "facts" because "imitators" needed to be "deterred." In response, a Zurich lawyer filed a formal suit.[30] He wrote: "As stated in Ganzfried's article in *Die Weltwoche,* we are dealing not with the book of a mentally ill man but with a 'cold-blooded swindle' perpetrated by several persons, which is why I am filing a suit against Dössekker and consorts on my own behalf as an aggrieved party. I have been deprived of the book's price, since I would never have bought it had it been publicly offered as a novel. Moreover—beyond the strictures of the law—I have been cheated of a portion of my life and maliciously tricked into feeling sympathy for this topic." Disappointment at having been misled into feeling sympathy for the author of a fabricated story of suffering is an understandable motive, reminiscent of the hurt of an ill-used lover. Actual material fraud should also be punished. The question remains, however, whether delegating the affair to the public prosecutors is not more likely to cover up the countless problems it poses.

The suit appears to me to be a symptom of the way in which Wilkomirski's story of victimization has assumed an opposite function. As a result of the criticism of Switzerland's anti-Semitic past presented day after day in the media, the victim could function as a fetish—offering, that is, a way of being on the right moral side, of joining in the chorus of accusers, and even of agreeing with demands for massive sums of money by Jewish voices. Wilkomirski was an individual victim who suddenly emerged like a personification of the past, hitherto taboo; he burst from an unobtrusive middle-class life with the horrifying dimension of a double existence. As such, he was splendidly suited for treatment by the media, since he focused complex issues into a single face and an emotional, dramatic, Manichaean story. But with the turnabout in public and published opinion, it now became opportune to renounce sympathies previously felt as having been evoked by "malicious swindle."

Ganzfried was in no way an exponent of this new discourse.

His charges of fraud were, on the one hand, an expression of justified indignation and concern for the defilement of remembrance of the Shoah that Wilkomirski had committed. On the
other hand, they were also the result of his outrage at Wilkomirski's publishers and literary agent for not acting sooner on
the basis of his own research. I do not agree with the charge by
Wilkomirski's defenders that Ganzfried was providing grist for
the mills of those who deny the Holocaust—a claim that pun-
ishes the messenger for bearing the bad news. And the position
taken by Jewish weeklies—that it would be better to stomach a
public hoax than to accept Ganzfried's disclosures, thereby providing encouragement to those who claim that Auschwitz is a
lie[31]—reflected a dubious understanding of public enlighten-
ment. Ganzfried's disclosures were necessary and courageous and
essential to the integrity of our remembrance of the Shoah. But
they likewise occurred at a point when it had become passé to
make a fetish of a concentration-camp victim and, in symbolic
unity with him, to overcome a negative side of one's own history.
Discussion about Switzerland's past has changed quite indepen-
dently of Wilkomirski. But both his rise and his fall were suited
to personify this trend in a way that played into media hype.

Media It was the media that hyped Wilkomirski as the incarnation of the true concentration-camp victim. Reports in the media
were characterized by a lack of any sort of critical distance, so that
Wilkomirski's perspective was transmitted unbroken—and that
had consequences. At least some people in the media knew of the
doubts, but they kept silent. But in uncovering the truth, it was
also the media, with Daniel Ganzfried in the vanguard, that
played the decisive role. My research corroborated the factual
basis behind all of Ganzfried's claims about Wilkomirski's identity; only in the matter of his mother's estate is the truth more
incriminating than his critic assumed. It is worth noting how
long the media simply cribbed off Ganzfried without doing their

own research. In addition, substantial contributions regarding the basic questions involved were few and far between, though this was probably due in part to a justifiable reticence at making a definitive judgment before all the facts were in.

Not a few journalists have adopted Wilkomirski's dualistic worldview, which allows only the poles of victims and villains, of saviors and persecutors. This leads to the paradoxical situation that in attempting to free themselves from Wilkomirski's deceptions and put an end to them, his fiercest critics have been more than willing to play the game by his Manichaean rules. The literary critic Klara Obermüller, who has constantly changed sides on the issue, sometimes even within the same text, is likewise lost in this dichotomized world. She praised the book in a review that simultaneously sowed doubts and warned against their being pursued. She promoted the book and as the president of the Zurich Literature Committee defended it against the doubters. At the same time she helped to spread rumors questioning its authenticity and was indirectly responsible for putting Ganzfried to work on his disclosures—only to advise a short time later against any publication of his research. Unable to come to a decision, she has been torn between the opposing sides.

The Struggle over Memory In the eyes of many of the active parties, societal order is apparently endangered—and maintaining it is the purpose of the media debate, and now of legal measures. I have come to this conclusion in part because of the enormous excitability and passion that I have encountered in the course of my work. Countless conversations—including telephone calls at every hour of the day and night—with representatives of the media, with witnesses from the past and others involved, have sometimes left me with the impression that for them Wilkomirski's deceptions are the most important and dramatic issue in the world. At the very least, remembrance of the Shoah has been jeopardized. But is that really so?

For the Western world, remembrance of the Shoah is a constitutive part of its self-understanding. That is especially true for the worldwide community of Jews, for Israeli and German society, but it also holds for France and the United States. In his fantasies Wilkomirski took narcissistic possession of that remembrance and with the grace of a sleepwalker exploited the collective ritual of remembering. If this had been restricted to his therapy and those closest to him, we might perhaps have pitied this misguided man, but the public needn't have bothered about his fantasies. His conduct turned highly explosive only because he became a public figure and entangled publishers, schools, museums, the media, self-help organizations, and readers in his game. By uncovering Wilkomirski's true identity and exposing his act as a farce, Ganzfried also laid bare the weaknesses of this culture of remembrance, revealing the dangers and excesses that threaten it.

This happened at a time of heightened nervousness, when people were searching for new modes of dealing with this period of the past. Symptoms of the same thing can be seen in Germany, in the debate about Martin Walser's acceptance speech for the Peace Prize awarded by the German booksellers; in the bitter controversy about the Wehrmacht exhibition of the Hamburg Institute for Social Research; in the no less emotional arguments about Daniel Goldhagen's *Hitler's Willing Executioners;* and in the lengthy discussions about the meaning and form of a proposed Shoah memorial in Berlin. The same upheaval is evident within Switzerland in the criticism leveled at Swiss complicity in Nazi crimes, an issue that has occupied domestic and foreign media for several years now. And finally, in Israel a new generation of historians are attracting notice for their denunciation of all exploitation of the Shoah for whatever political goals, and for drawing a critical picture of their past during the Nazi regime and the period of Israel's founding as a state.

Although the rewriting of history is part of the normal process of historiography, and any culture of remembrance is always in flux, as those who were alive at the time slowly die off, it is only logical that in the case of the Shoah insecurities should become heightened. This is a delayed consequence of the traumatic events themselves. In such a context, it is equally understandable that Wilkomirski's violation of norms would be upsetting. It is partly the result of people's fear that such an example could be imitated, that a good many copycats—such as Grabowski—might start popping up.

It appears to me that a far more important reason why people are upset is that they have not yet freed themselves of arguments to which Wilkomirski gives his false interpretation. He says: I am a representative of Shoah survivors; in rejecting me you reject all victims. He thus equates belief in his personal story with belief in the Shoah. Ganzfried suggested the same thing when he referred to *Fragments* as being related to the claims of those who call the Holocaust a "lie," and warned of an "erosion of the facticity of Auschwitz." On another occasion he said explicitly that if we can let someone invent the Holocaust, we can also let someone deny it.[32] That is a false analogy. Those who deny the Holocaust deny the story of the Shoah in its entirety, especially the stories of all its victims. Wilkomirski, however, is lying about his personal story, replacing reality with a falsified Holocaust biography. Between the fabrication of one personal story and the denial of millions of others lies not just a quantitative but above all a qualitative difference.

Finally, behind this uneasiness is a misunderstanding of what the memories of witnesses from the past actually accomplish. When former concentration-camp inmates tell and write about what they had personally experienced, they provide the public with knowledge to which it would have no other access, not even through historical research. We now know how they experienced life as victims and how they interpret it today. That is what testimony from the past really accomplishes. Frequently, however, these witnesses are charged with another burden. They are asked not just to document and interpret this reality as they themselves experienced it, but to prove it as well. This is not just to demand something superfluous—solid research on the Shoah fills whole libraries and there is more than enough proof of all the essential events—but to demand something impossible. The reports of witnesses are ultimately texts as well—representations of events, not the events themselves. At the moment when some remembered cruelty is written down, a text emerges out of memory. James E. Young says that in the arm forever bearing the tattooed number of a death camp is embodied the connection between the text, the author, and the past event that is the basis of all testamentary literature. The written text is proof that a survivor has written about the Holocaust. It proves the survival of the writer, proves his existence in the here and now—a proof that no survivor of those crimes ever takes for granted.[33] But the documentary text is not proof of the Holocaust itself, and does not need to be. Thus for the facticity of the Shoah there is no significance whatever if one such text, as in the case of Wilkomirski, is discovered to be a fabrication.

That does not mean, of course, that it is irrelevant when a fictional Shoah biography presents itself as genuine. First, there will soon no longer be any survivors who can tell the world of their specific experiences. It is important that this precious part of our collective memory not be falsified. Second, by his deceptions Wilkomirski has sown many doubts and thus done considerable harm to the believability of the witnesses in general. Third, he has once again abused that very group of people whose lives have been instrumentalized over and over again in so many different ways.[34] At times this misuse took on parasitic forms—one need think only of Karola and the other survivors whom Wilkomirski directly involved in his story. His presentation of the image of the eternal victim, moreover, perpetuated a view of the victim that incorporates various anti-Semitic stereotypes.

Finally, it is not simply a matter of images, it is a battle over who occupies and owns what memories and with what right.

The Hungarian writer and concentration-camp survivor Imre Kertész notes, with a sidelong glance to Wilkomirski, whom he calls an "Auschwitz swindler" and a "Holocaust guru": "The survivor is told how he must think about what he has experienced, completely independent of whether and to what extent this way of thinking corresponds to his real experience. The authentic witness is soon merely in the way, an obstacle to be shoved aside."[35] Along with the faction that feels misused, there is another group of survivors who are still committed in their defense of Wilkomirski because they see their own experiences expressed in *Fragments* and mirrored in attacks on its author. Thus, paradoxically, in the arguments of both Wilkomirski's sympathizers and his critics, one feels the afterthroes of a story that will not disappear.

And all the while, the debate is being nourished by two opposing interpretations—one might term them historical and anthropological. While Ganzfried is the advocate of a historical understanding, the shocked reception that many readers gave to *Fragments* was based upon an ahistorical and ultimately anthropological reading. Ganzfried says that if Auschwitz is ever to be grasped in both its origins and its meaning, then it must be analyzed as a concrete event in the context of the historical conditions of the period. He criticizes a position that takes Auschwitz as a metaphor, or declares that Eichmann is in everyone, or suggests that every individual has the right to interpret and use the experiences of Shoah victims in his or her own personal way—a position that psychologizes away the historical conditions and procedures of this singular mass crime and, so to speak, anthropologizes and universalizes it. Ganzfried detects this attitude in the reception that *Fragments* received, which was primarily emotional and ignored the question of facticity, so that almost no one noticed the countless incongruities. It is perhaps no accident that on the one hand Wilkomirski was very impressed by Kosinsksi's book, while on the other the historian Raul Hilberg was among its sharpest critics, for the historian had made a name for himself with his meticulous analysis of the bureaucratic process that first made this mass crime possible. In contrast, Kosinski's book—much like *Fragments*—offers an ahistorical, metaphorical presentation of the Holocaust: these cruelties are the consequence of human nature; the persecuted protagonist is "everybody's victim" (in Elie Wiesel's words).

As long as the public believed Wilkomirski's story, it was part of the collective memory essential for the identity and self-presentation of any group. But when we look at those involved in the dispute about Wilkomirski, it turns out to be—despite the ongoing expansion of the remembrance of the Shoah—primarily an inner-Jewish matter. For it was Jewish institutions that played the main role in receiving and honoring the book; it was not by chance that all the important prizes came from that quarter. And almost all those who were involved in rejecting or defending Wilkomirski's memories were Jewish: his critics (Ganzfried, Stabinsky, Hilberg, Gourevitch, Lappin, etc.) as well as his defenders (Balint, Bernstein, Matta, Koralnik, van Messel, Althof, etc.). The highly emotional defense mounted by many survivors, as well as their inability to distance themselves from the story, reveals how fragile their lives and security seem to them within the normalcy of the present, and how deep their (post)traumatic experiences still reach.

The success of many memoirs and diaries demonstrates the public's desire to secure a hold on history by means of autobiographical narratives. It evidently corresponds to a deep human need to make the past present in the colorful and emotional yet concrete reality of an individual—a desire that scientific history seldom satisfies. This need for what is subjective has a special justification in the remembrance of the Shoah, since it wrenches individual suffering and death from the world of anonymous, assembly-line murder and restores names and stories to those faceless numbers. Without the readiness to hear the voices of the victims and to save their stories, Wilkomirski's alleged biography never would have been received as it was. Its author's successful abuse of this need does not speak against its legitimacy, but it does reveal many of the mechanisms by which literature written by eyewitnesses achieves its effect. In fact his text demonstrates many of the hallmarks that—for good reason—apply to the reports of genuine witnesses: the offer of identification with the victim, a division of the world into victims and villains, the rhetoric of facticity. And the book's reception and believability were based—just as was its later defense against doubters—on the norms that have developed in our dealings with survivors. No small portion of the upheaval that followed Wilkomirski's unmasking may well be explained by the fact that his book's success was founded primarily on mechanisms that are valid for true Shoah autobiographies.

As an objective event the Shoah can certainly be described, and in that regard a high level of knowledge has been achieved through historical research by now. There are also individual survivors such as Primo Levi or Paul Celan who have expressed their experiences in a masterly manner. And yet most of the victims of those days—presumably including those just named—suffer under the unbearable realization that they can neither integrate their experiences into their personal life stories nor express them in appropriate and communicable ways. This torment made many of them receptive to the idea of seeing *Fragments* as an authentic story of someone condemned to the concentration camps. Their eagerness manifests a great need to make the impossible possible and to transform the meaningless events of the Shoah into a meaningful narrative.

The rise and fall of the figure of Binjamin Wilkomirski reveals more than just the mechanisms that are now part of the Shoah and its remembrance, and it would be wrong to discuss the phenomenon only within that framework. Nonetheless it can be said that the Wilkomirski phenomenon, from the origins of his memories to their reception and exposure, is a litmus test revealing how we all—depending on the nature of our involvement—deal with its aftermath. These aftereffects arise from the uncomprehended and incomprehensible nature of the Shoah. In the end, this fictive "autobiography" of an alleged victim of the death camps reflects the very core structures of the Shoah itself.

AFTERWORD

At the end of July 1999, I revealed the results of my research at a meeting with Binjamin Wilkomirski, Verena Piller, and Eva Koralnik. On 7 October 1999, I sent an interim version of my report to the Liepman Agency and the publishing houses concerned. At that point Suhrkamp, Schocken, and Calmann-Lévy withdrew *Fragments* from the bookstores; owing to a lack of sales, several other publishers had already ceased to offer it even before Ganzfried's disclosures. The agency relinquished its authorization to represent *Fragments* and its author. Wilkomirski sent me—as had been agreed before my research began—a written statement in response to my findings. In every sentence—beneath the wounds, the anguish, and the insecurity—one could hear the voice of a person who had become very aggressive, who felt willfully misunderstood, offended, and belittled by almost every page of my report, with the exception of my description of Bruno Grosjean's first four years of life. Any corrections he suggested as to content have, wherever plausible, been included in the text as it now stands. Other critical points that I could not accept have been included in the notes. In his accompanying letter, Wilkomirski rejected my work on principle: "Even if it were true that my memory and my inner images have deceived me since my youth, that would not improve or legitimate Mächler's report."[1]

Bruno Grosjean has probably fallen silent forever—that is, unless it is he who is speaking through Wilkomirski's words.

EPILOGUE

Since Binjamin Wilkomirski's book was most widely distrib-
uted in English, I am of course pleased that the results of my
own research, which present a challenge to his text, are now
available in that language. When *Fragments* was first published
in the United States, the Holocaust was already a long-debated
and highly public issue. It is my contention that this fictitious
concentration-camp autobiography is but one manifestation of
the darker side of this preoccupation. What does this mean?

During the immediate postwar period, there was scant interest in the history of the genocide of the Jews, but it became and
has remained the center of attention since the 1960s and 1970s.
Today, the Holocaust is surely the most researched, debated, and
depicted issue in world history. It occupies its most prominent
place in the United States, and there not only among Jews but
in the American culture at large. The Holocaust memorials in
almost every big city, the numerous prestigious museums dedicated to the subject, and, not least, the cultural-industrial
exploitation that has turned the Shoah into big business, testify
to this.[1]

This enormous attention is certainly attributable to the
abnormal dimensions of the historic events themselves. Yet the
historian Peter Novick is right when he questions why it is
greatest in the country that did not participate directly in the
Holocaust and was far distant from the places where the horror
was perpetrated. The obsessive preoccupation, he explains,
stems from Israel's Six-Day War of 1967, which clearly showed

the influential Jewish community in the United States how fragile the State of Israel was and how its continued existence could be secured by instrumentalizing the Shoah.[2]

But political mechanisms such as these cannot by themselves account for this focus on the Holocaust. A decisive factor was that the history of victimization has become the most important common identifying mark of American Jewry. In Novick's opinion, it is "a symbol well designed to confront increasing communal anxiety about 'Jewish continuity' in the face of declining religiosity, together with increasing assimilation and a sharp rise in intermarriage, all of which threatened demographic catastrophe." Falling back on the shared history was an obvious move, since Jewishness cannot be defined by attendance at synagogue, geographical location, cultural elements, or physical characteristics. Like all ethnicity, it has no natural referent. Consequently, common distinguishing features other than this history of suffering would have been hard to find. It is also worth adding that images of "survival" and "survivors" have been emerging in American popular culture since the late 1960s, so that everyday persistence and coping, as much as actual life-and-death struggle, have been liberally described in such terms. This culture of victimization, in Novick's view, "didn't *cause* Jews to embrace a victim identity based on the Holocaust, it *allowed* this sort of identity to become dominant."[3] Thus, the Holocaust, seen as a unique history of suffering, became the very epitome of Jewish self-perception and self-representation.

For some time now, this fixation upon the history of victimization has prompted growing criticism within the Jewish community. Norman Finkelstein has recently accused the Jewish elite of using the Holocaust as an "extortion racket," of acting out of power and profit motives and quite illegally, in order to appropriate money from European governments, banks, and economic enterprises and from the survivors themselves. His pamphlet, which unleashed a massive outcry in Europe, is based, however, partly on false or unsubstantiated premises and facts, and is hardly conducive to constructive debate.[4] An older and more justifiable concern is that focusing on the history of suffering perpetuates an image of the Jews as eternal victims, reduces thousands of years of Jewish history to the few years under the Nazi terror, and so affords the perpetrators a posthumous victory. In 1988, the historian and child survivor Yehuda Elkana went so far as to plead for an end to the constant preoccupation with the Holocaust and for a renewed commitment to life. (Admittedly, this plea was mainly directed, provocatively, at the Zionist instrumentalization in Israel.) Elkana wrote: "The very existence of democracy is threatened when the memory of the victims of the past takes an active part in the democratic process. . . . Democracy is about cultivating the present and the future; cultivation of the 'remembered' and an addiction to the past undermine the foundations of democracy."[5]

Criticism of the rhetoric of victimization also targets the two typical manifestations that have become established in the last two decades. On the one side, the survivors are venerated as if they were heroes or secular saints, whose survival amounts to a triumph or even to redemption. The most celebrated exponent of such a mythological interpretation is Elie Wiesel, who sees the religious significance of the Holocaust as being "equal to the revelation at Sinai" and claims that "any survivor has more to say than all the historians combined about what happened." On the other side, a psychological debate on traumatization and victimization has emerged, which stereotypes the survivors—a problematic, simplistic term, which I only use for want of an alternative. They are reduced to being cases of what is now generally known as posttraumatic stress disorder (PTSD), diminished into mere victims of a dreadful past. Their multiple and individual personality traits vanish in this perspective, as do the lives they led before and after the years of terror.[6] To be sure, this fixation upon the victims' experience is not always voluntary. Indeed, where the people directly affected and their offspring are concerned, it is the result of chronic and profound pain caused by the disaster. Yet criticism of the permanent preoccupation with victimization is justified when it is leveled at the instrumentalization of suffering. This would not be the case, of course, if it had been leveled by representatives of the perpetrator societies just to deny their own past, their liability, the consequences of their actions.

This emphasis upon the victims' experience is a central element of the way in which the Holocaust is commemorated, not only among Jews, but also in American society in general. An impressive illustration of this is the United States Holocaust Memorial Museum, located in the heart of the Mall in Washington, D.C., which exemplifies the official side of the remembrance culture—and for which Wilkomirski went on a fund-raising tour. This focus is immediately apparent at the entrance to the museum, where the visitor is asked to equip himself or herself with the identity card of a Holocaust victim. The intention of the exhibition's designers was to enable visitors thus to relate personally to the historic events portrayed. In the permanent exhibition they then encounter scenes of racism, intolerance, dictatorship, and persecution under the Nazi regime; America is portrayed as the liberator in 1945 and as a refuge for survivors in the postwar period. The nature of the presentation and the identification with the victims allows visitors to distance themselves from the victimizers and to take up their own position on a moral high ground. "It is a European event," according to the Holocaust scholar Tim Cole, "which can be included in American natural history, but within the parameters that Americans were the 'liberators' and 'Nazis' the 'perpetrators,' and therefore it can be observed from outside." This "most un-American of crimes" constitutes the negative foil to the fundamental tale of pluralism, tolerance, democracy, and human rights that America tells about itself. Such a culture of remembrance makes it possible not only to display one's own values, but to ignore the real problems of one's own history. Eyes trained on Auschwitz cannot discern and confront the Vietnam

War, slavery, or the genocide of Native Americans. "Allowing a foreign trauma to take up a central position means that national traumas may be dealt with in the shadow, or ignored"—fascination with the Holocaust as screen memory in the Freudian sense.[7]

The nature of this remembrance culture at least partially explains the reception of *Fragments* in the United States. For one thing, Wilkomirski, with his alleged experience of Switzerland's anti-Semitism and blindness to its own past, is the perfect embodiment of an image that the American media have projected in their campaign against the major Swiss banks. In addition, Wilkomirski is ideally placed in the twofold debate on survival as irreversible damage or (conversely) as heroic triumph. In his self-appointed victim's role, he personifies the notion of a horribly abused and ruined life, as well as that of an authoritative commentator with privileged insight into the truth about the genocide. The first way of construing his book is typified by the numerous voices that describe his story as an impressive example of traumatized memory. The other, as it were, liturgical function became apparent in his public readings, for instance at the international conference "Humanity at the Limit: The Impact of the Holocaust Experience on Jews and Christians," held at Notre Dame University in South Bend, Indiana. There he described to the audience how historians had contested his memories of the "children's quarantine" block in Majdanek. "They really tried to make a fool of me," Wilkomirski said. "It was very hard. And I said, 'I was there, not you, but I was there.' "[8] Historical knowledge is replaced by fabrication claiming to be a higher authority.

This increasing tendency to sentimentalize, sanctify, and commercialize events, severing them completely from their historical links, is in fact the greatest danger for the remembrance of the Holocaust. In Tim Cole's view, the "Shoah business" has actually given rise to the Holocaust lie, instead of preventing it. "In many ways 'Holocaust denial' has emerged only within the context of the emergence of the myth of the 'Holocaust.' It was not until the 'Holocaust' emerged as an iconic event that it was perceived to be an event which was deemed to be worth denying."[9]

Cole criticizes the products of this remembrance industry "because they tend to blur the critical distinction between reality and representation." He is completely right in this. Yet the problem is that historical realities are by definition past and absent, and can only be confronted in the representations made of them since. Where the Holocaust is concerned, this problem is made more acute by the very nature of the events. Although they have been researched and described in great detail, they elude definitive and convincing analysis. This void remains the insoluble problem. But for this, there would not be so many self-contradictory efforts, protracted over decades, to find an explanation, nor the need to draw from the events the most varied lessons for the present. There would not be the countless attempts to give shape to the uncomprehended, nor all these processes of instrumentalization and mythologization, these embittered debates. But for this void, Wilkomirski would surely have chosen another vehicle for his morbid fascination, and his misuse and imposture would not have been successful. This, of course, by no means excuses it.

When the German edition of this book appeared, it prompted a reaction from many people who were more or less directly involved in Wilkomirski's story. Among them was Bruno Berti, who provided me with a plausible explanation for the toys and food that were, according to Wilkomirski's account, traces of the boy with whom he claims to have been exchanged. At that time Berti had been commissioned as an architect to inspect the damaged attic room in which the objects were found. The food dated from the war, when people were obliged to store emergency rations, and the toys were relics of Frau Dössekker's own childhood. Older residents of Nidau confirmed the circumstances in Bruno Grosjean's foster family at the time. According to them Frau Aeberhard was a strange, unpredictable, domineering woman, who often beat Bruno. Neighbors were reported to have given the famished boy a bite to eat out of pity on more than one occasion. A further letter mentioned that there was a town moat in Nidau, confirming my suspicion that Wilkomirski's memories not only of the Polish farmyard but also of the frozen moat in Riga really originated in Switzerland.[10]

In addition to information about the authentic backgrounds for Wilkomirski's biography, there were references to literary and cinematic sources. In his warning letter to Suhrkamp, Hanno Helbling, who had anticipated subsequent events with almost prophetic accuracy, explained the scene in which Binjamin hoards bread in the Swiss children's home as if, like a concentration-camp inmate, he has to ward off starvation. An almost identical episode can be found in the classic children's book *Heidi,* by Johanna Spyri, which Bruno, with his carefully protected, middle-class upbringing, must have read. The literary scholar Eva Lezzi discovered a literary model for the story of Jonah and the whale that Motti allegedly told his brother Binjamin: in 1980, the recollections of Jona Oberski, who had been interned in a concentration camp as a small child, appeared in German translation. He recounts what he lived through between his fourth and seventh years, writing in a style, and from a strictly maintained child's perspective, which are strikingly reminiscent of *Fragments.* Wilkomirski was writing his own memoirs at the very time that Oberski's autobiographical narrative was filmed under the title *Jona che visse nella balena* (Jonah, who lived in the whale). "In the prologue to the film," Lezzi wrote, "the protagonist related how his mother told him the story of Jonah and the whale. Whenever he was afraid, he was to think of this story." The story finds its analogy in *Fragments,* where little Binjamin loses his fear when he listens to the end of Motti's telling.[11]

Besides this corroborative material, there was also criticism. Samuel Althof, spokesman for the Contact Point for Children of Survivors of the Persecution of the Jews, objected to the way I had presented him. After conceding the falsity, he explained that in defending Wilkomirski, he was acting purely out of concern for his "great need" and "grave personal conflict." At the same time, he claims, he urged him repeatedly to face up to the truth. Moreover, in November 1999 he begged him—in vain, as it turned out—to apologize publicly out of "respect and solidarity toward the Shoah survivors and their children."[12]

All the institutions that honored Wilkomirski have since retracted their awards. Only ORTHO has, to date, not seen fit to act accordingly. In response to the accusations of fraud, an examining magistrate has been working on the case in Zurich since the beginning of the year; whether charges will be made and against whom has not yet been decided.

Zurich, September 2000

NOTES

1. Wilkomirski was a cosigner of the contract and, promising his full cooperation, also signed an authorization allowing me unlimited access both to documents restricted under privacy laws and to any persons previously sworn to silence. I was specifically charged with investigating whether

- Binjamin Wilkomirski alias Bruno Dössekker is the same person as Bruno Grosjean, born 12 February 1941, registered in Saules, canton of Bern;
- Binjamin Wilkomirski was exchanged as a child with said Bruno Grosjean, and/or to what extent such an act is probable both in and of itself and within its specific historical context;
- any evidence exists either proving or contradicting the biography described by Binjamin Wilkomirski in *Fragments.* In this context, greater weight is to be given to circumstances related to Switzerland.

In the course of his research, the commissioned historian is to give as much consideration as possible to the history of how Binjamin Wilkomirski's manuscript and recollections arrived at their present form.

The charge of fraud brought against "Dössekker and accomplices," which first became public toward the middle of November 1999, shortly before the completion of my manuscript, was not included in my commission, nor was any possible responsibility on the part of publishing houses or the literary agency. Cf. Daniel Ganzfried in *"Binjamin Wilkomirski und die verwandelte Polin"* (Binjamin Wilkomirski and the transformed Polish woman), *Die Weltwoche,* 4 Nov. 1999, and the formal suit filed with the public prosecutor of the canton of Zurich by the attorney Manfred Kuhn on 13 Nov. 1999.

2. Binjamin Wilkomirski, *Fragments: Memories of a Wartime Childhood,* trans. Carol Brown Janeway (New York: Schocken Books, 1996)*, pp. 377–78. German edition: *Bruchstücke: Aus einer Kindheit 1939–1948* (Frankfurt: Jüdischer Verlag im Suhrkamp Verlag, 1995).

THE STORY OF BRUNO GROSJEAN

1. Documents of inquiry for the private suit filed by Yvonne Grosjean, resident of Biel, against Henri Robert, resident of Neuenburg, for traffic violations and gross negligence resulting in grievous bodily injury, 1940–1942 (Staatsarchiv Bern, BB 15.1.458, Dossier 529 A).

2. Ibid.; files found at the Biel Guardianship Authorities concerning Bruno Grosjean.

3. Conversations with Max and Edeltraut Grosjean, 6 May and 4 July 1999.

4. For more on the still barely researched history of the boarding of orphans, see Jürg Schoch, Heinrich Tuggener, and Daniel Wehrli, *Aufwachsen ohne Eltern: Verdingkinder, Heimkinder, Pflegekinder, Windenkinder; zur ausserfamilären Erziehung in der deutschsprachigen Schweiz* (Growing up without parents: indentured children, orphanage children, foster children; the raising of children outside their families in German-speaking Switzerland) (Zurich: Chronos Verlag, 1989), pp. 39–40 and 138–9.

5. Birth certificate of Bruno Grosjean, issued 20 February 1941 (files of the Biel Guardianship Authorities).

6. Conversation with Rudolf Z., 20 July 1999.

7. Paternity records from 14 May 1941; cf. Stauffer, petitions to the Biel Guardianship Authorities, 9 June 1941 (files of the Biel authorities).

---

*The complete text of *Fragments* follows these Notes. The page references given here refer to the text of *Fragments* that appears in this book.

8. Ibid.

9. Cf. the investigation reports against Henri Robert (Staatsarchiv Bern, BB 15.1.458, Dossier 529 A); official report by Römer for 1941–1942, Legal Adviser File (Biel Guardianship Authorities).

10. Dr. Schmid in a letter to the general agent of Swiss Accident Insurance, 5 May 1941 (Staatsarchiv Bern, BB 15.1.458, Dossier 529 A).

11. Stauffer in a letter to the convalescent home in Langnau i. E., 18 June 1941; the convalescent home's letter to Stauffer, 14 July 1941 (Biel Guardianship Authorities).

12. Progress report of Dr. Wendling, 28 Aug. 1941; Dr. Schmid in a letter to Swiss Accident Insurance from 13 Feb. 1942 (Staatsarchiv Bern, BB 15.1.458, Dossier 529 A).

13. Notation by Stauffer, 2 Feb. 1942. Where not otherwise indicated, the following is taken from the files of the Biel Guardianship Authorities.

14. Römer in a letter to the Biel authorities, 30 July 1941 (Biel Guardianship Authorities).

15. Compilation of visitation report, File No. 191; Stauffer in a letter to Madame Rossel-Vaucher, 13 June 1944 (Biel Guardianship Authorities).

16. Telephone conversation with René Aeberhard and his daughter Marijke Meyer, 20 May 1999.

17. Conversation with René Aeberhard, 1 June 1999. Unless otherwise indicated, the following is taken from the same conversation.

18. Report by Stauffer, 17 February 1945 (Biel Guardianship Authorities).

19. Biel Child Welfare Office to Yvonne Grosjean, 9 March 1945 (Biel Guardianship Authorities).

20. Unless otherwise indicated, the following is from the files of the Biel Guardianship Authorities.

21. Brochure and additional information from Frau Rechsteiner-Güller of Heiden, an employee of the orphanage at the time.

22. Draft for authorization and memorandum (presumably by Stauffer), 17 May 1945 (Biel Guardianship Authorities). The state secretary for justice of the canton of Zurich took the position that birth parents had the right to personal interaction with their child not only during foster care but also after adoption. Cf. Otto Fehr, "Die Zustimmung der

leiblichen Eltern zur Kindesannahme" (Consent of birth parents in handing over a child), in *Zeitschrift für Vormundschaftswesen* (1947), pp. 130–135, p. 134. My thanks to Kurt Affolter, director of the Biel Guardianship Authorities, for this information.

23. Dössekker in a letter to the Biel Guardianship Authorities, 28 June 1945; Welfare Office of the City of Zurich, Department of Inquiries, 19 June 1945 (Biel Guardianship Authorities).

24. Declaration of Yvonne Grosjean, 27 June 1945; she signed the authorization for adoption on 22 June 1945 (Biel Guardianship Authorities).

25. Stauffer in a letter to Dössekker, 2 July 1945 (Biel Guardianship Authorities).

26. Stauffer in a letter to the Sonnhalde Children's Home, 7 July 1945 (Biel Guardianship Authorities).

27. Kurt Dössekker in a letter to Stauffer, 24 July 1945; Stauffer in a letter to Herr and Frau Dössekker, 21 July 1945 (Biel Guardianship Authorities).

28. The following is taken from a conversation with Max and Edeltraut Grosjean, 6 May 1999.

29. Yvonne Grosjean went to work for Ryff & Company in Bern on 4 July 1945, as noted in the firm's books for 26 June 1945 (Biel Guardianship Authorities); cf. the entries for arrival and departure at the respective registry offices.

30. Stauffer in his guardian visitation report, 28 August 1945; compilation of visitation reports, File No. 191, paragraph dated 18 December 1945 (Biel Guardianship Authorities); for the date of arrival, cf. the entry under his name in the files of the registry office in the Zurich municipal archives. The entry for his departure in the registry files at Adelboden is dated 20 October 1945.

31. Stauffer in his guardian visitation report, 25 July 1947; compilation of visitation reports, file No. 191, paragraph dated 14 Feb. 1947 (Biel Guardianship Authorities).

WILKOMIRSKI TELLS HIS STORY

1. Unless otherwise indicated, the following is taken from my conversations with Wilkomirski on 22 and 29 April, 14 May, 2 and 19

June, and 15 July 1999, as well as from his written statement of 22 Nov. 1999. Other sources and any splicing of material or departures from these conversations will be noted.

2. Video interview, Survivors of the Shoah, Visual History Foundation, 20 March 1997 (6 tapes), tape 6.

3. Binjamin Wilkomirski, *Fragments: Memories of a Wartime Childhood* (New York: Schocken Books, 1996, p. 470). Unless otherwise indicated, the following is taken from the same book (pp. 470–73).

4. Conversation with Verena Piller, 14 May 1999; video interview with the Shoah Foundation, tape 6.

5. Conversation with Wilkomirski, 14 May 1999; Elena Lappin, "The Man with Two Heads," *Granta,* no. 66 (Summer 1999), pp. 28–65.

6. Wilkomirski in a letter to Thomas Sparr, 4 March 1995 (Suhrkamp files).

7. Stauffer in a report, 14 February 1947 (Biel Guardianship Authorities).

8. Wilkomirski, *Fragments*, pp. 404–5.

9. Ibid.; video interview, Shoah Foundation, tape 1.

10. Video interview, Shoah Foundation, tape 1.

11. Video interview, Holocaust Memorial Museum, Washington D.C., 26 Sept. 1997 (6 tapes; interview in English), tape. 2; cf. Wilkomirski, *Fragments*, pp. 381–82.

12. The following is taken from video interview, Holocaust Memorial Museum, tapes 2 and 6; video interview, Shoah Foundation, tape 1; Wilkomirski, *Fragments*, pp. 395–403; and conversation with Wilkomirski, 15 July 1999.

13. Video interview, Shoah Foundation, tapes 1 and 4; cf. Wilkomirski, *Fragments*, pp. 395–96, 403.

14. Wilkomirski, *Fragments*, pp. 397–98; video interview, Holocaust Memorial Museum, tape 2.

15. Video interview, Holocaust Memorial Museum, tape 2; video interview, Shoah Foundation, tape 1.

16. Wilkomirski, *Fragments*, pp. 399–400.

17. Wilkomirski, *Fragments*, pp. 400–403. Wilkomirski's remark about the meaning of the word in Polish is from the video interview, Shoah Foundation, tape 2.

18. Video interview, Shoah Foundation, tape 2; Wilkomirski, *Fragments*, p. 403; video interview, Holocaust Memorial Museum, tape 2.

19. Video interview, Shoah Foundation, tape 2; video interview, Holocaust Memorial, tape 2.

20. Ibid.; Wilkomirski, *Fragments*, pp. 431–32.

21. Ibid.; Wilkomirski, *Fragments*, pp. 453–54.

22. Wilkomirski, *Fragments*, pp. 406–7, 443.

23. Ibid., pp. 416–17. He fingers the bump several times, e.g., in the video interview for the Holocaust Memorial Museum.

24. Wilkomirski, *Fragments*, pp. 436–37; cf. video interview, Holocaust Memorial Museum, tape 4.

25. Wilkomirski, *Fragments*, pp. 422–26.

26. Ibid., pp. 410–411.

27. Video interview, Shoah Foundation, tape 2.

28. Video interview, Holocaust Memorial Museum, tape 3.

29. Wilkomirski, *Fragments*, p. 452.

30. Video interview, Holocaust Memorial Museum, tape 5.

31. Video interview, Holocaust Memorial Museum, tape 5; conversations with Wilkomirski, 22 and 29 April 1999; video interview, Shoah Foundation, tape 3.

32. Video interview, Shoah Foundation, tape 5; Wilkomirski, *Fragments,* p. 453.

33. Wilkomirski, *Fragments*, pp. 459–64.

34. Ibid., p. 464.

35. Ibid., p. 465; video interview, Shoah Foundation, tape 5.

36. Video interview, Holocaust Memorial Museum, tape 5.

37. Video interview, Shoah Foundation, tape 5.

38. Karola ("Mila" in *Fragments*) is this character's true name.

39. Wilkomirski, *Fragments*, p. 467.

40. Ibid., pp. 438–40.

41. Ibid., p. 468; cf. video interview, Shoah Foundation, tape 6.

42. Wilkomirski, *Fragments,* p. 468.

43. Video interview, Shoah Foundation, tape 5.

44. Video interview, Holocaust Memorial Museum, tape 5.

45. Wilkomirski, *Fragments*, pp. 383–84, 468; video interview, Shoah Foundation, tape 5.

46. Video interview, Shoah Foundation, tape 5; Wilkomirski, *Fragments*, pp. 385–90.

47. Wilkomirski, *Fragments*, p. 427; video interview, Holocaust

Memorial Museum, tape 1; video interview, Shoah Foundation, tape 1; conversation with Wilkomirski, 22 April 1999.

48. Wilkomirski in a letter to Thomas Sparr, 4 March 1995 (Suhrkamp files).

49. Conversation with Wilkomirski, 22 April 1999.

50. Video interview, Shoah Foundation, tape 6.

51. Walter Dössekker in letters to Martha and Kurt Dössekker, dated 30 July and 4 August 1946. Emphasis in the original.

52. The fathers of Kurt and Martha Dössekker in a letter to them, 5 April 1951. Emphasis in the original.

53. Wilkomirski in a letter to Sparr, 4 March 1995 (Suhrkamp files).

54. Ibid.; video interview, Shoah Foundation, tape 6.

55. Wilkomirski to Sparr, 4 March 1995 (Suhrkamp files).

56. Wilkomirski, *Fragments*, p. 493.

57. Conversation with Wilkomirski, 22 April 1999; video interview, Holocaust Memorial Museum, tape 1.

58. Video interview, Holocaust Memorial Museum, tape 1.

59. Wilkomirski, *Fragments*, p. 475.

60. Video interview, Shoah Foundation, tape 6.

61. The episode is recounted in Wilkomirski, *Fragments*, pp. 481–84.

62. Ibid., pp. 475–80.

63. Video interview, Holocaust Memorial Museum, tape 1; Wilkomirski, *Fragments*, pp. 473–74.

64. Wilkomirski, *Fragments*, pp. 486–89; interview with Peter Zeindler, "Bei mir war es eine Baracke" (To me it was a barrack), *Zürcher Tages-Anzeiger*, 29 May 1997; video interview, Holocaust Memorial Museum, tape 4.

65. Video interview, Holocaust Memorial Museum, tape 1; Wilkomirski, *Fragments*, p. 495; conversation with Wilkomirski, 22 April 1999; video interview, Holocaust Memorial Museum, tape 1; *Tages-Anzeiger Magazin* (Zurich), 9 Dec. 1995.

66. Conversation with Wilkomirski, 22 April 1999; Wilkomirski to Sparr, 4 March 1995 (Suhrkamp files); video interview, Holocaust Memorial Museum, tape 6; Wilkomirski on film in Esther van Messel, *Fremd geboren* (Born a stranger) (Zurich, Dschoint Ventschr: 1997).

67. Conversation with Wilkomirski, 29 April 1999; van Messel, *Fremd Geboren;* video interview, Holocaust Memorial Museum, tape 1. In speaking

with me, he dated the beginning of his revenge fantasies to age fifteen; in the Holocaust Memorial Museum interview, to age seventeen or eighteen.

68. Video interview, Holocaust Memorial Museum, tape 1; conversation with Wilkomirski, 29 April 1999.

69. Wilkomirski, *Fragments*, p. 490; video interview, Holocaust Memorial Museum, tape 1.

70. Wilkomirski, *Fragments*, pp. 490–92, 494.

71. Video interview, Holocaust Memorial Museum, tape 1.

72. Wilkomirski, *Fragments*, p. 494. This passage is not found in the German edition.

73. Video interview, Holocaust Memorial Museum, tape 1.

74. Ibid. He does not explain which memories he talked about.

75. Video interview, Shoah Foundation, tape 6; conversations with Wilkomirski, 22 April and 19 June 1999.

76. Wilkomirski in a letter to Sparr, 4 March 1995 (Suhrkamp files); conversation with Wilkomirski, 22 April 1999; video interview, Shoah Foundation, tape 6.

77. Video interview, Holocaust Memorial Museum, tape 6; video interview, Shoah Foundation, tape 6.

78. Video interview, Holocaust Memorial Museum, tape 6; conversations with Wilkomirski, 22 April and 15 July 1999; written statement by Wilkomirski, 22 Nov. 1999.

79. Jerzy Kosinski, *The Painted Bird* (Boston: Houghton Mifflin, 1965). German version: *Der bemalte Vogel* (Bern: Scherz-Verlag, 1965).

80. Wilkomirski, *Fragments*, pp. 439–40; several conversations with him between 22 April and 15 July 1999.

81. Interview with Ursula Eichenberger, "Ich versuchte, ein guter Schauspieler zu werden, damit niemand etwas von meiner wahren Identität merkte" (I tried to be a good actor, so that no one would notice anything of my true identity), *Sonntags-Zeitung,* 18 May 1997; Wilkomirski in the television film *Das gute Leben ist nur eine Falle. Ein Besuch bei Binjamin Wilkomirski* (The good life is only a trap. A visit with Binjamin Wilkomirski), directed by Eric Bergkraut, producer (3 sat, 1997); van Messel, *Fremd geboren.*

82. Interview with Zeindler, *Zürcher Tages-Anzeiger,* 29 May 1997.

83. Video interview, Holocaust Memorial Museum, tape 6; interview with Eichenberger, *Sonntags-Zeitung,* 18 May 1997.

84. Van Messel, *Fremd geboren.*

85. Ibid.

86. William G. Niederland, *Folgen der Verfolgung: Das Überlebenden-syndrom Seelenmord* (Consequences of persecution: the survivor syndrome—murder of the soul) (Frankfurt: Suhrkamp, 1980).

87. Passages are marked throughout the book in dark ballpoint pen. I have included only a selection of the marked passages; page numbers are noted in brackets.

88. Conversation with Wilkomirski, 15 July 1999; cf. van Messel, *Fremd geboren.*

89. Conversations with Wilkomirski, 22 and 29 April 1999; video interview, Shoah Foundation, tape 6.

90. Fernando Colla, letter to the Committee of Experts of the Film Department, Federal Office of Culture, Bern, April 1983; Wilkomirski's files; also in Swiss Federal Archives, Bern, BAR: E 3010 (A) 1990/160 vol. 46, dossier 531.3 Binjamin (Fernando Colla).

91. Eberhard Fechner, *Der Prozess* (The trial), part 1: *Anklage* (Indictment), 89 min.; part 2: *Beweisaufnahme* (Presenting the evidence), 92 min.; part 3: *Das Urteil* (The verdict), 88 min.(Norddeutscher Rundfunk, 1984).

92. Video interview, Shoah Foundation, tape 6; Wilkomirski in a letter to Elena Lappin, 20 Dec. 1998 (Liepman files).

93. Wilkomirski showed me the videotape and provided commentary on 14 May 1999.

94. Conversation with Wilkomirski, 22 April 1999; video interview, Holocaust Memorial Museum, tape 5.

95. Van Messel, *Fremd geboren;* video interview, Holocaust Memorial Museum, tape 5.

96. Video interview, Holocaust Memorial Museum, tape 5; conversation with Wilkomirski, 14 May 1999.

97. Conversation with Wilkomirski, 22 April 1999; video interview, Holocaust Memorial Museum, tape 5.

98. Danuta Czech, *Kalendarium der Ereignisse im Konzentrationslager Auschwitz-Birkenau 1939–1945* (Reinbeck bei Hamburg: Rowohlt, 1989), p. 987. Available in English as *Auschwitz Chronicle* (New York: Henry Holt, 1990).

99. Conversations with Wilkomirski, 22 April and 14 May 1999.

100. Interview with Zeindler, *Zürcher Tages-Anzeiger,* 29 May 1997; conversations with Wilkomirski, 22 April and 14 May 1999; video interview, Holocaust Memorial Museum, tape 6.

101. Conversations with Wilkomirski, 22 April and 15 July 1999;

video interview, Holocaust Memorial Museum, tape 6; video interview, Shoah Foundation, tape 6.

102. In a telephone conversation on 23 July 1999, Edward Deskur confirmed to me that he had given Wilkomirski the materials circa 1995 or 1996—i.e., after the visit to Majdanek in 1993.

103. Wilkomirski in a letter to Elena Lappin, 20 Dec. 1998 (Liepman files); video interview, Shoah Foundation, tape 1; conversations with Wilkomirski, 22 April and 14 May 1999. The "cleansing" is documented in a volume of collected materials, *Majdanek 1941–1944,* ed. Tadeus Mencel (Lublin, 1991), p. 503.

104. Conversation with Wilkomirski, 15 July 1999; video interview, Shoah Foundation, tape 3; video interview, Holocaust Memorial Museum, tape 3.

105. Conversation with Wilkomirski, 14 May 1999.

106. Wilkomirski to Lappin, 20 Dec. 1998 (Liepman files); conversations with Wilkomirski, 22 April and 14 May 1999.

107. Conversation with Wilkomirski, 22 April 1999; Binjamin Wilkomirski and Elitsur Bernstein, "Die Identitätsproblematik bei überlebenden Kindern des Holocaust: Ein Konzept zur interdisziplinären Kooperation zwischen Therapeuten und Historikern" (The problem of identity for child survivors of the Holocaust: A concept for interdisciplinary cooperation between therapists and historians), in *Überleben der Shoah—und danach. Spätfolgen der Verfolgung aus wissenschaftlicher Sicht* (Surviving the Shoah—and afterward: Later consequences of persecution from a scientific viewpoint), ed. Alexander Friedmann, Elvira Glück, and David Vyssoki (Vienna: Picus, 1999), pp. 160–72.

108. Wilkomirski has only the Hebrew version (there is also one in English), which I viewed with him. Bernstein later gave me a cassette of the film so I could analyze it in greater detail. My thanks to Paul Russak and Daniela Kuhn for their translations of the Hebrew.

109. Conversation with Wilkomirski, 22 April 1999; video interview, Holocaust Memorial Museum, tape 6; video interview, Shoah Foundation, tape 6. The photograph is also shown in both interviews.

110. Conversation with Wilkomirski, 14 May 1999. According to Balint, the meeting took place on 1 Sept. 1994.

111. Conversation with Wilkomirski, 22 April 1999; video interview, Shoah Foundation, tape 5.

112. In English in the film.

113. Bergkraut, *Das gute Leben ist nur eine Falle.*

114. Written statement sent by Wilkomirski to his publishers, 5 October 1998 (Liepman files).

115. Wilkomirski in a contribution to the *Annual Report for 1994 of the Association for the Advancement of the Chair for German Studies at the University of Ostrava,* pp. 15–16. The association is a joint Swiss-Czech project founded in 1993. Its purpose is to support said chair both by providing financial aid and by promoting interaction among persons and institutions.

116. Ibid., pp. 11–12.

117. Ibid., p. 13; other presentations in 1997: at a conference in Vienna on the topic "Surviving the Shoah—and Afterward," organized by the Jewish ESRA-Foundation; at the fifth Multi-disciplinary Conference, Jerusalem; at a lecture for the Society of Psychoanalysis, Bern. In 1998, Holocaust symposium, University of Notre Dame, South Bend, Ind.; at a lecture for the Psychoanalytic Seminar, Zurich. The paper was first published as Elitsur Bernstein and Binjamin Wilkomirski, "Die Identitätsproblematik bei überlebenden Kindern des Holocaust" (The problem of identity for child survivors of the Holocaust) in *Werkblatt. Zeitschrift für Psychoanalyse und Gesellschaftskritik,* no. 39 (1997), pp. 45–57.

118. Video interview, Holocaust Memorial Museum, tape 6; conversations with Wilkomirski, 22 and 29 April 1999.

119. Wilkomirski and Bernstein, "Identitätsproblematik bei überlebenden Kindern des Holocaust," pp. 169–170.

120. Conversation with Wilkomirski, 22 April 1999; video interview, Holocaust Memorial Museum, tape 6.

121. Video interview, Holocaust Memorial Museum, tape 6 (slightly edited).

122. Video interview, Shoah Foundation, tape 6; conversation with Wilkomirski, 15 July 1999; cf. video interview, Holocaust Memorial Museum, tape 6; Bergkraut, *Das gute Leben ist nur eine Falle.* It has, in fact, been translated into only nine languages.

THE ORIGINS OF *FRAGMENTS*

1. Esther van Messel, *Fremd geboren* (Born a stranger) (Zurich: Dschoint Ventschr., 1997).

2. The following is from a conversation with Verena Piller, 14 May 1999.

3. In his written statement of 22 Nov. 1999, Wilkomirski corrects Piller, stating that he started to talk about his past only once. This was shortly before his marriage to his first wife.

4. Unless otherwise indicated, the following is from a conversation with Elitsur Bernstein, 24 May 1999. In his written statement of 22 Nov. 1999, Wilkomirski says that Piller was warned by only two women.

5. Elena Lappin, "The Man with Two Heads," *Granta,* no. 6 (summer 1999), p. 42; Philip Gourevitch, "The Memory Thief," *The New Yorker* (14 June 1999), pp. 48–68.

6. Conversation with Piller, 14 May 1999.

7. The following is taken from conversations with Bernstein, 24 May and 14 June 1999.

8. Conversations with Piller, 14 May 1999; with Bernstein, 24 May and 5 July 1999; with Wilkomirski, 15 July 1999.

9. The agency represents, e.g., the Polish authors Ryszard Kapuściński, Hanna Krall, and Ida Fink; the Russian Andrei Bitov; Hugo Claus of Belgium; Aleksander Tišma of Serbia; Norman Manea of Romania; Abraham B. Jehoshua of Israel; György Konrád of Hungary; and André Brink of South Africa.

10. As to the history of the agency, cf. Ruth Liepman, *Vielleicht ist Glück nicht nur Zufall* (Maybe luck is no accident) (Munich: Knaur, 1995); Eva Koralnik, "Das richtige Buch zur richtigen Zeit: vom Tun und Lassen der Literaturagenten" (The right book at the right time: what literary agents do and leave undone), in *Buchbranche im Wandel: Zum 150-jährigen Bestehen des Schweizerischen Buchhändler- und Verleger-Verbandes* (The book business in transition: 150 years of the Swiss Booksellers and Publishers Association), ed. Rainer Diederichs, Ulrich Saxer, and Werner Stocker (Zurich: Orell Füssli, 1999), pp. 187–198; as to the biography of Koralnik, cf. her speech in honor of Dr. Harald Feller (who helped her flee in 1944), Bern, 6 Sept. 1999.

11. Unless otherwise indicated, the following is taken from a conversation with Koralnik, 20 July 1999.

12. Sparr in a letter to Wilkomirski, 20 Sept. 1994 (Liepman files); Koralnik had previously received Sparr's oral acceptance of the manuscript.

13. Hanno Helbling in a letter to Dr. Siegfried Unseld of Suhrkamp Verlag, 9 Feb. 1995 (Suhrkamp files).

14. Sparr in a letter to Wilkomirski, 22 Feb. 1995 (Suhrkamp files).

15. Conversation with Bernstein, 5 July 1999.

16. Monika Matta in a letter to Sparr, 26 Feb. 1995 (Suhrkamp files).

17. Bernstein in a letter to Sparr, 2 March 1995 (Sandberg files).

18. Wilkomirski in a letter to Sparr, 2 March 1995 (Suhrkamp files).

19. Wilkomirski in a letter to Sparr, 4 March 1995 (Suhrkamp files).

20. Koralnik in a letter to Unseld, 28 Feb. 1995 (Suhrkamp files).

21. Statement by Löwinger (original in Hebrew), 12 March 1995 (Sandberg files).

22. Conversation with Bernstein, 5 July 1999.

23. Statement by Balint (original in Hebrew), 12 March 1995 (Sandberg files).

24. Conversation with Koralnik, 20 July 1999.

25. "Notarized statement" by Sylwester Marx, 21 March 1995 (Suhrkamp files).

26. Wilkomirski in a letter to Rolf Sandberg, 30 March 1995 (Sandberg files).

27. Sandberg in a letter to Sparr, 10 April 1995 (Sandberg files).

28. Unseld in a letter to Sandberg, 20 April 1995 (Suhrkamp files).

29. Confirmation by Dr. Miroslava Kyselá, Ph.D., Chair of German Studies, University of Ostrava, 21 March 1995 (Suhrkamp files); confirmation by I. Barlatzki, Head of the Testimonies Division, Yad Vashem, 30 April 1995 (Suhrkamp files).

30. Wilkomirski in a letter to Sandberg, 17 May 1995 (Sandberg files).

31. Wilkomirski in a letter to Sandberg, 7 July 1995 (Sandberg files).

32. Wilkomirski, *Fragments*, p. 496.

33. Conversation with Koralnik, 20 July 1999.

A GLOBAL LITERARY EVENT

1. Conversation with Klara Obermüller, 24 June 1999.

2. Klara Obermüller, "Spurensuche im Trümmerfeld der Erinnerung" (Seeking traces in the rubble of memory), *Die Weltwoche,* 31 Aug. 1995.

3. Klara Obermüller, "Einführung zum Buch von Binjamin Wilkomirski 'Bruchstücke' " (Introduction to *Fragments,* a book by Binjamin

Wilkomirski), given as an address at a publishing party, Puppentheater, Zurich (3 Sept. 1995).

4. Conversation with Obermüller, 24 June 1999.

5. Eva-Elisabeth Fischer, "Binjamins Wahrheit: Ein Kind, das die Lager überlebt" (Binjamin's truth: A child who survives the camps), *Süddeutsche Zeitung,* 19 Dec. 1995.

6. Taja Gut, "Mit nichts zu verbinden: Binjamin Wilkomirskis Suche nach seiner Kindheit im KZ" (Beyond connections: Binjamin Wilkomirski's search for his childhood in the concentration camp), *Neue Zürcher Zeitung,* 14 Nov. 1995.

7. Urs Ruckstuhl, "Das gute Leben ist eine Falle" (The good life is a trap), *Wochenzeitung,* 3 May 1996.

8. Jonathan Kozol, "Children of the Camp," *The Nation,* 28 Oct. 1996. This review is also quoted on the cover of the book's American edition.

9. Anne Karpf, "Child of the Shoah" and Katharine Vinder, "Great Art from the Terror," both in *The Guardian,* 11 Feb. 1998.

10. Video interview, Holocaust Memorial Museum, tape 6.

11. Klara Obermüller, "Werkjahre und Ehrengaben im Bereich Literatur 1995" (Grants and awards in literature for 1995), laudatio of the president of the Literary Committee of the City of Zurich.

12. Gary Mokotoff in a letter to Arthur Kurzweil, 6 Dec. 1996; cf. Elena Lappin, "The Man with Two Heads," *Granta,* no. 66 (summer 1999), p. 49.

13. Jean-François Forges, *Éduquer contre Auschwitz: Histoire et mémoire* (Educating against Auschwitz: History and memory) (Paris: ESF, 1997), cf. pp. 34–35.

14. Conversation with Wilkomirski, 29 April 1999; *Frankfurter Allgemeine Zeitung,* 28 Jan. 1996; S.H. in a letter to Wilkomirski, undated, early 1996.

15. Letter from I.H. to Wilkomirski, 15 July 1997; student reactions are likewise evident from letters addressed to Wilkomirski.

16. Daniel Goldhagen is quoted on the back jacket copy of the American edition of *Fragments.* The remarks by Wolfgang Benz and James Edward Young are in Jörg Lau, "Ein fast perfekter Schmerz" (An almost perfect pain), *Die Zeit,* 17 Sept. 1998.

17. Conversation with Wilkomirski, 29 April 1999; Wilkomirski, "Answer to some aspects of CBS's 60 *Minutes.*"

18. Jörg Lau, "Ein fast perfekter Schmerz"; Mark Pendergrast, "Recovered Memories and the Holocaust," as of 14 Jan. 1999, at www.stopbadtherapy.com/experts/fragments/fragments.html; Langer in an e-mail to me, 21 Dec. 1999 (including his term "powerful novel").

19. Video interview, United States Holocaust Memorial Museum, Washington, D.C.; video interview, Yad Vashem (25 April 1995); video interview, Survivors of the Shoah, Visual History Foundation; Esther van Messel, *Fremd geboren* (Born a stranger) (Zurich: Dschoint Ventschr., 1997); Eric Bergkraut, director, *Das gute Leben ist nur eine Falle* (The good life is only a trap) (3 sat, 1997).

20. E.C. of L., 7 Dec. 1997.

21. H. and E.G. of A., 28 Sept. 1995; T.W. of S., 21 May 1998.

22. B.H. of L., 2 April 1997.

23. These sales figures have been rounded off and refer to various sales periods (the low sales of the last few months of 1999 are missing, in part). Schocken (U.S.) and Picador (England): April 1997 to March 1999; Mondadori (Italy): April to December 1998; Suhrkamp (Germany): Aug. 1995 to Nov. 1999; Calmann-Lévy (France): Jan. to Dec. 1997; Ohtsuki Shoten (Japan): up to Dec. 1998, 3,300 copies sold; Companhia das Letras (Brazil): Feb. 1998 to Dec. 1999, 1,500 copies; Miskal-Yediot-Aharonot (Israel): July 1997 to Dec. 1998, 1,500 copies; Bert Bakker (Netherlands): April 1996 to Dec. 1998, 500 copies; Gyldendal Norsk (Norway): April 1997 to Dec. 1997, 400 copies; Forum (Denmark): Oct. 1996 to Dec. 1998, 300 copies. There were two other contracts with a South American publisher for a Spanish translation and with a publisher in Sweden, but those editions never came out. Wilkomirski received standard author's royalties, an average of 8% of the retail price; the literary agency in turn received between 10% and 15% of the author's income. Wilkomirski received in total a sum of 110,000 U.S. dollars (over five years, from all the different language editions, including advances); the Liepman A.G. received 19,000 U.S. dollars in total commissions. For a book to be put on a bestseller list in Germany, it must sell about 30,000 to 40,000 copies within a few months; in the U.S., 250,000 to 300,000. All data are taken from the bookkeeping records of Liepman AG.

24. Conversation with Wilkomirski, 15 July 1999; cf. video interview, Holocaust Memorial Museum, tape 6.

25. Bergkraut, *Das gute Leben ist nur eine Falle.*

26. Van Messel, *Fremd geboren;* Miriam: cf. video interview, Holocaust Memorial Museum, tape 6.

27. K.M. in a letter to H., 27 Jan. 1998; the documented name and birthplace of this woman are known to me, though she prefers to remain anonymous (italics in the original); interview with K.M. by Wolf Gebhardt, 14 April 1999; speech by Wilkomirski at the awarding of the ORTHO Prize, April 1999.

28. K.M. in a letter to H., 27 Jan. 1998 (italics in the original); interview with K.M. by Wolf Gebhardt, 14 April 1999, and by me, 21 October 1999.

29. Conversation with Wilkomirski, 29 April 1999.

30. Naomi Pfefferman, "Memories of a Holocaust Childhood," *Jewish Journal,* 24 April 1998; Bob Passantino and Gretchen Passantino, "Lauren Stratford: From Satanic Ritual Abuse to Jewish Holocaust," *Cornerstone,* 28, no. 117 (Oct. 1999): 12–18.

31. Lauren (the signature here is not "Laura") Grabowski in a letter to Mr. and Mrs. Benjamin, 15 July 1997.

32. Passantino/Passantino, "Lauren Stratford: From Satanic Ritual Abuse to Jewish Holocaust"; Pfefferman, "Memories of a Holocaust Childhood"; Wilkomirski in a letter to Sandberg, 6 Jan. 1999.

33. Wilkomirski in a letter to Sandberg, 6 Jan. 1999; conversation with Wilkomirski, 29 April 1999.

34. Conversation with Leon Stabinsky, 30 Sept. 1999; the following is taken from film footage provided by the BBC, which originally planned a film on child survivors with Wilkomirski as its central figure. The director was Christopher Olgiati; the research was done chiefly by Wolf Gebhardt, who, along with Sue Summer, is listed as producer. A few months later, in the wake of Daniel Ganzfried's revelations, the film took a totally different direction; it was broadcast by the BBC on 3 Nov. 1999, under the title *Child of the Death Camps: Truth & Lies.*

35. Pfefferman, "Memories of a Holocaust Childhood."

THE PLUNGE INTO THE ABYSS —
AUTOBIOGRAPHY OR FAKE?

1. Daniel Ganzfried, "Die geliehene Holocaust-Biographie" (The borrowed Holocaust biography), *Die Weltwoche,* 27 Aug. 1998.

2. Conversation with Verena Piller, 14 May 1999.

3. Wilkomirski in an interview with Peer Teuwsen, "Niemand muss mir Glauben schenken" (Nobody has to believe me), *Tages-Anzeiger,* 31 Aug. 1998; Teuwsen had previously offered a portrait of Wilkomirski, "Ein langer Weg" (A long road), *Tages-Anzeiger,* 9 Dec. 1995.

4. Thomas Sparr quoted in Konrad Tobler, "Es steht im Nachwort" (It's in the afterword), *Berner Zeitung,* 1 Sept. 1998; Daniel Ganzfried, "Fakten gegen Erinnerung" (Facts vs. memory), *Die Weltwoche,* 3 Sept. 1998.

5. Suhrkamp press release, 7 Sept. 1998, signed by Siegfried Unseld.

6. The inaccurate implication that Balint was an employee of Yad Vashem may have been based on a phrase in a letter from Bernstein to Sparr, dated 2 March 1995: "Frau Balint, a historian who works at Yad Vashem . . ." (Suhrkamp files). In two letters to Sandberg, dated 23 and 29 March 1995, Wilkomirski also represents her as "Lea Balint of Yad Vashem"; the files do not clearly indicate whether he ever referred to her in this fashion to Suhrkamp. In her own writings, Frau Balint describes herself correctly. In his written statement from 22 Nov. 1999 Wilkomirski claims that he merely pointed out that Lea Balint had made intensive use of the archives at Yad Vashem. For Kurek-Lesik's doctorate and research, cf. Sylwester Marx's "notarized" statement of 21 March 1995, and Wilkomirski in a letter to Sparr, 20 March 1995 (both Suhrkamp files), as well as a personal communication to me from Tomasz Kranz, Research Department, Majdanek Concentration Camp, 12 July 1999. The statement of Yad Vashem: I. Barlatzki, Head of the Testimonies Division, in a letter to Wilkomirski, 30 April 1995 (Suhrkamp files); Yehuda Bauer in a letter to me, 30 June 1999.

7. Lea Balint in her statement of 4 Sept. 1998.

8. Laura Grabowski in an e-mail to Lea Balint, 14 Nov. 1998.

9. Jörg Lau, "Ein fast perfekter Schmerz" (An almost perfect pain), *Die Zeit,* 17 Sept. 1998.

10. Raul Hilberg's statements were disseminated by the DPA and SDA news agencies and picked up by the media in that form.

11. Peter Bollag, "Unnötige Debatte" (Unnecessary debate), *Israelitisches Wochenblatt,* 3 Sept. 1998; Gisela Blau, "Mehr als nur eine Wahrheit?" (More than just one truth?), *Jüdische Rundschau Maccabi,* 3 Sept. 1998.

12. Eric Bergkraut, "Der anderen Hypothese eine Chance" (A chance for the other hypothesis), *Die Weltwoche,* 10 Sept. 1998.

13. Samuel Althof in a letter to Blake Eskin, 13 Dec. 1998; Samuel Althof and Irene Hubermann in a letter to the *Aargauer Zeitung,* 10 Sept. 1998; Althof and Hubermann in a letter to the *Basler Zeitung,* 22 Sept. 1998, and to the *Frankfurter Rundschau,* 17 Sept. 1998.

14. Wilkomirski's petition: press release by Suhrkamp Verlag, 16 Sept. 1998.

15. M.M. in a letter to Wilkomirski, 1 Sept. 1998; commission's refusal: cf. Jacques Picard, "Recht haben allein genügt nicht" (Being right isn't enough), *Zürcher Tages-Anzeiger,* 7 Oct. 1998, and J.L., "Wilkomirski," *Frankfurter Allgemeine,* 17 Sept. 1998.

16. Conversation with Max and Edeltraut Grosjean, 6 May 1999.

17. Conversation with Eva Koralnik, 20 July 1999.

18. Conversations with Eva Koralnik, 20 July and 25 Oct. 1999; as to the agency's attempt to clarify matters by a DNA test, there is also an undated note by Ruth Weibel of the Liepman Agency concerning an inquiry made to the Institute for Forensic Medicine, University of Zurich, on 15 Sept. 1998. As to Sandberg's attempts at clarification, independent of the Liepman Agency: Sandberg in a letter to the Institute for Forensic Medicine, 1 March 1999; Walter Bär in a letter to Sandberg, 2 March 1999; Sandberg in a letter to Wilkomirski, 11 April 1999. As to the same suggestion by the Biel Guardianship Authorities: minutes of "Conference with Herr Bruno Dössekker, born 12 Feb. 1941, at the Biel Guardianship Authorities, 10 December 1998." On 1 Nov. 1998, Annie Singer, a friend of Wilkomirski's from his youth, had suggested the possibility of a DNA test in a letter to *Die Weltwoche,* noting also that Wilkomirski's "attitude toward such a test would be very illuminating." Daniel Ganzfried repeated the suggestion in a letter to the *Neue Zürcher Zeitung,* 7–8 Nov. 1998.

19. Daniel Ganzfried, "Bruchstücke und Scherbenhaufen" (Fragments and debris), *Die Weltwoche,* 24 Sept. 1998; Koralnik in a letter to Wilkomirski, 2 Oct. 1998 (Liepman files).

20. Wilkomirski in a written statement sent to his publishers, 5 Oct. 1998 (Liepman files).

21. Conversation with Wilkomirski, 29 April 1999.

22. J.M. in a letter to Wilkomirski, 25 Oct. 1998; A.F. in a letter to Wilkomirski, 15 Nov. 1998 (capitals in the original); H.N. in a letter to Wilkomirski, 17 April 1999.

23. Guta Tyrangiel Benezra, *Mémoire bariolée Poetic paintings Glosy przeszlosci* (Ottawa: Legas, 1995).

24. Guta Benezra in a letter to the Hidden Child Association, New York, Federation of Children of the Holocaust, et al., attached in an e-mail to Wilkomirski, 4 Dec. 1998. Wilkomirski circulated Benezra's letters widely. As to her intervention with the Holocaust Museum and her request to Langer, Guta Benezra in an e-mail to Wilkomirski, 29 Nov. 1998; Langer in an e-mail to me, 21 Dec. 1999.

25. Conversation with Wilkomirski, 29 April 1999; Wilkomirski in a letter to Carol Brown Janeway, 25 Nov. 1998 (in which he describes the Contact Point as "my main help in Europe"); Samuel Althof in e-mails to Wilkomirski, 6 Dec. and 8 Dec. 1998 (capitals in the original).

26. Grabowski in an e-mail to Balint, 14 Nov. 1998; Grabowski in an e-mail to Wilkomirski, 5 January 1999.

27. Daniel Ganzfried, *Der Absender* (The sender of the letter) (Zurich: Rotpunktverlag, 1995; paperback edition, Frankfurt: Fischer Verlag, 1998).

28. Conversation with Daniel Ganzfried, 4 Sept. 1999. Unless otherwise indicated, the following is taken from that conversation. I have supplemented the excerpts with material from an interview Ganzfried gave to Daniela Kuhn, "Vor Auschwitz zählen keine Fakten mehr" (In the face of Auschwitz, facts don't count), *Israelitisches Wochenblatt,* 11 Sept. 1998.

29. Pro Helvetia's support is mentioned in the French edition.

30. Wilkomirski in a letter to Michael Guggenheimer, 24 June 1998; Rolf Sandberg in a letter to Ganzfried, 13 July 1998; Guggenheimer in a letter to Ganzfried, 20 Aug. 1998.

31. Conversation with Klara Obermüller, 24 June 1999.

32. Robert Dunki, archivist of the Zurich Municipal Archives, in a letter to Daniel Ganzfried, 19 Nov. 1998. In the same letter, Dunki notes that a foster child "is to be 'brought into contact' with its foster parents months before joining them.' . . . The first date known to the Zurich Municipal Archives is 7 June 1945." My later investigation has revealed that in the Biel authorities' records this date is stamped on a file that the authorities (the so-called Inquiry Service) opened on the Dössekkers after they first expressed an interest in adopting a child. The adoption of a particular child was not at issue at the time. The name Bruno Grosjean appears in that context for the first time on 2 July 1945.

33. Wilkomirski, "Answer to Some Aspects of CBS 60 *Minutes*" (undated copy; capitals in the original).

34. Minutes of "Conference with Herr Bruno Dössekker, born 12 Feb. 1941, at the Biel Guardianship Authorities, 10 December 1998." "Declaration of the Biel Guardianship Authorities," a statement released to the press on 8 Feb. 1999 by the Biel Guardianship Authorities, as per previous agreement with Wilkomirski's lawyer, Rolf Sandberg.

35. Elena Lappin, "The Man with Two Heads," *Granta,* no. 66 (Summer 1999), pp. 7–65.

36. Philip Gourevitch, "The Memory Thief," *The New Yorker,* 14 June 1999, pp. 48–68. His book on Rwanda is entitled *We Wish to Inform You That Tomorrow We Will Be Killed with Our Families* (New York: Farrar, Straus & Giroux, 1998).

37. Lea Balint in a letter to *The New Yorker* (Mrs. Josselin Simpson), 10 June 1999, first draft of a translation from the Hebrew into English. The date given in her letter is probably wrong, because the text is her reaction to an article which was not published until 14 June.

38. Lea Balint, written statement, 4 Sept. 1998 (Suhrkamp files). The text mistakenly says that Balint has been part of Children Without Identity since 1993; the English version, from 13 Nov. 1998 (Liepman files), gives the correct year, 1991.

39. Conversation with Balint (in the original English) in Zurich, 13 July 1999.

40. Balint in an e-mail to me, 28 July 1999.

41. ORTHO announcement of event, undated (Liepman files).

42. Gale Siegel, executive director of ORTHO, in a letter to Wilkomirski, 24 Feb. 1999; Gourevitch, "The Memory Thief," p. 65; conversation with Bernstein, 14 June 1999.

43. Harvey Peskin in a letter to Carol Brown Janeway, 9 March 1999. Peskin, "Holocaust Denial: A Sequel. The Case of Benjamin Wilkomirski's *Fragments*," *The Nation*, 19 April 1999. For a comparable argumentation, cf. Sarah Traister-Moskovitz, "Account of a Child Survivor: Fact or Fiction?—Does It Really Make a Difference?" *Martyrdom and Resistance,* International Society for Yad Vashem, May–June 1999.

44. Langer in e-mails to me, 21 and 24 Dec. 1999. Langer had written about Kosinski as early as 1975, though without addressing doubts that would arise later. Lawrence L. Langer, *The Holocaust and the Literary Imagination* (New Haven and London: Yale University Press, 1975). Cf. Lawrence L. Langer, *Holocaust Testimonies: The Ruins of Memory* (New Haven: Yale University Press, 1991).

45. Blake Eskin, "Wilkomirski Defends Holocaust Memoir," *Forward,* 16 April 1999.

46. The following is taken from the manuscript of Wilkomirski's speech, ORTHO, Arlington, Va., April 1999.

47. Eskin, "Wilkomirski Defends Holocaust Memoir."

48. Cf. Cathy Caruth, ed., *Trauma. Explorations in Memory* (Baltimore: Johns Hopkins University Press, 1995), introduction pp. 3–12; Bessel A. van der Kolk and Onno van der Hart, "The Intrusive Past: The Flexibility of Memory and the Engraving of Trauma," in ibid., pp. 158–82.

TRACKING DOWN THE TRUTH—
THE HISTORICAL RESEARCH

1. Vestermanis in a letter to me, 29 May 1999. A little later, Elena Lappin's article appeared, where some of Vestermanis's arguments were presented for the first time. Lappin, "The Man with Two Heads," *Granta,* no. 66 (Summer 1999), p. 52. Unless otherwise indicated, the following is from Vestermanis's letter.

2. Vestermanis in a letter to me, 29 May 1999 (emphasis in the original). Lipke's rescue operations are documented in David Silberman, "Jan Lipke: An Unusual Man" in *Muted Voices: Jewish Survivors of Latvia Remember,* ed. Gertrude Schneider (New York: Philosophical Library, 1987), pp. 87–111; also in Marģers Vestermanis, "Retter im Lande der Handlanger: Zur Geschichte der Hilfe für Juden in Lettland während der Endlösung" (Saviors in the land of the henchmen: On the history of help provided to Jews in Latvia during the Final Solution), in *Solidarität und Hilfe für Juden während der NS-Zeit, Regionalstudien 2, Ukraine, Frankreich, Böhmen und Mähren, Österreich, Lettland, Litauen, Estland* (Solidarity and help for Jews during the Nazi period, regional studies 2, Ukraine, France, Bohemia and Moravia, Austria, Latvia, Lithuania, Estonia), ed. Wolfgang Benz and Juliane Wetzel (Berlin: Metropol, 1996), pp. 231–72, 263, 269–71. Bernstein made a tape recording of the August 1994 trip, summarizing the day's experiences, including notes on people with whom they had spoken. He mentions Vestermanis's statement about how Jews were transported by boat to the concentration camp at Stutthof in 1944; he did not record anything about Lipke, perhaps because he (correctly) saw no connection between him and

Wilkomirski's flight. A transcript prepared by Bernstein of his tape recording is in my possession.

3. Perhaps Wilkomirski confused the date of the ghetto liquidation with 25 Oct. 1941, when the ghetto was closed off from the rest of the city. That is the date of the first snowfall, as one can read in the literature. Cf. Bernhard Press, *Judenmord in Lettland, 1941–1945* (Murder of the Jews in Latvia) (Berlin: Metropol, 1992), p. 76.

4. In his statement of 22 Nov. 1999, Wilkomirski denies having spoken of his childhood memories of the library with the clock. In our conversation of 22 April 1999, however, he explicitly mentions that he had given Bernstein this description *before* his trip to Riga. In his statement, Wilkomirski also repudiates the criticism that the term "Latvian militia" was not in use at the time. According to Wilkomirski, the Russian word from which the term "militia" is derived was familiar at the time, since Latvia had been Russian up to the October revolution. Hilberg and Vestermanis are not, however, concerned with the term militia as such, but with the fact that, contrary to Wilkomirski's account, the call Latvian militia would not have been used. In addition, Wilkomirski says that he could not have known the nationality, thereby implicitly correcting his own memory and bearing his critics out.

5. The entry is found in a "House Book" under the address Brivibas Street 125; copies of the original documents from the Riga state archives, 10 Sept. 1999.

6. Wilkomirski in an interview with Ursula Eichenberger, *Sonntags-Zeitung,* 18 May 1997.

7. Conversation with Wilkomirski, 29 April 1999.

8. Conversation with Verena Piller, 14 May 1999.

9. Conversation with Tomasz Kranz, 12 July 1999; Zofia Murawska, who has done research on children and the sanitary conditions at the camp, also knows nothing about a plague of rats. As to Jankl's advice about rats, cf. Wilkomirski, *Fragments*, p. 406. In his statement from 22 Nov. 1999, Wilkomirski claims he "never spoke of a *plague* of rats." In his video interviews for the Shoah Foundation and the Holocaust Museum in Washington, however, he speaks repeatedly of the many rats, likewise in *Fragments.* This can be compared with Verena Piller's quoted statement. Wilkomirski denies localizing the rats in the Majdanek concentration camp, despite his story involving Jankl, who allegedly gave him tips in that camp for keeping these vermin at bay.

10. As to Fischer and König, M.A. Jerzy Wróblewski, director of the State Museum of Auschwitz, in a letter to me 29 July 1999. Conversation with Annette Dössekker, 26 July 1999; in his statement of 22 Nov. 1999, Wilkomirski claims that the bump was the result of someone striking his son on the head, but names no names.

11. Elena Lappin, in researching her article "The Man with Two Heads," found no former residents of these homes who could confirm Wilkomirski's account or remember him personally. She likewise has plausible doubts as to Löwinger's testimony. Since she does not find herself in a position to reveal her sources to me, I have researched some of the factual background in greater detail myself.

12. Conversation with Balint, 13 July 1999.

13. Maria Hochberg-Mariańska and Noe Grüss, eds., *The Children Accuse* (London: Vallentine Mitchell, 1996), pp. xxxii–xxxiii. The Jewish Historical Commission, Kraków, published the book in Polish in 1946.

14. Ibid., p. xxv; Pelegia [Hochberg-]Mariańska, "Children in Hell," 8 May 1945 (typescript translated for my use from the Polish by Maggi Król).

15. Pelagia [Hochberg-] Mariańska, "Children in Hell"; Hochberg-Mariańska, *The Children Accuse,* p. xxii.

16. Conversation with Misia Leibel, 7 July 1999; material from the German minutes of a conversation in Polish that I commissioned Maggi Król to have with her, 29 June 1999. Unless otherwise indicated, the following is taken from Leibel's statements in these conversations.

17. Maria [Hochberg-] Mariańska in letters to the Central Department of Child Supervision in Warsaw (*Do Centralnego Wydzialu Opieki nad Dzieckiem, przy C.K.Z.P. Warszawa*), 3 and 5 Aug. 1946; letter with list of orphans, dated 3 Aug. 1946; there is no indication that the list might be incomplete. (All documents in Polish, copies in my possession.) [Hochberg-] Mariańska regularly visited her niece, who lived in the home on Augustiańska Street; conversation with Karola, 10 Sept. 1999. In his statement from 22 November 1999 Wilkomirski offers an explanation of why his name does not appear on any list. A historian at Yad Vashem and former inmate of the home on the Dluga (Wilkomirski names him) explained that only a small number of the surviving children are listed. In my view, even the existence of incomplete lists does not explain the remarkable circumstance that there are no written traces

whatsoever of the young Wilkomirski. This is next to impossible for Jewish child survivors. Wilkomirski also contests the recorded date of the move from the Dluga to the Augustianska in August 1946. According to him, older children had already gone to the new place in January 1946 to help renovate the building. He provides no proof and in any case he himself would not have been among these older children.

18. Conversation with Balint, 13 July 1999.

19. Conversation with Wilkomirski, 14 May 1999. According to Balint, the meeting took place on 1 Sept. 1994.

20. Conversations with Nuna and Salek Elbert (who remains in the background, with Nuna translating for him), 8 July 1999; with Emanuel Elbinger, 5 and 18 July 1999; with P. Ch., 5 July 1999; with Karola, 18 Aug. 1999.

21. Conversation with Nuna and Salek Elbert, 8 July 1999.

22. Lappin, "The Man with Two Heads," p. 110; Wilkomirski, *Fragments*, p. 467.

23. Löwinger in his statement, 12 March 1995 (Suhrkamp files). Conversation with Löwinger, 22 June 1999.

24. Conversation with Vered Berman, 22 June 1999. Berman says the scene can be viewed in the rushes of the film. In my conversation with Nuna and Salek Elbert, 8 July 1999, they confirmed the episode by volunteering this information on their own. Wilkomirski maintains, in his statement from 22 November 1999, that my presentation is "false." He had looked at the photos with Bernstein and Löwinger before the arrival of the television crew. Berman, the director, had then replayed the scene, so that it was no longer "authentic." Nevertheless, the rushes and the accounts of witnesses establish the fact that Wilkomirski identified Karola in the photos by a name that was unknown to the former inmates of the Augustianska. It would have been even stranger if he had done this in a reconstructed scene.

25. Conversation with Bernstein, 24 May 1999.

26. Wilkomirski, *Fragments*, p. 468; video interview, Shoah Foundation, tape 5; video interview, Holocaust Memorial Museum, tape 5; conversation with Bernstein, 14 June 1999; Wilkomirski in his written statement, 22 Nov. 1999.

27. Conversation with Ema Haber, a former attendant of home on Miodowa Street, 10 Sept. 1999; Wilkomirski in his written statement, 22 Nov. 1999.

28. Anna Cichopek, "Z dziejów powojennego antysemityzmu—pogrom w Krakowie 11. 08. 1945" (Unpublished master's thesis, Faculty of History, Jagiellonian University, Kraków, 1998), pp. 50 ff.

29. Rafal Żebrowksi and Zofia Borzymińska, PO-LIN, Kultura Żydów Polskich w XX wieku (Zarys) (Warsaw: Amarant, 1993), pp. 302–3. My thanks to Dr. J. L. Stein for this information.

30. At 26 Miodowa Street; cf. Cichopek, "Z dziejów powojennego antysemityzmu—pogrom w Krakowie 11. 08. 1945"; Wilkomirski, Fragments, pp. 464–65.

31. Conversation with Balint, 13 July 1999. In the video interview with the Shoah Foundation, tape 5, the sequence of his residences is: Miodowa, Długa, Augustiańska, from where Frau Grosz then rescues him from the pogrom. Both in the video interview with the Holocaust Museum, tape 5, and in our conversation of 22 April 1999, he witnesses the pogrom on Długa Street. Of the three streets, the Miodowa is the only one I can locate inside the Jewish quarter, where the pogrom occurred, whereas Wilkomirski, in his statement from 22 November 1999, claims that Augustianska Street is situated "in and on the fringe of the Kazimierz district, Dluga Street very close to it" (emphasis in the original).

32. "Misia and Olga . . . who used to take us for walks," in Wilkomirski, Fragments, p. 468. In his statement from 22 November 1999 Wilkomirski writes "Here too, Mächler assumes that I, a child, should have been able to clearly recognize the 'hierarchy' among the adults!!!!! Olga was 14 years old, he says. From my perspective, a 14-year old was a grown woman, who accompanied me on a walk which I remember." How then was Wilkomirski able to make the distinction with Karola, who was older than Olga, and to see her as an older playmate?

33. Leibel in a letter to me, 18 July 1999 (translated from the Polish by Maggi Król).

34. The following is taken from the Annual Report of the Swiss Red Cross (SRK) for 1945 (Documentation Office of the SRK, Bern), pp. 86–95.

35. As to the total number of children arriving illegally: cf. Guido Koller, "Entscheidung über Leben und Tod: Die behördliche Praxis in der schweizerischen Flüchtlingspolitik während des Zweiten Weltkrieges" (Life-and-death decisions: official practice in Swiss refugee policy during World War II), in Die Schweiz und die Flüchtlinge (Switzerland

and the Refugees) (Bern: Paul Haupt, 1996), pp. 17–106, 88; as to children's trains and illegal refugee assistance, Antonia Schmidlin, *Eine andere Schweiz, Helferinnen, Kriegskinder und humanitäre Politik 1933–1942* (Another Switzerland, helpers, children of war, and humanitarian policy) (Zurich: Chronos 1999), esp. chaps. 5–7; Jacque Picard, *Die Schweiz und die Juden 1933–1945* (Switzerland and the Jews 1933–1945) (Zurich: Chronos, 1994), pp. 435–40.

36. Henrich Rothmund in a letter to Federal Councilor J. Baumann, chief of the Federal Justice and Police Department, 15 Sept. 1938 (Swiss Federal Archives, Bern, BAR E 4800 (A) 1, box 1).

37. Rothmund to Minister Rüegger, 14 May 1947 (BAR 4800 [A] 1, box 6); as to continuation of anti-Semitic policies, cf. Stefan Maechler, "Kampf gegen das Chaos, die antisemitische Bevölkerungspolitik der eidgenössischen Fremdenpolizei und Polizeiabteilung 1917–1954" (Struggle against chaos, the anti-Semitic population policy of the Federal Police for Foreigners and Police Division 1917–1954), in Aram Mattioli, ed., *Antisemitismus in der Schweiz 1848–1960* (Anti-Semitism in Switzerland 1848–1960) (Zurich: Orell Füssli, 1998), pp. 357–421.

38. As to the journal kept by the Basel police: cf. Jean-Claude Wacker, Humaner als Bern! Schweizer und Basler Asylpraxis gegenüber den jüdischen Flüchtlingen von 1933 bis 1943 im Vergleich (More humane than Bern! A comparison of asylum practices in Basel and Switzerland in dealing with Jewish refugees from 1933 to 1943) (Basel: Kommissionsverlag Friedrich Reinhardt, 1992), pp. 22–23. The journal and the files of the canton Fremdenpolizei (Police for Foreigners) are in the State Archives, Basel. My thanks to the deputy state archivist, Dr. Ulrich Barth, for his research. My thanks to Frau Sabina Tresise and Frau Hélène Marbarcher of the Swiss Red Cross, Bern, for research in the files of the Swiss Red Cross, Aid to Children (which today may be found in the Swiss Federal Archives under the designation J II. 15).

39. Data bank for files of the Federal Police Department in the fields: place of residence, sojourn, refugees (N-series). My thanks to Guido Koller of the Swiss Federal Archives, Bern, for this search.

40. Warsaw: Légation suisse à Varsovie (1945–51), BAR: E 2200; Police Department, support provided to returning Swiss citizens, BAR: E 4264 1984/172; tracking center for Swiss citizens abroad, BAR: E 4265; Welfare service for Swiss citizens abroad, BAR: E 7179. My

thanks to Frau Christine Lauener of the Swiss Federal Archives, Bern, for this painstaking search.

41. Unless otherwise indicated, the following is taken from conversations with Frau Hilb, 22 July and 26 August 1999. In his statement from 22 November 1999, Wilkomirski comments that Hilb did not object to his story before the Ganzfried article. In his view, witnesses like her are negatively influenced by reports in the media, whereas I presented their testimony as "the absolute truth," which he found questionable. This example, he further admonishes, shows the "absurdity" of treating "an early childhood memory" as the "considered, expert report of an adult witness." He could not remember every detail nor had he understood the things that happened at the time. But this is just what people reproached him with, also Hilb in this case. Wilkomirski says that the first page of his book clearly emphasizes that he is merely recording in writing "how a child's memory preserves traumatic experiences, without the ordering logic of grown ups." For this very reason he did not artificially clarify the "contradictory nature of memories" with the help of his present knowledge. The issue at stake in this chapter is not contradictory representation, but the historic impossibility of an alleged entry into Switzerland.

42. Hilb later sent me an original index card used by the Red Cross, of the sort that every foreign representative had to fill out for each vacation child before he or she could be included in a transport. A space is reserved for a photograph, and there are preprinted entries for personal information, the address of the intended foster family, as well as the notation that such an individual permission corresponds both to information on a complete list of all children and to a collective visa. In order to enter Switzerland illegally, a person would have had to supply all such data by using falsified identity papers. Hilb in a letter to me, 27 Aug. 1999.

43. Conversation with Balint, 13 July 1999.

44. The charge of assassination of Jewish children was made by J. Sternbuch in a letter dated 14 Nov. 1945 to the VSJF, or Verband Schweizerischer Jüdischer Fürsorgen (Jewish Refugee Committee). Sternbuch was a member of the SHJEFS, Schweizerischer Hilfsverein für jüdische Flüchtlinge im Ausland (Alliance of Swiss relief for Jewish refugees abroad). The VSJF was the most important Jewish relief agency

and was closely allied with the SIG, the Swiss Federation of Jewish Communities. I found this document in 1990 in the cellar of the VSJF in Zurich, as part of the board of directors' minutes of 1944–47 (it has presumably now been transferred to the Archives of Contemporary History of the ETH, Zurich). Wilkomirski used the phrase "ideology of despair" in his statement to his publishers, 5 Oct. 1998. In his statement of 22 November 1999, Wilkomirski writes that "immediately after the war there were many Jewish intellectuals who held such views." He furnishes no evidence, especially none relating to Switzerland in the post-war period. For the controversy about children in Switzerland, cf. Picard, *Die Schweiz und die Juden,* pp. 444–51; for a sympathetic view of the Orthodox position, cf. Joseph Friedenson and David Kranzler, *Heroine of Rescue: The Incredible Story of Recha Sternbuch, Who Saved Thousands from the Holocaust* (New York: Mesorah Publications, 1984), pp. 207–9. In his statement from 22 November 1999, Wilkomirski claims that "until the end of the 40s, *Jewish children* and young people without established family ties were *forbidden* to enter Switzerland. If at all, then entry was only possible illegally. Relief organizations arranging the transport of holiday children had to guarantee that there were *no Jewish children* among them!!!!!" (emphasis in the original). Wilkomirski refers to the historian Jacques Picard in his statement. However, the latter merely describes in his work how Jewish holiday children were not welcome up until 1943. He has not investigated the later period which is relevant here, since Wilkomirski claims to have entered Switzerland after the end of the war. Finally, Wilkomirski mentions a further argument in support of his narrative: "A former member of a small organization which attempted to smuggle children out of Eastern Europe in the years 1945 to 1948 explained why Switzerland and Holland were the most desirable, albeit illegal destinations for children who could not be taken to Israel (Palestine), namely because they provided the best medical care for the children. That was the only consideration which counted—the children had to survive at all costs, no matter how or as what." Wilkomirski gives neither the name of the organization, nor that of his informant, so that I cannot verify his statement.

45. Hilb in two letters to me dated 23 July 1999. The quotation is taken from Nettie Sutro, *Jugend auf der Flucht 1933–1948. 15 Jahre im Spiegel des Schweizer Hilfswerkes für Emigrantenkinder* (Youth on the run:

Fifteen years in the mirror of the Swiss Committee for Emigrated Children) (Zurich: 1952), pp. 115–16.

46. Conversation with Wilkomirski and Eva Koralnik, 28 Feb. 1999; Wilkomirski in a letter to Elena Lappin, 20 Dec. 1998. Siegfried was the Swiss Red Cross's delegate to the SHEK; information provided by Liselotte Hilb, 3 Sept. 1999.

47. Cf. Walter Leimgruber, Thomas Meier, and Roger Sablonier, *Das Hilfswerk für die Kinder der Landstrasse: Historische Studie aufgrund der Akten der Stiftung Pro Juventute im Schweizerischen Bundesarchiv* (The relief agency for children of the road: Historical study based on the files of the foundation Pro Juventute in the Swiss Federal Archives) (Swiss Federal Archives, Dossier 9, Bern: 1998).

48. Swiss Federal Archives, electronic data bank, "Children of the Road."

49. Conversation with Bruno Berti, 23 April 1999. In his statement from 22 November 1999, Wilkomirski questions Berti's comments on principle. He says that when he was introduced to Berti, he himself had long been attending school and saw him on only about five occasions up until 1963. Berti knew him only "by hearsay, through his later wife, who clearly disliked me." Berti denied these allegations to me. Wilkomirski is indignant that I should use remarks of Berti's that are critical of him, on the grounds that these are "out of place in a historical investigation." He continues: "The aim here, as in countless other instances in this report, is clear: to 'sensationalize' the story in the style of the tabloid press and to display my personality in the worst possible, defamatory light." Wilkomirski asks further how Berti could have seen him as early as December 1945. For even Kurt Dössekker's parents complained in the summer of 1946 that they had not been informed about accepting a child. Their complaint also shows, according to Wilkomirski, that the photos of himself and relatives of his foster parents are incorrectly dated in summer of 1946. I have not used the photos as evidence. But there is no reason to dismiss the possibility that the grandparents were photographed in the same summer in which they met him for the first time.

50. School ID made out for Bruno Dössekker, school records 1947–1948, class of Ruth Giger (City of Zurich Archives). His foster parents had just received permission from the Police Department of the

canton of Bern to assign their own name to their foster child on his first
day of school. They had submitted such a request to the canton government in Bern the previous December, but were not successful until the
second try. Cf. request to the Bern Governmental Council by Kurt
Dössekker for a change of name, 24 Dec. 1946, and the subsequent correspondence, Biel Guardianship Authorities.

51. Conversation with Ruth Akert-Giger, 31 May 1999, supplemented by telephone conversations, 22 May and 19 June 1999.

52. As to his "block-warden teacher," Wilkomirski provided me with
the name of a person who in fact never taught him. He asked me not to
contact the woman in question, since she had once substituted in his
son's class at the Heubeeribüel School and at a parents' evening had
embarrassed him in front of everyone. It is true that Akert substituted at
that school at the time, but she has no memory of any incident with
Wilkomirski. On the contrary, she has pleasant recollections of other
chance meetings with him. It is impossible that Wilkomirski could have
meant any other teacher besides Akert as the "block warden." According
to the research of Wolf Gebhardt of the BBC, the teacher who followed
Akert also knows nothing of these episodes, and after that, Wilkomirski's teacher was a man. All of his schoolmates whom I contacted dispute his accounts as well.

53. The following is from a conversation with Sylwester and Christine Marx, 5 July 1999, as well as from a letter from Sylwester Marx to
me, 9 Aug. 1999.

54. Conversations with Annette Dössekker, 26 July 1999; Ch. B., 31
Aug. 1999; and Sybille Schuppli, 9 Sept. 1999.

55. Conversation with Wilkomirski, 15 July 1999.

56. Telephone conversation, 19 Aug. 1999. The following is taken
from several telephone conversations over the next few months.

57. Wilkomirski, *Fragments*, pp. 385, 439.

58. The criticism of Lappin refers to "The Man with Two Heads,"
p. 57.

59. Daniel Ganzfried, "Binjamin Wilkomirski und die verwandelte
Polin" (Binjamin Wilkomirski and the transformed Polish woman), *Die
Weltwoche,* 4 Nov. 1999.

60. Conversation with Koralnik, 4 Nov. 1999. Koralnik presented
her position, which was published in *Die Weltwoche,* 9 Dec. 1999.

61. The following is taken from a telephone conversation, 13 Nov. 1999.

62. Karola wrote a letter to *Die Weltwoche* on 15 Nov. 1999 in which she denies Ganzfried's presentation of her conversation with Koralnik. The newspaper did not print her correction. I received a copy of the letter.

63. Conversation with Karola, 5 Oct. 1999. In his statement from 22 November 1999, Wilkomirski claims that Karola told him and Verena Piller that she had to speak German to me, and therefore she had not understood half of our conversation. Wilkomirski also writes that I did not make the changes to my text that Karola had demanded. In fact my conversation with Karola was conducted in French and without any language problems. I had sent her the exact text of the chapters in which she is mentioned. On 5 Nov. 1999, she sent me additional written confirmation that my presentation was correct. I then sent her a revised version in Dec. 1999.

64. Bernstein in an e-mail to me, 13 March 2000.

65. Conversation with Bernstein, 5 July 1999; for the biographical data about Appelfeld, cf. Lawrence Langer, ed., *Art from the Ashes: A Holocaust Anthology* (New York: Oxford University Press, 1995), p. 271.

66. Conversations with Bernstein, 24 May 1999; with Balint, 13 July 1999; and with Wilkomirski, 29 April 1999; Wilkomirski in an e-mail to Lappin, 20 Dec. 1998; he has said much the same to me on several occasions.

67. The following is taken from a detailed documentation that I received from Stabinsky, 23 September 1999; also from several telephone conversations with Stabinsky in Sept. and Oct. 1999. Disclosures about Laura Grabowski as Laurel Rose Willson alias Lauren Stanford are well documented in Bob Passantino and Gretchen Passantino, "Lauren Stratford: From Satanic Ritual Abuse to Jewish Holocaust," *Cornerstone* 28, no. 117 (Oct. 1999): 12–18. Stabinsky is not included in their article, since he decided only after its publication to make public his own role in exposing her. My thanks to the BBC and Daniel Ganzfried for the tip about the connection between Grabowski, Stratford, and Willson.

68. Bob Passantino, Gretchen Passantino, and Jon Trott, "Satan's Sideshow: The True Lauren Stratford Story," *Cornerstone* 18, no. 90 (Oct.–Nov. 1989): 23–28.

69. Passantino and Passantino, "Lauren Stratford: From Satanic Ritual Abuse to Jewish Holocaust"; John Johnson and Steve Padilla, "Satanism: Skeptics Abound," *Los Angeles Times,* 23 April 1991.

70. Lauren Stratford and Johanna Michaelson, *Satan's Underground: The Extraordinary Story of One Woman's Escape* (Eugene, Ore.: Harvest House, 1988; reprint, Gretna, La.: Pelican Publishing, 1991).

71. Lauren Stratford, *Satan's Underground,* p. 146.

72. In 1998 and 1999, Grabowski received a total of over $2,000 from the Jewish Family Services of Los Angeles. The documents are in my possession, but my informant would like to remain anonymous.

73. As to Lauren's early years and the following biographical material, cf. Passantino, Passantino, and Trott, "Satan's Sideshow"; as to her Polish grandparents, Passantino and Passantino, "Lauren Stratford: From Satanic Ritual Abuse to Jewish Holocaust."

74. Lauren Stratford, *I Know You're Hurting: Living Through Emotional Pain* (Gretna, La.: Pelican Publishing, 1993; Gretna, La.: Harvest, 1989); Lauren Stratford, *Stripped Naked: Gifts for Recovery* (Gretna, La.: Pelican Publishing, 1993).

75. Lauren Stratford, *I Know You're Hurting,* p. 246. As for interest in the Shoah and/or the ostensible parallels, cf. pp. 29 ff., 119, 161, 212, 221, 245.

76. Lauren Stratford, *Satan's Underground,* pp. 123–24.

77. Ibid., pp. 15–18.

78. Ibid., pp. 178 and 124; Wilkomirski, *Fragments.*

79. Monika Muggli, in an e-mail to Jen Rosenberg, 6 Nov. 1999, and to Ganzfried, 8 Nov. 1999. For this information, my thanks to Ganzfried, to whom Muggli reported her gift of $1,150 after reading his *Weltwoche* article of 4 Nov. 1999.

80. Jerzy Kosinski, *The Painted Bird* (Boston: Houghton Mifflin, 1965).

81. As to the initial reception of Kosinki's book, cf. James Park Sloan, "Kosinski's War," in *Critical Essays on Jerzy Kosinski,* ed. Barbara Tepa Lupack (New York: G. K. Hall, 1998), pp. 236–46, 237, and James Park Sloan, *Jerzy Kosinski: A Biography* (New York: Dutton, 1996), pp. 222–23; Elie Wiesel, "Everybody's Victim," *The New York Times Book Review,* 31 Oct. 1965, reprinted in Lupack, *Critical Essays on Jerzy Kosinski,* pp. 47–49; Langer, *The Holocaust and the Literary Imagination,* p. 178.

82. Wilkomirski in a letter to Lappin, 20 Dec. 1998. He made similar statements in a conversation with me, 29 April 1999.

83. Sloan, *Jerzy Kosinski: A Biography,* pp. 388 ff. and pp. 207 ff.; Sloan, "Kosinski's War," p. 237.

84. For details, cf. Sloan, *Jerzy Kosinski: A Biography,* pp. 4–8, 21–38, 49–58, 108–109, 167, 190–95, 209.

85. Yakov Maroko, *Sha'agat Me'una* (Tormented scream) (Bnei Brak: self-published by Maroko, no date), p. 16 (the quotations were translated for me by Paul Russak); conversation with Bernstein, 5 July 1999; Bernstein in a letter to Lappin, 27 Dec. 1998.

86. Maroko, *Sha'agat Me'una,* p. 16. Maroko gives the date of his first thinking about Lerner as early February 1995. This seems somewhat too late to me, since the film was broadcast on 24 Nov. 1994 and Wilkomirski's first letter to Maroko is dated 12 Feb. 1995.

87. Maroko, *Sha'agat Me'una,* p. 18.

88. Ibid., p. 19.

89. Ibid., p. 20.

90. Ibid., pp. 296, 298.

91. Bernstein in a letter to Lappin, 27 Dec. 1998.

92. Maroko, *Sha'agat Me'una,* p. 298.

93. Ibid., p. 300.

94. Ibid., p. 316.

95. Ibid., p. 322.

96. Ibid., p. 319, 320.

97. Conversations with Bernstein, 14 June and 5 July 1999; Bernstein in a letter to Lappin, 27 Dec. 1998.

98. *Wanda's List,* part 2, 1995; Maroko, *Sha'agat Me'una,* p. 322; conversation with Bernstein, 14 June 1999; Bernstein in a letter to Lappin, 27 Dec. 1998.

99. Cf. Maurice Halbwachs, *Das Gedächtnis und seine sozialen Bedingungen* (Memory and its social conditions) (Frankfurt: Suhrkamp, 1985).

100. Maroko, *Sha'agat Me'una,* p. 327; conversation with Bernstein, 14 June 1999.

101. In response to Lappin, Wilkomirski claimed on 20 Dec. 1998: "Since I long assumed that I arrived in Basel in winter, this date was made my birthday. This has not been confirmed, however, upon examination of the Grosjean documents." At this point in time Wilkomirski had not even seen the Grosjean dossier; both he and his lawyer saw it for

the first time in the spring of 1999. Wilkomirski denies this in his statement on 22 November 1999, but compare note 112 below.

102. Wilkomirski in a written statement to his publishers, 5 Oct.
1998 (Liepman files); cf. draft of afterword to *Fragments,* May 1995
(Sandberg files).

103. Wilkomirski in a statement to his publishers, 5 Oct. 1998
(Liepman files).

104. Children adopted in Switzerland prior to 1 April 1973 received,
like Wilkomirski, an abbreviated birth certificate, which also listed the
birth parents. According to the new law, only the adoptive parents are
listed. Wilkomirski's rudimentary birth certificate is thus more detailed
than a "normal" one! Moreover, all persons generally receive only excerpts from the birth registry and not an original birth certificate, as he
presumes in the afterword to *Fragments.* As to the legal basis, cf.
Zeitschrift für Zivilstandswesen (May 1999), p. 142; my thanks also to Frau
Rickli, director of the Biel Registry Office, for further explanations provided in letters, 18 June and 7 Sept. 1999, as well as in telephone conversations, 4 and 24 June 1999. Rolf Sandberg requested and received
excerpts from the family register of the Grosjean family in Saules and of
the Rohr family (husband of Yvonne Berthe Grosjean) in Hunzenschwil
(Sandberg files). Wilkomirski describes my presentation as "untenable"
in his statement from 22 November 1999. He says that even though
this may not be the case today, most of the people he knows of his generation are in possession of a "detailed, complete birth certificate." On
his "abbreviated birth certificate" the birthplace of all the people concerned was missing. This information is indeed missing. But is was no
secret; Wilkomirski could have found it out from the family register, for
instance.

105. Wilkomirski in a letter to Sandberg, 30 March 1995; Sandberg
in a letter to Sparr, 10 April 1995. As to the legal issues involved: cf.
Cyril Hegnauer, "Dürfen dem mündigen Adoptierten die leiblichen
Eltern gegen den Willen der Adoptiveltern bekanntgegeben werden?"
(May an adult adoptee be informed about birth parents against the will
of adopted parents?), *Zeitschrift für Vormundschaftswesen* (*ZVW*), no. 46
(1991), pp. 101–3; Franz Werro, "Quelques aspects juridiques du secret
de l'adoption" (Some legal aspects of adoption privacy), *ZVW,* no. 49
(1994), pp. 73–85; and Vormundschaftskammer des Obergerichts des
Kantons Aargau, "Einsichtsrecht in altrechtliche Vaterschaftsakten"

(Access to paternity files under the old law), *ZVW*, no. 52 (1997), pp. 128–29; cf. the decision of the Federal Court on 24 June 1999, in the case of J.H. My thanks to Kurt Affolter, Biel Guardianship Authorities, for his guidance.

106. Sandberg's petition for access to guardianship and adoption files to the Biel Guardianship Authorities, 10 May 1995; Sandberg's admonishments, 9 and 28 June 1995. Reply by Graber, Biel Guardianship Authorities, 30 June 1995; personal response of Affolter, Biel Guardianship Authorities, 3 Sept. 1999.

107. Graber, Biel Guardianship Authorities, in a letter to Sandberg, 13 Oct. 1995, enclosed the letter (rendered anonymous) from Rudolf Z., 11 Oct. 1995; Graber, Biel Guardianship Authorities, in a letter to Sandberg, 26 Oct. 1995, enclosed the letter (rendered anonymous) of Rudolf's daughter M.Z., 24 Oct. 1995.

108. Wilkomirski in a fax to Sandberg, 9 Nov. 1995.

109. Wilkomirski in a letter to Sandberg, 11 Dec. 1995 (date uncertain; incomplete) (Sandberg files).

110. Graber in a letter to Sandberg, 30 July 1995. Graber in a note regarding a telephone call, 30 Oct. 1996 (Biel Guardianship Authorities); Sandberg in a letter to Graber, 30 Oct. 1997.

111. Wilkomirski in a statement to his publisher, 5 Oct. 1998 (Liepman files). Wilkomirski attempts to lend plausibility to his idea of an exchange of children by repeatedly stating that he never once saw his guardian, Stauffer. In his statement of 22 Nov. 1999, he also suggests that Stauffer's first personal visit to the Dössekkers was on 14 Feb. 1947. There is no evidence to support either claim, and both are highly improbable. In October 1945 two people from the Biel Guardianship Authorities traveled to Zurich for an "inspection visit" at the Dössekkers; in December 1945, it was one person alone. On the first visit the inspectors were presumably Stauffer and Forster, who wrote up the report, and the second was certainly Stauffer, who wrote the report himself this time. It is factually true that Stauffer wrote no reports during the period of the alleged exchange; but evidence for that period is found in expense-account receipts (cf. Stauffer's guardian visitation report for the period of 17 June 1945 to 17 June 1947; compilation of visitation reports, File no. 191). It is also clear from later visitation reports that Stauffer personally visited the Dössekkers in the succeeding years. Moreover, photographs of Bruno Grosjean were passed on by the Dössekkers

through the guardian's hands; this is documented for the period between January 1947 and February 1949. Stauffer would surely have noticed if the child had been exchanged for another (Stauffer in a letter to Max Grosjean, 23 Jan. 1947; Stauffer in a letter to Dr. Dössekker, 17 Feb. 1949). In his statement from 22 November 1999 Wilkomirski furnishes an additional argument for the alleged exchange. From 1942 the reports of the guardianship authorities had spoken "without exception of a normal boy who was developing well." But suddenly in June 1949, there was a different note: "Bruno is a delicate child, who causes his foster parents some trouble in this respect." A year later the report asserts that the boy "needs continuing good care and attention." At this point Wilkomirski adds the observation that "on at least two occasions" his foster father had applied to the primary school for a holiday extension on medical grounds. He criticized me for deliberately withholding this information, despite my knowing about these requests, since I claimed to have studied all the school records. For the period following the alleged exchange, the guardianship authorities describe the boy as far from sickly. In February of 1947 and 1952 Bruno is described in identical language on both occasions as "healthy, cheerful and developing satisfactorily" (compilation of visitation reports, File no. 191.) I never came across the holiday applications of the foster father, perhaps because I did not study all the school material on file. I never claimed to have done so.

112. Wilkomirski, *Fragments*, p. 496. In his statement from 22 November 1999, Wilkomirski accuses me of giving a *"distorted presentation."* The question was to check whether papers were genuine or fake. In August 1995 "this question had already been long answered for me, and the matter was closed, which made *further steps pointless."* (Emphasis in the original.) However, according to Sandberg, his lawyer (conversation on 9 June 1999), he and his client first viewed the files of the Biel Guardianship Authorities in April 1999. The head of the office, Kurt Affolter, had stated this fact to me on 28 April 1999. The most comprehensive and important information on Bruno Grosjean's early years was on file at this office. Hence in 1995 neither Wilkomirski nor Sandberg checked whether the most important papers pertaining to Grosjean were genuine. Further steps to inspect the records would have been imperative. It is also debatable whether the question posed applied merely to the genuineness of the documents. In February 1995 Helbling had confronted Suhrkamp and the Liepman AG with the suspicion that Wil-

komirski's autobiography (he did not know his name) was a fabrication. Helbling did not raise the question of forged papers. It was in fact brought up by Wilkomirski to defend his story. Claiming an exchange served to make his alleged autobiography plausible. The actual central questions would have been whether Wilkomirski's concentration camp memory was correct and whether he had been swapped with Bruno Grosjean, genuine or fake papers aside.

113. The following is from a conversation with René Aeberhard, 10 June 1999.

114. The following is taken from conversations with René Aeberhard, 28 June, 8 and 31 July 1999. The plans and video sequences can be found in Wilkomirski's video interview with the Holocaust Memorial Museum, tapes 2 and 6. In his statement from 22 November 1999, Wilkomirski comments that one could "compare two biographies at random and invariably find a number of chance correspondences and similarities." According to him I had presented hypothesis and conjecture demagogically as facts; I had simply ignored what did not tally. He itemizes a series of divergences between the situation in Nidau and his Polish memories: Motti had been younger than René Aeberhard; there had been no foster father living on the Polish farm, nor had there been any rabbits there; the sledge had not been a Davos model but a Swedish one, etc. Wilkomirski adds that Aeberhard identified the small Wilkomirski as Bruno Grosjean only because he had already seen Wilkomirski's photo in the press. I sounded out this possibility with Aeberhard before he knew why I was contacting him, so I can exclude it.

115. This is the age mentioned in the script for the Colla project, and it matches Wilkomirski's statement that after this meeting he was transferred to Field 3 and thus escaped the Field 5 massacre of November 1943. He dates his birth to circa 1939; cf. *Fragments*, pp. 410–415. video interview with the Holocaust Memorial Museum, tape 3; video interview with the Shoah Foundation, tapes 1 and 3; the script written by the Colla brothers, BAR: E 3010 (A) 1990/160, vol. 46, dossier 531.3, Binjamin, Fernando Colla.

116. Conversation with Frieda Churchod-Rohr, 29 May 1999.

117. Conversations with Wilkomirski, 2 June and 15 July 1999; Lappin, "The Man with Two Heads," pp. 26–27.

118. Last will and testament of Yvonne Berthe Rohr-Grosjean, 16 Sept. 1979 (Tax Office of the Canton of Bern, Dept. ESN).

119. Letter of Bruno Dössekker (my italics) to the Chancellery of the City of Bern, Testamentary Office, 3 Nov. 1981 (Inheritance Office of the City of Bern); inventory of the estate of Yvonne Berthe Rohr née Grosjean, 17 Feb. 1982 (Tax Office of the canton of Bern, Dept. ESN).

120. Telephone conversation with Annette Dössekker, 26 July 1999. In his statement from 22 November 1999 Wilkomirski criticizes me for using his divorced wife and "her hanger-on" (he must be referring to Annie Singer) as a source of historical information. I questioned them on factual matters in which they were involved or which they had witnessed. Prior to that I had listened to Wilkomirski's point of view.

121. Conversation with Rudolf Z., 20 July 1999.

122. Interview conducted by Wolf Gebhardt with Rosa Käppeli, a friend of Egloff's, 21 and 23 March 1999; according to Käppeli, Egloff began service with the Dössekkers in 1945. Wilkomirski's statement that she did this solely for his sake is another indication that he was already in Zurich at the time and could not possibly have been at the Augustiańska Street home, since it first opened in the summer of 1946. Annie Singer in a letter to the editor, Die Weltwoche, 1 Oct. 1998.

123. Conversations with Annie Singer, 18 April 1999; Lukas Sarasin, 28 April 1999 (interviewer: Wolf Gebhardt); Annette Dössekker, 26 July 1999; Jürg Wagner, 25 March 1999 (interviewer: Wolf Gebhardt); Chr. B., 31 Aug. 1999. There are numerous credible examples of fabricated stories. Sarasin, Dössekker, and N.N., another grade-school friend (name known to the author, conversation, 2 Nov. 1999), confirmed the improbability of the ski-lift episode. In his written statement of 22 Nov. 1999, Wilkomirski says these witnesses first came to know him only after the diesel motors that had panicked him at the ski slope had been replaced by electric motors.

124. Conversations with Jürg Wagner, 25 March 1999; Nika Derungs, 21 May 1999; Verena Zollinger, 22 May 1999; Ruth Akert, 31 May 1999.

125. Conversation with Annie Singer, 18 April 1999; with Annette Dössekker, 26 July 1999.

126. Conversation with Annette Dössekker, 26 July 1999.

127. Conversations with Chr. B, 31 Aug. 1999; Annette Dössekker, 26 July 1999; as well as a letter from Wilkomirski to Birgit Littmann, 16 Feb. 1983. As to genuine illness, cf. medical attestation of Wilkomirski's general practitioner, 30 Nov. 1998.

128. Conversations with Peter Indergand, 17 June 1999; Fernando Colla, 3 May 1999; Rolando Colla, 6 May 1999. The statements of all three are in verbatim agreement in places. The following is based on those statements.

129. Despite any rumors to the contrary, a profit motive probably played no role for Wilkomirski in his film project. Given production conditions in Switzerland, it is almost impossible to make a commercially viable film. The script written by the two Collas and Indergand was entitled *Binjamin,* and two versions of it, which do not differ substantially, were submitted as part of two different requests for funding to the Federal Office for Culture. Material cited in the following is taken, unless otherwise indicated, from the second version (the funding request of 21 April 1983). Funding requests by Fernando Colla to the Federal Department of the Interior, Federal Office for Culture, 12 Feb. and 21 April 1983. Since the filmmakers themselves no longer had copies of the documents, my thanks to Fernando Colla for permission to review them in the Swiss Federal Archives, Bern, BAR: E 3010 (A) 1990/160, vol. 46, dossier 531.3, Binjamin, Fernando Colla.

130. First version of the script (the funding request of 12 Feb. 1983).

131. E.g., interviews with Ch. B., 31 August 1999; Sybille Schuppli, 9 Sept. 1999.

132. In his written statement of 22 Nov. 1999, Wilkomirski explains the discrepancies between the Colla project and his later version as follows: "I told the Collas only rudimentary things, since I had not yet begun my own detailed research at that point and was not prepared at the time to surrender all the images in my memory." He also comments that one does not tell one's life story to someone one has known only for a few days or weeks. However, the scripts which he helped to put together over many months include intimate details from his life. Wilkomirski's statement neglects, moreover, to mention that he told the filmmakers not only "rudimentary things" but also things that were later omitted from his history. It is plausible that the later stories only arose as a consequence of the "detailed research" that followed, but this would contradict Wilkomirski's claim that he always told the same memories (while confirming my own impression that his story only gradually came into being).

133. Jerzy Kosinski, "Notes of the Author on The Painted Bird" in *Passing By: Selected Essays, 1962–1991* (New York: Random House,

1992), pp. 201–22, 202. The notes were written in English as an appendix to be translated for the German-language edition of his novel in 1965, the same year they were published in English separately under the imprint Scientia-Factum. The following is taken from pp. 203–12 of the reprint in *Passing By.* Italics in the original.

134. Eberhard Fechner, *Der Prozess* (The trial), part 1: *Anklage* (Indictment), 89 min.; part 2: *Beweisaufnahme* (Collecting the evidence), 92 min.; part 3: *Das Urteil* (The verdict), 88 min. (Norddeutscher Rundfunk, 1984).

135. Rauff's document can be found in the book of the film script of Claude Lanzmann, *Shoah* (Cambridge: Da Capo Press, 1995). Thomas Kranz, director of research for the museum at Majdanek, has informed me that some trucks or tractors were used in the camp to drown out the screams of those being murdered.

136. Parallels between Frau Grosz and his biological mother, Yvonne Grosjean, are also evident in the same syllable contained in the two surnames.

137. Wilkomirski, *Fragments*, pp. 377–78.

138. Eric Bergkraut, *Das gute Leben ist nur eine Falle;* conversation with Wilkomirski, 22 April 1999.

139. He used the term "self-experiment" in conversation with me and also explained that what was now needed was a modification of the concept, in which examples from his own story would be replaced with the experiences of other people, thus detaching it from his own person. Conversation with Wilkomirski, 29 April 1999. In contradiction to this assertion, he says in his written statement of 22 Nov. 1999 that not all the examples in his therapy concept were taken from his own story.

140. Binjamin Wilkomirski, outline of a lecture, "Das Kindergedächtnis als historische Quelle für die Zeitgeschichte am Beispiel von überlebenden Kindern der Shoa (Holocaust)" (Childhood memory as a historical source for contemporary history, with examples of child survivors of the Shoah [Holocaust]), 11 October 1995. Unless otherwise indicated, the following is taken from this document.

141. Cf. Wilkomirski, *Fragments*, pp. 380–81.

142. Wilkomirski and Bernstein, "Die Identitätsproblematik bei überlebenden Kindern des Holocaust," p. 170; cf. video interview, Shoah Foundation, tape 4, and Wilkomirski, *Fragments*, p. 450.

143. Conversation with Wilkomirski, 29 April 1999.

144. Cf. Wilkomirski and Bernstein, "Die Identitätsproblematik bei überlebenden Kindern des Holocaust," p. 164.

145. Wilkomirski in an interview with Peter Zeindler, *Tages-Anzeiger*, 29 May 1999.

146. Monika Matta in a letter to Thomas Sparr, 26 Feb. 1995 (Suhrkamp files). Wilkomirski and Bernstein, "Die Identitätsproblematik bei überlebenden Kindern des Holocaust," p. 169.

147. Philip Gourevitch, "The Memory Thief," *The New Yorker*, June 14, 1999, p. 54. Emphasis in the original.

148. Mark Pendergrast, *Victims of Memory: Incest Accusations and Shattered Lives* (Hinesburg: Upper Access, 1995).

149. Edition published by Picador. A similar statement can be found in the Hebrew edition. Cf. Mark Pendergrast, "Recovered Memories and the Holocaust," revised 14 Jan. 1999, at www.stopbadtherapy.com/experts/fragments/fragments.html.

150. Lyn Laboriel, Catherine Gould, and Vicky Graham Costain, in Stratford, *Satan's Underground*, p. 238.

151. Cf. eds. Kathy Pezdek and William P. Banks, *The Recovered Memory/False Memory Debate* (San Diego: Academic Press, 1996); eds. Paul S. Appelbaum, Lisa A. Uyehara, and Mark R. Elin, *Trauma and Memory: Clinical and Legal Controversies* (New York: Oxford University Press, 1997); Elizabeth Loftus and Katherine Ketcham, *The Myth of Repressed Memory: False Memories and Allegations of Sexual Abuse* (New York: St. Martin's, 1994).

152. Siegfried Schmid, ed., *Gedächtnis: Probleme und Perspektiven der interdisziplinären Gedächtnisforschung* (Memory: Problems and perspectives of interdisciplinary memory research) (Frankfurt: Suhrkamp, 1991); Siegfried Schmid, "Gedächtnis—Erzählen—Identität" (Memory—narrative—identity), in *Mnemosyne. Formen und Funktionen der kulturellen Erinnerung* (Mnemosyne: Forms and functions of cultural memory), eds. Aleida Assmann and Dietrich Harth, (Frankfurt a. M.: Fischer, 1993), pp. 378–397; Gerhard Rusch, *Erkenntnis, Wissenschaft, Geschichte: Von einem konstruktivistischen Standpunkt* (Perception, science, history: From a constructivist standpoint) (Frankfurt: 1987). For psychoanalysis, cf. Matthias Kettner, "Das Konzept der Nachträglichkeit in Freuds Erinnerungstheorie" (The concept of deferred action in Freud's theory of memory), *Psyche*, no. 4 (1999), pp. 309–42. For a view aimed at combining the two: Stefan Granzow, *Das autobiographische Gedächtnis: Kogni-*

tionspsychologische und psychoanalytische Perspektiven (The autobiographical memory: Cognition psychological and psychoanalytic perspectives) (Berlin and Munich: Quintessenz, 1994).

153. Loftus and Ketcham, *The Myth of Repressed Memory,* pp. 92–93.

154. Cf. Bessel A. van der Kolk, "Traumatic Memories," in Paul S. Appelbaum et. al., eds., *Trauma and Memory: Clinical and Legal Controversies,* pp. 243–260, 245.

155. Cf. Bessel A. van der Kolk, "Trauma and Memory" in *Traumatic Stress: The Effects of Overwhelming Experience on Mind, Body, and Society,* ed. Bessel A. van der Kolk, Alexander C. McFarlane, and Lars Weisaeth (New York and London: Guilford Press, 1996), pp. 279–302, 287–89, 296.

156. Bessel A. van der Kolk, "Trauma and Memory," pp. 296–97.

157. Ibid., p. 283.

158. Wilkomirski and Bernstein, "Die Identitätsproblematik bei überlebenden Kindern des Holocaust," pp. 170–171 (italics mine). In his statement from 22 November 1999 Wilkomirski disputes that this example stems from his own history. But cf. note 139 above.

159. Wilkomirski, *Fragments,* pp. 401–2; video interview, Shoah Foundation, tape 2; video interview, Holocaust Memorial Museum, tape 2.

160. Wilkomirski and Bernstein, "Die Identitätsproblematik bei überlebenden Kindern des Holocaust," pp. 162–66.

161. Binjamin Wilkomirski, outline of a lecture, "Das Kindergedächtnis als historische Quelle für die Zeitgeschichte am Beispiel von überlebenden Kindern der Shoa (Holocaust)."

162. Wilkomirski and Bernstein, "Die Identitätsproblematik bei überlebenden Kindern des Holocaust," pp. 161 and 164; cf. video interview, Shoah Foundation, tape 6.

163. For example, video interview, Shoah Foundation, tape 6; conversation with Wilkomirski, 14 May 1999; Wilkomirski and Bernstein, "Die Identitätsproblematik bei überlebenden Kindern des Holocaust," p. 167.

164. The historian Wolf Gebhardt has given me a digest of circa 50 pages written by this woman, some of it as letters, most of it as a journal. I also received an audiotape of an interview he conducted with her on 14 April 1999. I myself spoke at length with the woman several times by telephone between the middle of October and late November 1999. Wolf Gebhardt received these texts from the woman whom

Wilkomirski calls Sabina Rapaport on condition that he use them only in such a way that neither her name nor her place of residence could be recognized. I call these materials the K.M. file. The following is taken from that file and from my conversations with K.M.

165. L414 was the number of the house in which Ruth Klüger was housed. Cf. Ruth Klüger, *weiter leben: Eine Jugend* (Go on living: A childhood, 8th ed.) (Munich: Deutscher Taschenbuch Verlag, 1999), p. 87.

166. In his statement from 22 November 1999 Wilkomirski claims: "In many shared discussions we gradually came to the subject of 'names'; I merely confirmed what she probably already assumed." Compare this, however, with his ORTHO talk on page 159 in this book. It refers to the sentences: "and would promptly feel better. 'You know,' he told her, 'Rapaport is a well-known Jewish name! If this word. . . .' "

167. She sent me a copy of her protest note to Wilkomirski, dated 27 Oct. 1999, which contained a portion of what she had told me on the phone.

168. Bernstein in e-mails to me, 13 and 15 March, 2000.

THE TRUTH OF THE BIOGRAPHY

1. Daniel Ganzfried, "Binjamin Wilkomirski und die verwandelte Polin" (Binjamin Wilkomirski and the transformed Polish woman), *Die Weltwoche,* 4 Nov. 1999.

2. Cf. Stefanie Mimra, *Adoption, eine Herausforderung für die Identität: Adoptierte zwischen Verleugnung und Integration ihrer biologischen Herkunft* (Adoption, a challenge for identity: Adopted children between denial and integration of their biological origins) (Linz: edition pro mente, 1997), pp. 227–30.

3. Cf. Steven Jay Lynn, Judith Pintar, Jane Stafford, Lisa Marmel-stein, and Timothy Lock, "Rendering the Implausible Plausible: Narrative Construction, Suggestion, and Memory," in *Believed-In Imaginings: The Narrative Construction of Reality,* ed. Joseph de Rivera and Theodore R. Sarbin (Washington, D.C.: American Psychological Association, 1998), pp. 123–43.

4. Wilkomirski in his statement of 22 Nov. 1999. Cf. Michael Kenny,

"The Proof Is in the Passion: Emotion as an Index of Veridical Memory," in *Believed-In Imaginings: The Narrative Construction of Reality,* pp. 269–93.

5. Ganzfried, *Jie Geliehene Holocaust Biographie*; as to May as a pathological liar, cf. Claus Roxin, *Karl May: Das Strafrecht und die Literatur. Essays* (Karl May: criminal justice and literature) (Tübingen: Klöpfer & Meyer, 1997), pp. 52–55, 86, 118–80; my thanks to Dr. Ernst Piper for this idea.

THE TRUTH OF THE FICTION

1. Peter von Matt, *Verkommene Söhne, missratene Töchter: Familendesaster in der Literatur* (Degenerate sons, daughters gone astray: Family disasters in literature) (Munich: Deutscher Taschenbuch Verlag, 1997), p. 36.

2. Wilkomirski, *Fragments*, pp. 377–78.

3. Ibid., p. 495.

4. As to the social conditions of even the most private memories, cf. Maurice Halbwuchs, *Das Gedächtnis und seine sozialen Bedingungen* (Memory and its social conditions) (Frankfurt: Suhrkamp, 1985; originally published in French, 1925), p. 71.

5. Cf. Tanja Hetzer, *Kinderblick auf die Shoah: Formen der Erinnerung bei Ilse Aichinger. Hubert Fichte und Danilo Kiš* (A child's view of the Shoah: Forms of memory in the works of Ilse Aichinger, Hubert Fichte, and Danilo Kis) (Würzburg: Königshausen & Neumann, 1999). By way of exception, there is one autobiographical concentration-camp memoir narrated from the child's perspective: Jona Oberski, *Kinderjahre* (Childhood years) (Vienna: Paul Zsolnay, 1980).

6. Sarah Traister-Moskovitz, "Account of a Child Survivor: Fact or Fiction?—Does It Really Make a Difference?" *Martyrdom and Resistance,* International Society for Yad Vashem, May–June 1999.

7. Ruth Klüger, "Kitsch ist immer plausibel" (Kitsch is always plausibel), *Süddeutsche Zeitung,* 30 September 1998.

8. Ibid.

9. James Edward Young, *Writing and Rewriting the Holocaust: Narrative and the Consequences of Interpretation* (Bloomington: Indiana University Press, 1988), p. 169.

10. Von Matt, *Verkommene Söhne, missratene Töchter,* p. 37.

11. E.M. in a letter to Wilkomirski, 4 Oct. 1995.

12. Peter Surber, "Dichtung, Wahrheit" (Poetry, truth), *St. Galler Tagblatt,* 11 Sept. 1998.

13. Wilkomirski, *Fragments*, p. 496.

14. Ruth Klüger, *weiter leben: Eine Jugend* (Go on living: A childhood), 8th ed. (Munich: Deutscher Taschenbuch Verlag, 1999), p. 112.

15. Cf. Andrea Reiter, *"Auf dass sie entsteigen der Dunkelheit": Die literarische Bewältigung von KZ-Erfahrung* ("That they may rise from the darkness: Overcoming the concentration-camp experience through literature") (Vienna: Löcker Verlag, 1995).

16. Birgit R. Erdle, "Traumatisiertes Gedächtnis und zurückgewiesene Erinnerung" (Traumatized memory and rejected memories), in *Figuren des Fremden in der Schweizer Literatur* (Strangers as characters in Swiss literature), ed. Corina Caduff (Zurich: Limmat Verlag, 1997), pp. 153–74, 163.

17. Ruth Klüger, "Dichten über die Shoah: Zum Problem des literarischen Umgangs mit dem Massenmord" (Writing about the Shoah: Literature's problems dealing with mass murder), in Gertrud Hardtmann, ed., *Spuren der Verfolgung: Seelische Auswirkung des Holocaust auf die Opfer und ihre Kinder* (Traces of the persecution: Psychological effects of the Holocaust on its victims and their children) (Gerlingen: Bleicher Verlag, 1992), pp. 203–21, 218.

18. Cf. Peter Novick, *The Holocaust and Collective Memory: The American Experience* (London: Bloomsbury, 2000).

19. Cf. James Edward Young, *Writing and Rewriting the Holocaust: Narrative and the Consequences of Interpretation* (Bloomington: Indiana University Press, 1988), esp. part 2; and Novick, *The Holocaust and Collective Memory,* pp. 241–44.

20. Cf. Young, *Writing and Rewriting the Holocaust,* esp. part 2.

21. Cf. Novick, *The Holocaust and Collective Memory,* pp. 235–236.

22. Video interview, Holocaust Museum, tape 6.

23. Hans Keilson, *Sequentielle Traumatisierung bei Kindern: Deskriptiv-klinische und quantifizierende-statistische Follow-up-Untersuchung zum Schicksal der jüdischen Kriegsweisen in den Niederlanden* (Sequential traumatization among children: Descriptive-clinical, quantifying statistical follow-up investigation of the fate of Jewish war orphans in the Netherlands) (Stuttgart: Ferdinand-Enke-Verlag, 1979).

24. Comparable arguments can likewise be found in William G. Niederland, *Folgen der Verfolgung: Das Überlebenden-Syndrom Seelenmord* (Consequences of persecution: the survivor syndrome—murder of the soul) (Frankfurt: Suhrkamp, 1980); cf. Hans Keilson, "Die Reparationsverträge und die Folgen der 'Wiedergutmachung' " (Compensation agreements and the consequences of "reparation"), in *Jüdisches Leben in Deutschland seit 1945* (Jewish life in Germany since 1945), ed. Micha Brumlik, Doron Kiesel, Cilly Kugelmann, and Julius H. Schoeps (Frankfurt: 1986), pp. 121–39; Helga Fischer-Hübner and Hermann Fischer-Hübner, eds., *Die Kehrseite der "Wiedergutmachung": Das Leiden der NS-Verfolgten in den Entschädigungsverfahren* (The reverse side of "reparations": What people persecuted by the Nazis suffered during suits for compensation) (Gerlingen: 1990).

25. Harvey Peskin in a letter to Carol Brown Janeway, 9 March 1999; Bernstein in a letter to Wilkomirski, 21 Nov. 1998 (this letter was circulated among Wilkomirski's defenders at the time); Monika Matta in a letter to Sparr, 26 Feb. 1995 (Suhrkamp files).

26. Cf. Philippe Lejeune, *Der autobiographische Pakt* (The autobiographical pact) (Frankfurt: Aesthetica, edition Suhrkamp, 1994).

27. Daniel Ganzfried, "Die geliehene Holocaust-Biographie," *Die Weltwoche,* 27 Aug. 1998.

28. Cf. Independent Commission of Experts: Switzerland–Second World War, *Switzerland and Gold Transactions in the Second World War: An Interim Report* (1998); *Switzerland and Nazi Gold* (1999); *Switzerland and Refugees in the Nazi Era* (1999); all available from the Eidgenössische Druck-Materialzentrale, Bern. Cf. also Pierre Weill, *Der Milliarden-Deal* (The billion-dollar deal) (Zurich: Weltwoche ABC-Verlag, 1999).

29. *Focus,* no. 44 (30 Oct. 1999), p. 333; *Sonntagsblick,* 17 Oct. 1999; *Neue Zürcher Zeitung,* 19 Oct. 1999; Graf on Wilkomirski: "Die Demontage Wilkomirskis: Oder was Ganzfried vergessen hat" (The dismantling of Wilkomirski: Or what Ganzfried forgot), at http://www.ruf-ch.org/Archiv/1998/5/Wilkogra.html. In the election of 23–24 Oct. 1999, the Swiss People's Party received 22.54 percent of the votes, with the Social Democratic Party only slightly behind at 22.47 percent.

30. Daniel Ganzfried, "Binjamin Wilkomirski und die verwandelte Polin" (Binjamin Wilkomirski and the transformed Polish woman), *Die*

eryl(cm

Weltwoche, 4 Nov. 1999; a formal suit was filed by the attorney Manfred Kuhn, resident in Uster, Switzerland, with Dr. M. Bertschi, prosecutor for the canton of Zurich, on 15 Nov. 1999. Cf. Michael Meier, "Strafanzeige gegen Autobiograf Binjamin Wilkomirski" (Formal suit against autobiographer Binjamin Wilkomirski), *Tages-Anzeiger*, 16 Nov. 1999.

31. Cf. Peter Bollag, "Unnötige Debatte" (Unnecessary debate), *Israelitisches Wochenblatt*, 3 Sept. 1998; Gisela Blau, "Mehr als nur eine Wahrheit?" (More than just one truth?), *Israelitisches Wochenblatt*, 3 Sept. 1998.

32. Daniel Ganzfried, "Binjamin Wilkomirski und die verwandelte Polin"; for parallels between Holocaust inventions and denials, see Daniel Ganzfried in Christopher Olgiati, *Child of the Death Camps: Truth & Lies* (BBC, 3 Nov. 1999).

33. Young, *Writing and Rewriting the Holocaust*, pp. 23–39.

34. Cf. Moshe Zuckermann, *Zweierlei Holocaust: Der Holocaust in den politischen Kulturen Israels und Deutschlands* (Twofold Holocaust: The Holocaust in the political cultures of Israel and Germany) (Göttingen: Wallstein, 1998); Solmon Z. "From Denial to Recognition: Attitudes Toward Holocaust Survivors from World War II to the Present," *Journal of Traumatic Stress*, no. 8, pp. 215–28.

35. Imre Kertész, "Wem gehört Auschwitz?" (Whom does Auschwitz belong to?), *Die Zeit*, 19 Nov. 1998.

AFTERWORD

1. Written statement by Wilkomirski, 22 Nov. 1999.

EPILOGUE

1. Cf. Tim Cole, *Selling the Holocaust: From Auschwitz to Schindler; How History Is Bought, Packaged, and Sold* (New York: Routledge, 1999), esp. pp. 1–5.

2. Peter Novick, *The Holocaust and Collective Memory: The American Experience* (London: Bloomsbury, 2000). In a book otherwise remarkable for its furious polemics, Norman G. Finkelstein, in *The Holocaust Indus-*

try (London: Verso Books, 2000) offers a variation of this argument: the Six-Day War revealed not the weakness but the strength of Israel as a potentially useful partner in the Middle East. That is the reason why American foreign policy became directed toward the Jewish state and the Jews in America became such ardent supporters of Israel—a commitment that now strengthens their own position as good American citizens, whereas earlier they would have been accused of divided loyalties. In this context, Finkelstein argues, American Jewish elites began to instrumentalize the Holocaust as a weapon with which to ward off criticism. Finkelstein's thesis seems greatly oversimplified and in part reminiscent of long-familiar conspiracy theories.

3. Novick, *The Holocaust and Collective Memory,* pp. 7, 190; cf. Hilene Flanzbaum, "The Imaginary Jew and the American Poet," in Hilene Flanzbaum, ed., *The Americanization of the Holocaust* (Baltimore and London: Johns Hopkins University Press, 1999), pp. 18–32, 30.

4. Finkelstein, *The Holocaust Industry.* Cf. Ulrich Herbert, "Vorschnelle Begeisterung" (Premature enthusiasm), *Süddeutsche Zeitung,* 18 August 2000.

5. Yehuda Elkana, "Bizhut ha-shihehad" (In praise of forgetting), *Haaretz,* 2 March 1988, quoted from Omer Bartov, *Mirrors of Destruction: War, Genocide, and Modern Identity* (Oxford: Oxford University Press, 2000), p. 183.

6. Wiesel, quoted by Novick, *The Holocaust and Collective Memory,* p. 201; cf. Henry Greenspan, "Imagining Survivors: Testimony and the Rise of Holocaust Consciousness," in Flanzbaum, ed., *The Americanization of the Holocaust,* pp. 45–67, esp. pp. 58–59.

7. Cole, *Selling the Holocaust,* pp. 157, 14; cf. Novick, *The Holocaust and Collective Memory,* p. 15.

8. Martin DeAgostino, "He Accepts Memories of Holocaust," *South Bend Tribune,* 29 April 1998.

9. Cole, *Selling the Holocaust,* pp. 187–88.

10. Conversation with Bruno Berti, 8 June 2000; Lotti Teuscher, "Der Beweis fand sich im Grasgarten" (Evidence was found in Grasgarten), *Bieler Tagblatt,* 4 July 2000; Lotti Teuscher, Nidau, in an e-mail to me, 2 August 2000; Hedwig Schaffer, Nidau, in a letter to me, 19 June 2000.

11. Hanno Helbling in a letter to me, 7 July 2000; Eva Lezzi in an e-mail to me, 17 August 2000; Jona Oberski, *Kinderjahre* (Childhood

years) (Vienna: Paul Zsolnay, 1980); the corresponding film, *Jona che visse nella balena,* directed by Roberto Faenza, Italy, 1993, 91 min.; cf. *Fragments*, p. 387.

12. Conversation with Samuel Althof, 24 June 2000; Althof, in an e-mail to me, 24 June 2000.

SELECT BIBLIOGRAPHY

Caruth, Cathy, ed. Introduction to *Trauma: Explorations in Memory,* pp. 3–12. Baltimore and London: Johns Hopkins University Press, 1995.

Cichopek, Anna. *Z dziejów powojennego antysemityzmu—pogrom w Krakowie 11. 08. 1945* Master's thesis, Faculty of History, Jagiellonian University, Kraków, 1998.

Eichenberger, Ursula, "Ich versuchte, ein guter Schauspieler zu werden, damit niemand etwas von meiner wahren Identität merkte" (I tried to be a good actor, so that no one would notice anything of my true identity), *Sonntags-Zeitung,* 18 May 1997.

Ganzfried, Daniel. "Die geliehene Holocaust-Biographie" (The borrowed Holocaust biography), *Die Weltwoche,* 27 Aug. 1998.

———. "Bruchstücke und Scherbenhaufen" (Fragments and debris), *Die Weltwoche,* 24 Sept. 1998.

———. "Fakten gegen Erinnerung" (Facts vs. memory), *Die Weltwoche,* 3 Sept. 1998.

———. "Binjamin Wilkomirski und die verwandelte Polin" (Binjamin Wilkomirski and the Transformed Polish Woman), *Die Weltwoche,* 4 Nov. 1999.

Gourevitch, Philip. "The Memory Thief." *The New Yorker,* 14 June 1999, pp. 48–68.

Halbwachs, Maurice. *Das Gedächtnis und seine sozialen Bedingungen* (Memory and its social conditions). Frankfurt: Suhrkamp, 1985; originally published in French, 1925.

Klüger, Ruth. *weiter leben: Eine Jugend* (Go on living: A childhood). 8th ed. Munich: Deutscher Taschenbuch Verlag, 1999.

Kolk, Bessel A. van der. "Trauma and Memory." In *Traumatic Stress; The Effects of Overwhelming Experience on Mind, Body, and Society.* Edited by

Bessel A. van der Kolk, Alexander C. McFarlane, and Lars Weisaeth. New York and London: The Guilford Press, 1996, pp. 279–302.

Kolk, Bessel A. van der, and Hart, Onno van der. "The Intrusive Past: The Flexibility of Memory and the Engraving of Trauma." In *Trauma: Explorations in Memory.* Edited by Cathy Caruth. Baltimore and London: Johns Hopkins University Press, 1995; pp. 158–82.

Kosinski, Jerzy. *The Painted Bird.* Boston: Houghton Mifflin, 1965.

Langer, Lawrence L. *The Holocaust and the Literary Imagination.* New Haven and London: Yale University Press, 1975.

Lappin, Elena. "The Man with Two Heads." *Granta,* no. 66 (summer 1999); pp. 7–65.

Loftus, Elizabeth, and Ketcham, Katherine. *The Myth of Repressed Memory: False Memories and Allegations of Sexual Abuse.* New York: St. Martin's, 1994.

Lupack, Barbara Tepa, ed. *Critical Essays on Jerzy Kosinski.* New York: G. K. Hall, 1998.

Maroko, Yakov. *Sha'agat Me'una* (Tormented scream). Bnei Brak: self-published by Maroko; n.d.

Matt, Peter von, *Verkommene Söhne, missratene Töchter: Familiendesaster in der Literatur* (Degenerate sons, daughters gone astray: Family disasters in literature). Munich: Deutscher Taschenbuch Verlag, 1997.

Niederland, William G. *Folgen der Verfolgung: Das Überlebendensyndrom Seelenmord* (Consequences of persecution: the survivor syndrome—murder of the soul). Frankfurt: Suhrkamp, 1980.

Novick, Peter. *The Holocaust and Collective Memory: The American Experience.* London: Bloomsbury, 2000.

Passantino, Bob; Passantino, Gretchen; and Trott, Jon. "Satan's Sideshow: The Real Story of Lauren Stratford." *Cornerstone,* 18, no. 90 (Oct.– Nov. 1989): 23–28; and at http://www.cornerstonemag.com.

Passantino, Bob, and Passantino, Gretchen. "Lauren Stratford: From Satanic Ritual Abuse to Jewish Holocaust." *Cornerstone,* 28 (Oct. 1999): 12–18. First published in *Cornerstone Magazine Online,* 13 Oct. 1999. http://www.cornerstonemag.com/features/iss117/lauren.thm.

Pfefferman, Naomi. "Memories of a Holocaust Childhood." *Jewish Journal,* 24 April 1998.

Picard, Jacques. *Die Schweiz und die Juden* (Switzerland and the Jews). Zurich: Chronos, 1994.

Rivera, Joseph de, and Sarbin, Theodore, eds. *Believed-In Imaginings:*

The Narrative Construction of Reality. Washington: American Psychological Association, 1998.

Sloan, James Park. *Jerzy Kosinski: A Biography.* New York: Dutton, 1996.

"Kosinski's War." In *Critical Essays on Jerzy Kosinski.* Edited by Barbara Tepa. New York: G. K. Hall, 1998; pp. 236–46.

Stratford, Lauren, and Michaelson, Johanna. *Satan's Underground: The Extraordinary Story of One Woman's Escape.* Eugene, Ore.: Harvest House Publishers, 1988. Reprint: Gretna, La.: Pelican Publishing, 1991.

Wilkomirski, Binjamin. *Fragments: Memories of a Wartime Childhood.* Translated by Carol Brown Janeway. New York: Schocken Books, 1996. German original: *Bruchstücke: Aus einer Kindheit 1939–1948.* Frankfurt: Suhrkamp, 1995.

Wilkomirski, Binjamin, and Bernstein, Elitsur. "Die Identitätsproblematik bei überlebenden Kindern des Holocaust: Ein Konzept zur interdisziplinären Kooperation zwischen Therapeuten und Historikern" (The problem of identity for child survivors of the Holocaust: A concept for interdisciplinary cooperation between therapists and historians). In *Überleben der Shoah—und danach: Späfolgen der Verfolgung aus wissenschaftlicher Sicht* (Surviving the Shoah—and afterward: Later consequences of persecution from a scientific viewpoint). Edited by Alexander Friedmann, Elvira Glück, and David Vyssoki. Vienna: Picus, 1999; pp. 160–72. Same article with minor changes, *Werkblatt* 39 (1997); 45–58.

Young, James Edward. *Writing and Rewriting the Holocaust: Narrative and the Consequences of Interpretation.* Bloomington: Indiana University Press, 1988.

Zeindler, Peter. "Bei mir war es eine Baracke" (To me it was a barrack). *Zürcher Tages-Anzeiger,* 29 May 1997.

ARCHIVES

Schweizerisches Bundesarchiv Bern/Swiss Federal Archives, Bern
Schweizerisches Rotes Kreuz Bern/Swiss Red Cross, Bern
Staatsarchiv Baselstadt/State Archives, City of Basel
Staatsarchiv Bern/State Archives, Bern
Stadtarchiv der Stadt Zürich/Municipal Archives of City of Zurich

State Archives, Riga
Vormundschaftsamt Biel/Biel Guardianship Authorities

FILMS AND DOCUMENTS

Bergkraut, Eric. *Das gute Leben ist nur eine Falle. Ein Besuch bei Binjamin Wilkomirski* (The good life is only a trap. A visit with Binjamin Wilkomirski). Directed by Eric Bergkraut; produced by 3 sat, and Schweizer Fernsehen DRS, Beta SP, 1997. 46 min.

Fechner, Eberhard. *Der Prozess* (The trial); Part 1: *Anklage* (Indictment), 89 min.; Part 2: *Beweisaufnahme* (Presenting the evidence), 92 min.; Part 3: *Das Urteil* (The verdict), 88 min. Produced by Norddeutscher Rundfunk, 1984.

Messel, Esther van. *Fremd geboren* (Born a stranger). Produced by Dschoint Ventschr, Zurich, 1997. 52/60 min., Beta SP/35mm, color.

Olgiati, Christopher. *Child of the Death Camps: Truth & Lies.* Produced by BBC One, 1999.

Survivors of the Shoah, Visual History Foundation. Video interview, 20 March 1997. 6 tapes (in German).

United States Holocaust Memorial Museum, Washington, D.C. Video interview, 26 Sept. 1997. 6 tapes (in English).

The author possesses copies of all documents not available to the public. I have included locations of sources in my notes only for those institutions open to the public, as well as the files of the Liepman Agency and Suhrkamp-Verlag.

CONVERSATIONS WITH WITNESSES AND OTHER INFORMANTS

Most interviews and conversations are preserved on tape recordings or in transcriptions; some, however, are documented in the form of notes taken during a conversation. Several conversations took place by telephone. People who provided only point-for-point confirmation are not included in the following list.

Aeberhard, René—Lompoc, CA, USA

Affolter, Kurt—Biel Guardianship Authorities, Biel, Switzerland

Akert-Giger, Ruth Elisabeth—Zurich, Switzerland

Balint, Lea—Jerusalem, Israel

Berman, Vered—Jerusalem, Israel

Bernstein, Elitsur—Bat Yam, Israel

Berti, Bruno—Zurich, Switzerland

Colla, Fernando—Winterthur, Switzerland

Colla, Rolando—Zurich, Switzerland

Curchod-Rohr, Frieda—Froideville-Le Jorat VD, Switzerland

Deskur, Edward—Küsnacht, Switzerland

Dössekker von Gonzenbach, Annette—Zurich, Switzerland

Elbinger, Emanuel—Kraków, Poland

Ganzfried, Daniel—Zurich, Switzerland

Grosjean, Max Albert—Horgen, Switzerland

Grosjean, Edeltraut (Trauti)—Horgen, Switzerland

Hilb, Liselotte—Zurich, Switzerland

Indergand, Peter—Winterthur, Switzerland

Karola—in P. (last name and address known to the author)

Koralnik, Eva—Zurich, Switzerland

Kranz, Thomasz—Pánstwowe muzeum na Majdanku (State Museum, Majdanek), Lublin, Poland

Leibel, Misia (Emilia)—Kraków, Poland

Löwinger, Julius—Petach Tikwa, Israel

M. K. ("Rapaport, Sabina")—L., Switzerland (real name and address known to the author)

Marx v. Prądzyński, Christine—Bochum, Germany

Marx v. Prądzyński, Sylwester—Bochum, Germany

Obermüller, Klara—Zurich, Switzerland

Piller-Altherr, Verena—A., Switzerland

Rechsteiner-Güller, Augusta Charlotte—Heiden, Switzerland

Sandberg, Rolf—Zurich, Switzerland

Schuppli, Sybille—Zurich, Switzerland

Singer, Annie—Zurich, Switzerland

Stabinsky, Leon—Chatsworth, CA, USA

Widmer-Dietz, Brigitta—Lindau, Switzerland

Wilkomirski, Binjamin/Dössekker, Bruno—Amlikon, Switzerland

Z., Rudolf—L., Switzerland

PERMISSIONS ACKNOWLEDGMENTS

Grateful acknowledgment is made to the following for permission to reprint previously published material:

American Society for Yad Vashem: Excerpt from "Account of Child Survivor: Fact or Fiction? Does It Really Make a Difference?" from *Martyrdom and Resistance* by Sarah Traister-Moskovitz (May–June 1999). Reprinted by permission of the American Society for Yad Vashem.

Cornerstone: Excerpt from "Satan's Sideshow: The True Lauren Stratford Story," by Bob Passantino, Gretchen Passantino, and Jon Trott (*Cornerstone*, 18, n. 90 (Oct./Nov. 1989) pp. 23–28). Reprinted by permission of *Cornerstone*.

Forward: Excerpts from "Wilkomirski Defends Holocaust Memoir" by Blake Eskin, *Forward* (April 16, 1999). Reprinted by permission of *Forward*.

Georges Borchardt, Inc.: Excerpt from "Everybody's Victim" by Elie Wiesel. Copyright © 1965 by Elie Wiesel. Originally published in the *New York Times Book Review*. Reprinted by permission of Georges Borchardt, Inc., for the author.

Schocken Books: Excerpts from *Fragments* by Binjamin Wilkomirski, translated by Carol Brown Janeway. Translation copyright © 1996 by Carol Brown Janeway. Copyright © 1995 by Binjamin Wilkomirski. Reprinted by permission of Schocken Books, a division of Random House, Inc.

Scientia-Factum, Inc.: Excerpts from "Afterword" to *The Painted Bird* by Jerzy Kosinski. Copyright © 1965, 1976 by Jerzy Kosinski, published by Grove Press. Reprinted by permission of Scientia-Factum, Inc.

ABOUT THE AUTHOR

Stefan Maechler was born in Aargau, Switzerland, in 1957 and now lives in Zurich. He studied history and German at the University of Zurich. He has published several studies on anti-Semitism and Switzerland's policies on asylum and refugees.

FRAGMENTS

BY

BINJAMIN WILKOMIRSKI

ONE

I have no mother tongue, nor a father tongue either. My language has its roots in the Yiddish of my eldest brother, Mordechai, overlaid with the Babel-babble of an assortment of children's barracks in the Nazis' death camps in Poland.

It was a small vocabulary; it reduced itself to the bare essentials required to say and to understand whatever would ensure survival. At some point during this time, speech left me altogether and it was a long time before I found it again. So it was no great loss that I more or less forgot this gibberish which lost its usefulness with the end of the war.

But the languages I learned later on were never mine, at bottom. They were only imitations of other people's speech.

My early childhood memories are planted, first and foremost, in exact snapshots of my photographic memory and in the feelings imprinted in them, and the physical sensations. Then comes memory of being able to hear, and things I heard, then things I thought, and last of all, memory of things I said.

"He who remembers nothing gambles away his future," a wise man once said.

If you don't remember where you came from, you will never really be able to know where you're going.

My earliest memories are a rubble field of isolated images and events. Shards of memory with hard knife-sharp edges, which still cut flesh if touched today. Mostly a chaotic jumble, with very little chronological fit; shards that keep surfacing against the orderly grain of grown-up life and escaping the laws of logic.

If I'm going to write about it, I have to give up on the ordering logic of grown-ups; it would only distort what happened.

I survived; quite a lot of other children did too. The plan was
for us to die, not survive. According to the logic of the plan, and
the orderly rules they devised to carry it out, we should have
been dead.

But we're alive. We're the living contradiction to logic and
order.

I'm not a poet or a writer. I can only try to use words to draw
as exactly as possible what happened, what I saw; exactly the
way my child's memory has held on to it; with no benefit of perspective or vanishing point.

The first pictures surface one by one, like upbeats, flashes of
light, with no discernible connection, but sharp and clear. Just
pictures, almost no thoughts attached:

It must have been Riga, in winter. The city moat was frozen
over. I'm sitting all bundled up with someone on a sled, and
we're running smoothly over the ice as if we're on a street. Other
sleds overtake us, and people on skates. Everyone's laughing,
looking happy. On both sides tree branches are bright and heavy
with snow. They bend over the ice; we travel through and under
them like through a silver tunnel. I think I'm floating. I'm
happy.

But this picture is quickly scared off by other ones, dark and
suffocating, which push into my brain and won't let go. They're
like a wall of solid black between me and the sparkling and the
sun.

For the first time, the feeling of deathly terror in my chest and
throat, the heavy tramp of boots, a fist that yanks me out of my
hiding place under the covers at the bottom of the bed and drops
me onto the floorboards in the middle of an otherwise unfur-
nished little room.

At the window, straight as candles and by order of height, four or five boys.

My brothers, maybe.

In a shadowy corner, the outline of a man in hat and coat, his sweet face smiling at me.

Maybe my father.

Uniforms, boots, screaming at him, hitting him, leading him out of the door. A cry of terror echoing down the staircase:

"Watch it: Latvian militia."

Doors slamming.

The man is taken downstairs. I crawl after him, grab on to the banisters, clamber down. They take the man outside, I follow them, and look up in the icy street. Uproar everywhere, lots of people milling around. More uniforms everywhere, angry shouting from all sides. I see a solid wooden barrier, the street is blocked off like a cul-de-sac.

They've put the man against the wall next to the front gate. The uniforms climb noisily onto a transport that's parked on the street. They wave their arms in the air, swing sticks, make faces of terrible rage. And they keep yelling something that sounds like "Killim, killim, killim."

The transport starts to move. It gains speed, heading for us and the wall. The man doesn't move, he's still leaning against the wall right beside me. I'm sitting on the ground, half under the gate, half against the wall, and looking up at him. He looks down at me and smiles.

But suddenly his face clenches, he turns away, he lifts his head high and opens his mouth wide as if he's going to scream out.

From down below, against the bright sky, all I see is the line of his jaw and his hat falling backward off his head.

No sound comes out of his mouth, but a big stream of something black shoots out of his neck as the transport squashes him with a big crack against the house.

I'm sad and very afraid because he turned away from me, but I feel that he didn't do it because he doesn't love me anymore.

His own upset must have been too much for him, and he only turned away because something unknown was even stronger than he was.

All at once I realize:

From now on I have to manage without you, I'm alone.

It takes a while for me to feel I'm able to look over there, but the man is gone. Nothing there to see anymore but a little mound of clothes, blood, and snow on the side of the road.

I see a tiny room, darkened, the only window hung with bits of cloth. In the middle, a small table, two men and a woman sitting around it. On the table a huge piece of paper that rustles when they put their elbows down with their heads in their hands. A kerosene lamp burns in the middle, lights up the faces. Soft words, almost whispering. Fingers following lines on the paper.

On the floor in the corner of the room, an oval woven basket, filled with rags. I sit on the woman's lap, look over the edge of the table, watch the faces. After a time the woman lifts me down and puts me to bed in the basket.

It's night, terribly cold. A woman is carrying me, there's someone with her, and several boys who know how to walk already. We hurry past walls of houses, we stop and wait several times at crossroads, looking carefully around the corners, then we hurry on again. There's another long wait, I think I see a street sign.

"Now! Move!" I hear suddenly, and we race across a huge, empty square and reach the harbor.

I sit on the dock on a bollard that has a ship tied up to it. We sit in the dark, and we have to wait a long time.

My clothes are all wet through to the skin. I'm horribly cold. At last the time comes, we climb three, four steps up a ladder, and group ourselves in the bow of the boat. Carefully coiled ropes lie there, making a hollow shape in the center. I am set down in this, as if I'm in a pan. The woman sits down on the edge, the boys lie in a circle on the deck.

On my left, there's a tiny bit of light coming up on the horizon, and I can already make out the clear shape of the city spires against the sky as the ship casts off from the bank. We move past the city for a bit, and I guess the way we came and the part of town we escaped from tonight. The woman spreads a cloth over me, and I can't see anything anymore. In spite of being cold and shivering, I fall asleep.

There's a station in my memory. We have to go through a barrier, papers are shown and looked at—maybe false ones.

Sighs of relief and we're standing on the platform and it's sunny. I have the feeling that a danger has passed, but I don't know what danger. People are standing about, waiting, lots of them women, all clean, in pretty clothes, smiling, and with different kinds of funny little hats on their heads, nothing I've ever seen before.

I'm surprised by this peaceful scene. People are strolling up and down, calm and relaxed, and I think:

How is this possible? They don't seem to have any idea what was going on back there.

And something tells me:

This isn't real peace. There's something wrong—it's only *their* peace!

We stand on another track, waiting again. There's no platform, no proper station either, just a little house. We stand next to the rails as if we're in open country. Lots of people are standing with us; we stand and wait, the sun above us is burning hot, I'm thirsty.

At last I see the train, it hisses and smokes, comes slowly to a halt. But it's already full up. People are standing on the steps, hanging there like bundles. There are even uniforms sitting up on the engine, and I'm very surprised that they can sit there in spite of the heat.

It seems to me impossible that we can get into one of the passenger cars. There's a lot of pushing and pulling, and somehow we manage.

A journey begins, and seems never to end. Endless fields, endless woods, and endless terrible thirst. But there seems to be some vague hope as well. I don't know where it comes from, even though the woman explains it to me. But I gather that it has something to do with Lemberg.*

I don't know what Lemberg is. It's some kind of magic word, that stays hanging and swaying in my head. It seems to be a place, maybe a town, that has something to do with something important we're all expecting, maybe someone we have to find there, or meet, who's going to help.

We never reached Lemberg, and we never found the mysterious person who was supposed to help us. Instead, this was the beginning of years that I only slowly came to understand, when someone tried to talk hope into me again, and took me on another long journey.

*Lvov.

TWO

The passenger car was stifling hot, and absolutely full.

"Not long till Basel," said Frau Grosz, who had got me out of an orphanage in Kraków and brought me with her this far.

I looked at her. She was staring at her hands and seemed to be a long way away. Something important, something that couldn't be changed, was going to happen. Basel. The word sounded as if it didn't know whether it was meant to be hopeful or threatening; either way, that's where we were going.

I looked out of the window and thought back to the house in Kraków, and the other children, the ones I'd watched as they played, the ones I'd fought with.

Frau Grosz might have been one of our children's nurses, or maybe she just came often to visit—I don't remember anymore.

One day she took me aside from the other children when we were playing in the little courtyard. She was rough with the others when they got curious, and shooed them away, and when we were alone, she said:

"I'm going back home, it's a long way away. I come from Switzerland, I came to Poland to get married before the war, my husband is dead, now I'm going home again. Switzerland is a beautiful country."

Her Yiddish had a funny sound; I didn't understand what she was talking about.

"I know they've been very nasty to you, you have to get away from here," she began again, and I wasn't sure what she meant.

Especially because I had never said a word about the children's camp or the children's barracks, never told anyone anything about what happened then. All I'd done was to keep asking about my brothers. That's all I ever said.

"Would you like to come too? I mean, you must say that you're my son, that way I can take you with me," and "Switzerland's a beautiful country."

She was repeating herself.

"People will be nice to you. Do you want to come?" she asked more urgently, because I still wasn't saying anything.

I was getting afraid. Away? From here? Could she be trusted?

"No, no, I don't want to," I started to scream hopelessly as loud as I could. "No, no, I don't want to go away. I belong here. This is where I live!"

I yelled and struggled. But to my complete astonishment, there wasn't a sound. And in the middle of the silence, I heard a voice saying quietly and clearly, "Yes, I'll come too."

This unknown voice! Or was it my voice? I heard myself wondering.

I was horrified. I tried again. I took the deepest breath I could manage. I wanted to scream so loud that everyone would hear!

"No—I belong here! I live here! I don't want to go away!"

And again I heard the unmistakable sound of my own voice, as if it was someone else's, loud and clear:

"Yes, I'm coming too."

That seemed to settle everything. Frau Grosz went away.

I felt as if I'd been defeated, disgraced. I was going to go away, all secretly, just go, leaving the rest of them in this mess.

I could feel the guilt like a lump in my throat. I didn't say a word to anyone. Not even Mila.* I liked her. When there was

---

*In the German edition this character's name is Karola. After she protested, Wilkomirski changed her name to Mila for the English edition (Stefan Maechler).

fighting at mealtimes, she always took care of me. Sometimes she even hugged me. She was older than I, and I think I'd known her from before, somewhere.

So here I was in a railway passenger car next to Frau Grosz, who was still staring at her hands and not saying anything.

We'd been traveling for days and days, and this is what I can remember about the last day of the journey:

There was a destination, and it was coming close, it wasn't *my* destination, but I let it happen, I was tired, apathetic maybe, no thought of resisting. I thought about the friends I'd left behind. And often about Mila, who was certainly still running through the streets of Kraków, asking the grown-ups about her mother or her father.

Can anyone tell, just by looking at me, that I'm a traitor, a deserter? My face began to burn, I couldn't hold my head up or look up.

Things started to stir on the train. The journey was almost over. Frau Grosz stood up purposefully, took my hand, and began to pull me through the crush of people from one car to the next and then the next. I just let it happen. I was tired out, despite all the bustle I couldn't keep my eyes open.

I woke up because of loud noises. How long had I been asleep? I looked around. Something must have happened while I was asleep.

This was another car, not where I'd been sitting with Frau Grosz before. And this one was full of children the same age as me, who were pulling down parcels from the racks, all tied up with string, and running up and down excitedly. There were some grown-ups too.

Lots of yelling and calling at one another in a language I didn't know. The voice of a conductor rose above the hubbub, and someone answered: "These children all French" was all I understood, and to my amazement, I noticed that there was a

string tied around my neck. Flapping down from this was a
label with a red border, just like all the French children had.

How did I get one? I looked around. Frau Grosz was nowhere
to be seen.

The train rolled slowly into the dark station hall. Strong arms
took hold of me, and set me down on the platform in the row with
everyone else, and then we were marched off into a waiting room.

Absolute chaos. Packages were being undone and spread out
by ladies, then tied up again. In the middle of everything, children running around and yelling.

People looked at the labels around our necks.

I sat in a corner on a bench, clutching my bundle, though I
had no idea what was inside it.

"Those are your things" was all Frau Grosz had said.

Gradually the to-ing and fro-ing settled down. One after
another, children were called, then led away out of the waiting
room by women in white and red aprons.

I gasped for air—more children were led away by grown-
ups—and I couldn't see where they were being taken.

That was the way it had been before, too. Only then it was
gray uniforms that took them away with angry gestures. The
gray uniforms carried sticks and whips. The ones they took away
never came back. But this time the grown-ups were friendly. I
tried to push away the tiredness.

Don't go to sleep! Keep watch!

I tried to make sense of what was going on here, but couldn't.
The children looked happy, a lot of them were laughing.

Maybe this is all just to confuse me; it's dangerous when
grown-ups are friendly to children, I say this to myself.

I struggled to remember, and I thought about the big gray
man. The big gray man was a warning to me.

The big gray man guarded us back then, whenever we were
allowed out of the barracks into the open air, and we played the
games we made up, as we stumbled and hesitated in the bright
daylight.

He didn't like us, the big gray man, and sometimes he kicked us or hit us. His gray uniform was all dirty and creased, and his eyes had a dangerous glint in them.

When he was standing there in the middle of us, all bored, I used to think how to cheer him up, so that he wouldn't kick us. He always kicked us when he was bored.

Very carefully at first, then more boldly, I began to dance around him, skipping up to him, then jumping away again, the way you do when you're playing tag. I kept trying and at last he looked at me. His eyes gradually lost the dangerous shadow they had. Astonished, I saw his mouth begin to twitch; only very slowly and just a little at first, but quite definitely. I felt a rush of pride and utter joy. I'd done it! I'd made the angriness go away from his face, and he was joining in my game.

I'd beaten him!

First he grabbed hold of my hand, we danced around in a circle, and he laughed. It sounded funny and rough, but that was just while he was laughing the angriness out of himself. Then he gave a great swing and lifted me onto his shoulders and I rode him like King David on his snow-white horse. We galloped faster and faster in circles and I was so happy, I couldn't even describe it: he'd been all angry, and now he was playing our games with us.

The others stood around absolutely astonished.

But suddenly he began to run crazily straight ahead, and I got frightened. He broke through the circle of amazed children, running for the wall that marked off our playground, took tighter hold of my feet, lifted me up over his head, and came to a stop for a moment at the wall. He was still holding on to my feet in the air and I flew forward like a loose bundle, clean over his head, until my forehead hit the stone. That's when he let go of me and went away.

He was still laughing.

I lay on the muddy ground, crippled with disbelief and shock at this betrayal. It was some time before I felt the pain. I climbed to my feet and ran screaming at the top of my lungs into the barracks.

A female guard, perhaps a block warden, looked at me, bent over me yelling, and pointed at the freshly mopped, scoured floorboards. Another one stood there beside her, grinning.

I looked behind me.

A trail of blood marked the way I'd come. She threw a big, heavy cloth at me. She ordered me to clean the floor. I bent down and tried to wipe up the blood. Again and again and again. It seemed never-ending. Every time I bent over to wipe, more blood fell down from my forehead, and I wiped and wiped, and I thought:

This is how it's going to be, forever and ever, until everything's dripped out of me, and then I'll be dead.

I don't remember how it actually ended.

So—careful! Friendly grown-ups are the most dangerous, they're best at fooling you, I thought.

I never saw the big gray man in the dirty uniform again.

Maybe he's here, in amongst all these other friendly grown-ups? I'll be ready for him. I'll bite him when he shows up!

I thought about this. I felt afraid, and angry. I squeezed myself deeper into my corner.

The waiting room had gone all quiet meantime, there was only one group of grown-ups talking off in a corner. Bundles of papers were being passed around, then carried out.

The "operation" seemed to be over.

The waiting room was empty.

"Why am I always the one who's left behind?" I wondered.

We'd arrived early in the morning, shortly after dawn. Now the sun was already high, shining through the glass roof. I was still sitting alone in my corner, holding tight to my bundle, looking at the empty room. Frau Grosz was nowhere to be seen. I was freezing cold, even though it was mild. I felt helpless and alone. For the first time in a long time, I began to cry. It felt strangely warm as the tears ran down my face.

I had cried sometimes in the last years, yelled out whatever rage or powerlessness was in my lungs, screamed in physical pain or fear. But when was the last time I'd really cried because I was so sad?

It must have been a long time ago, because nobody was allowed to be sad in the camps. Whoever was sad, even for a minute, was weak. Whoever was weak, died.

But I remembered, and it seemed a long way away and a long time ago. It was in the farmhouse, away somewhere in amongst the Polish forests, where I lived for a little while with my older brothers, long before I was taken to the children's camp. That's where I had my first clear memories from.

I can still see it exactly:

We were all sitting around the table in the main room, and for some reason I was crying. Motti, my eldest brother, stood up and bent over me. His face was full of love and concern, his broad back curved down over me like a great safe shield, and I listened to his comforting voice.

A blissful moment—I had to cry all over again.

But Motti had gone away a long time ago. So had my other brothers. In their place, a strange woman was suddenly bending over me. I looked up.

"I've never seen this uniform before," was my first thought. I felt uneasy.

"So, did they forget you?" she asked, and the way she spoke was strange, I could barely understand her.

I swallowed, couldn't answer, didn't want to, either.

She went away again, shaking her head, with my label in her hand.

"It's blank," she said out loud, turning around.

"Where did you come from? Who gave you this?"

I choked and clenched my teeth. I shook my head, and shrugged.

I won't say anything, ever, to anybody. I have to keep quiet, I mustn't give anything away.

When she came back, she was talking at me fast, and all upset.

I didn't understand a word, but I could tell that she was very cross, that I must have done something wrong, and that the thing "was not so simple," that they "hadn't been expecting" me, that there was "no spot" for me.

But then she went away again, and other people came and asked the same things:

"Where did you come from? Who brought you here? What's your name? We don't know anything about you! You're not on our list. We have to make a phone call."

I stayed brave, and kept my mouth shut.

From the opposite corner of the waiting room there were sounds of agitated conversation. The waiting became a torture; fear and disappointment washed over me, I had to fight for air.

Eventually, a long time later, another lady came in, pushed a stuffed teddy bear into my arms, and said:

"We finally managed to find a place in an orphanage, but we have to go there by train. Hurry, they're expecting us at lunchtime."

"I want to go to Frau Grosz," I murmured, and started to cry.

She shook her head and looked at me puzzled.

"Who's Frau Grosz?"

Oh—I almost gave myself away.

I shut my mouth tight, I didn't say another word, I just shrugged, and she pulled me off the bench.

This one wasn't wearing any uniform. So I took my bundle and the teddy bear, and we ran to the train.

We were late getting to the orphanage. I was led into a big room, where the last children were just getting up from a huge long table. Someone said I was to wait here. I looked at the table, everyone had gone and I was standing there alone.

The table looked different from what I was used to. It was covered with a big cloth, which hung way down over the edge. The children's plates were still lying there, they'd just left them. But the plates weren't the usual gray tin ones, they were white. Plates like that for children?

I was surprised, and I went closer.

What I saw was so completely amazing that I couldn't understand it, but there was no time to think. I had to do something at once.

The children hadn't eaten everything on their plates! They'd left bits in strips around the edges. These leftovers were all over everywhere, and apparently nobody was guarding them.

I looked around, but there was nobody to be seen. I quickly hid myself under the table behind the protection of the cloth and by reaching out just one arm, began to feel around on top to where the plates were, and I collected the leftover strips. I put as many as I could into my mouth, and as many as I could into my pockets and into my shirt. The strips were chewy, but they tasted delicious; the most delicious things, aside from bread, that I'd ever smelled or eaten. It was like being drunk. I had to get more, everything that I could fit into my shirt.

You could eat enough to be full, and even lay in a supply for another week, maybe longer, I thought.

In just a few seconds, to be able to find enough food to last for days without worry—it was beyond me.

These stupid kids! I thought.

How can anyone be dumb enough to leave food lying around unprotected? They don't seem to have a clue. Maybe they're new here, and they don't know yet that surviving means laying in supplies, finding a good hiding place, defending your food. Never ever leave food unguarded, that's what Jankl always told me.

I was thinking this, and chewing and chewing, and breathing

in the wonderful smell when suddenly a hand seized my arm as I groped for another plate.

A hard yank, and I was pulled out from under the table.

I sat there on the floor, mouth full, clutching the last delicious bits in both fists, looking at fat calves and the hem of a white apron. A second yank, and I was hauled up onto my feet. Some of the strips fell out of my shirt.

I raised my head.

I was looking into staring, pale, angry eyes. First they looked at the floor and the strips I'd dropped, then at my fists, then at my mouth crammed full, with the spit running down, and after a moment of silent shock the angry screaming started:

"Cheese rinds! He's eating cheese rinds! Monster!"

I didn't know what a monster was, but I both understood what it must mean—and didn't understand at all. Her mouth twisted with disgust.

Why should it be forbidden to eat what was edible, that nobody was guarding as theirs, and that tasted so good? Maybe the strips belong to her? Does she want to take them back, so she can eat them herself? I wondered.

I pulled free and ran away, determined to defend my booty to the last. So I raced through the room, right around the table, then under it and out the other side, behind a sort of counter, but then, summoned by the screaming, a second pair of fat calves under a white apron came at me.

I fell onto the floor, arms tried to grab hold of me, quick as a flash I tried to bite one of the calves. But all I got was a mouthful of apron. I pulled down on it, got all tangled up, and then there was more screaming and they had hold of me.

I couldn't breathe, so I had to spit out the last of the strips, which produced yet more screaming.

"What's been going on here?" asked a quiet voice from somewhere.

It was the lady who'd brought me.

"He's spitting and biting and fighting, and eating scraps," said one of the white aprons angrily.

She'd already got my shirt open, and now she shook my whole gathered treasure out onto the floor.

Another one came with a pail and dustpan and brush and took everything away.

I didn't understand anything anymore.

They were taking my food away, but not because they wanted it themselves. They didn't seem to be hungry. No, they were just throwing food away right in front of my eyes. Was this how they wanted to punish me?

One of the aprons gave orders, and I was put into a solitary room, as they called it.

"Only till you quiet down," they said, and shut the door.

Only now did I realize that in all the uproar I'd lost my bundle—and the stuffed bear was gone too.

I tiptoed to the door, but it was locked.

I looked around. The only things in the room were a bed, a single one but huge, a table, and a chair. On the bed was a great big cover, all full of air like a cloud. I sniffed. The cloud smelled sweet and clean and tempting.

I didn't dare touch it.

I thought:

The only person who'd be allowed to sleep here must have extra-special privileges, and be very powerful and strong. How else could he defend a place like this? He must be someone with a specially important uniform, one with shiny buttons. I haven't seen any of the black or gray uniforms here, but you can't be sure.

Oh—but what if he finds me here? Will he beat me, because he thinks I'm trying to take over his property and his place? Everyone here seems to be stronger than I am.

Then I thought again about my defeat, about the food I'd lost, and the lost bundle, and the lost stuffed bear, and I was afraid that the uniform might already be standing on the other side of the door.

I listened, but the whole house was quiet.

They're taking everything away from me here.

A lump thickened in my throat.

Perhaps it's not just the food, perhaps they're going to take my clothes too. It's winter. Perhaps they're going to leave me here to starve. Switzerland isn't a beautiful country, the way Frau Grosz said. Frau Grosz lied to me! Frau Grosz has left me all alone. I hate Frau Grosz!

Hungry and exhausted, I crawled under the bed and went to sleep.

THREE

Did I have four brothers or five, which seems righter? I can't say for sure anymore. But they're in all my earliest memories, the ones I'm halfway sure about.

Shards of recollection, holding my brothers fast inside, like flakes of feldspar in a great rockslope of childhood memory.

A farmstead, a cluster of small buildings arrayed in a rectangle to make a courtyard in the middle. A house facing an empty stable, a barn for the horsecart minus horse, standing open on the side facing the courtyard, and another barn for grain, now as empty as the stable.

The only grown-up is the farmer's wife, severe, rough, full of punishments. She supervised us, fed us, some kind of porridge out of a big pot.

We sat at a long table in order of our ages. At one end was me, as the youngest, then Daniel; at the other end was Motti or "Mordechaiiii," the way the woman sounded whenever she yelled for him, as the eldest. The others in between, only shadowy pictures of them.

Opposite us, in the middle of the other long side of the table, the farmer's wife, who ordered us never to open the doors or even leave the house without permission, never to look out of a window, and always to duck down when going past one—"because of the bullets that could come through the glass," she said.

The way she looked at us, so dark and angry, as she said this, told us how bad the punishment would be if we disobeyed. But there was also something else in her eye, which made me much more uneasy—I think it was fear. This powerful muscular woman with her big arms and heavy hands, who embodied absolute power over us children—could there be something that was even more powerful than she was? Something even she was afraid of?

How we spent our days in the house, I've almost no idea anymore. I remember Motti's endlessly repeated warnings to crouch before I went past a window, and occasional forays into the open air once evening came.

Once Motti put together a glider out of paper and sticks. I was allowed to watch. He set it out to dry on the little wood stove, warned me not to touch it, and went into the kitchen. But my curiosity was stronger than his warning, and as I touched it, it fell onto the floor and broke.

Motti didn't hit me, he never hit me, he didn't even say anything bad, he just explained calmly what had happened. Then he showed me how you repair an airplane.

When the farmer's wife was away from the house, Motti took over from her as the guardian of us younger ones. This was always a wonderful time. Motti always took special care of me. To me, he wasn't a child anymore. He was strong, the protector who never got angry or yelled. He could comfort too, and he meant warmth and safety.

A canal ran past the farmstead. We had to cross a small footbridge over a weir to get to a meadow where we were sometimes allowed to play. There was only one rail and it was too high for me, and I was afraid of the deep whirlpool under my feet.

But mostly I was afraid of the whale, the one Motti had told us about.

There was this whale that swallowed Jonah when he didn't want to do what God said—or so said Motti. I knew I didn't always do what people said either, and I thought that one day God was going to say to the whale:

See over there, that farm's where Binjamin lives, he's disobe-
dient. Swim up the canal, and next time he's crossing the weir,
jump out of the water and swallow him and bring him to me!

Shaking with fear I kept peering down into the water to see if
this time the whale was waiting for me.

Motti was the only person I could tell about what I was afraid
of. But Motti laughed and said that wasn't the whole story, and
he'd explain why I didn't have to be afraid.

This is what he told me:

"The whale spat Jonah out again, because Jonah said he was
sorry. God was very pleased with the whale, because it had done
its work so well. And then there came a time when more and
more people didn't do what God said. God remembered the
whale, and sent him out to swallow all the bad people and only
spit out the ones who said they were sorry. But not many people
did, and so the whale got bigger and bigger and rounder and fat-
ter. When the whale got old and died, it was huge. And then
God had an idea: he saw the poor Jews in the world, and he saw
that a lot of them were starving. So he gave them the dead
whale, so that once a week for a thousand years they could all eat
whale. That's why we Jews always eat gefilte fish on Sabbath."

"But I've never eaten gefilte fish," I said, and Motti said,
"Maybe the whale's all eaten up by now—and that's also why
there's a war now, because there's been no whale for a long time
now to swallow up the bad people" . . .

That's how I lost my fear of the whale in the canal and found
out what war was.

But soon various things happened to shatter the peaceful time at
the farm. One day we heard a man's voice, loud and deep, half
singing, half roaring in front of the house. In spite of it being
forbidden, we peered furtively out of the window.

Motti said it was a soldier and explained to me what a soldier
was. Motti recognized the uniform and explained to me about

uniforms. The soldier was carrying a gun, and Motti explained what he used it for.

As the soldier came up to the house, we fled in fear into the kitchen, where the farmer's wife was fussing about. The soldier appeared outside the kitchen window and looked in. He began yelling something again that I didn't understand, and I saw his arm swing back, then hit right in the middle of the window-pane.

The whole window splintered into the kitchen and the soldier climbed in. The woman and the soldier were screaming words at each other in a language I didn't know.

"Out, get out," the woman spat at us, and her voice sounded different, something new about it.

We ran into the living room and listened. We heard terrible noises, crashing and blows, the woman screaming, the man cursing in his deep voice. Then it was silent.

We kept waiting, we didn't dare move, we waited a long time.

Then we heard a soft whimpering coming from the kitchen. Cautiously we slipped into the room. The woman was sitting on the floor in the middle of the room, her clothes all torn and her hair in a mess, and she was crying.

The farmer's wife could cry!

The farmer's wife, this strong woman who could be so bad-tempered and frightening. The stern judge who ruled us children and thought up such painful punishments—she could cry?

I was dumbfounded.

There she was, sitting on the floor surrounded by bits of crockery, between the smashed chairs and the overturned kitchen table.

"Out, out!" she screamed at us again angrily, but it sounded forced, and she tried to push the hair off her wet face and out of her eyes, but couldn't.

So we left her alone and crept back into the other room. We

never said a word about it, not ever, but we knew that the war had sent us its herald.

When winter came, there soon wasn't anything to eat anymore. Every two days or so, Motti led us out of the house once it got dark. Without the woman, we'd cross the frozen canal in the snow and go into the nearby woods. We crawled our way under snow-covered branches, pushed through bushes until we reached a clearing, where a little house stood in a hollow. Other, unknown children would arrive from all directions too, sliding down the snow into the hollow, and going into the house.

There was just one room inside. In the middle on an open fire was a huge pot bubbling with soup. The air was sticky, so full of steam you almost couldn't see a thing. Every child got a bowl, and the soup smelled wonderful.

We went there often, and mostly I came back crying. The way through the snow was almost more than I could manage. Motti always made us go as fast as we could, only he seemed to know why this was.

When we got to the hut, I always burned my fingers on the hot tin dish, and my lips on the hot soup. Most often we had to leave again before I had a chance to drink all of my bowl. But it seemed to be more important to leave really promptly.

Spring came and the ground began to thaw, the weather got warmer, then really hot. We didn't have to freeze anymore.

Then one day it happened. The war reached us.

Sounds of gunfire came echoing out of the wood and we heard the rumble of engines. The noise came closer.

"Under the table! Lie on the floor! Not a sound!" called the woman.

So I lay between Motti and Daniel, my next-eldest brother, I hardly remember the others at all, and we listened to a rattling noise that came closer and closer until it turned into a horrible din. Then there was a dull explosion, and the whole house seemed to shake. The racket died down, there were one or two more scattered shots—then silence. We waited, holding our breath, we waited and waited, but nothing happened, no soldier came into the house, everything stayed quiet, it all seemed to be over.

Having to stay still under the table was slowly getting more and more uncomfortable. Slowly but surely my curiosity was getting the better of my anxiety.

"I have to pee," I whispered and crawled carefully out from under the table.

The toilet was in a little outhouse which you could get to from the main room. I went in, climbed carefully onto the seat, and pulled myself up to the little window. I looked out.

To one side, halfway through the broken rear wall of the house, was some kind of vehicle I'd never seen before. It was huge, looked as if it was made of iron, a gray black monster with a round lid that was standing open. There was smoke and a bad smell coming out of the hole. I could see quite clearly that there was the body of a soldier hanging out into the air from under the lid, and it wasn't moving. Another two soldiers were lying just as still between the fruit trees in the meadow.

A loud noise behind me dragged me away from my observations. The woman had pulled the door open—I'd been gone too long. She cried out when she saw me up there, more furious than I'd ever seen her. She dragged me down from the window and slapped me in a way she'd never done before.

"I'm going to lock you up alone in the cellar for this. No sleeping with your brothers tonight!" she gasped and pulled me onto the floor.

It was already late morning when I woke up on a pile of sacks that smelled of fruit. The tiny cellar was almost dark. The only light came from two tiny windows that opened to the air at ground level. I could see that the sun must already be high. The door to upstairs was locked.

Why doesn't she come and get me—or else Motti—if it's daytime already? I wondered, and listened as hard as I could for footsteps. Everything stayed quiet, there wasn't a sound in the house. I climbed up on a crate and looked out.

It must have been midday by the time I managed, after endless trying, to pull myself all the way up and scramble out into the courtyard.

Everything seemed peaceful and quiet, but there was nobody to be seen. None of my brothers, and not the woman either. I went through the empty house, all the doors were open and the pot still had some of yesterday's porridge in it.

I went back out into the courtyard, back into the house, back out to the courtyard again; I started calling, but nobody answered.

Where could they have gone? Why didn't they take me with them? I thought.

I felt very sick. I was afraid when my brothers weren't there, and without Motti's protection.

Two, maybe three days went by before I heard any noises. I was standing outside next to the horsecart without the horse.

I detected a roaring sound that was coming closer and closer. A truck drove slowly into the courtyard, followed by a group of strange men on foot. Green uniforms with guns were running alongside them. Green uniforms got out of the cab of the truck, and made a circle around it, and they had weapons too.

On the back of the truck lots of people were standing, all pushed together so that they swayed oddly as they looked down at me. They looked tired and dusty. I stood and stared in amazement, I'd never ever seen so many people before. They were almost all grown-ups, just a few children, bigger than me.

A shape detached itself from the standing group and came over to me slowly. It was a woman. You could see she was different from the others, because she was all dressed in gray. She looked like a soldier on top because she had a peaked cap and a jacket with beautiful shiny uniform buttons. But on her bottom half she wasn't wearing trousers like the ones in green, she was wearing a skirt. And she had boots—I'd never seen any as grand as hers.

The gray uniform was made of some kind of material I didn't know—smooth and clean, no tears, no holes, no stains. She must be someone special.

She stood there, a great gray shadow, and said something to me. I shook my head, because I couldn't understand a single word. She stopped, then she started speaking again, and this time it sounded like the way Motti spoke.

"What are you doing here?" she asked. "Are you alone?"

"Yes," I said, "and I'm looking for my brothers."

Hope was beginning to rise.

Maybe she knew where Motti and Daniel and the others had gone. She just nodded, went into the house, came out again, and said:

"I'll take you to your brothers, come with me," and she took my hand.

I was ready to whoop with joy, but her grip was too hard, somehow, and her hands reminded me of the hands of the farmer's wife.

She pushed me over to the others where they were waiting, the truck started up, and we followed it away across fields and along roads where I'd never been before.

"Where to?" I asked the gray uniform, clutching on to the edge of her skirt to keep pace.

"Majdan Lublin—Majdanek," she said, and "You can play there."

Her voice sounded oddly harsh, and she pushed my hand roughly off her skirt.

"Where to?" I asked again.

"Majdan Lublin—Majdanek," she said again abruptly, and I looked up at her.

"And my brothers?"

"You'll see them all again," she said, looking down at me, and now she was smiling.

She was smiling, but her smile kept turning into a sort of grin, and I wasn't sure what to make of it.

"Majdanek, Majdan Lublin, Majdanek," I said, over and over again. The name was so pretty.

My anticipation of seeing my brothers banished all suspicion.

I pictured how it was going to be in Majdanek, with no angry farmer's wife, just together with my brothers. We would play— that's what the gray uniform lady had said—we'd play, in a big, sunny field outside in the light, with shady trees all round. No more being shut up in that stuffy room, day after day.

Motti must certainly have taken his handmade glider with him, I thought, and maybe the ball too.

I couldn't wait.

How long the journey went on, I've no idea. Suddenly people were saying "We're here"—perhaps that same day, perhaps the next.

I do remember: it was evening already, and the day had been hot. I was terribly thirsty.

We went down a dusty path, past a big snow-white house. I'd never seen such a high house. It wasn't made of wood, it seemed to be made of stone, and I was surprised that I couldn't see a roof. A short distance past the strange house we waited for a long time at a wooden fence with barbed wire on it.

I saw a gate being opened, I saw a wooden tower, I saw a street leading upward, a whole sea of long-shaped houses built of wood.

There were soldiers standing around. One of them was right next to me, and I looked him up and down, curiously.

"What's that funny weapon you've got?" I asked him.

I pointed at a thing that was hanging down from his belt.

Quick as a flash he turned around, just as quickly his arm

shot up in the air with the strange thing in his fist, and something whizzed across my face with such burning heat that I thought I'd been cut in two. That's how I learned what a whip is, and I understood:

The gray lady was lying: Majdanek is no playground.

FOUR

The peaceful calm of that first sleep in the new children's home was shattered by a nightmare. The nightmare would repeat itself mercilessly in the years that followed, image by image, detail by detail, night by night, like an unstoppable copying machine.

I was in half darkness, and I was the only child on earth. No other human being, no tree, no grass, no water—nothing. Just a great desert of stone and sand.

In the middle of the world, a cone-shaped mountain loomed up against the dark sky. The peak of the mountain was capped with a black, metallic, glinting, ominous helmet.

At the foot of the mountain was a hut with a sort of canopy in front. Under the canopy were a lot of coal cars on rails. Some of the cars were full of dead people; their arms and legs stuck out over the edges. A narrow rail track ran straight up to the peak and in under the helmet, into a gaping jawbone with filthy brown teeth. The cars cycled uphill, disappearing into the jaw under the helmet, then cycled back down again, empty.

All over the plain around the mountain, hordes of biting insects suddenly came crawling out of the ground. Everything was covered with them thicker and thicker, as far as the eye could see, until the plain looked like a sea of evil creatures.

The bugs crawled over me. Ants, lice, beetles; they crawled up my legs, and over my stomach; they flew against my head, and scrabbled in my hair, and ears, eyes, nose, and mouth.

My skin began to itch and burn. I knew I was their last meal on earth. Where could I go to save myself? I saw that the only places they avoided were the iron cars. They slid off them.

But it was no use fleeing to one of the cars. They traveled as unstoppably and regularly as clockwork up the mountain and tipped their contents into the awful gullet under the helmet. Jumping onto one of the cars would only postpone the end.

I awoke with a sense of despair, and the absolute certainty that there was no way out. Any relief is not real, it's the last false hope before the inevitable arrival of death. And I knew it would be both slow and agonizing.

I lay there awake for a while. It was early, everything was quiet in the orphanage, and I had to think about the kennel.

It was during the time when I was living with a horde of other children in the big barracks.

Once, overcome by curiosity, I had gone off a long way from the others; without anyone apparently noticing, I left the inner fence perimeter along with a women's work detail. I went along the road in the camp that led downhill from our zone, which was for women and children, past the next fenced-in zones and toward the big main gate.

In front of the store barracks, where mountains of suitcases and clothes were piled up, I turned off to watch a man in a brownish green uniform. A ragged man next to him was hacking at a strip of earth alongside the path. I wandered slowly past behind them, without noticing that I was losing my direction.

Perhaps they want to plant some flowers, I thought, the way the farmer's wife did when we lived with her.

Behind the freshly dug strip of earth was a fence, and behind that was a row of kennels. I was terrified of the brownish black dogs. But now the kennel doors were open, and the kennels were empty. So I moved closer to the man, to see what he was doing.

Both men turned around and stared at me. The ragged man dropped his pick, and the brownish green man let out a roar of rage and charged at me, cursing and waving his arms like a madman. He pointed to the earth and to my feet. I looked. I was standing right in the middle of the freshly turned strip of earth. Apparently this was a big crime.

I wanted to run away, but the man grabbed at me. He grabbed for my head, his hands reaching for my ears, and lifted me off the ground. A stabbing pain went through my head and neck, and I felt as if my face was being torn in half. But the more I fought, the worse the pain got. I was lifted higher until I swung between the big fists on either side of my face, over the fence in the direction of the kennels. The fists pushed me in, and the entrance was barred with a plank.

Bent over, half standing, half sitting, I waited for the pain to go away. I waited and waited, but nothing else happened. Everything had gone quiet outside, nobody seemed to have heard me crying or calling. A little light came through a crack in the plank, and it was getting weaker, and I knew night was coming.

If only they don't bring the dogs back, I thought, frightened, if only rats don't come once it gets dark.

Rats were what I was most afraid of, because they came when you were asleep. To drive them away, I began to stamp my feet in a steady rhythm, the way Jankl had showed me.

But the rats weren't what was worst that night.

The kennel was full of bugs. The darker it got, the more I began to sweat with fright, the more I tried to brush the creatures off my body, and the more greedily they seemed to start crawling up my legs again. Lice began to run over my face in racing, ticklish streams to my nose, mouth, and eyes. No amount of wiping or scratching helped. They always came back.

But the most disgusting were the hard, fat, triangular beetles that flew buzzing at my head and crawled into my clothes. I tried to protect my hands at least, and pushed them into the semicircular pockets of my child's overalls. But there were beetles in there too, and when they were squashed they gave out a horrible smell.

I was overcome with nausea. My stomach was empty and

nothing came up but a sour liquid, and it was even worse than before. The lice were crawling over my face again. They seemed to be in even more of a hurry than before. Neither blowing my nose nor spitting could stop their assault on my face.

At some point the crack in the wood got light again. Somebody took the plank away from the entrance.

I don't know who fetched me out. As I was pulled into the daylight, hot pain shot through my eyes deep into my head. What had happened to my eyes? I could hardly make anything out. The light stabbed like needles, even through my closed eyelids. Guided by the shoves I was given, and blinking down at the ground now and then, I crawled rather than walked until I reached the rescuing darkness of my barracks.

FIVE

The first days in the orphanage were all confusion. There were so many new rules to learn, and most of them made no sense to me. Everything seemed to happen as endless contradictions.

The nurses were friendly, they didn't yell, they didn't hit us, they helped without being asked, and they brought clothes and food. Especially food!

It took your breath away. Every morning, mountains of unfamiliar luxuries were piled up on a sideboard, and there was enough for everyone—more than we all could eat.

On the other hand, I was always being forbidden to stick to the most important rules of survival. I had learned that stuff from Jankl in the big barracks, and I took such care not ever to forget any of it.

I knew that everything depended on it. But the nurses and the other children seemed to have forgotten it all. I often got the feeling that they'd never known the rules at all. They did everything with such dangerous carelessness.

Finally, nobody can know how long there'll be enough to eat. It can all come to an end any day. And maybe it's all just a trap, I said to myself.

I knew for sure that I had to be on the alert, because it was the clueless ones who always got into trouble first, and had the worst of it. Each meal could be the last for a long time. But nobody seemed to worry about this.

They always caught me stealing supplies, they always found my hiding places, they always saw through my plans to run away, and took their precautions. But oddly, they didn't punish me, at least not right away. And that was what was so unsettling. What were they planning?

Perhaps, I thought, they were holding off punishing me until they could catch me in a moment when I wasn't paying attention, and that would make it even worse.

I lived in a state of anxiety and watchfulness, all mixed up with breathless enjoyment of this temporary abundance.

But one thing in particular hurt me—I wasn't able to make any friends. I had always been friends with the ones like Jankl, who shared food with me.

Jankl used to steal food, when we were about to collapse from hunger. Jankl knew he'd be killed if he got caught. Jankl didn't eat what he'd stolen all himself, he gave me some, he always shared. Jankl was my friend.

But here, nobody wanted to share.

Once one of the older girls sat next to me at breakfast. She had the most beautiful eyes, and a soft voice. I held out half of my thick-buttered bread, but she just laughed at me and took her own piece of bread from the huge mound on the table.

As for the mound of bread on the table: an almost indescribable feeling went through me when I saw it that first morning after I arrived at the orphanage.

I was the last to arrive in the dining hall, because I didn't know that there would be food for us every morning. Only a few children were still sitting around the table.

I was shown where to sit. I sat down and waited. When no further signal came, I slowly looked up and glanced around cautiously—and there it was! Right in front of me on the table.

A big platter holding a mountain of bread. Clean-cut, even slices all beautifully stacked up in towers and turrets, and behind the towers, more, more than I could even count. I stared in awe, as if it were a holy relic.

Who could it belong to? I thought to myself. Who could be that powerful, and control so much bread? And why was it lying here unguarded? And would this person, whoever he was, give me a piece? Or should I try to steal one?

I looked at the bread and dilated my nostrils. A wonderful smell was coming in my direction, and suddenly I recognized this smell from before. But this time it was much stronger, and it enveloped me.

I remembered. It all came back in pictures which took me back to the day when I learned what the smell of bread was.

It was a day when the door to the barracks was opened. Bright light flowed in. My eyes still hurt.

"Binjamin! Is there a Binjamin here? Come out! Quick!" came a rough woman's voice from out of the light.

Hesitantly I stood up and went over, blinking, to the silhouette that stood in the open door. The dark outline told me that this was the same gray uniform that had brought me here from the farm. The same high boots, the same thick stockings, the same skirt hem that I had run alongside for so long.

"You're . . . ?" I nodded.

"Today you can see your mother, but—only dahle."

I didn't understand what she was saying. What did "dahle" mean? I still have no idea today. She pronounced it with a very long, broad *aah.* And what did "mother" mean?

I couldn't remember.

I had certainly heard other children using the word "mother" from time to time. I'd heard some of them crying, and calling out for mama. And they fought about it.

Some of them said "everyone has a mother."

The others objected to this, and insisted that there were no mothers anymore, that it had only been that way once, back then, a long time ago, in another world, before all the children had been brought together behind the fences and in the barracks. But since then there hadn't been any mothers, and the other world had disappeared long ago, forever. They said:

"There's no more world outside the fence!"

And I believed it.

They screamed at each other and called each other liars.

They began to strike out at each other bitterly.

All I understood was that a mother, whether you had one or not, must be something immensely important, something that was worth fighting for, the way you fought over food.

"Do you understand? You're going to see your mother! Do you understand?" the uniform lady said again.

I began to be afraid of her impatience. I shook my head and shrugged.

"You're going to come with me, and from now on you're not to talk. It is absolutely forbidden to say a single word, not now, not when you see your mother, not afterward either. You won't ever talk about it to anyone ever, do you understand? Anyone, do you understand, do you?"

The last words came out almost in a shout. I shook my head and shrugged again.

Then she took hold of my chin and pulled it up to make me look at her. All I could see was a shape and a blur that must be the peaked cap on her head. She bent down, stared into my eyes for a moment, and said in a clenched, soft voice:

"And if I so much as see you open your mouth, then I'll . . ."

And she made a terrible gesture over my head.

Now I nodded, and I knew she would kill me.

She took hold of my arm and dragged me off with her. I really didn't want to go. My knees were hurting, my eyes even more. I opened them briefly now and again, but the dazzling light burned and stabbed, and I could only see the path through a watery haze.

We walked and walked forever, big gates in the fence were opened, then closed behind us again. At every gate she said something very quietly to the guards.

The brilliant reflection of the sun off the yellowish white sandy path burned in my eyes, and I was thirsty. My tongue felt like a lump, and my mouth was glued shut.

After a long time of miserable hurrying, stumbling, falling down, and hurrying on again, the woman suddenly stood still. I opened my eyes, she put her finger to her lips and looked at me severely. I nodded again. We were standing in front of a huge, dark barracks door. The sandy area in front of it glittered white in an ominous way.

Slowly and quietly she opened the door.

"All the way at the back, against the wall, on this side," she said, pointing to the left.

She shut the door behind me quickly, without making a sound.

The dim light in the barracks felt good. I could make out a long central walkway, but there were no high wooden bunks down the two long sides: the walls were bare.

At first I thought the room was empty. But then I saw that there were people lying on the floor on covers over a bit of straw, on both sides of the walkway.

They seemed to be all women. They were hardly moving, and when they did, it was very, very slowly. I went carefully down between the bodies toward the wall.

At the foot of the last sleeping place, I came to a stop. I turned slowly toward the side that the uniform had pointed to.

I made out the shape of a body under a gray cover. The cover moved. A woman's head became visible, then two arms laying themselves slowly on top of the cover.

I bit my lips so as not to cry out. I looked unblinking into a face that looked back at me with huge eyes.

Was this my mother, my dahle?

One of the children had once said that if you have a mother, she belongs just to you! So this woman belonged to me, just me? I wondered.

But I wasn't allowed to ask. I wanted to tell her that I wasn't allowed to speak, that they'd kill me if I said anything to her— but I couldn't do that.

So I stood there in silence, clenching my teeth together, and didn't dare move. I didn't look away from her once. For just a moment the face seemed to smile, but I couldn't be sure.

I don't know how long I stood there like that. A loud creak broke the silence, the door opened a crack—the sign that time was up. At that moment, the woman moved one of her arms, groping with her hand under the straw and the lumps between her and the wall, as if she was looking for something. The hand re-emerged, clutching something. She motioned for me to come closer.

I kept standing there without moving. I was waiting, I was afraid. She beckoned faster, more urgently. Slowly I fought down my shyness. I went up to her.

Now I could see the face more clearly, it was shiny and wet, and I saw that it was crying. Without saying a word she reached out her hand to me and indicated that I should take what she had brought out from under the straw. For a single moment I touched her hand—it felt hot and damp.

I took the object, clutched it tight against me, and went toward the door, which now stood wide open, silhouetting the dark waiting shape of the gray uniform skirt and the peaked cap.

We went back the way we'd come. The woman held my arm, dragging me along behind her. I used my free hand to grope the unknown object with curiosity. It had jagged edges and corners, and felt coarse and hard.

"What is this?" I asked the gray uniform as we reached my barracks.

"That's bread," she said, and "You have to soften it in water, then you can eat it." Then she went away.

I spent a long time chewing on the softened bread and then dunking it again into the little ration of water in my mug, and chewing again, over and over again, until the water was all used up and the crust had shrunk to a tiny little ball.

Finally all that remained was the indescribably delicious smell of bread on my fingers as I held them to my nose again and again.

I only ever saw the lady in the gray uniform once again. I recognized her by the rhythm of her stride. She was hurrying somewhere and I ran up to her. I thought she would look for me and take me to my mother. She stood still for just a moment and looked at me. It took her a second to recognize me.

"Oh, it's you . . . you can't see your mother again . . . it's not possible anymore."

She hurried off without a further thought.

I observed the other children. They were taking some kind of thick red stuff out of a jar and putting it on their bread before they ate it.

I didn't dare take a slice from the bread pile in front of everyone. So I picked up my spoon and went over to the jar with the red stuff. I dipped the spoon in and licked it off.

It tasted so sweet! I tried it again. But a smack on my hand stopped me. A white apron bent over me.

"You're not allowed to do that. Only with bread!" she said severely.

"But the bread doesn't belong to me," I said. My eyes began to smart, I felt tears coming and I was ashamed.

"Here's a piece of bread for you and now you can . . ." was all she had time to say.

"I only take bread from my mother," I screamed at her in tears of fury, and ran from the room.

But where to? I didn't know the building. The nurse followed me and took me by the shoulders. I wondered whether to bite her or not, but the situation seemed hopeless, so I clutched one arm over my stomach to protect it and held the other over my head and waited for the blows, but nothing happened. I took a quick look up at her—and saw that she was smiling.

So I let myself be led back to the table, but I didn't drop my guard. She took another piece of bread from the mound and used a knife to smear it with a thick layer of the good sweet stuff.

"This is my present to you," she said.

I was hungry, and hesitantly I began to eat.

SIX

I had got used to the ringing of the bell, which summoned us to our walk after breakfast. Like the other children, I'd been given real winter shoes, beautiful new ones of real leather, with soles so thick they'd never get holes.

Everything turned into bustle and hurry when the bell rang the second time. The children got ready to set off.

I was one of the last to leave the table, and I rushed to the row of cubbyholes where each of us had a place to keep his own shoes and socks. It was almost empty—already.

I reached into my place and got a fright: there was nothing in there, no shoes, only socks.

"My shoes, where are my shoes, someone's stolen my shoes," I cried.

I should have guarded them more carefully.

Panic set in.

I hunted through every compartment, but my shoes had definitely gone. The last children had all collected theirs and I could hear voices from the courtyard where everyone was waiting. My heart was pounding as if it would burst.

It's happened again! No—not again. I can't have to run through the snow without shoes again, I thought in despair.

Once before, in the barracks, my shoes had disappeared, and I had to go out into the snow with rags on my feet. Rags that Jankl tied on for me. I remembered only too well.

We were driven out of the barracks in tremendous haste, and then we had to run along a narrow path in the snow, keeping in a column, I no longer remember where to or why. But staying in step was the most important thing.

Whoever had shoes managed better. If you fell behind, you were driven on with blows; if you didn't catch up, you . . .

I ran and ran, but I fell further and further behind, I couldn't catch my breath anymore, I was afraid I'd choke. The children behind me saw that the gap in the column was getting wider, and began screaming at me in fear and anger, to drive me on.

But I had no shoes and the rags on my feet gave me no sure footing. One of them came undone and then it happened. I stumbled, slid out of line, and landed to one side of the path.

It was a raised path. I rolled some way down the bank, sinking further and further in soft snow. I struggled convulsively to pull myself back up, but I couldn't.

The column came to a halt.

The sound of deep men's voices yelling cut into the shrill yelping of my friends. Then I heard a noise.

I raised my head to find myself looking straight at the tip of a black boot that was aimed at my face. I was quick enough to turn away, so it only hit the back of my head. The blow lifted me and threw me clean back onto the path.

Two of the older children who'd been running ahead of me came back, took hold of my arms, and hauled me along behind them, pursued by brownish green uniforms.

My shoes, my shoes, I kept thinking despairingly. The children were racketing around outside.

I reached for the back of my head, where I could feel the big ridge that had formed as a result of the blow.

I thought feverishly.

I have to find rags. Rags for my feet. Rags in snow are still better than socks would be!

I ran to the scullery.

Here there were cleaning cloths. Lots of them, without holes, big, thick, warm ones. I took the first best ones I could find and wrapped them around my feet and calves the way Jankl had taught me in the big barracks. A quick search and I found string to hold everything together. I gasped with relief. I ran downstairs as fast as I could.

"There he is! He's coming!" called one of the waiting children.

I stepped outside. The confusion of voices suddenly broke off. An unearthly silence suddenly met me. A wordless semicircle formed as they all gaped at me openmouthed.

I stood there petrified, not understanding. Something here was wrong. But now, as if on command, there was a roar of mocking laughter, poisonous and ugly. The children were pointing at me. They yelled and catcalled and clutched their stomachs. I stood there speechless, still not understanding.

What had happened? Why were these children suddenly pushing me away and making such a fool of me?

I began to feel afraid of the unruly mob. I bit down hard and ran back into the house. I reached my bed all out of breath, crawled under the covers, and listened anxiously to see if they were following me.

It was some time before I heard a single set of footsteps, but they sounded calm, not as if they were in pursuit. I looked out. One of the older nurses—she had white hair—came in smiling, lifted the cover, and said calmly:

"It's nothing . . . nothing. Just your feet—people aren't used to that here."

She seemed to understand. Finally someone who understood! She took my hand and led me into the laundry drying room.

"Look," she said, "here are your shoes. Why didn't you ask? They were so wet from yesterday's walk that I put them in here to dry."

SEVEN

One day two new boys were brought to the orphanage. They sat opposite me at breakfast and I watched them curiously and tried to eavesdrop on what they were saying to each other.

They were speaking in a mixture of Yiddish and Polish. I was so frightened that I got goose pimples and began to sweat. My stomach clenched with fear. I stared at them.

Haven't I seen them somewhere before, in the chaotic throng of children in the half-light of the big barracks?

"No," I decided, yet I wasn't absolutely sure.

My neighbor at table nudged me and asked something.

I bit my lips and didn't reply.

Do not say a word right now. They mustn't hear my voice. They could recognize me by my voice. And if they recognize me and tell everyone where I came from, then it's all over. Either they'll kill me themselves, out of revenge, or they'll betray me to one of the gray uniform women in Poland, and they'll come and get me and throw me into the furnace.

My head was hammering.

I tried to think clearly, but the anxiety kept rising in me.

Without eating my breakfast or saying a word to the child next to me, I ran back into the empty dormitory, jumped onto my bed, and bit down on the pillow so as not to cry out. Panic.

I couldn't stop the vivid memories of the new boy in the big barracks. They forced me to lie still and for the thousandth time I had to be a spectator at what had happened to the new boy in front of the barracks, and how it was my fault and my crime.

At the beginning there was no one in the big barracks who took charge of organizing things or keeping anything clean. We were alone most of the time—a hundred, a hundred and fifty, maybe two hundred children. At that time there was no roll call.

Most of the children were older than I. When we weren't allowed for long periods to go outdoors, we had no choice but to relieve ourselves in the long passageway between the two-tiered racks of bunks. Nobody cared, nobody cleaned up, until the shit was ankle deep.

Hunger was a torment, but thirst was worse. Even the stone washtubs remained empty for a long time. Then once a day a few women in torn clothes and rags started coming to our door from the neighboring barracks and they brought us water in buckets, although it was forbidden. So we were able to fill our mugs at least once a day, but sometimes there was only enough for half.

But the worst thing during that time was the stink. I often thought I was going to suffocate in it.

Once I had to get down from my bunk, and sank up to my calves in shit. I was disgusted, I gasped and retched, but mostly I cried.

"What are you bawling about? Stop that noise," one of the older boys snapped at me.

He seemed to know everything already and to have been here for some time.

It was Jankl.

I think that was the first time I saw him. He was something like a leader, or a ringleader, and you could ask him things, and he helped, and he taught us lots of tricks. He became my friend, my counselor, and my protector. He knew how to steal food and where to get it, and he shared with me.

Jankl looked at me.

"If you stand in it, it's warmer. It'll stop your feet from freezing so quickly."

I was amazed at his wisdom, fell silent, and fought down my need to be sick.

Then at some point after that, we were all driven outdoors one day. It wasn't so cold anymore. The ground was thawing and getting soft. The big barracks was scrubbed out with buckets of water by faceless ragged gray figures who hurried in with full buckets and out again with empty ones in an unending chain. All I can remember is their strange shapes.

It was almost evening when the endless hurrying came to a stop. The big barracks was clean.

But our good fortune was short-lived. New barracks regulations were introduced; new rules of the game, and you survived only if you learned them right away.

By day, you had to go outside to relieve yourself, but only if you could run far enough to reach the latrine ditch near the big fence. We soon found out what could happen to anyone who didn't reach the ditch in time.

The image of the two boys in front of the barracks door is burned into my mind.

They were forbidden to come back into the barracks. They were meant to be a warning to the rest of us. Huddled over, crying constantly, they knelt in the filth. I stared horrified at their trousers, which were all spotted with red.

The older children explained:

On the way to the latrines they hadn't been able to hold their water anymore. Two of the block wardens had caught them as they were peeing against the wall behind one of the barracks. As a punishment, they'd taken little sticks and pushed them up into the boys' penises as far as they'd go. Then the block wardens had hit their penises, making the sticks break off. The wardens had laughed a lot and had a good time.

"Now all they'll do is pee blood," said one of them.

When evening came they were still whimpering. Then people came and took them away.

_____

But at night, nobody was allowed to go to the latrines.

So nights became much scarier even than the days. Regulations provided for a single metal bucket to be put out in the passageway down the big barracks each evening. But it was far too small for all of us. It soon filled up.

A big block warden watched over the bucket. Her uniform was like the uniform that had brought me here from the farm and the one that had brought me to my mother, only much dirtier and without any shiny buttons. She too always had a peaked cap on her head, and we knew that when she pulled the cap forward was when she was most dangerous.

If a child got up in the night and went to the bucket, her torch switched itself on.

Woe betide the one who first made the bucket overflow in the dark, or knocked it over. He would be grabbed, dragged down the passageway while being yelled at, and taken outside. No one this happened to ever came back. But the uniform left us on our own for the rest of the night. We all knew at those times that we couldn't go anymore, and everything had to stay absolutely quiet.

Those silences were unearthly, and it was a great torture, because lots of us had diarrhea.

The new boy they brought during the day was pale, small, and very shy, and didn't know how anything worked.

He was given a bunk on the other side of the passageway, diagonally opposite me. At that time we were sleeping four or five to a bunk section on torn sacks oozing straw and insects. We had one cover, and everyone tried to pull as much of it over himself as possible.

It was only his first night and the new boy began to moan, softly at first, then louder and louder, and sometimes cried out. He wanted to go to the bucket, but the bucket had already been taken away, and he had taken in the strict instructions. He complained louder and louder about the pains in his stomach.

"What shall I do? I need the bucket, I can't hold on any longer," he kept saying, and "I can't anymore! Help me, help!"

But nobody answered. There was nothing anyone could say.

We crawled as far under our covers as we could and tried not to make a sound. We were trembling, and the anxiety was terrible. The new boy could be the end of us all with his screaming.

If the guards hear the noise, we're done for, and the death carts will pick us up in the morning, I thought.

Now he was calling out again, and I put my hands over my ears. It didn't do any good. I thought my heart was going to jump right out of my body.

"Help me! What should I do?" the new boy screamed, louder than ever.

Then he was quiet for a moment.

But the sudden quiet was as frightening as his noise had been—I listened hard, and thought I could hear footsteps coming closer to the barracks. Panic took hold of me.

Still nobody answered the new boy.

"Just go in the straw, right where you are," a loud voice said suddenly.

At first I was stunned, then I shook—that sounded like my voice. It *was.*

With horror I realized that I'd said right out loud, really loud, what I only thought I was thinking.

Everyone listened tensely. The footsteps went away again. The new boy whimpered quietly, but it didn't sound like pain anymore, it sounded like relief and exhaustion, and soon we were all asleep.

It was early morning, at first light. We were already standing in a long double row outside on the swampy assembly ground, being counted perhaps. We were standing, and not allowed to move. It went on for an eternity. Apparently the barracks was being inspected.

We looked at each other.

Way out in front, right opposite, but hard to make out, was the shape of a block warden or a gray SS assistant, and next to it, big, threatening, booted, a black uniform.

The sun slowly rose behind the roofs of the blocks at the other end of the assembly ground. It shone directly into our faces. Our eyes hurt; we weren't used to the bright light. But nobody dared to turn away.

Behind us there was a creaking and groaning.

Don't turn around, I thought, they're bringing the cart that collects the corpses.

It came every morning.

More waiting.

Then, suddenly, quick footsteps approaching from our barracks. They went up to the black uniform.

A second's expectant hush, then a terrible roaring:

"Who soiled the straw last night? Whatever swine is responsible, identify yourself."

Silence.

I began to sweat. The whole world was waiting. My chest started to hurt. I was so terrified, I could hardly breathe. I guessed what was coming next.

I tried to think.

Should I identify myself? Protect the new boy? Should I say it? Yes, I should say I was the cause of it.

I stood frozen, didn't say a word, didn't step forward, and knew in despair that my fear and cowardice were winning out.

"Who?" the voice roared again out of the light. "Who was the swine?"

Slowly a small figure detached itself from our row—it was the new boy.

Head down, huddled over, arms waving loosely, he shuffled over to the gray and the black uniforms.

It seemed an endlessly long distance, and it seemed to take forever.

At last he stood there in front of them. I could hardly even see him anymore. The sun was higher and my eyes hurt.

The new boy was now just a shadow that melted into the dark outlines of the two uniforms.

Should I identify myself now? I can still do it. It's not too late yet! I could say I caused it, that it wasn't the new boy's fault.

I shook. I knew this was the absolute last moment to save the new boy.

What should I do, what should I do?

The moment passed. I gasped for air.

A new fear took hold of me.

The new boy can still betray me. He can say, "He's the one who told me to do it." How long will he hold out before he talks?

Fear and guilt choked off my breath. I couldn't stand it anymore. I wanted to sink into the muddy ground, become invisible. I tried to scuffle backward out of the row, barefoot, and deeper into the mud.

I wanted to sink into the mud forever!

But it didn't work.

"Halt," someone yelled behind me.

And I was back in the row again.

It was one of the brownish green ones, a Ukrainian perhaps, an assistant of the black uniform. They often arrived together. The Ukrainian stepped forward. He inspected us angrily, walking down the row.

I listened up ahead, but I couldn't hear anything. I looked anxiously. I trembled. All I could see was shadows. They were standing right in the sun, which was now fully risen, and my eyes burned and teared over.

We waited.

The group seemed to be discussing something.

Has the new boy already betrayed me? Is he talking to the uniforms now?

I listened. Nothing—just silence.

There was movement in the group, and finally we heard a loud *Jawohl* from the Ukrainian.

Silence again. We waited, motionless. Then there was a crack of bones, then hard footsteps and the sound of something being dragged toward the block in the rear.

I saw nothing; I couldn't make out a thing against the sun. My inflamed eyes kept weeping.

I listened. Nothing but a rattling noise as they threw the bodies onto the cart.

Another moment's silence, then the creak of wheels.

Not one of us made a sound, the only thing audible was the scraping of our feet as we went back into the barracks.

I'm guilty, I'm a murderer. If it hadn't been for me, it wouldn't have happened. And they'll know it was me by my voice.

The thought hit me like a blow.

Admittedly it had been dark in the barracks when I said the lethal words, none of the children had seen me, but they'd all heard me.

They'll take revenge if they recognize my voice, I thought.

If they recognize my voice, they'll betray me for a bowl of soup or a mug of water. I can't let anyone hear my voice again— anyone at all. I mustn't speak! Just keep absolutely silent. I'm a coward. A murderer. I killed the new boy. I'm scared they'll find me out. I mustn't talk anymore. I'll be an outcast, and it'll serve me right, I handed him over, I'm guilty. I'm afraid of the revenge. I knew perfectly well that children's revenge can be terrible.

I crawled into the darkness of my bunk. I felt the finality of what I'd done and the irredeemability of my guilt.

The memory flashed past me and was gone. I pushed the torn pillowcase aside and thought. Everything in the house was quiet.

Did the two new Polish kids come to look for me? Could they even recognize me? No—or yes?

If they don't hear my voice, I'm still safe. But I mustn't attract attention. They mustn't find out I came from Poland, from the camp, from the big barracks. No one must find out.

And I made lots of plans for keeping out of their way.

But after a few days they went away. I breathed again. But I had to stay on the alert.

I made no objection when I was punished for tearing the pillowcase because I didn't want anyone asking dangerous questions.

The days and weeks that followed in the orphanage were calm. I mostly sat on my own, I didn't like playing the others' games. So I had lots of time to remember.

Again and again I thought back through all my memories. I didn't want to lose or forget anything, because I wanted to run away from here, I wanted to get back, somehow. I thought the only way I'd find my way back would be if I remembered every place, every street, every house, and every barracks.

Then I compared the world I came from with the world Frau Grosz had brought me to—Frau Grosz, who'd tricked me, secretly abandoned me, and handed me over to this place.

No matter how hard I tried, I couldn't pull these two worlds together. I hunted in vain for some thread I could hold on to.

I could only get away from this unbearable strange present by going back to the world and the images of my past. Yes, they were almost as unbearable, but they were familiar, at least I understood their rules.

EIGHT

It was already evening, and bitterly cold in the barracks. I was lying on my bunk—we were lying together in fours, squashed together to keep warm. We were almost at the front, near the entrance.

We'd hardly gone to sleep when footsteps came up to the door, it opened, and an icy wind blew in. A figure became visible. It threw in two bundles. The door was shut again.

No way to know who had thrown the bundles in at us—a uniform, a block warden, or just one of the women prisoners from the barracks next door.

The bundles were on the floor, leaning against our rack of bunks. Cautiously I peered over the edge. The bundles moved, two heads, two white faces became visible, and huge dark eyes. They were tiny babies, they had their first teeth, but they couldn't talk yet.

Were they supposed to sleep in here with us? On the floor? I'd never seen such tiny children up close before.

I thought.

The bunks were beyond capacity already.

Maybe they'll give them somewhere to sleep tomorrow, I thought, and looked at them again.

They were moving again. They lifted their thin little arms up out of the rags and I got a shock. They were white, like their faces; only the hands and in particular the fingers were black, and I couldn't see any fingernails.

"Frozen," whispered Jankl next to me.

Cautiously we nudged them. They didn't react. They sucked on their black fingers, perhaps to warm them, I thought, and they looked off into the far distance out of big eyes, as if searching for something.

I woke up when it got light. I worked my way over to the edge of the bunk and looked down: they were still there, just like the night before, as if they hadn't moved. I leaned forward, not believing what I was seeing. Both of them were holding their hands up stiff in front of their faces, in front of their glassy, half-closed eyes. But they weren't proper hands. What I saw made no connection with anything I knew.

Their hands were black, as they were the night before, but now their fingers were white—snow-white. Except they weren't proper fingers. What I could see were tiny little white sticks that looked broken, each pointing in a different direction.

I pulled anxiously on Jankl's arm.

"What's that, Jankl—look—their hands!" I said, and Jankl took a long look over the edge of the bunk.

"Bones," he said, "just bones, that's what you look like inside, you have bones like that all over, everywhere that it feels hard. That's what holds you together, but you mustn't break them."

I touched my body, my hands, my arms, my knees. I felt the hardness, and for the first time I could picture what my bones looked like. I felt a sense of superiority, as if I'd just made a great discovery.

"But—why are those two's bones outside? I've got skin holding me together. Are they ill?" I asked, beginning to feel anxious.

Something seemed to be not right. Jankl chewed on his lip.

"Are they ill?" I asked again, and Jankl said:

"Yes, it's a sickness called hunger. Frozen fingers don't hurt.

Sometime in the night they chewed their fingers down to the
bone—but they're dead now."

Jankl had spoken in a quiet, soft voice, but for the first time
since we'd been together, I heard something sad and bitter in
his voice, and as I looked at him in surprise, I saw that he was
crying.

NINE

Jankl was good.

It was Jankl I had to thank for everything. If I say this, it's because I mean it quite literally.

I owe my life to Jankl. I should write a whole book in his honor, not just one pitiful little chapter. I'm ashamed, but too little has stayed in my memory.

How our friendship started in the big barracks, I don't remember either.

Jankl was already big—maybe twelve. To me, he was already a grown-up. He was always there when I needed him. He protected me, he gave me advice, he taught me a lot, he alerted me to dangers.

He showed me patiently how to tie a knot, and why this mattered.

When it got cold, he was good at wrapping my bare feet and legs in bits of cloth. Nobody knew where he got them.

"Now you tie the knots yourself," he said.

It took a lot of tries before I managed it, but he didn't get impatient, and showed me over and over again.

He reminded me of Motti.

Jankl didn't say much. He knew I didn't understand much of his strange dialect anyway. So most of the time he taught me silently, just by the way he moved his hands.

Sometimes he disappeared for long periods, and each time he came back he took me to my bunk, then carefully untied the strings he'd tied around his trouser legs at the ankles. And immediately the most unbelievable things lay between his feet: fresh potato peels, sometimes even a whole potato, or half, and sometimes a huge cabbage leaf.

He divided everything carefully, slowly, without making a sound. Then he always pushed one half over to me with a look, a mischievous smile, and a nod.

"I know all the places," he once said, and "Never get caught, or . . ." and he made a wringing movement with both hands around his neck and crossed his eyes.

I understood.

He taught me not to eat everything at one go but, whenever possible, to divide out the food over the whole day, or longer.

He taught me to hide my supplies and how to guard them.

He taught me to avoid the uniforms, and if necessary, to pick the right moment to run away from them, but only ever on his signal—and always alone, never in the same direction as everyone else, and never to scream like the other children when I was running.

But one day Jankl didn't come back.

After I'd waited a long time, I saw there was a whole crowd of agitated children outside. I went over slowly. Something must have happened, I felt afraid, but curiosity still pulled me closer. The children were standing in a semicircle and I could see that they were shrieking at each other—I could see it, but I was amazed to realize that I couldn't hear a sound—just deathly silence.

What's happened? Why can't I hear anything? Where are my ears? I've lost my ears . . .

I went even closer.

There was a grown-up standing in the middle of the semicircle, in shirtsleeves, but wearing boots. Shirtsleeves seemed to be in an absolute fury, he was yelling and pointing to a boy on the edge of the semicircle, and I saw it was Jankl.

I was panic-stricken, even though I didn't know where the danger was.

Run, Jankl, run away, I wanted to scream, but no sound came out of my throat and not a sound could get through to my ears.

Deaf and dumb and frozen to the spot, I stood there and watched.

Jankl stood there, feet together, arms and hands straight down and pressed tight to his sides, like a soldier. He stood motionless, as if turned to stone, and then—then he slowly tipped forward, still stiff, the way he'd been standing, without bending, without putting out his arms to break his fall. He fell so slowly it seemed to go on forever.

As his face hit the mud, sending up a huge spray, shirtsleeves in the boots turned and left, and the children dispersed.

Jankl lay there peacefully, not moving.

I got down on the ground, crawled over to him, and saw his face sinking into the mud, slowly, deeper and deeper, till just his ears and the back of his head were visible.

I watched, staring at him.

Why aren't you breathing? You have to breathe, and then a bubble will come up through the mud and go plop, and then you have to lift your head, so you can breathe in again, I thought anxiously.

I wanted to touch him, take hold of him, pull his arm—whether I did or not, I don't remember.

I waited and waited—no plop came, nothing moved, his ears were now out of sight too, only a tiny bit of the back of his clean-shaven head still showed above the mud.

Two of the bigger children pushed me from behind; I looked around. They seemed to be talking to me, all upset, but I still couldn't hear a thing. I was deaf. So they took me under the arms and dragged me backward across the assembly ground.

I looked back at Jankl, getting smaller and smaller until he finally looked like any other little bump of earth between the mud puddles. As I was pulled into the barracks, I couldn't even see him anymore.

I felt absolutely helpless, crippled, I was beginning to turn freezing cold. What had happened?

I didn't understand.

All I knew was that I was alone now.

TEN

I don't remember any longer where it was, or when. But it was one of the few days when we children were allowed out of the barracks into the open air. We jumped about, some of us crawled on the ground, others just lay there, warming themselves in the sun. In among them, a powerful, bull-necked man, who slowly took off his uniform jacket.

I'd never seen such thick, strong arms. They were astonishing.

Suddenly I can see something, there's an object the children are throwing high up in the air. It looks like a ball, but seems to be much heavier—maybe it's a wooden ball.

As I watch, it rolls between the children, they all race to pick it up and throw it again. Bull-neck watches them, his arms crossed. I'm chasing the ball too, I'd like to throw it once as well.

The ball rolls to a stop at bull-neck's feet.

The game freezes for a moment and I'm spellbound.

What's he going to do? I wonder.

He kicks the ball away with his boot. It rolls in amongst the others, and now one brave child pushes it back at bull-neck, and he shoves it back again.

The spell is broken.

He's playing with us! And as long as he's playing, he won't do anything to us.

There are several back-and-forths. We lose our shyness, and I too come closer and closer to bull-neck.

I'd like to get the ball too. I'm standing with some others right near him, and we want to catch the ball. But he's quicker. He lifts the ball into the air. We reach up our arms and hop and jump, but none of us can reach it.

I glance at the boy next to me, the little one who's leaping up with his arms high, calling, "Me, me, give it to me," with his head tilted way back to try to see the ball in bull-neck's raised hand.

The little one seems possessed.

Then I see the huge, thick arm lifting itself even higher in the air with the ball, I see the arm swung back, I see bull-neck's face suddenly grimace, then I see the arm come hurtling down in a huge swing.

I hear a strange crack—and someone beside me drops to the ground without a sound.

In disbelief and horror I stare at the little boy. His face lies there in the sun, absolutely white, but no blood on it. I'm surprised there's no blood. But his forehead is all pushed in, there's a deep hollow in it, exactly the same size as the ball.

I keep looking down—still no blood, but I know the little one is dead.

Rage and despair explode in me, I can't think anymore.

Kill him, kill him, I'm screaming inside me, and I can see bull-neck's slack arm right above me and his self-satisfied, grinning face.

Do it like a dog—a dog! Kill him—the voice inside me screams again.

Yes—I'm a dog now, I'm a wolf.

Hands out, I take a flying leap. I grab the bare forearm, open my jaws as wide as I can, and bite with all my strength.

Harder! Deeper! You've got to kill him, I think, my jaws grinding as best they can.

Then I want to let go and run away. I loosen my hands, want to let myself drop, but my jaws won't open, they feel locked shut. They're still grinding, independent of my control. So I'm hanging from this arm by my teeth and it's pulling me upward by brute force, then coming down again, then it's carrying me away and the roaring and screaming is deafening.

Blood and spit are running down me, and my stomach begins to heave.

My memory stops at the moment when my back is slammed hard against something.

How I came out of it, I have no idea. Maybe bull-neck thought I was already dead when I hit the ground.

ELEVEN

Mila* was somewhat older than I was. I recognized her when we met each other again in the orphanage in Kraków. I didn't have to be afraid of her.

We knew each other from somewhere, from one of the many barracks probably, we weren't sure anymore, and we never talked about it.

We just looked at each other, and that was enough.

Just once, I asked her what had happened when she was taken away with her mother, and this, more or less, is what she told me:

They were already moving in the column of people who were being led from the barracks through the camp, Mila and her mother, with uniforms in attendance, all selected to die.

It was a long way, the column kept stopping and starting, past unfamiliar barracks, and mounds of bodies, then more barracks and more mounds of bodies.

Then the column had to halt again. Mila and her mother stood still and waited.

They were standing next to a stacked pile of corpses. The SS men were patrolling impatiently up and down.

Then something completely extraordinary happened. A uniform, a young one, came slowly up beside Mila's mother, looked her up and down for a moment, then grabbed hold of her and with a single heave threw her on top of the corpses that were

*In the German edition, this character's name is Karola (Stefan Maechler).

next to them. Mila was being held tight by her mother's hand, so she was carried along with her.

They lay there, frozen with terror, on the cold bodies. They didn't understand what had happened, or why; it had all happened so fast. But they did understand that now there was a way out.

They lay there, playing dead, absolutely still so as not to be discovered, all day until night came. Once it was dark, they slid down and mixed themselves back in among the living, but as fake living people, struck off all the lists, because they were supposed to be dead.

It was hard, because they didn't dare to be recognized either dead or alive.

Later Mila and her mother got separated after all, and neither got further news of the other.

Now Mila kept looking everywhere and asking.

And now we were together in this orphanage in Kraków, at least some of the time. I don't know anymore whether I lived there too, or whether I was just put there during the day, and got something to eat and was allowed to play. I was afraid of the other children, they were older than I, and their games were often cruel and dangerous. They imitated the uniforms, and were obviously practicing to be grown-ups.

If that's how it is, I don't ever want to grow up, I thought, and being with Mila gave me some sense of safety and peace.

I don't know why, but nobody ever dared come near her to do anything bad, she never got trapped into quarrels, she was untouchable.

Years later, when we were both grown up, we met quite by chance. She was working as a translator, and I'd become a musician.

Mila had managed to find her mother, and we went together to visit her—she was old by now—in a hospital. She died soon after that.

Mila and I saw each other regularly now—we often had long talks. We discussed the present, but what we really meant was our past. Both of us were living among the living, yet we didn't really belong with them—we were actually the dead, on stolen leave, accidental survivors who got left behind in life.

We loved each other, and our love was fed by our sadness. But it was always accompanied by a fear of touching what actually bound us together.

So, inevitably, we lost each other again.

TWELVE

I'm sitting in rain-softened clay near the door to the barracks, waiting. For what, I don't know. I watch the little streams of water. They flow past me on either side, taking strange winding paths through the mud, then they flow together again in front of me and make a bigger stream, which shimmers with the most unusual colors. I dip my forefinger into it and move it to and fro, watching the strings of color change shape and make bright whirlpools.

It's quieter these days, now that most of the children are no longer here. I don't know where they are. I can't remember where I was when they were taken away. I miss them—why didn't I go with them? Now there are only a few children in the barracks, other children, bigger and stronger. And it's not the same barracks anymore, either.

But it's the same place, same surroundings, same stink, same smoke in the air, that burns your eyes and leaves an oily deposit on your face.

The same factory stands there up on the hill, outside the fence, with the big chimney—only perhaps this one's a little smaller, a little further away, I'm not sure.

Suddenly there are lots of women here, they die in the night, then more come and they die, too.

Every morning the bodies are thrown in a pile at the corner of each barracks by the ones who are going to die during the next night.

And every morning the cart comes by, pulled by gray people in rags. They're grown-ups but they don't have any definite shape, you can't tell if they're men or women. They throw the dead women on the cart and move on again.

But the cart didn't come today, not yesterday either. The women are still lying there in a tangle. The heap is bigger than it used to be. They're lying there quite naked. I've seen it for myself—the dead ones give their clothes to the ones who are still living.

The block warden—or maybe it was the chief warden—hurries past; her stiff, high boots make the mud splash into my face. She always does that, but it's not bad. We children are just dirt, she always says, so it doesn't make any difference.

I sit here, and because there are no other children here, I go on playing with the dirt. I stir it around sometimes, to make waves in the shimmering, tinted water, and I wait to see where it will run over, and start making a colorful new canal.

Sometimes I look over at the dead women. Some of the older children have told me that little children grow in women's bellies before they're born, and I wonder: everyone keeps saying I'm so small, that must mean that I grew in a belly too. I think about my mother, I think about the one time the gray uniform took me to a woman and said:

"You can see your mother."

Does that mean all mothers have to die once they've had children?

It must be true, otherwise why would new children keep coming, and more women keep dying every night?

I look over again.

Something catches my eye, yet the mountain of corpses is just lying there, as usual. But didn't something just move over there?

That's strange. Dead women aren't allowed to move.

I look at the woman lying right on top of all the others. She's on her back, her body hanging down a little, her arms are wide open, and her breasts are tipped to one side like little sacks above her ribs, which stick out a lot, and her belly seems all swelled up.

Is my mother lying like that now?

Something *is* moving! It's the belly. I don't dare stand up, and I can't take my eyes away. I can't believe it. I inch forward cautiously on my knees. What's happening here?

"Children move inside the belly, that's how the mother knows they want to come out," one of the older girls in the big barracks once said, once when we were still all together.

Is a child trying to come out of this belly? How is that possible? The woman's dead.

I crawl closer, I want to know.

Now I can see the whole belly. There's a big wound on one side, with something moving in it. I get to my feet, so that I can see better. I poke my head forward, and at this very moment the wound springs open, the wall of the stomach lifts back, and a huge, blood-smeared, shining rat darts down the mound of corpses. Other rats run startled out of the confusion of bodies, heading for open ground.

I saw it, I saw it! The dead women are giving birth to rats!

Rats—they're the deadly enemies of the little children in the camp. Rats that attack us at night, that bite us, leaving painful wounds that never heal, that nobody knows how to heal, and that make the children's living bodies start to rot away.

"Mother, mama, my mama, what have you done?"

I open my mouth to scream, in shock and fear, but nothing comes out of my throat. It feels as if my gullet is being squashed into my chest, and I hear a noise deep inside me, a sort of ringing and crackling, like something fragile being stepped on. Then there's a long silence.

After a time I try to get up. My mind is empty, I've forgotten everything. I don't know who I am. Who am I?

I touch my legs again and again. I undo the rags around my calves and feel the skin. Is it skin, or do I actually have gray fur?

Am I a rat or a human? I'm a child—but am I a human child or a rat child, or can you be both at once?

Still staring at the women, I kneel in the mud with my mouth open, and I can't close it.

Everything inside me comes loose and seems to flow away; I flow away along with my blood and vomit in the bright, muddy runnels of water, down the street of the camp to wherever the runnels peter out.

Nothing connects to anything else anymore. Nothing is in its right place. Nothing has any value.

Is this what it's like to die? Am I dying?

There are no feelings left. I can't feel if I'm breathing, I can't feel my ever-present hunger, or thirst.

I'm just an eye, taking in what it sees, giving nothing back.

But I'm cold.

Many years later I went with my wife for the birth of our first son. I wanted to be there with her, to support her.

The first thing that slowly became visible was the half-round of the baby's head. As a first-time father, I didn't know how much dark hair a newborn baby can have. I wasn't ready for this little half-head of hair. All I could do was stand still and stare at it, and once again, like an echo from before, I heard the ringing and crackling noise in my chest.

I must have looked pretty bad as I left the birthing room. I walked down the long corridor, past the open dayroom where the nursing sisters were sitting having coffee and eyeing me curiously and giggling.

As I went out into the open air, their mocking commentary still rang in my ears.

They had been murmuring something about men—and weaklings who had no stomach for things.

THIRTEEN

The morning routine of standing, counting, and having the roll called had gone on longer than usual. I no longer remember how it came about, but I found myself in a group that was going "on the transport." That's what they said.

Anxious about the unusual alteration in the day's routine, I found myself almost immediately standing in a car so packed with people that I couldn't move, or see out. I'm not even sure whether it was a truck or a railcar. Such dizziness came over me that I couldn't make out anything much—at some point I must have gone to sleep.

All I remember is the end of the journey, and the memory is full of holes, muddled, in broken pictures with no order to them, too many pieces missing.

A terrible noise startles me awake, jerking me back into consciousness. I am hemmed in between grown-ups; I'm shaken, pushed, shoved. I can't see a thing. Above the general din there's a constant, overriding yelling and screaming from what sounds like a thousand people.

What's happened? All I can see is legs and stomachs, none of them with any idea that I'm down here, that I don't want to be trampled, that I need air. With enormous effort, I manage to get my arms up, so that I can put them over my face. The sharp elbows take effect. I can breathe a little.

But the pressure starts getting worse again right away. People keep leaning more and more to the side, and over me.

Where are we? Are we still in the car? Is the car tipping over and taking us with it?

I'm hot. The pressure becomes unendurable. It's stopping me from breathing. Then suddenly I'm not inhaling air anymore, it's smoke, and the smoke is getting stronger.

Where am I? I have to get out of here. Is the car on fire? I'm suffocating! There's fire somewhere, and we're burning up!

Panic seizes me.

Why is everyone wedged so tight together? Why aren't they moving? Why don't they notice that we're on fire? Why doesn't anyone open the car? Are we still in the car? Do something!

Nothing moves, everything has turned still, the noise has stopped, the screaming has died down. Only now do I see that the legs and backs and stomachs that pen me in are naked. I'm amazed.

Suddenly in front of me a glimmer of light, something opens, there's a little air.

That must be the way out, I think, and:

Why isn't anyone getting out? Why isn't anyone making space? I want to get out—I don't want to burn up!

With a wild fury that I've never felt in myself before, I begin to struggle and kick, to make a space for myself, and then I draw breath, deeper than I've ever drawn breath before, and I begin to scream with all my strength as I've never screamed before.

At this very moment, like an answer to my great long scream, something behind me moves. Two big, strong hands seize me under the arms. They throw me forward, up over everyone else, to where the light is, and air. I fly out over the motionless bodies, fall to earth somewhere.

I'm in the open air, I can see the sky.

What happened? Have I been lying here long? I wake up as if from an anesthetic. I look around:

Behind me, a great high shadow, maybe the car that brought us here.

In front of me a steep embankment that stands lit up by the sun with a straight, sharp edge against the sky. All around people are lying, lots of them, nobody moving, nobody to help me, they all look dead.

Why are they so naked? Some of them all naked, others half naked. When did they get undressed? And why? It's not hot out here, I think, puzzled again.

Something terrible has happened, but I don't know what. I want to get away from here. I'm afraid. I want to go up there, where the sun's shining, out of this shadow. I look up again.

Up on the edge, something moves: I make out the shape of a man, waving and calling. Then he starts running to and fro. His waving gets more urgent.

There are dead bodies on the embankment, too. But now one of them begins to move, slowly at first, and timidly. Then he starts flailing his arms and legs; he climbs up to the other man who's still standing up there, waving.

Like a beetle up a wall, I think.

Carefully I work my way over the bodies to where the embankment begins. I want to get up to the two men standing in the sun. They've seen me, they're calling and yelling, and now both of them are waving, I'm to come up as quickly as possible.

The slope is steep and full of loose earth. I try to hold on to scattered clumps of grass to pull myself up, but I slide backward more than once. The clumps don't hold. I don't understand, they don't seem to have taken root. So I have to hang on to the arms and legs of the corpses on the slope. Slowly I work my way up again.

If only they hold, and don't come crashing down with me, the way the clumps of grass did . . .

I fight down panic and a feeling that I'm going to faint. I'm almost at the top, I can almost see over the ridge already. My legs are shaking and they ache. I start to tremble, I lose my balance.

Off at an angle below me, there's a big man lying as if he'd been hung up on the wall like a picture, his huge bare stomach a shiny white in the sun.

He's all there is between me and falling. I have to put my bare feet on his stomach for support. But I don't want to—I'll hurt him. And if he starts to slide, and takes me with him, he could squash me, is what flashes through my head.

Then I tread, or rather jump, onto the big white stomach. My foot sinks right down in it. I go up and down and sway as if I'm on a seesaw, but the corpse doesn't fall. I begin to retch, I want to be sick, but I can't, my stomach's empty.

With one last effort I drag myself up over the edge of the embankment. My hands get a firm grip. I pull myself forward on my stomach, until only my legs are swinging over the void.

I've done something terrible, I think. I trod on a dead man. He couldn't defend himself. Can dead people feel pain? The dead man saved me, and I wanted to be sick on him.

I feel guilty. Can a dead person forgive you?

Slowly I realize that what I'm lying on up here is a railway embankment. My hands are holding tight to a rail. I wait, exhausted, my mind's a blank. I have no strength left.

After a while I turn myself around carefully and look back. I see the bodies I climbed over, lying as if glued to the steep slope. Looking further back, back over the car, I can see the place where I was thrown by the big hands. Those bodies here. I can't count them, there are too many. They're lying every which way. There's still smoke in the air, my eyes smart, and the smell makes me sick.

A little further away I see the vague shapes of what seem to be three railcars. They're standing off-center, slightly crazily, not in a straight line.

What is all this? Did we come in these cars? And why are they down there in the field and not up here on the embankment, on their rails? I lie down again on the railbed.

To my right there are people running along the embankment,

four or five of them. Some are already a long way away, but I can still hear them yelling. They all seem to be running in the one direction, as if they know where they're going. They keep pointing, yelling again, waving their arms in the air, gesturing urgently in the same direction they're running.

Then I look left.

At first all I see is smoke and empty space. The tracks end right next to where I am, the embankment stops abruptly, like the end of a military fortification. My eyes are burning and watering. I look over the edge into the bottom of the trench, then out over it. I can't understand what I'm seeing through the billows of smoke, and at the same time I do understand, but it doesn't connect up with anything I know, either in pictures or in words. I just feel that this is a place where everything ends, not just the embankment and the rails. This is where this world stops being a world at all.

Someone's yelling:

"Come on, get up, come back here—now!"

I put my head on my arm and look down at the pebbles between the rails. I don't care, I don't want to hear. They can yell and run around, but leave me alone. I've had enough, I can't anymore.

My legs seem to be dead, I can't feel them anymore. That means I can't run anyhow, and there's nowhere I want to run.

All that seems to be left of me is my eyes, my head, and two hands holding on. I want to go to sleep, just to sleep, nothing else.

For a moment, everything is quiet.

Then suddenly there's more yelling, this time right up close to my ear. I see a lot of legs standing around me. There's a woman. She bends over, she wants me to get up and come with them now, quickly, to the right, where the others are running along the embankment and are already all small in the distance.

For the first time, I consciously refuse. I don't want to obey anyone ever again. I shake my head, I don't know where my legs

are, I just want to sleep, I want to be left in peace, I don't want
to do what everyone else does anymore, I've had enough.

The confusion of voices over my head won't stop. Why don't
the grown-ups understand? I don't need them anymore. There
are no more questions, I know everything now—I've already
looked out over the end of the world.

The woman is yelling at me, she's very angry, and afraid, and
impatient. The others are yelling, too, I have to run, with them,
now, before it's too late.

The woman bends over me again. She's screaming at me, and
I feel her spit. I think she's going to slap my face. She hauls me
up by the wrist. She's rough and very angry.

So they simply drag me away with them, my numb feet trail-
ing in the gravel. They run.

I can't, I cry with fury. I just fall down, I'm picked up again,
this time by both wrists, so I'm being carried rather than running of my own accord.

This forced march went on and on and on. On my right, the sun
was already going down over the plain like a fireball that etched
itself like burning acid into my inflamed eyes. I could hardly see
where I was going.

Gradually the pace eased off into an endless monotonous trot.
The only time it was interrupted was when two or three people
came running across the fields. A farmer's wife waved a basket at
us, and after that my memory just turns into a long gray fog.

It wasn't till long afterward, when it had turned cold and the
first snow was falling, that my mind began to work again, and I
became aware of my surroundings.

The world was full of barracks again, there was another block
warden and a chief warden. But now it was more often men who
guarded us. Men who did nothing but yell, and sometimes hit
us, and also sometimes took away other children and didn't
bring them back again.

For the first time, however, the thirst wasn't as bad as the hunger whenever I could push a handful of snow into my mouth without being seen.

The place was always crowded to bursting, and the air was often full of smoke. I knew that smell.

I had my usual barracks again, like before, but this one seemed to be in a different place.

Who brought my barracks here? And why?

This one wasn't at the top of a slope anymore. And the enormous chimney was no longer up there on the hill, where the barracks ended and the big fence began. There was no more hill. Here everything was as flat as a plate.

And here the barracks streets went on forever, far further than I could see.

Maybe, no, not just maybe, they go right to the end of the world, to the edge of the plate, and nobody here knows what it's like there.

"What's it like?" I demanded of a big boy who was next to me. I knew. But he didn't know. He didn't say anything, just stared up at the sky.

FOURTEEN

I'd lost all sense of place a long time ago. It was a long time since I'd been in Majdan Lublin, in Majdanek. The barracks all around me were different, they kept on changing, yet they were always the same, sometimes the place changed too, I don't know anymore. But my barracks always stayed the same, it seemed to follow me everywhere.

Outside the big fence, there was nothing anymore, just flat fields and a pale wood, which was mostly covered in mist.

There were always new children around me. I could almost never understand what they were saying, and even less from the grown-ups. Everything seemed to be dissolving, murky, a blur. I didn't know enough to make sense of it, the constant changes confused me. The days suddenly had no set order, none of the regular timetable they'd had before. There didn't seem to be any rules anymore. I have some shreds of memory still, like a brief flash of light, but their meaning is much less clear.

For a time I wasn't allowed out of the barracks. I didn't know why. When it was time for roll call and everyone hurried outside, I was forbidden to go too. Each time someone grabbed hold of me and pushed me into a corner, or maybe it was a hole. A cover was put over me, and then a plank, and I wasn't supposed to move. I struggled, I didn't understand why they wouldn't let me, I didn't want to be left alone. I was afraid and began to cry.

A slap took care of that.

It went on that way for quite a long time, day after day, every morning and every evening. Everyone who lived in the barracks ran outside, two grown-ups stayed with me, I got the slap, then the cover, then the plank, then the two of them ran out as well; I knew it was them by the sound of their wooden clogs.

Another time a group of women took me outside with them. We ran past a jumble of unfamiliar barracks and lots of unknown faces.

Suddenly we were in a column, we had to wait, and one of the women made a sign for me to hold on tight to her leg. Then she spread her skirt over me. We waited like that for a time, and then began to move on again.

It went on for a long time and it was freezing cold. Eventually they brought me into a room that was quite different from any room I knew.

This room was big and high and had a window on one wall. Against each of the other three walls a huge pile of pieces of cloth, rags, maybe clothes, towered all the way up to the roof. Right in front of the middle pile, opposite the window, there was a table.

Two women were standing barefoot at the table. One of them was throwing clothes or rags from one of the piles, and the other turned them this way and that, and took them away again.

I was pushed through under the table to the foot of the mountain of clothes. Hands groped around in the mountain, hollowed out a nest, and I crawled into it. This was my new home. I liked the quiet in the room. I liked the strange soapy smell and the unaccustomed warmth. There were only three or four women there by day. They talked to each other quietly, they were friendly, and they made signs that I wasn't allowed to speak or call out to them, that I was safe as long as I stayed in my burrow under the mountain.

Once a day, I was allowed to crawl out. Each time there was a tin bowl standing ready on the edge of the table, at eye height. I pulled the spoon out of my clothes and began to eat. This spoon was my single most precious possession, and I'd carried it and a mug on a chain under my shirt for a long time now.

Then one of the women would prepare a cloth under the table, for me to relieve myself on. Then I crawled back into my cozy burrow, the woman bundled up the cloth and took it away. This happened every day, always the same. Was it a few days, a few weeks, a month, longer? I have no idea.

But the last day in the room is embedded in sharp contours in my mind, indelibly.

The women came as they always did, just before dawn. As always, I heard their whispered conversation, their footsteps, the rustling of material and clothing as they sorted them out. As always, the tin bowl stood ready and the cloth was under the table.

I was long gone back under the mountain of rags when I was startled by loud, hard footsteps, loud, deep men's voices, and terrified cries from the women. I inched forward and spied through the cloths. I saw the legs of the table, and between me and the table the hem of a skirt, two bare legs and feet. Very carefully I looked between the legs out into the room.

The loud men's voices and the noise of boots were now mixed in with high screams that were getting louder and louder. I saw pairs of black boots and naked legs running this way and that. Suddenly, the screaming died away into a soft whimpering, the sound of boots slowed down but got more threatening, the noise subsided—I peered out and listened as intently as I could.

The boots all came to stand together in front of the mountain of clothes on the right-hand wall. It was quiet for a moment, then I was absolutely amazed to hear the shrill cries of children. There must have been several of them, including big ones.

The boots and bare feet started to run again.

Other children in here? I couldn't believe it. I was sure I'd been alone.

The crying of the children, the women's screams, and the men's yelling mingled with the thumping and trampling until it filled the room. A full hunt seemed to be under way. I heard blows and dragging sounds that got further away. Then it got quiet again. I slid further forward, lifted a few more of the cloths away from my face and looked out again under the table legs to where the bare calves were still standing, only now they were closer to me.

I saw the room, I saw the open window opposite. Outside the window, the shapes of men swinging something—weapons or sticks—through the air. Inside, over to my right, in front of the other mountain of clothes, several pairs of boots still standing.

Uniform jackets, bending over, came into my field of vision; arms were stirring through the bottom of the mountain almost directly opposite me.

Two small, wriggling bundles were pulled out by large hands; the noise got louder again, more yelling from the boots, then a big swing and the bundles flew clear across the room, all spread out in the strangest way as if they were trying to flap their wings, through the window, and out.

Silence for a second—and in the silence, from outside, twice over the unmistakable sound of breaking skulls.

The calves in front of me moved, a bare foot came up, set itself against my face, and shoved me hard back into my burrow. The foot stayed there for a bit, squashing my nose and mouth together. I struggled for air. Then the foot was lifted away and I drew breath as carefully as I could. I could hear the echoing stamp of boots and the thud of bare feet slowly going away until there was no more sound.

Deathly silence. The storm seemed to have passed as quickly as it had come. It was only now that I felt any fear. I waited and listened for what seemed like forever. The room appeared to be empty.

It must have been late afternoon when the door opened and quiet footsteps approached. I heard whispering.

The rags over my head parted and women's arms reached around carefully for me. A woman's head, all shaved, bent down, kissed me, and I was lifted up out of my burrow with a smile and a sigh. Two more women were standing in the room. They looked at me questioningly, in disbelief. They shook their shaved heads slowly, went "tz-tz-tz," but they were smiling too.

The biggest woman began saying something to me quickly and urgently. All I understood was that we had to get out of the room and this barracks as fast and as quietly as possible, without being seen, that she would go first, that I had to do everything she did, and that we had to go out one by one, past the house, past the window, then run behind the barracks next door. She'd be waiting there.

We stood in a row behind the doors leading to the outside, and listened. The big one was in front, the others behind me. We peered out and waited. It was getting dark, it was foggy and raining. There were patches of snow.

The big woman set off at a run. I stuck my head out, looked left down the wall in the direction she'd taken. She'd already passed the window, now she disappeared around the corner.

"Don't worry—quick—now!" said an urgent whisper behind me.

But I was frightened, really frightened, I clung tight to the door frame. But my hands were pulled loose and I was given a gentle push.

Now I started to run too, as fast as I could, the length of the barracks wall, with a concentration born of terror.

Don't fall, don't stumble now—falling would be disaster, I thought, with my eyes fixed on where I had to go.

Then everything in me froze, turned into a single enlarged moment of time:

What I saw on the ground, up against the wall, was the two bundles, still lying there, or rather, what was left of them. The pieces of cloth were undone, lay around all torn, and in amongst them the babies on their backs, arms and legs outspread, stomachs all swollen and blue. And where once their little faces must have been, a red mess mixed with snow and mud.

Nothing else to see—except the skulls were smashed open.

A mass of yellow, sticky-shiny stuff had flowed out and was splashed against the wall, on the ground, and right across the path I had to follow. My stomach heaved with horror and disgust.

Can I jump over, without treading in the yellow stuff, or slipping in it and falling down?

I mustn't fall down. If I jump and fall, that's it. A block warden might hear, or a chief warden—it would all be over. I have to get past—I just have to jump.

I fought to stop my legs seizing up, fought to keep the moment from freezing me there for all eternity. It seemed to take forever until I was over the bodies and past them, and I felt all alone.

Who was there to help? I could hardly feel my legs anymore. They seemed to have solidified into shapeless lumps. I ran and ran, for hours it seemed, until I reached the corner and saw, between the next barracks, almost invisible in the fog, the shadow of the big woman waiting for me.

I've never been able to free myself of this picture, or of any of the others. They came back again and again, still do today—and this one in particular.

In the orphanage in Switzerland, there was also a room for nursing babies and little children. I once found myself in there by accident. When I saw the babies, it all came back, the numbing, crippling, freezing sensation that crept up from my feet, up past my knees, into my thighs and up against my innards. I slipped out cautiously, and never once went into that room again.

I still feel it today, whenever I catch sight of very small children, feel myself tensing to jump over the two bundles. I see them clearly. I see them vanish from under me as I fly over them with my legs stretched wide, as if in slow motion. In such dreadful slow motion that I think I'm going to fall right onto them.

I often reproach myself, I can't understand how I could have felt nothing for the little ones back then. Although I was just a child myself, was I already so brutalized that there was nothing left in me, no sympathy, no pity, not even anger?

Because I felt nothing then, nothing but disgust and my own icy terror.

FIFTEEN

Children were being taken away again every day, as so often before. We were just a little group now, maybe ten or twelve of us.

The interior of the barracks was now divided in two. One part was for us, in the other were women, who sometimes appeared like shadows out of the darkness, took care of us, then disappeared again behind hanging pieces of cloth into their territory.

Lots of the bunks stayed empty; we were colder than before. I didn't understand what was happening. I couldn't understand the remaining children, either; they spoke languages I didn't know. I hardly took them in at all—except for one child, that is, I can remember something about that one. I'm not sure if it was a boy or a girl. This one was older than I, perhaps, and called something like Kobo, or Kola or Kala—I'm not sure anymore. He or she seemed to be the favorite of the others, and I remember a round head on a long, thin neck. He/she liked to play and make faces, and sometimes even laughed.

But one day, I noticed that Kobo had vanished, along with the others.

Why have I been left on my own? Have I missed something again, or slept through something? Why am I always the last to see what's going on? It felt bad.

I didn't know what to do. The unaccustomed silence in the barracks was unsettling, everything around me seemed to be dissolving into inexplicable disorder.

I saw people going away, crowds of them. Most of them

seemed to be going however they chose, not in step and not in the usual column. Most of them seemed to know where they were going; they didn't turn around as they went past, nobody paid any attention to me, and I watched them go until they were swallowed up in the sea of barracks.

Despair grew and grew.

They're all going off somewhere, they all seem to know something I don't know. Why am I always the only one who doesn't understand? Why doesn't someone tell me? Where are they all going? I don't have anywhere to go, I'm hungry and I'm freezing cold.

There were only three or four women left in my barracks. They didn't say anything, just silently passed me something to eat now and then.

There were no orders, no rules to define the day the way it was before, no roll call, nobody bothered. The block warden seemed to have disappeared, no chief warden came by anymore, even the big men in the fancy uniforms stayed away, the ones who used to look for children and take them away.

Then, all at once, I felt the silence. No orders being given, no yelling, no crying, no standing still in rows in the morning and at night; the indistinguishable tumult of voices that used to fill the air had gone quiet. I stayed where I was and spent the days half asleep.

I was shocked out of my daze only once. There was a fire somewhere, barracks were burning down, but it didn't worry me for long. I didn't care. I went back to sleep. I was tired.

But there's one morning I do remember, as clear as glass. I was standing outside, in the cold. I was waiting at the corner of one of the neighboring barracks, looking down the street of the camp. I don't know what I was waiting for, and why I was standing in the cold. I scratched a hole in the slushy ground so that I could put my feet into the mud, which was warmer. In the distance I heard shots, lots at first, then not so many; they didn't come any nearer, and I stopped being afraid, and stayed where I was.

Again I saw people I'd never seen before. Most of them weren't in orderly rows, most of them went by in a confusing, disorganized mob. There were women, sometimes men too, and sometimes big children, but I didn't know them. They all came from the same direction. They turned ahead of me into a side street and disappeared between the barracks toward the horizon, the end of world.

For a long time, all morning maybe, I froze and watched the puzzling activity, and I saw that the women from my barracks were also joining one of the groups, and then they slowly disappeared out of my view. They walked slowly through the rows of barracks toward the wires, to the fence, where it was forbidden to go.

What do they all want there? That's where the world ends, there's nowhere further to go. What should I do? I just waited, without any idea, without knowing what I was waiting for.

Then another group came. Women, a few children, a very few men, and they turned off in front of me, just like the others. I looked after them. A few rays of sun broke through and began to warm me.

Then suddenly, the group comes to a halt. One of the women turns around, detaches herself from the knot of people, runs back along the path, and she's screaming. She throws her arms up in the air so wildly that her rags slip off and you can see her white breast. But she doesn't notice, she keeps waving and calling and calling and her voice is falling over itself:

"Binjamin," she's screaming. "Binjamin, oy Binjamin," and she keeps running in my direction.

Spellbound, I stare at her. What's the matter with her? She's quite close to me now.

"Binjamin—is it you?" she calls again, all excited, her whole voice like a question.

Suddenly it hits me—I'm the person she's calling, I *am* Binjamin, she means me. I'd almost forgotten that I have a name.

The woman bends over me, I look up into a round face that seems to be saying "You—here?" as she stares disbelievingly at me.

"Binjamin, Binjamin," she keeps panting, and hugs me so tight it hurts. What does it mean? Who is she? It doesn't make any sense to me, all I do know is that I *am* Binjamin, that she does mean me, but I have no idea who she is, I don't remember her at all.

"Come with me, come quick, before anyone sees you here," she gasps and pulls me toward the waiting group at a run.

What's happening? Why do I have to leave? Why can't I just stay here? I've been standing here all morning. I'm hungry. Will she give me something to eat?

I'm too tired to ask, I just let it all happen. The shapes in the group take me into the middle as we move on, so I get only glimpses of where we're going.

We pass through row after row of unfamiliar barracks, where I've never been before. Near a cross street and a passage between the fences, there's an open gate. We come to a halt.

Another surprise: just next to a barracks I see a group of women half dressed, naked almost, washing themselves out in the open air—in spite of the cold. They stand barefoot in a big puddle of water, snow, and muck, looking after us without saying a word.

After a brief pause we follow the passage between the fences, and then we're on an even bigger street. As we get closer and closer to the outer fence, I begin to get suspicious; it's what the other children call the End of the World.

The thought terrifies me—we're not on our way to a new barracks, or looking for food: we're actually going to go to the other side, outside the big fence, out of this world. Over there, in the fields, there's nothing anymore, there was a world once, but it disappeared long ago, the older children always said so. But how can you go somewhere that's disappeared, that no longer exists? There's nothing out there on the other side of the fence—everything came to an end out there. As I keep thinking this, my anxiety rises. We're doing something that's impossible. Or does this actually mean we're going out there to die? Is this we're doing now what the big children called "the death walk"?

In spite of the cold, I'm sweating.

We're almost at the fence, close to the last buildings. A uniform is standing by the side of the road. The group slows its pace. We go by. He doesn't do a thing. He doesn't shoot. He doesn't yell. He just turns around with both hands in his pockets and stares wordlessly after us.

I can't make out what they're saying in the group, but the voices get louder and more excited as we pass the fence, go through the gate and out into the open country.

I'm dead tired, my legs feel dull and numb again, as if they don't belong to me, just my knees ache. But the unknown woman who knows my name pulls me along relentlessly. When do I get to die? Why does she go on hurting me? I can't feel my feet anymore. I stumble. I fall. I lie with my face in the snow, beating the frozen ground with my fists.

There's nothing here anymore, nothing, just fields and fog. No barracks to sleep in, nothing left to eat. We're on our way to nothing, it's all over, the world's over. I've left it! I can't go back, I'll starve, it's the end now. I want to go to sleep—leave me alone! I'm not hungry anymore, I don't want to see anyone ever again, I want to be alone, I just want it all to stop, I want to go to sleep.

My memory stops here; maybe I really did fall asleep.

The next thing I have any recollection of was months later, and even that is hazy. The unknown woman who knew my name kept me with her. We walked for a very long time, sometimes we ran, sometimes we sat on a horse-drawn cart. After a long time we came to a small town high up on a mountain. The strange woman who knew me had been talking for days about Sandomierz and how we absolutely had to get there—just for a few days, she said. I understood that it was something to do with papers that she had to arrange.

During the day, she locked me in the tiny attic room where we lived. She left in the early morning, always carrying lots of printed and handwritten papers. She was away all day.

It was a good time. I sat for hours on the window ledge, looking out. I could see way down to the flat land under the cliffs at Sandomierz and to the river, glittering between the trees. It was spring already, the snow had melted, and I watched all the birds flying over the valley and the river below me. I daydreamed about flying with them, soundless and free.

"We have to go back to Kraków now—it's all settled," she said one night.

Back? To Kraków? Isn't that where we were to begin with, after we went through the big fence? I brooded about it, I wasn't sure of myself, I didn't dare ask questions, I didn't even want to try; I didn't talk anyway.

Nothing has stayed with me about the journey to Kraków. On the other hand, I retraced the route from the station to the Miodowa synagogue like a sleepwalker twenty years later, the first time I ever went back to the city.

For several days we kept going back and waiting in front of this synagogue. The woman who knew me wanted to speak to someone, she said it was about me, that she was going to "deliver" me here.

At last the huge doors opened. An impressive-looking man in a long black coat and a big black hat looked down at me and smiled. The woman spoke to him vehemently. I only understood the first words she said.

"I'm bringing you the little Wilkomirski boy, Binjamin Wilkomirski." She took me by the shoulders and pushed me forward, so that he could see me better. He nodded.

I was very surprised and proud that I now had two names.

The woman kept talking. The rabbi's face turned serious, then he smiled at me, then turned serious again. I began to trust him. I felt he belonged with us, that he was one of the barracks people too.

He took my hand, led me into the garden behind the synagogue and up some stone steps at the back of the house, to a sort of balcony or arcade. His hand was firm and felt good, it didn't grab or push. It said things, it comforted and calmed and conveyed safety. Since the time of Motti, and then Jankl, I hadn't felt a hand like that.

Up on the balcony there were two older men sitting at a table, and they had black hats, too. They had papers in front of them. The rabbi went away, and the two men inspected me.

They began to ask questions, lots of questions, but I don't know what they were anymore. All I do know is that, without knowing how, I suddenly began to talk in a way I'd never talked before. I heard myself talking, as if it was someone else inside me. I talked like a waterfall, but I have no idea anymore what I said. But at some point it was enough, there was only a sick feeling in my throat, I stopped talking and everything inside me was quiet again, the way it was before.

The two men got up in a hurry and went away. One of them came back after a time; he looked different, there were drops of water still hanging in his beard and his face was a sort of gray-green color.

Looking straight in front of him and not at me, and without saying another word, he took me down the stone stairs again into the garden.

"Wait in front of the entrance, you're going to be collected," said the rabbi, who'd come back to meet me down there. He stroked my shoulder and back, which made a great impression on me, then he disappeared.

Where was the woman who knew my name? She'd gone—I never saw her again.

———

Where they took me, and who took me—I've no idea. It's all a blur.

Sometimes I was with lots of children, then with just a hand-ful—probably I kept moving from one place to another. I do know that I kept running away, that I wanted to find my bar-racks, where I belonged.

The city, other people, other children, all put me in a panic. A tangle of questions kept gnawing at my brain like acid, tor-menting me more and more, sometimes flooding my head like molten lead. I couldn't say the questions out loud, they choked my throat and mouth and set my heart racing, or else threatened to make it stop altogether; I couldn't get anything out, so there was no hope of any answer.

What kind of people are these? A lot of them have strange uniforms, different ones. They're all nicely dressed, they live in whole houses, which are warm, and not in ruins or in barracks. I don't belong with them.

The people who live in whole houses and don't wear striped shirts and have everything to eat, as much as they want, they're the ones who kill the others. They're the ones I have to fear, the ones with fat faces and strong arms and legs and terrible big hands. They're the ones who sometimes grab children and take them away and throw them into the fire, so as to make room for new children.

I don't want to live with these people! What are they plan-ning? Where's my barracks?

I can hardly believe what the grown-ups and a lot of the chil-dren have to say—according to them, the city isn't new. It was always here, even during the time I was in the barracks. The city and the world outside the fence didn't disappear, the way I was told. Some of the children say they were never in a barracks, and that they've lived here for a long time. Lots of them also say that they hid outside the fence in other places that didn't disappear.

Others say they're going to wait until they're picked up by papa, or mama, or their older brothers and sisters.

My mama's dead.

Oh God—I had brothers too once, I did—I remember now. Where are they?

My brothers will come and get me out of this city where the murderers live—where are Motti and Daniel? Why don't they come now, before it's too late?

But then, why weren't we all together in the barracks behind the big fence? Why me? Why Jankl? Why did they tell me the world outside the fence had disappeared, and that it was better to live in the barracks than to be thrown in the fire? Why were the other children thrown in the fire? Why didn't they get to me? Did they forget me? Or are they still waiting? What will they do when they find me?

Why are there even children who say they never had to hide at all?

Something here doesn't make sense—they've tricked me. They've all tricked me. Maybe I didn't need to live behind the fence at all. Or Jankl either. But Jankl's dead.

Was it all about nothing?

Now I have warm clothes and hot food. That's nice. But I'm living with cheats and murderers! And the grown-ups all lied to me. Best not to listen to them ever again.

Not even Mila can give me the answers. She's the only one I'd believe. But she only knows what I do.

Wouldn't it be better for me to get back to the barracks, before anyone notices that I'm here in the city, still alive? But where is my barracks? They took it away. Here there's nothing but stone houses—everywhere—and no grandpa, no mama, no brother to take me away. Where can I go, what can I do?

Many years later I recognized some of the streets in Kraków again: Miodowa Street and its synagogue in the Jewish quarter. The Dluga and Paulinska Street. The house on Augustianska Street with the big staircase and the exercise bars in the playground.

The faces of Mischia and Olga resurface; they used to take us for walks. I also recognized Jozefinska Street and the Limanovskiego, which oddly are somewhere else entirely, namely Podgorze, the ghetto area built by the Nazis, on the other side of the Vistula. I begged there once. Number 38, Zamoiskiego also comes back to me—what was there? Nowadays there's a new building on the site.

I remember that I begged on the streets every time I ran away from somewhere, and that it was hard, because the bigger children savagely defended the best begging places.

I also remember a Purim festival, more precisely I just remember the bit about "killing Haman." Lots of children were sitting squashed around a long table by candlelight. I beat with my stick as hard as I could, and didn't want to stop, until two soft hands took hold of my arms from behind, and a voice spoke to me soothingly.

Then, suddenly, I think it was already autumn, and cool, a house, almost empty rooms, iron bedsteads. Sudden uproar in the house. Children running to the windows, me too. We leaned over the windowsills and looked down into the street. A deafening racket rose up at us, coming from a black mass of stamping, yelling people surging through the street. They were swinging planks and sticks through the air and roaring like drunkards. A warning memory took hold of me and I climbed down from the windowsill and went to hide in the corner behind an open door. I heard grown-ups' voices, very upset; in the house, someone called:

"They're killing Jews again."

It wasn't long after that when Frau Grosz appeared and asked me:

"Do you want to come? I'll say—you must say that you're my son, that way I can take you with me," and:

"Switzerland is a beautiful country."

SIXTEEN

I was standing waiting, staring at the rails and streaming sweat. A children's nurse from the Swiss orphanage had brought me here to the station of the nearest town. She was holding tight to my sleeve, in case I ran away.

There had been a terrible row before that, in the orphanage. A strange woman had visited the day before, and had a long talk with the director of the home; a doctor was there too. He examined me, wrote lots of things down on a piece of paper, nodded, and said:

"In a few days this lady will fetch you, you're going to live with her, you're getting foster parents." And then, turning to the strange lady, he said:

"And what have you thought about transport?"

And the strange lady said:

"I think we'll take the train."

I didn't listen to another word; I began to scream and yell, I jumped at the strange lady, hit her with my fists in a frenzy of rage and fear, and ran away before anyone could catch me. It was the beginning of a wild hunt through the building, and they overpowered me. Biting, kicking, hitting—none of it was any use, they had an iron grip on me. It was the first time I was ever hit in this house—for my "appalling behavior," they said.

"No, no transport, no—I won't go on any transport," I screamed despairingly. "I want to go home, let me go home. Not the transport, please!"

Lots of people talked to me but I didn't understand what they said—I didn't want to understand anything. They would only lie to me, like the gray uniforms who took me from the railway station before.

They tried to give the word "transport" other names, but I didn't let myself be fooled. After all, I knew the word from personal experience and from what lots of children had told me. Whenever I asked them about their parents or brothers or sisters, it was always the same:

"They were put on the transport."

And that always meant they'd gone forever. Almost nobody ever came back who'd been on a "transport."

I was forced to recognize that running away was impossible; my transport was already "written down," as they said.

I lost all hope in the days that were left. I had to stay in the house. I was constantly watched; they ran to lock doors behind me and in front of me, so that I wouldn't get away from them at the last moment.

And now I was standing here on the platform of a little town in Switzerland, waiting for my transport. The nurse was holding me by the wrist now, because I was making fists; I didn't want to give her my hand.

The train pulled in, the strange lady got out, all that changed was the hand holding my wrist. We waited in silence, another train came, and we went to the place where the strange lady lived.

It was a big house, in a big garden, and there weren't any other children. But the husband of the strange lady was there. He greeted me with a rather awkward smile. Apart from him, there didn't seem to be anybody in the house.

It was evening already, they gave me food, nothing I knew; absolutely everything was unfamiliar. The food took a whole series of strange journeys: first it was in a frying pan, then it was in a bowl, then it was on a plate that got put on another plate. This all happened with three different frying pans, three bowls and plates, and then yet another plate, separate, that one was only for uncooked vegetables—I had to eat salad, they said, it was healthy. It tasted so sour that my stomach went tight. At the end I sat bewildered in front of a reddish yellow ball that was put in front of me on another new plate. Why all the new plates? This was the fourth already.

"Don't you like oranges?" they asked, and I shrugged my shoulders. I didn't know what they meant.

The man took the ball, peeled it, and divided it into slices. I almost choked when I swallowed the slice without chewing.

Then it was time to sleep. Some doors were opened.

"This is your room," they said, and the man went away. The room was enormous, and the idea of sleeping there alone without any other children next to me was frightening.

I lay down on the bed.

"Now you must learn to say 'good night' to me properly," the strange lady said.

"What's that?" I said.

"Good night, Mother—that's what you must say to me now," she said.

"No, I won't," I cried, upset.

"Yes, I'm your mother now."

"No, no—aunt!" I screamed.

"Not aunt—you must call me your mother," she said forcefully.

"No, I know who my mother is. You're not my mother. I know where my mother got left. I want to go back, I want to go home," I yelled as loud as I could. "I want to go back to where I came from." I didn't dare to say the name of the place, in case she would be able to find me there again.

"You must forget that now. Forget it—it's a bad dream. It was only a bad dream," she kept saying. "You must forget everything. I'm your mother now."

I jumped up and wanted to get dressed again, get my shoes on, most of all get out of here, get away, get out of this terrible house.

But she wouldn't let me and there was a sort of wrestling match all around my bed, with both of us screaming. I cried and yelled and bit and scratched and kept trying to reach my clothes. But she was stronger and she had longer staying power.

At some point I was exhausted and gave up, and sobbed out some muttered noise that sounded like "mother," and she relented and turned out the light.

I cried for a long time. I thought about my mother's face as she lay there and how she sort of smiled as she gave me the bread.

I felt more ashamed than I had ever felt in my life. I felt as if I'd become a criminal, my mother's betrayer. I felt filthy and wretched, and my skin began to crawl and itch again.

Now I've really turned into a bad person.

Nobody will want me anymore, nobody will like me. What should I do? I would need to ask Motti, or Jankl. They'd know what to do. But they'd maybe chase me away. Nobody wants to be friends with a traitor. I won't ever be able to go back to my people—they'd have so many reasons to take revenge on me. No amount of talking can cover up the terrible thing I just did, there's no way to forgive it.

And here? I can't stay here, it'll just go on like this—I've ended up on the wrong side.

Thinking that, I fell asleep, and dreamed the terrible dream again about the dead world, the black sky, the insects eating me, and the iron cars going up the mountain in their endless chain and disappearing into the yellowish brown jaw under the helmet.

Next day the lady took me through the house and the big garden. She explained to me that I wasn't allowed to tread in the flower beds, and that I could walk on the grass, but not sit— grass stains are very hard to wash out—if I wanted to sit, there was the garden bench.

She showed me the fruit trees, and told me not to get any

ideas about pulling fruit down off them. Above all, I was to take care of my new clothes and always take off my shoes after I'd been playing, and wash my hands. She said a lot else, but I don't remember it.

But there was something else—she also showed me the high fence surrounding the garden, and I was told never to climb over it. I looked at her mistrustfully, but nothing moved in her face.

Then we went back into the house and she wanted to show me the cellar.

"This is the laundry room," she said, "and this is the drying room, and that's the food cellar with fruit."

She opened a heavy door, and a dim light was switched on. I could hardly believe my eyes.

There were wooden bunks. And on the wooden bunks were apples, but the bunks looked like the bunks I knew.

I didn't believe anything she said anymore.

Take away the apples and they look just like the stacks of bunks in the barracks! Only smaller, just right for children. I was terrified. What's going on here? Something's not right. Be careful.

She shut the door again.

"And now the coal furnace for the heating. We also heat the water that way," she said without any expression.

She opened another door, this one even heavier. We went around a heap of coal, and there it was.

All I understood about heating until then was that a stove was something in which you burned little bits of wood, and you cooked on it, and warmed your hands.

But this was a huge, black monster, far taller than I was.

The lady opened a semicircular cover, took the shovel, threw some coal inside, and I could see the flames. In deathly fear I stared at the monster.

So—my suspicions were right. I've fallen into a trap. The oven door is smaller than usual, but it's big enough for children. I know, I've seen, they use children for heating too.

Wooden bunks for children, oven doors for children, it's all too much. As I thought this, I suddenly raced up the cellar stairs and into my room. My thoughts were falling over each other. I was right. They're trying to trick me. That's why they want me to forget what I know. The camp's still here. Everything's still here.

They've only got to carry the "fruit racks," the bunks, into the wooden garden house, they've only got to take the cast-iron oven with the children's door and install it out on the stone forecourt outside, the garden's already fenced in, and it would all be just the way it was before, except that this time I'd be alone, totally alone.

The camp's still there, they just hid it. They'll bring it out if I don't obey them.

"Mama, Motti, Jankl, what do I do?" I cried silently into the pillow, but nobody answered.

Years later, the coal system was replaced by a small, modern oil-fired one and I breathed easier: at least this danger seemed to have been banished, but that didn't mean people were to be trusted.

SEVENTEEN

"He has to go to school as soon as possible," my foster parents said, and that was the beginning of a bad time.

School was full of talk, but nobody had the faintest idea about life—still less about death—not even the teacher. They all behaved as if they were going to live forever.

People talked about things and learned things that simply didn't exist. Mostly, I couldn't understand a thing. I could understand most of the words quite quickly, but when I put them together, they made no sense, no shape that I could project. So I dozed along in class, mostly baffled by what was going on around me.

The strangest problems were explored for hours on end, and the questions asked struck me as completely unreal. Why should I care how many pairs of shoes I can buy with so-and-so much money, if one pair costs such-and-such? Who needs so many shoes? I've only got two feet. And lots of people have no shoes at all, and that's when you get strips of cloth to tie around your feet. Or sometimes you trade your shoes for soup or a mug of water.

"Which stories of Swiss heroes do you all know?" asked the teacher.

Heroes? Did she say heroes?

From somewhere, once, I'd picked up the phrase "heroes of the German Reich," and who they meant were the black uniforms. Are there heroes like that here too? Aren't heroes always the people who kill you?

"Stories of Swiss heroes?" she asks again, and she's pointing at me. I stand up and they're all looking at me. What am I supposed to say? What does she want me to say? I begin to sweat.

"I—I didn't know these heroes were Swiss"—the girls in the benches behind me snicker, and one or two of the boys begin to boo.

The teacher looks at me resignedly, the way she always does when she doesn't understand my answers, and then she unrolls a big colored poster.

"What do you see here?" she asks again.

"Tell! William Tell! The arrow!" they're calling from all the benches.

"So—what do you see? Describe the picture," says the teacher, who's still turned toward me.

I stare in horror at the picture, at this man called Tell, who's obviously a hero, and he's holding a strange weapon and aiming it, and he's aiming it at a child, and the child's just standing there, not knowing what's coming.

I turn away. What has school got to do with me? Why is she showing me this terrible picture? Here in this country, where everyone keeps saying I'm to forget, and that it never happened, I only dreamed it. But they know all about it!

"You're supposed to be looking at the picture—what do you see?" she asks impatiently, and I make myself look at the picture again.

"I see—I see an SS man," I say hesitantly, "and he's shooting at children," I add quickly.

A gale of laughter in the classroom.

"Quiet," barks the teacher, then turns back to me.

"I'm sorry—what did you say?" and I can see that she's getting angry.

"The—the . . ." I'm stuttering now. The girls behind me snicker even louder. They always do that when I stutter.

"The hero's shooting the children, but . . ."

"But what?" the teacher says fiercely. "What do you mean?" Her face is turning red.

". . . But . . . but it's not normal," I say, trying not to cry.

"Who or what isn't normal here?" Now she's beside herself, and shouting. I force down the lump in my throat and try to concentrate. But I can't interpret what's going on. What's this about? Something's coming—what is it? I decide to observe her before I say anything else. I look straight at her face. I see the glittering eyes, the angry, twisted mouth—it's the block warden.

There she stands, legs apart, sturdy, hands on her hips. The teacher's a warden—our block warden. She's just in disguise, she's taken off her uniform. Now she's wearing a red sweater, she's trying to trick me.

"You children are just dirt," she always said. So why is she trying to force me to explain this picture now? She's known all about it forever—she knows what it means.

I try again.

"It's not normal, bec—because . . ." I'm stuttering again.

"Because why?" she says loudly.

"Because our block warden said, 'Bullets are too good for children,' and bec-bec-because only grown-ups get shot . . . or they go into the gas. The children get thrown in the fire, or killed by hand—mostly, that is."

"How do you . . ." she screeches, losing her composure.

"How?—well, using the hands, around the neck, the way they do with hens."

"Sit down and stop talking drivel."

"Drivel?"—another incomprehensible word, but clearly not a good one.

I look over the warden-teacher, standing there shaking with anger, standing there in front of the big blackboard, her hands still on her hips. My eyes begin to smart, and the big blackboard turns watery, gets bigger and bigger until it surrounds the whole classroom and turns into a black sky, and the warden-teacher is standing in front of the black sky in her red pullover, and the red pullover is dripping red blood down in a stream over all the benches. "Red warden—bloody warden," I hear in my head.

She was so feared, the block warden who watched over us back then, and kicked us with her hard boots or "decorated" (as she called it) our stomachs and backs with bloody stripes—the bloody warden, who deliberately poured the little ration of soup so that it missed your bowl and went onto the floor. And took away children, children she swore at and called "dung" or "cameldung" and never brought back again.

"Cameldung"—whatever that was—meant something absolute, something irretrievable, it was the announcement of the end. Lots of us were cameldung.* Now she's found me, too. Now she's ridiculing me, while I have to describe the picture of her hero, the one who shoots children.

I can tell: one day there'll be a banging at the school doors and her hero Tell will come in. He'll say a friendly hello to the warden and she'll say:

"Look, there he is, I found him. That's him! He made the new boy do it, and he's responsible for his death. He's the one who ate the stolen potatoes with Jankl, and managed to get out of the barracks world. I leave the rest to you." And as she's saying it, she points at me.

And Tell will thank her just as politely, then he'll lead me along the long school corridors and down into the courtyard, and take aim at me.

I take another look at the warden-teacher's blood-red sweater, and it slowly turns into a fiery red ball—a huge fire against the black horizon up on the hill, behind the big fence near the big smoking chimney, where the blackboard used to be.

---

*In Majdanek, inmates in the last stages of starvation were called "camels" because their spines were bowed.

The class has gone wild, they're all yelling. The girls are laughing right out loud now, high mocking laughter, and tapping their foreheads, while the boys point at me and make fists and yell:

"He's raving, there's no such thing. Liar! He's crazy, mad, he's an idiot."

The warden has trouble restoring order. She explains that Tell isn't shooting children, he's shooting the apple on the child's head.

I look at the child. The child's barefoot. No shoes, not even rags on his feet, he's so poor. He hasn't got long to live anyway, I think, without shoes, or rags against the cold and the rats. His feet will freeze to the ground at roll call. And look at his clothes: only a long shirt, tied around the middle, sleeveless, no trousers—he can't survive.

And anyway—SS men don't shoot apples—that's just stupid. It's just another piece of cruelty: the child's hungry, and he's not allowed to eat the apple. A child who's about to die doesn't need an apple. Tell will eat it once he's killed him.

The warden-teacher must know this. She's lying to us, and the other children obviously believe her. How can they? I don't believe one word.

The lesson continues, and I no longer understand what they're saying. The only thing that's clear is that they're all full of awe and admiration when they talk about this hero and SS man Tell, who shoots children.

An SS man doesn't ever aim without firing. I hate the picture. I'll tear it up sometime, secretly.

The warden-teacher didn't hit me as a punishment, she left that to the rest of the class after school. They fell on me in a swarm on the way home—what could I do, against so many? I sat down on the edge of the pavement and let them beat me.

Why do the children ally themselves with her? That's what hurts most, and makes me sad. Why do they do it? Why do they fight me? They're children too. Why doesn't one of them help me?

Then, to save myself, I fly away in my head, and soar through the air, over the houses and roofs, over the evil city and away, following the birds, far away over endless birch forests, lakes, and rivers, I circle pure white clouds and fly on over hills and valleys, I wave at Motti, my eldest brother, who's in a sunny field throwing his handmade airplane—and it's all beautiful. Motti waves back.

At some point, I realized that the beating had stopped and that the children had gone away. I stood up and went home.

"You're late," my foster mother said angrily, as she looked suspiciously at my dirty clothes. "Why do you always keep getting into fights?"

I shrugged.

"What did you do in school?"

"Nothing special. Just drivel." And I went to my room.

EIGHTEEN

I'd only been at school for a few weeks when the teacher said there was going to be an outing. There was a Folk Fair, and we could all go.

"They have a whole town of booths. We'll go there too," she said.

I couldn't imagine what this might be, but I was excited.

"This afternoon we're going to the town," is all I said at home. I didn't want to show my ignorance.

I was excited, but a little frightened too. All sorts of unexpected things could happen, and I would have no grip on them, and they could betray me.

In spite of all the misfortunes I'd had at school, none of the children had got suspicious of me. None of them had hinted that I might belong to the ones with no right to be here, that I belonged to the ones who had no right to share in their comforts.

The fairground was a dazzling sight. I'd never seen so many colors, and everything seemed to be turning or moving in one direction or another.

Children were sitting on brightly painted horses, on fairy-tale animals, others sat in little coaches, in red cars, in little ships—and they all went around in circles, laughing and waving. Lots of them were sitting on little benches that were lifted up high in the air by a huge wheel and then came swaying down again. In amongst all this were colorful market stalls.

"We'll meet at five o'clock at the exit. Don't let anyone be late," called the teacher.

The class split up into individual groups and little clusters and scattered in all directions. The children seemed to know their way around already, and they were holding shiny coins which they showed each other and compared.

I was uncertain. Which way should I go? After a suitable interval, I followed some of the boys, secretly so to speak, in case they noticed that I didn't know how you were supposed to behave here. I wanted to watch what they did and how they did it.

It wasn't easy to follow them through the crowd, but they soon stopped at one of the stands. I hid opposite, behind a black metal bucket on three legs, which was steaming and smelled wonderful. I looked carefully over to the other side—they were still standing there.

"Do you want a hot chestnut?" asked a man's voice.

I just looked at him, and was too shy to ask what a "chestnut" was.

Chewing and smacking his lips, he held out a round hot brown thing to me.

"Thank you," I said and bit into it.

It crunched, and I thought I was chewing wood fibers.

The man roared with laughter and said, "You're so hungry you don't even want to peel it?" and I was ashamed as I spat the shell out onto the ground.

I took another quick peek over at the boys on the other side. They were still there. They were right up at the counter now, and then with a terrible shock I saw that one of them was holding a gun in his hand.

Are there soldier-children here? Have I just found out what they've been hiding from me? was my first thought. The others were talking excitedly to the marksman and pointing at something inside the stall—a painted lady was standing there.

Oh no—is he going to shoot her?—and at that moment I

heard the shot. It sounded a bit thin perhaps, but definitely a shot. I looked over, and was relieved—the painted lady was still standing there. So close, and yet he still missed her? Maybe he just wanted to put a scare into her. But I thought it would be advisable to find my own way and stop following the group.

So I wandered around for a long time on my own, marveling at all the activity. It was wonderful how much there was to see and to smell. There were stalls with amazing sweet things, in endless quantities. How did you get some?

I observed the grown-ups and the children. They handed over the coins and got what they wanted, then walked on, chewing.

I didn't have any coins—that was obviously their privilege—but I'd started to feel hungry. People were taking so much away from the stalls. Maybe someone will have something left over, I thought, and remembered the way it had been before:

There were whole days of hunger back then, and I would sit at a street corner, on the steps of an entryway, protected from the rain by the overhang of a balcony, with my hand outstretched and my cap at my feet. I sat that way for hours. Sometimes I got a potato or a piece of turnip, or someone would throw an onion into the hat; sometimes I just got a kick, or someone would spit into my cap.

Suddenly I was hauled roughly up off the ground. A fist pulled at my ear. "What sort of disgusting behavior is this?" someone was barking over my head. "People don't beg! It's forbidden! Have you gone mad? You should be reported to the police!" It was the man from the stall next door.

Laughter and mocking remarks all around me. Some children in my class had found me, they were grinning in a nasty, scornful way. Where am I? was my first thought, then I came to, and realized.

I hastily grabbed the handkerchief that was still lying in front of me on the ground. I'd spread it out in front of my feet, since I had no cap. None of the children wore caps here.

The handkerchief was empty.

I've no idea how long I'd been sitting on the ground between the stalls, in among all the passing legs.

News of my unheard-of behavior soon spread through the whole school, even my foster parents heard about it, and they were scandalized: I'd disgraced them, there was no need to beg, they gave me plenty to eat, after all, I had everything I needed— what people must think of them now didn't bear thinking about.

Months later, whenever the children in school caught sight of me, they'd begin their chant:

Beggar kid, beggar kid.
There's never enough for the yid.
Beggar kid, beggar kid.

NINETEEN

I was maybe ten years old, or twelve, I just don't know. During school term I lived with my foster parents, and in the holidays I went back to the Children's Home. But that winter I was taken to another home on the Lenzer Heath, and for the first time I saw the Alps in the snow. It was a beautiful house above the village, near the edge of the woods. The director of the house and two women looked after us—we were about fifty children.

I didn't know any of them, and I was alone a lot. The snow was piled high, and I didn't like walking on the paths that the director, whom they also called the "ski instructor," plowed and shoveled clear. What I liked was wading along beside the paths and the space for traffic in the deep snow, under the weighed-down fir trees. That's what I was used to, and it made me feel safe.

As I was doing my big circle one gray, overcast afternoon, walking along through the silence, a girl suddenly stepped out from behind a tree and stood there a few feet in front of me, without saying a word, staring into my face.

She was from the Children's Home, but I'd only seen her once before, briefly, from behind. She was about my age, thin face. I looked back at her silently. I didn't dare move, just returned her stare, mesmerized. I saw her wide-open eyes, and all of a sudden I knew: these eyes knew it all, they'd seen everything mine had, they knew infinitely more than anyone else in this country. I knew eyes like this, I'd seen them a thousand times, in the camp and later on. They were Mila's eyes. We children used to tell each other everything with these eyes. She knew it, too; she looked straight through my eyes and into my heart.

We were still standing there, motionless.

"I prefer not using the path, just walking in the snow through the wood—it's beautiful," I said.

She nodded.

"It's a little like home," she said softly, and I knew she was thinking of the huge forests we'd left so far behind. Slowly, not talking, but holding hands tightly, we did another big circle around the Children's Home before we went back inside.

The next day the sun came out, the sky was bright, and the snow glittered.

"We can all take a turn on the ski lift today—go and get ready," announced the director–ski instructor. I shrugged—I didn't know what a "ski lift" meant.

They tied wooden boards under my feet—you used them to get through the snow more easily. All the children gathered themselves into a double column outside in front of the house. The girl was suddenly standing in front of me. They'd tied pieces of wood under her feet too. We walked silently in the long line side by side. The director ran up and down the line, supervising.

I kept watch on him. Something about him looked more and more disturbing. Under his long jacket, he was wearing strange battlefield-gray trousers, and on his feet were some new kind of heavy shoes. Something was wrong. In anxious silence I hurried along with the girl. The further we went through the wood, and the closer we got to the valley floor, the more loudly we could hear an unfamiliar noise. It was just a humming at first, but then it got louder and louder, ominous and threatening. The thunder of what was clearly a huge engine filled the air until it threatened to suffocate everything in its roar.

I came to a terrified halt in the shelter of the last line of trees, and looked down into the clearing. The girl stopped beside me, shaking, and reached for my hand. The other children pushed past us, laughing. In the clearing was a little house, open on one side. An immense iron wheel was turning inside like some merciless, indifferent mill. The wheel moved two fat steel ropes that ran up the mountainside opposite.

"The death machine," I heard myself saying. My nightmare was coming true.

"Yes," the girl whispered. "This time we've had it." She was crying without a sound. We stared hypnotized at the thundering monster.

"The director," I thought suddenly. I had been right to feel anxious about him. We could see double wooden hooks hanging down off the steel rope. We watched as the director and an assistant kept attaching pairs of children to the hooks. A jolt, and the children were carried off up the mountain by the rope.

My eyes followed the rope, and what I was able to see through the fir branches was the last proof of the horror that was under way: there was a house built into the mountain way up there. But the front of the house was missing—there was only a huge, yawning black hole that led right through the house and into the mountain—and disappearing into it was the steel rope with the children on the hooks.

The girl followed my look. She leaned against me, and I could feel her fingers digging into my arm. I turned my head—she wasn't crying anymore. When I looked at her eyes, I saw the eyes I remembered very well, of children who won't come back.

"The grave's inside the mountain," she said slowly, and I nodded.

"We'll go together?"

I nodded again.

"It's caught up with us," I said.

So the director was also the executioner, and he did his work fast. The area down there was emptying. We clutched each other as tightly as we could, and slowly we reached the death machine, the last ones. A brief feeling of happiness came over me. That must be what people call love, I thought.

We were the only children who knew the truth, and we could rely on each other absolutely, and we were ready to hold hands as we went toward the end.

The executioner positioned us under the steel rope and I saw the double wooden hook coming up on us from behind. The executioner tried to push the hook underneath us. We clung on to each other even tighter. There was a great jerk and we were thrown forward. The hook didn't hold, it seemed to be too big for us. The hook slid upward, banging us on our backs and heads, and disappeared into the air. I thought there must be a chance. The next hook was on its way.

"Lie flat," I whispered.

We fell down in the snow as the hook knocked us from behind again and disappeared. The executioner began to curse furiously in a language I didn't know. We sprawled in the snow, half on our knees and half on our stomachs. Squinting sideways, I saw the executioner's heavy shoes next to me.

"Stay down," I whispered again.

The girl reacted quickly, the way we'd learned. She forced her face down in the snow, closed her arms over her head for protection, and tensed her back. I did the same, and we waited for the blows. But nothing happened, except that the death machine sounded even hungrier.

I was afraid that the girl would not be able to hold her head down for long enough. If you brought your head up too soon, there was the danger that you'd get a boot in your face, which could throw you right over so that you landed on your back, leaving your face and stomach unprotected for a moment. But still nothing like that happened.

Suddenly we heard the executioner cursing again. He hauled us up with rough hands and set us ungently on our feet again. We were to return immediately to the Children's Home, he yelled at us with a red face and little yellow eyes. He took the wooden boards off our feet and we ran. We could hear him still calling:

"City kids . . . weaklings . . . scaredy-cats."

We came to a halt under the protective cave of the first trees and looked back, trying to work out what had happened. The clearing down there was empty, with just the roar of the death machine. The girl held tight to my hand and we stared at the double wooden hooks come swinging empty down the mountain.

"You see—nobody's coming back," I whispered, "no one ever comes back."

"They're all dead," said the girl. "We're the only ones who know the secret."

We looked at each other, and we knew we'd never give it away. We walked slowly back through the woods. Suddenly she stopped and I saw that she was crying.

"Aren't you happy?" I asked. "Isn't it better to be alive than dead?"

She looked at me sadly.

"No," she said, "both are terrible. A car is coming to take me away tomorrow. We'll never see each other again."

Sadness poured over me, and I wondered if it had been a good idea to cheat the executioner. It was my fault that instead of dying, we were now going to be alone, each of us, without knowing how we were going to bear it. What had I done?

Next morning I waited under a tree from which I could see the road the car would have to take to get here and go away again with the girl—the road shoveled clear by the executioner.

The car windows were iced over, I couldn't see anything. I don't know if the girl saw me, or if she waved back when I waved to her.

I never once asked her her name.

By noon the sun was shining again and everything was quiet in the home. I saw the executioner—so-called ski instructor—lying out on his deck chair on the sun terrace. I looked down from the window at him as he slept unawares.

"I have to find a way to kill him."

TWENTY

I was already in one of the senior classes at high school, and we had a teacher for both history and German whom I really admired. A tall old man with bushy white hair. He had once been a theater director and producer in Germany, until the Nazis expelled him as an undesirable alien. So he had his own reasons for taking us very thoroughly through twentieth-century history.

When we discussed the Nazi system and the Second World War, I soaked up every word he said, asked endless questions, followed up every suggestion to get hold of additional books, which I then secretly read. My foster parents must not find out. They reacted allergically to all these things, and the entire subject was taboo.

I wanted to know everything. I wanted to absorb every detail and understand every connection. I hoped I would find answers for the pictures that came from my broken childhood memory some nights to stop me going to sleep or to give me terrifying nightmares. I wanted to know what other people had gone through back then. I wanted to compare it with my own earliest memories that I carried around inside me. I wanted to subject them to intelligent reason, and arrange them in a pattern that made sense. But the longer I spent at it, the more I learned and absorbed empirically, the more elusive the answer—in the sense of what actually happened—became. It made me despair.

Why had I, in particular, survived? I hadn't earned that right. I had brought too much guilt on myself for that.

I had handed over the new boy; I was inextricably caught up in the fact of his death. It was only because I was a coward that they killed the new boy. I might perhaps have been able to save him, and I didn't do anything.

I had betrayed my mother and now called a stranger "mother."

I had given up the search for my brothers out of a fear of discovering the truth.

I had deserted the colors, and abandoned my friends in the orphanage in Kraków to their fate. I was sitting here in safe, stuffed Switzerland. I had food, I had clothes, while they were under the stamp of Stalin in Poland, and still belonged among the unwanted.

A bad conscience and the fear of discovery were my daily companions. History lessons helped me to sort it out, and increased my confusion, all at the same time. In one of our last lessons, the teacher showed us a documentary film about the Nazi period and the camps. Especially the camps. I hardly dared to look. I sat there, numb. I was afraid of giving myself away. Nobody must find out that I came from all that filth and madness. I saw all the human shapes I remembered so well in the streets of the camps, the barracks, the bodies, the starving, the uniforms.

But then came something so unexpected as to be unreal, that I knew nothing about: the narrator made mention, full of pathos, of the liberation of the camps by the Allies. On the screen was the Mauthausen concentration camp near Linz.

The yard of the camp was filled with people, prisoners in their striped clothing. They were laughing and waving. You could see them sitting on all the walls surrounding the yard, in jubilation.

And then, the great moment: through the gates of the camp came an American tank with American soldiers on it, also waving. There seemed to be no words to describe the jubilation. Soldiers went over to the weakened prisoners lying on the ground.

They were embraced, comforted, kissed. You could see food being handed out; the sick were tended to and the wounded were being bandaged. And everywhere, over and over again, faces transfixed with happiness at being liberated.

"Liberation—it's not true! That's not how it was! It's a lie—that's not what happened." My hands were tight over my mouth to stop myself screaming at the class. I was shattered. And yet I was looking at what was undeniably documentary footage.

Goddammit—who got freed? And where was I when everyone else was being freed? I was there too, in a camp, and I didn't see anything. No one freed us, and nobody brought us food, and nobody tended us or stroked us the way it happened in the film.

So how was it, back then? We just ran away, without permission. The guards were the first to leave our part of the camp. They fled without a word. And the ones who stayed had no more ammunition to fire at us.

And the people outside the camp, in the countryside and the nearby town—they didn't celebrate when they saw us. They cursed us and said, "Go back to where you came from" and "We thought Hitler had gassed the lot of you—and now you come crawling back again."

These people sided with the uniforms. And they spat at me.

I puzzled furiously over what I could recall—but there was nothing there. No joyous liberation. I never heard the word "liberation" back then, I didn't even know there was such a word.

Nobody ever told me the war was over.

Nobody ever told me that the camp was over, finally, definitely over.

Nobody ever told me that the old times and their evil games and rules were over and I could go forward without fear or threat into a new time and a new world, with new peaceful games and new rules. Not even later.

My foster parents just kept repeating:

"You must forget it all. Forget it, the way you forget a bad

dream: you're not to think about it anymore. It was all a
dream . . ."

It was impossible for me to work out what they really wanted
from me. And if I tried to confide in other people, to tell them
about it, they would usually listen to the first sentence, then say,
"You're making it up!"

How can I forget what I knew? How can I forget what I'm
forced to think about every morning when I wake up, and every
evening when I go to bed and try to stay awake as long as possible, for fear of the nightmares? How can the scar on my forehead
and the knobbly ridge on the back of my head be nothing but
the results of a dream?

No, nobody ever said right out to me: Yes, the camp was real,
but now it's over. There *is* another world now, and you're
allowed to live in it.

So I told myself: All right, you're still stronger than I am. I'll
pay constant attention, I'll learn the rules of your games, I'll
play your games, but that's all I'll do—play them—I'll never
become like you. You people, you profess to take these rules seriously. You preach honesty, and you're liars. You preach openness,
and you won't tell me the truth.

Making me play along, making me adopt your rules, is just
one of your tricks to soften me up and lull me into a false sense
of security. There are the real rules, about living and surviving,
that I learned in the camp, and that Jankl taught me, and you'll
never get me to forget those.

The good life is nothing but a trap. The camp's still there—
just hidden and well disguised. They've taken off their uniforms
and dressed themselves up in nice clothes so as not to be recognized.

But listen carefully and watch how they disregard their own
nice rules of the game. Just give them the gentlest of hints that
maybe, possibly, you're a Jew—and you'll feel it: these are still
the same people, and I'm sure of it. They can still kill, even out
of uniform.

I had had lots of this kind of long conversation with myself when I was a boy. And now I saw this incontrovertible documentary about the liberation of Mauthausen and other camps.

I went home as if anesthetized, threw down my schoolbag, and went out into the garden. As I often did when I wanted to be left alone to think through something, I climbed high up into one of the beautiful old fir trees and settled myself comfortably on a perch I'd knocked together up there.

From here I could look out over most of the town. The gentle swaying of the treetop was soothing. I was safe up there. Nobody could follow me; I could think.

I replayed the laughing faces of the freed prisoners, their look of relief on the film. Given that the film wasn't lying, given that these faces weren't lying, where was I? What did they conceal from me? Why wasn't I there, too? Did something really happen there and I knew nothing about it?

I became more and more unsure, and a terrible suspicion began to eat its way into me like a gnawing pain. It clawed into my stomach, lay heavily on my chest, and rose chokingly into my throat:

Perhaps it's true—somehow I missed my own liberation.

I often used to go back and visit my first great physics teacher, Salvo Berkovici, although I'd been studying in another city for a long time by then.

He was an old man, and a wise one. The last surviving member of a centuries-old family of Romanian rabbis, he had studied, among other things, music, physics, mathematics, philosophy, and medicine. He was my guide and mentor, the kind of father I would have wished for myself.

He was the only person with whom I could be open. He was the only person back then who understood if all I could dare do was to hint at past events.

He understood what I was really saying.

AFTERWORD

I grew up and became an adult in a time and in a society that didn't want to listen, or perhaps was incapable of listening. "Children have no memories, children forget quickly, you must forget it all, it was just a bad dream." These were the words, endlessly repeated, that were used on me from my schooldays to erase my past and make me keep quiet. So for decades I was silent, but my memory could not be wiped clean. Very occasionally I would make timid attempts to share at least some parts of it with someone, but these attempts always went wrong. A finger tapping against the forehead or aggressive questions in return soon made me fall silent, taking back what I'd revealed. It is so easy to make a child mistrust his own reflections, to take away his voice. I wanted my own certainty back, and I wanted my voice back, so I began to write.

It is only in recent years that the Children of the Holocaust societies came into existence in Warsaw and the United States, that the AMCHA organization was formed in Israel, and that historians and psychologists began to tackle the questions and the problems of children who survived the Shoah. I am in contact with many of them—historians, psychologists, and victims—and I have worked with some of them for years. Several hundred children who survived the Shoah have come forward. They are "children without identity," lacking any certain information about their origins, with all traces carefully erased, furnished with false names and often with false papers too. They grew up with a pseudo-identity which in Eastern Europe protected them from discrimination, and in Western Europe, from being sent back east as stateless persons.

As a child, I also received a new identity, another name, another date and place of birth. The document I hold in my hands—a makeshift summary, no actual birth certificate—gives the date of my birth as February 12, 1941. But this date has nothing to do with either the history of this century or my personal history. I have now taken legal steps to have this imposed identity annulled.

Legally accredited truth is one thing—the truth of a life another. Years of research, many journeys back to the places where I remember things happened, and countless conversations with specialists and historians have helped me to clarify many previously inexplicable shreds of memory, to identify places and people, to find them again and to make a possible, more or less logical chronology out of it. I thank them all.

I wrote these fragments of memory to explore both myself and my earliest childhood; it may also have been an attempt to set myself free. And I wrote them with the hope that perhaps other people in the same situation would find the necessary support and strength to cry out their own traumatic childhood memories, so that they too could learn that there really are people today who will take them seriously, and who want to listen and to understand.

They should know that they are not alone.

June 1995